# Contents

# Essentials of Production and Operations Management

**Second Edition**

**Ray Wild**

*The Management College, Henley
and
Brunel University*

Holt, Rinehart and Winston
London · New York · Sydney · Toronto

Holt, Rinehart and Winston Ltd: 1 St Anne's Road,
Eastbourne, East Sussex BN21 3UN

## By the same author

The Techniques of Production Management (1971)
Management and Production (1972) *(2nd ed. 1980)*
Women in the Factory
        *(with A. B. Hill and C. C. Ridgeway)* (1970)
Mass Production Management (1972)
Principles of Modern Management
        *(with B. Lowes)* (1972)
Work Organization (1975)
Concepts for Operations Management (1977)
Operations Management—A Policy Framework (1980)
Management and Production—Readings (1981)
Four children's books comprising the 'Read and Explain' series (1982)
How to Manage (1983)
Production and Operations Management—Principles and Techniques, Third Edition
(1984)

**British Library Cataloguing in Publication Data**

Wild, Ray
    Essentials of production and operations
    management.——2nd ed.
    1. Production management
    I. Title
    658.5        TS155

ISBN 0-03-910585-7

Typeset by Phoenix Photosetting, Chatham
Printed in Great Britain by Mackays of Chatham Ltd

Last digit is print number: 9 8 7 6 5 4 3 2 1

# Preface

This is a book about production and operations management. The production and operating functions within businesses are concerned with the conversion or transformation process. Such processes are technologically diverse and embrace the provision of both goods and services. This book is concerned with both of these aspects.

This is the second edition of the book, which is an abridged and somewhat modified version of *Production and Operations Management—Principles and Techniques*, Third Edition (Ray Wild, Holt, Rinehart and Winston, 1984). It has been designed specifically to meet the syllabus requirements of several professional bodies, institutions and examination boards. It complements the parent text in providing a somewhat different level of treatment but over a similar subject area and range.

This is intended as an economical and straightforward text. Unnecessary words have been kept to a minimum and 'padding' avoided. The intention throughout is to provide the student with a concise, readable, balanced and adequate introduction to the subject.

The book is structured in a semi 'life-cycle' form since it deals, in order, with the types of problems which would be encountered in establishing, designing, planning, running and maintaining a production or operating system. It aims to introduce the reader to the major problems and decisions facing the production and operations manager as well as introducing some of the techniques for the solution of these problems. It is intended specifically as a teaching text for use throughout a course, but this does not of course mean that other material cannot be used in conjunction with the text. Further reading material is suggested at the end of each chapter and assignment questions are also given. It is not a case study book but could be used in conjunction with a case study approach.

Unlike some books in this area, this text is not concerned solely with manufacturing situations. Nor, however, does the approach employed in the text make the assumption that similar problems are encountered in the management of different types of operating systems. The approach employed involves: identifying the principal types of operating systems which might be encountered; identifying the reasons for their differences, in particular the different problems encountered in managing different types of systems; and identifying different procedures and techniques for the solution of these problems, as well as considering those problems which have substantial similarity in different types of systems.

Teachers may wish to employ this book in conjunction with the parent book *(Production and Operations Management—Principles and Techniques,* Third Edition, 1984), using the latter themselves as a means of pursuing some of the subjects in greater depth, to be better able to teach and guide the student through the topics treated in this volume. It should be noted, however, that some additional topics have been introduced in this volume in order that the syllabus and examination requirements referred to above might be adequately treated.

## ACKNOWLEDGEMENTS

I am grateful for the many comments and suggestions offered by the users of the first edition of this book. I hope that they, in particular, find this edition useful.

Henley-on-Thames                                                                                           Ray Wild
England
1984

# PART 1

# OPERATING SYSTEMS AND OPERATIONS MANAGEMENT

# INTRODUCTION TO PART 1

*This part of the book is the principal foundation for subsequent chapters. Here we take a broad view of operations management. Definitions are developed and a categorization of types of operating systems is provided. The major problem areas, or decisions required of operations managers, are considered and three principal problem areas are identified. A model is presented to identify the factors influencing the operations manager's decision-making and role. And finally we consider the operations management decision-making process.*

*The chapter introduces several new concepts and ideas, and aims to encourage the reader to think about the fundamental nature of operating systems and the role of the operations manager.*

# CHAPTER 1

# The Nature of Operating Systems and Operations Management

## THE NATURE OF OPERATING SYSTEMS

### Operating systems: definition

> *An operating system is a configuration of resources combined for the provision of goods or services.*

Bus and taxi services, motels and dentists, tailors and mines, fire services and refuse removers, retail organizations, hospitals and builders are all operating systems. They all, in effect, convert inputs in order to provide outputs which are required by a customer. Physical inputs will normally predominate, hence operating systems convert physical *resources* into outputs, the *function* of which is to satisfy customer wants, i.e. to provide some utility for the customer.

### *Resources in operating systems*

Operations managers are principally concerned with the use of physical resources, so we shall take a physical view of operating systems and concentrate on the physical resources used by the system, which for convenience will be categorized as follows:

1. *Materials,* i.e. those physical items consumed or converted by the system, e.g. raw materials, fuel, indirect materials.
2. *Machines,* i.e. those physical items used by the system, e.g. plant, tools, vehicles, buildings.
3. *Labour,* i.e. the people who necessarily provide or contribute to the operation of the system, without whom neither machines nor materials are effectively used.

## Function of operating systems

Given this definition a large range and variety of systems may be considered as operating systems. The examples above illustrate this variety. Some form of categorization of such systems would be of value, if only for descriptive purposes. One useful categorization is afforded by a consideration of system function.

The function of an operating system is a reflection of the purpose it serves for its customer, i.e. the *utility* of its output to the customer. Four principal functions can be identified:

1. *Manufacture*, in which the principal common characteristic is that something is physically created, i.e. the output consists of goods which differ physically, e.g. in form or content, from those materials input to the system. Manufacture therefore requires some physical transformation, or a change in *form utility* of resources.
2. *Transport*, in which the principal common characteristic is that a customer, or something belonging to the customer, is moved from place to place, i.e. the location of someone or something is changed. The system uses its resources primarily to this end, and such resources will not normally be substantially physically changed. There is no major change in the form of resources, and the system provides primarily for a change in *place utility*.
3. *Supply*, in which the principal common characteristic is that the ownership or possession of goods is changed. Unlike manufacture, goods output from the system are physically the same as those input. There is no physical transformation and the system function is primarily one of change in *possession utility* of a resource.
4. *Service*, in which the principal common characteristic is the treatment or accommodation of something or someone. There is primarily a change in *state utility* of a resource. Unlike in supply systems, the state or condition of physical outputs will differ from inputs by virtue of having been treated in some way. (NB. It should be noted that this definition is somewhat narrower than that normally implied by this term.)

Many organizations comprise systems with different functions. For example, an airline will depend on operating systems whose purpose is transport, supply and service. A typical manufacturing organization will have internal transport and service systems. In fact, except in very small organizations, we are likely to be able to identify all four functions providing we consider small enough parts of the total system. For this reason the description of a complex organization as a manufacturing system, or transport system, etc., provides only a very general indication of its *overall* or principal purpose. A more detailed description necessitates the consideration of parts, or sub-systems, of the whole. These four principal functions can together be used in describing all operating systems and their sub-systems. They provide a basic language for operations management and permit the development of a slightly more detailed definition of an operating system:

> An operating system is a configuration of resources combined for the function of manufacture, transport, supply or service.

We can divide *manufacture* in two traditional ways. First, we can identify continuous, repetitive and intermittent manufacture. Theoretically, a *continuous* process will run for 24 hours a day, seven days a week and 52 weeks a year. Although this degree of continuity is often the objective, it is rarely achieved. Examples of this type of manufacture are steelmaking and petrochemicals. A *repetitive* process is one in which the product (or products) is processed in lots, each item of production passing through the same sequence of operations, as, for example, in the assembly of motor vehicles. An *intermittent* process is one in which very small lots, or even single products, are made in response to separate customer orders.

The second and similar classification divides manufacturing processes into process or mass, batch and jobbing. *Process* manufacture involves the *continuous* production of a commodity in bulk, often by chemical rather than mechanical means. *Mass* production (or manufacture) is conceptually similar to process manufacture, except that discrete items such as cars and domestic appliances are usually involved. A single item or a very small range of similar items is manufactured in very large numbers. *Batch* production occurs where the number of discrete items to be manufactured in a period is insufficient to enable mass production to be used. Similar items are, wherever possible, manufactured together in batches. Finally *jobbing* manufacture, although strictly consisting of the manufacture of different products in unit quantities, in practice corresponds to the *intermittent* process mentioned above.

The principal function of *transport* systems is that of changing the location of someone or something. Taxi or bus services, ambulance services, furniture removers, and refuse-removal systems can be categorized as transport systems. Within manufacturing organizations, transport systems may be employed for moving work-in-progress between manufacturing departments, removing waste materials, etc.

*Supply* systems have the principal function of changing the ownership or possession of item(s) which are otherwise physically unchanged. At an organization level, a retail shop, warehouse, petrol station and broker may be seen to have the principal function of supply. Within organizations, supply systems may be evident as internal stores, etc.

Dentists, fire services, launderettes, hospital wards and motels may be considered to have the principal function of *service*, i.e. the function of treating or accommodating something or someone. Within organizations a similar function may be performed by systems such as welfare departments and rest rooms.

No such categorization can be watertight. Inevitably there will be overlap and such an approach is of value only for descriptive purposes. Such descriptions indicate something about the purpose of and reason for systems, but of necessity we must develop a somewhat different approach if we are to explore the nature of operating systems from an operations management viewpoint.

## Structure of operating systems

Categorization by function identifies the scope of operating systems but tells us little about their nature. The nature of the operations manager's job will to some extent depend upon the nature of the system being managed. His or her role is partly influenced by the characteristics of the system. Not only what must be done, but the way in which it can be done, is influenced by the nature of the system. To explore the nature of operating systems we shall examine their structure or 'shape'.

Using simple systems terminology all operating systems may be seen to comprise inputs, processes and outputs in the manner of Figure 1.1. This simple system structure can represent any operating system and at any level of detail, e.g., an organization as a whole, or some part of it. As a descriptive device it is limited, so we

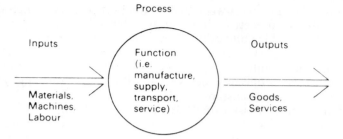

**Figure 1.1**   *A simple system model.*

must examine system structure in slightly more detail. The terminology of Figure 1.2 will be used for this purpose. With this simple approach we can identify four simple structures for *manufacturing* systems:

(a) '*Make from stock, to stock, to customer*', i.e. all input resources are stocked and the customer is served from a stock of finished goods.
(b) '*Make from source, to stock, to customer*', i.e. no input resource stocks are held, but goods are produced to stock.
(c) '*Make from stock direct to customer*', i.e. all input resources are stocked but goods are made only against and on receipt of customers' orders.
(d) '*Make from source direct to customer*', i.e. no input resource stocks are held and all goods are made only against and on receipt of customers' orders.

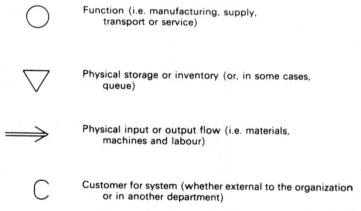

**Figure 1.2**   *System notation.*

Each structure shows how a system will provide for future output. Structure (d), for example, indicates that, in order to provide the next output for a customer, resources must first be acquired, whereas in (c) the next customer order will be satisfied through the use of already existing resources.

Now considering *supply* systems in a similar manner, by substituting 'supply' for 'make' in the above list, we may recognize the validity of these four simple structures. Both structures (a) and (b) require function in anticipation of order, i.e. structure (a) depicts 'supply from stock, to stock, to customer' and structure (b) depicts 'supply from source, to stock, to customer'. Neither case is common in supply operations, but both can exist. More commonly structures (c) and (d) will exist. Structure (c) depicts

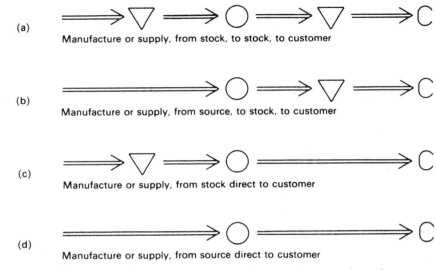

(a)

Manufacture or supply, from stock, to stock, to customer

(b)

Manufacture or supply, from source, to stock, to customer

(c)

Manufacture or supply, from stock direct to customer

(d)

Manufacture or supply, from source direct to customer

**Figure 1.3**    *Basic system structures for manufacture and supply.*

'supply from stock direct to customer'. These four basic structures for manufacture and supply systems are shown in Figure 1.3.

A slightly different situation applies in respect of both *transport* and *service*. All structures which require function in anticipation or in advance of receipt of a customer's order are not feasible, since, in the case of both transport and service, no physical output stock is possible. Consider transport. A taxi service cannot satisfy a customer's relocation or movement requirements before receiving the customer's orders. Similarly, ambulance, refuse or furniture removal services cannot build up a stock of outputs to satisfy future customer demands. Nor can a bus service perform its function of transporting individuals before those individual customers arrive. The bus can, and often does, move from stop to stop along its route even though no customers have arrived. In doing so, however, it has not performed its function of changing the location of customers. In fact, it has simply remained as an unutilized stocked resource, in need of customers. Nor can service systems, such as fire services, launderettes, hospitals and motels, build up a stock of outputs to satisfy future customer orders.

One further important structural difference is evident in the case of transport and service systems. Since the function of transport and service is to 'treat' the customer (whether a thing or a person), the customer is a resource input to the system, i.e. *the beneficiary of the function is or provides a major physical resource input to the function.* Thus transport and service systems are dependent upon customers not only taking their output and in some cases specifying what that output shall be, but also for the supply of a major physical input(s) to the function without which the function would not be achieved. For example, in transport, a taxi, ambulance or bus service moves customers or something supplied by them, e.g. a piece of luggage. In service systems, e.g. a hospital or motel, the customer is treated in person, while launderettes and fire services treat items which might themselves be considered as customers (e.g. burning houses) or whose supply is controlled by the customer.

In other words, unlike manufacture and supply, transport and service systems are activated or 'triggered' by an input or supply. The customers exert some 'push' on the system. In manufacture and supply the customers act directly upon output: they 'pull' the system, in that they pull goods out of the system whether direct from the function (structures (c) and (d)) or from output stock (structures (a) and (b)). In transport and service the customers push the system: they act directly on input. In such systems, therefore, some part of the resource inputs is not *directly* under the control of operations management. In these 'push' systems the customers control an input channel, and we must therefore distinguish this from that controlled by operations management.

Somewhat different structures are therefore required to represent transport and service systems. Three structures would seem to exist, as illustrated in Figure 1.4:

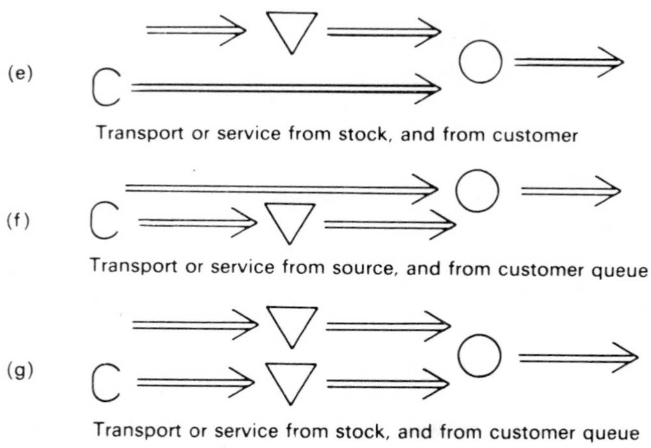

(e)

Transport or service from stock, and from customer

(f)

Transport or service from source, and from customer queue

(g)

Transport or service from stock, and from customer queue

**Figure 1.4**   *Basic system structures for transport and service.*

(e) *'Function from stock, and from customer'*, i.e. input resources are stocked, except in the case of customer inputs where no *queuing* exists.
(f) *'Function from source, and from customer queue'*, i.e. no input resources are stocked although customer inputs accumulate in a queue (or stock).
(g) *'Function from stock, and from customer queue'*, in which all input resources are stocked and/or allowed to accumulate in stocks.

Customer queues are physical stocks in the customer input channel, although they cannot be utilized by operations management in the same way as other resource stocks, for they are usually beyond their direct control. Queues comprise those customers who have 'arrived' at the system and await service or transport. They are the customers who at any one time have asked to be 'treated' by the system. The queue therefore represents known and committed future demand.

In total, therefore, we have seven basic structures for operating systems. They are simple system descriptions. For example, they deal only with single channels for input and output. However, this type of approach can be used to describe more complex systems. Furthermore, these basic system models can be used to describe operating systems at any level of detail—the organization, a division, a department, a section, etc.—depending on our particular focus.

## OPERATIONS MANAGEMENT

*Operations management is concerned with the design and the operation of systems for manufacture, transport, supply or service.*

The nature of certain of the problems which face operations management can be shown to be influenced by operating system structure, hence the role of operations management is in part influenced by the structure of the operating system. Thus, for example, an operations manager responsible for a system in which output stocks exist will face a somewhat different task if he or she moves to a situation in which there are no such stocks. Additionally, the role of operations management is influenced by the objectives which are adopted by or prescribed for operations management, since these, together with the characteristics of the system, necessitate the use of particular operations management strategies, i.e. the general approaches adopted for tackling problems. Figure 1.5 outlines these relationships between system structure, problems, objectives, strategies and the role of operations management. Recapping, this model or framework indicates that, because of the nature of certain (principal) operations management problem areas, particular operating system structures have distinctive problem characteristics. These problem characteristics, together with operations management's objectives, influence the strategies or general approaches which are adopted by operations management in tackling problems, and in turn the nature of the strategies employed and the circumstances in which they are employed influence the role of the operations manager.

Given the influence of the basic operating system structure, one principal aim of operations management will be to select the system structure to be employed or,

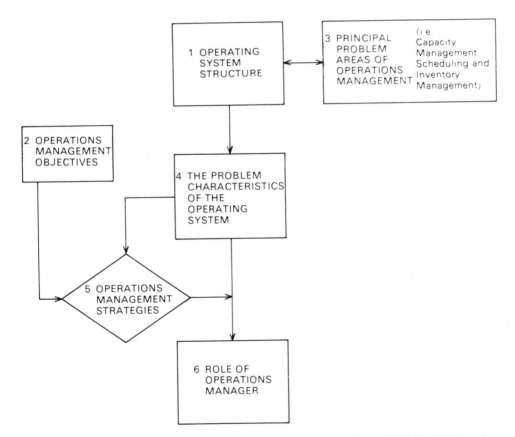

**Figure 1.5** *A framework of concepts for operations management. From Wild, R. (1977)* Concepts for Operations Management. *New York: Wiley. Reproduced with permission.*

failing that, to influence its selection. Operations managers may have *some* choice of system structure or be able to change structures, but only within certain feasibility constraints. The system structure which exists at a particular time is determined by both internal and external factors. External factors—largely beyond the direct control of operations management—determine feasibility, while internal factors—largely or partly under its direct control—will influence operations management's choice of system structure.

Figure 1.6 indicates the manner in which such factors influence system structure.

1. *Appropriateness.* The function of the system and the nature of customer influence (i.e. whether customers 'push' or 'pull') will determine the appropriateness of the structure. (For example there will be only four appropriate structures for manufacture and supply situations and only three for transport and service situations.)
2. *Feasibility.* Given appropriateness, feasibility will be determined by the nature of customer demand, in particular the predictability of the nature of the demand. Unless the nature of the product which will be required by future customers is certain, it will not be possible to operate in anticipation of demand and to provide output stocks. Unless there is some knowledge of the nature of the items which will be required by customers, it may even be impossible to stock resources. Similarly, unless the general nature of the service or transport required by customers is known, certain structures may not be feasible.
3. *Desirability.* The function of the system, the influence of customers on the system, and the predictability of the nature of demand are all factors which are normally beyond the direct control of operations managers, so we can consider these to be the *external* influences on system structure (Figure 1.6). Operations management

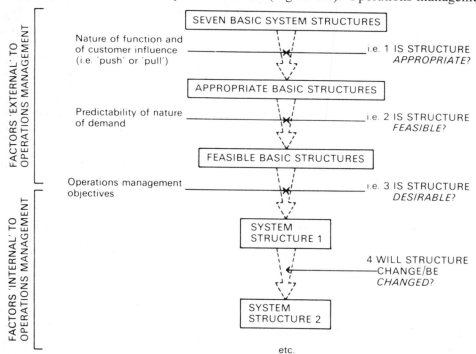

**Figure 1.6**   *Factors influencing system structure. From Wild, R. (1977)* Concepts for Operations Management. *New York: Wiley. Reproduced with permission.*

may choose only from feasible system structures. This choice will reflect the desirability of each of the feasible system structures, desirability in turn being influenced by objectives which are partly influenced by operations management. One particular structure may be desirable given the relative importance of customer service vis-à-vis resource productivity. For a different balance of importance between these two objectives a different structure may be considered to be more desirable.

4. *Change.* Once adopted, a system structure may be changed by operations management usually through changes in capacity, schedules or inventories. The question of structure change leads us to consider the influence of *time*. System structure can change over a period of time, and for this reason we should consider the structure of systems at a given point in time. If a system is designed to have, or if it must normally have, a certain structure, the strategies adopted by management should reflect the needs and constraints of that system structure. If the structure changes, for whatever reason, either the approach to the management of the system will remain basically unchanged or the approach will be changed. It is likely that in the case of temporary structure changes the approach to management will not change, but in the case of long-term change a corresponding management change will be desirable. Clearly a system may not always exist or work as it is intended to. For example, all customers must ultimately be prepared to wait or queue in a 'push' system. Even an emergency ambulance service may on occasion require customers to wait. However, it may be inappropriate or unnecessary to consider changing the system structure every time such a queue forms. The length of time customers are prepared to wait may be too short to permit the system to be run or managed in a different way. The way the system is managed, therefore, may not change at all, despite a temporary structure change. In practice the manner in which a dentist manages will not change simply because the non-arrival of a few patients causes the system structure to change temporarily. Short-term structure changes may affect customer service or resource productivity, but little else.

In certain cases different 'parties' may see systems in different ways. Customers may consider queues to exist, while operations managers may perceive a different structure. It is the latter which is of importance for us. The operations manager's perception of a system will influence his or her behaviour. We must therefore consider the normal, intended or actual system structure—whichever is appropriate—and consider system structure from the operations manager's viewpoint.

Given the general model shown in Figure 1.5, two aspects now attract attention: operations management objectives and principal problem areas.

## Operations management objectives

The objective of operating systems is the conversion of inputs for the satisfaction of customer wants. Customer satisfaction is therefore a key objective of operations management. Table 1.1 identifies the main aspects of customer satisfaction for each function. Customers will want the outputs of the operating system; this is the primary condition for their being customers. Secondary considerations, however, will exist and for simplicity these can be considered in terms of costs and timing. Thus, using the classic catch-phrase, one objective of operations management is to provide customer satisfaction by providing the 'right thing at the right price and at the right time'. We shall refer to this as the objective of *customer service*.

**Table 1.1**  *Aspects of customer satisfaction. (From Wild, R. (1977)* Concepts for Operations Management. *New York: Wiley. Reproduced with permission.)*

| Principal function | Principal customer wants | |
| --- | --- | --- |
| | Primary considerations | Secondary considerations |
| Manufacture | Goods of a given, requested or acceptable specification | Cost, i.e. purchase price or cost of obtaining goods |
| | | Timing, i.e. delivery delay from order or request to receipt of goods |
| Transport | Movement of a given, requested or acceptable specification | Cost, i.e. cost of movement |
| | | Timing, i.e. (1) duration or time to move (2) wait, or delay from request to its commencement |
| Supply | Goods of a given, requested or acceptable specification | Cost, i.e. purchase price or cost of obtaining goods |
| | | Timing, i.e. delivery delay from order to request to supply, to receipt of goods |
| Service | Treatment of a given, requested or acceptable specification | Cost, i.e. cost of treatment |
| | | Timing, i.e. (1) duration or time required for treatment (2) wait, or delay from requesting treatment to its commencement |

Given infinite resources any system, however badly managed, might provide satisfactory customer service. Many organizations have gone bankrupt despite having loyal and satisfied customers. The problem for operations management arises from the fact that operating systems must satisfy multiple objectives. Customer service must be provided simultaneously with the achievement of efficient operation, i.e. efficient use of resources, or *resource productivity*. Either inefficient use of resources or inadequate customer service is sufficient to give rise to the 'commercial' failure of the operating system.

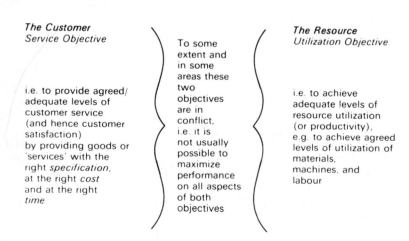

**The Customer Service Objective**

i.e. to provide agreed/ adequate levels of customer service (and hence customer satisfaction) by providing goods or 'services' with the right *specification*, at the right *cost* and at the right *time*

To some extent and in some areas these two objectives are in conflict, i.e. it is not usually possible to maximize performance on all aspects of both objectives

**The Resource Utilization Objective**

i.e. to achieve adequate levels of resource utilization (or productivity), e.g. to achieve agreed levels of utilization of materials, machines, and labour

**Figure 1.7**  *The twin (often conflicting) objectives of operations management.*

Figure 1.7 summarizes the twin objectives of operations managers. Operations management is concerned with the achievement of both satisfactory customer service and resource productivity. Operations managers must attempt to balance these two basic objectives. They will be judged against both, and the relative importance attached to each will in part be influenced by them. An improvement in one will often give rise to a deterioration in the other. Often both cannot be maximized, hence a satisfactory performance must be achieved for both and sub-optimization must be avoided. All of the activities of operations management must be tackled with these twin objectives in mind.

## Operations management problem areas

The scope of operations management is adequately indicated by the list of problem areas or fields of activity given in 'life-cycle' or chronological order in Table 1.2. Operations management will normally be responsible for the management of inventories, quality, the maintenance and replacement of facilities, and the scheduling of activities. Such responsibilities will be discharged in respect of an operating system, the nature, location, layout, capacity and staffing of which will have been determined largely by operations management. Managers working in this function will also normally have some influence on the design or specification of the goods or services,[1] processes, staffing policies and performance measurement.

**Table 1.2**   *The scope of operations management.*

|  | Problem areas |
|---|---|
| Design and planning | Involvement in design/specification of the goods/service<br>Design/specification of process/system<br>Location of facilities<br>Layout of facilities/resources and materials handling<br>Determination of capacity/capability<br>Design of work or jobs<br>Involvement in determination of remuneration system and work standards |
| Operation and control | Planning and scheduling of activities<br>Control and planning of inventories<br>Control of quality<br>Scheduling and control of maintenance<br>Replacement of facilities<br>Involvement in performance measurement |

Although each of these problem areas is of importance in the effective planning and operation of the system, we can identify three areas which have a particular significance for operations management. Three problem areas in particular will influence the nature of operations management. The type of problem faced by operations management in each of these three principal problem areas will be influenced by the operating system structure. These are the distinguishing or characteristic problem areas—unlike others, in which the nature of the problems faced by operations management is largely unaffected by system structure. Each basic system structure will have distinguishing characteristics because of the nature of the problems which occur in these three principal problem areas. Furthermore, decisions

---

[1] Throughout we shall use the term 'goods and services' to cover items, transport and services, i.e. the 'outputs' of all four functions.

in each of these areas may affect system structure. Operations managers working in different situations will probably have to use different strategies and techniques in tackling problems in the three principal problem areas. In contrast, when making decisions in other areas, operations managers may be able to rely on the same types of strategy and techniques in different situations. For this reason, in discussing decision-making techniques in the remainder of this book, we must, when considering the principal problem areas, ensure that we consider the appropriateness of techniques, while in considering other problem areas the matter of appropriateness is less of an issue.

### Principal problem areas

*Inventory management*

The problem of managing physical stocks or inventories is clearly a function of system structure, if only because certain structures provide for the existence of stocks while others do not. The location of inventories is a function of structure, as also is the nature of the inventory management problem. Defining inventory management as the planning and control of physical stocks, both aspects of the problem may be affected by structure and may also affect structure. The structure of an operating system will largely reflect the nature and location of inventories, and the management of such inventories will influence both resource productivity and customer service. The existence of output stocks may facilitate the provision of high customer service, at least in terms of availability or 'timing'. However, their existence may be costly. The provision of input resource stocks may benefit customer service, yet resource productivity may be adversely affected because more resources are idle. Few organizations can exist entirely without stocks of raw materials, work in progress or, where appropriate, output goods. The planning of inventory levels, the control of inventories and the maintenance of such stocks are expensive but necessary. Inventories will normally tie up considerable amounts of capital, thus there is a balance to be struck between obtaining the benefits of inventories, such as flexibility, high customer service, and insulation against demand fluctuations, on the one hand, and minimizing the costs of such stocks on the other.

*Scheduling*

The nature of some aspects of scheduling in operations management is characteristic of the system structure, and decisions made in scheduling can affect the structure. Scheduling is concerned with the timing of occurrences. *Operations scheduling* in its widest sense may therefore be considered to be concerned with the specification in advance or the timing of occurrences within the system, arrivals to and departures from the system, including arrivals to and departures from inventories within the system. Thus we can consider the inventory management problem to be a part of a wider operations scheduling problem. The nature and extent of this overall scheduling problem will therefore be influenced by the presence and location of inventories and the relationship between the customer and the system, all of which are characteristic of system structure. As with all characteristic problems, the procedures and methods deployed in scheduling may be influenced by structure, and the effectiveness of scheduling may in turn affect structure. If we consider operations scheduling to relate to the physical flow or transfer of resources or goods, then the nature or extent of the overall scheduling problem is clearly influenced by the number of stages involved in the system, and therefore by structure. Where output stocks exist, customer demand will be met by scheduled output from stock, such stocks being replenished by scheduled inputs. In the absence of such stocks customer demand will be met by scheduling output from the function, which in turn will necessitate the scheduling of resource inputs from either input stock or direct suppliers. Conventionally we take a narrower view of the scheduling problem. We normally focus on *activity scheduling,* which is concerned only with activities directly related to the function.

*Capacity management*

The determination and adjustment of capacity in an operating system is an important problem area, since decisions made here may intentionally or inadvertently change the structure of the system and/or affect the efficiency of operation of a particular system. Equally, decisions not made, or wrong decisions, may also result in structure changes and/or loss of efficiency, as for example following the failure to adjust system capacity to match customer demand changes. The planning and control of capacity is both important and complex, and furthermore the nature of the problem will often be affected by structure. In other words, for a given system structure the capacity management problem may well differ from that facing management in a different structure. Since structure affects the nature and complexity of the capacity planning problem, the methods, procedures and techniques appropriate for tackling the problem may also be influenced by structure. In all respects, therefore, we can consider capacity management to be a principal problem area, the nature of which is characteristic of system structure. The management of system capacity is of crucial importance in operations management. The determination of capacity is the key system planning or design problem and the adjustment of capacity is the key problem area in system control. Capacity decisions will have a direct influence on system performance in respect of both criteria, i.e. resource productivity and customer service. It is difficult to see how any organization can operate effectively without good capacity management. Excess capacity inevitably gives rise to low resource productivity, while inadequate capacity may mean poor customer service. Decisions made in other areas are unlikely to offset errors in this area. The capacity problem is often of a medium- to long-term nature. Since system capacity is a reflection of the nature and amount of resources available in the system, short-term adjustments are often impossible. Capacity management is concerned primarily with the matching of resources to demand. It is concerned, therefore, with the levels of resources and demand.

One factor adding considerably to the complexity of inventory, capacity and scheduling problems is their close interdependence. Decisions made in one will have a direct impact on performance in the others. Such interdependence is less evident in the other problem areas, a fact which tends to 'underline' the central importance of these three problem areas in the management of operations. In many respects the problems of inventory management and scheduling are subsidiary to the problem of capacity management. Capacity management decisions will determine how the operating system accommodates customer demand level fluctuations. Capacity management decisions will provide a context within which inventories and activities will be both planned and controlled. It will to some extent reflect operating policy decisions, while inventory and scheduling problems might be considered as more tactical issues.

## OPERATIONS MANAGEMENT DECISION-MAKING

We have made a distinction between what have been called the 'principal' or 'characteristic' problems, which necessitate the problem-solving procedure being tailored to the particular circumstances, and the 'common' problems, which may yield to the same type of problem-solving approach each time they are encountered. Much of the remainder of this book is about problem-solving in these areas and therefore about operations management decision-making. Before beginning to discuss the problem-solving strategies, procedures, techniques, etc., we can pull together some of the points made in the previous sections, and develop an overview of the operations manager's decision-making process. This will give a foundation for our discussion in the next part of the book, where we shall deal with operations management in the business policy context and the relationships between operations management and other functions within the organization.

For the purposes of this discussion we define the *operations management decision-making process* as 'the formulation of overall strategies for operations, typically involving interrelated areas of responsibility within operations management, and the making of decisions in these areas in pursuit of these strategies within the broader business context'.

Figure 1.8 provides a simple model of the operations management decision-making process. It is derived from our discussion above, in particular from Figures 1.5 and 1.6 and Table 1.1. The figure shows the decision-making process as a 'contingency' model. It suggests that operations managers' decision about: (a) the formulation of strategies for the solution of problems; and (b) particular problem-solving procedures is not a free, unconstrained process. It suggests, naturally, that operations managers' decisions are contingent upon other factors, and, deriving from our discussion above, suggests that the three sets of *contingent factors* or constraints might be categorized as follows:

1. *Feasibility.* The feasibility of choosing a particular course of action in the principal decision-making areas of operations management (i.e. capacity management, scheduling and inventory) will be influenced largely by the nature of the operating system, which in turn will be a function of the demand situation, the processes and outputs involved and the systems function (see Figures 1.5 and 1.6).

    We have seen that the predictability of the nature of demand (i.e. whether or not it is known what future customers want) will influence the feasibility of the existence of output stocks created in anticipation of demand, and ultimately the use of input stocks of particular resources. For example, an operating system established to satisfy demand which is totally unpredictable in nature will contain neither output stocks of finished (unsold) goods or services nor stocks of specialized input resources, e.g. specialized materials or equipment.

    The types of processes and outputs involved may influence the nature of the system. For example, in electrical power generation, even though the nature of future demand is known (i.e. for electricity of a particular voltage, etc.), it will not normally be possible to provide substantial output stocks.

    The function of the system will also influence its nature, since the configuration of transport and service systems will differ from that of supply and manufacturing systems, as in both the former cases the customers or some physical item provided by the customers will be a direct input to the process.

    Thus the nature of demand, process and outputs, and system function, and their relationship with the customer influence the nature of the system, which in turn will have a major feasibility influence on the approaches adopted by operations management for the management of such systems.

2. *Desirability.* The desirability of pursuing a particular approach in managing the system will be influenced largely by the operations manager's perceptions of desired outcomes, which in turn will be associated with explicit or implicit business objectives. Thus, considering the twin operations management objectives of providing customer service and achieving high resource utilization, an emphasis on the former will possibly encourage the adoption of particular strategies in capacity management, scheduling, etc., while an emphasis on resource utilization may encourage a different approach. For example, given feasibility, an emphasis on customer service will encourage the use of output stocks and possibly the maintenance of excess capacity, while an emphasis on resource utilization may mitigate against the use of output stocks and lead to a reduction in capacity. Although in general the operations manager's basic strategies may be seen as a

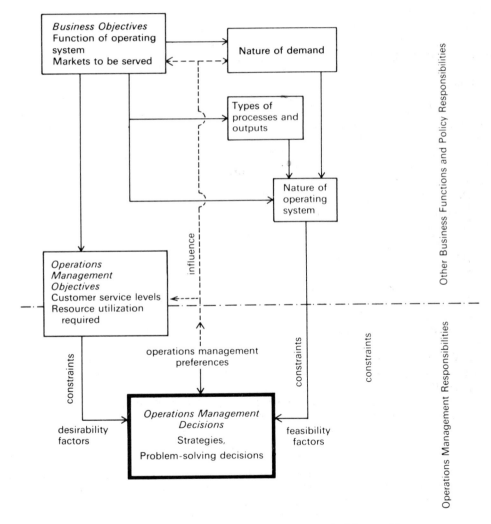

**Figure 1.8**   *A model of the operations management decision-making process.*

function of the given or required balance between customer service and resource utilization, other objectives, e.g. labour policies and pricing policies, will also have some influence. Most of these factors will be beyond the direct and total control of the operations manager. We can consider them to be policy-level decisions to which the operations manager will make some contribution.

3. *Preference.* Given feasibility and desirability, we would expect operations managers to have certain preferences. For example, the operations manager may prefer a situation in which his or her activities are in some way 'buffered' or protected from demand uncertainties. This, for example through the use of output inventories, permits the 'core' of the operating system to be in some way protected from uncertainties and thus to be run in a steady and efficient manner. In a labour-intensive situation the operations manager may prefer to minimize the amount of change in the labour force, hours worked, etc., thus minimizing the risk of labour/industrial relations problems. Or the operations manager may prefer to schedule work in such a way as to avoid the need to schedule each activity against a particular customer's 'requirement' date. All such approaches provide the operations manager with a far greater choice of strategies, etc, but the extent to which this approach might be employed is of course a function of both feasibility and desirability.

The operations manager who, for whatever reason, has greater 'power' within the organization is likely to be able to exercise his or her preferences to a greater extent than might otherwise be the case. Such power may be informal or formal. It may have been acquired, have evolved, or simply exist because of the broader circumstances, e.g. the existence of minimum feasibility and desirability constraints. This view associates 'power' with the scope, freedom of action and breadth of choice of the operations manager given certain feasibility and desirability constraints. This, however, is largely an internal perspective. We must recognize that such power, perhaps rather more broadly defined, may be exercised by the operations manager in seeking to influence both feasibility and desirability constraints which operate on him or her. Thus in certain circumstances the operations manager may be able to influence product/service design and/or marketing policy in order to make feasible the provision of output stocks of uncommitted goods. Further, he or she may seek to retain an overriding commitment to customer service and a tolerance of low resource utilization. Thus the extent to which the operations manager contributes to and influences these policy-level decisions will at least ensure that such decision-making takes into account the needs, constraints and abilities of the operations function, and at best ensure that constraints are minimized, thus enabling maximization of preference. This mechanism ensures that operations managers who are unable, or unwilling, to influence their policy-level decisions within the organization can be required to operate in highly undesirable situations, seemingly having to meet conflicting objectives while using resources in a diverse range of activities in a continually changing situation. In such circumstances the power of the operations manager clearly approaches zero: no preference is exercised, and the operations manager's decision-making process is entirely constrained by 'external factors'.

Summarizing, we can view the operations management decision-making process as a contingent/constrained process where outcomes are influenced by feasibility, desirability and preference factors. Such a view is presented in the simple model in Figure 1.8. The recognition of these relationships and the adoption of a suitable decision-making process are the prerequisites for effective operations management, and the solution of particular operations management problems must be seen as a subsidiary part of this decision-making process. The operations manager's responsibility within the broader business context must include the recognition of the fact that decisions in other functions will limit his or her own decisions, but, equally important, the operations manager must also seek to influence those factors which give rise to feasibility and desirability constraints on his or her decisions in the light of, and in order to exercise, his or her particular preferences.

In the next part of the book we shall look more closely at the policy decision-making context for operations management and the relationships of operations managers with those in other functions within the business.

## The significance of operations management

To some extent everybody is an operations manager. We all have some managerial responsibility for systems which produce, supply, transport or service. The housewife is both a manufacturer and a manufacturing manager when working in the kitchen. The student manufactures written documents and is responsible for managing that process. We have taken a comprehensive view of operating systems, hence, in our view, a wide range of people must have some operations management responsibilities. Even accepting that operations managers focus on the use of physical resources and the management of physical flows, such responsibilities are unlikely to be confined to those with operations/manufacturing production management job titles. Transport managers, and those involved in supply, service, warehousing, etc., will have some involvement with and responsibility for the decisions outlined above.

The restaurant manager is responsible for manufacturing and service systems. The hospital administrator may be responsible for transport, service and supply systems, and most senior managers in most organizations will have some responsibility for a variety of types of operating system. Indeed most organizations will depend on operating systems with most, and usually all, of the four basic functions. For this reason we cannot assume that, for example, manufacturing systems will be found only in what are known as the manufacturing industries, or that transport systems will be found only in industries such as rail, road or air transport. The various types of operating system will exist alongside each other in most types of organization.

Our broad view of operations management naturally gives considerable significance to the subject. Operating systems are ubiquitous, and operations management responsibilities are therefore pervasive. It is tempting to suggest that operations management *is* management—a claim which would rightly be denied by financial managers, personnel managers and others who deal with the common 'ingredients' of business. It is, however, undeniably true that operations management (whether primarily one, or some, or all of the four basic functions) is central to most business organizations, hence those concerned with the management of this function are of considerable significance within the business. Equally, since most activities might in some respect be considered as analogous to manufacture, supply, transport, or service systems, it is probable that managers in functions such as finance and personnel might find some relevance in our operations management approach. Our concept of operating systems and our approach to operations management therefore potentially afford a comprehensive and integrative treatment of business systems.

## FURTHER READING

Wild, R. (1977) *Concepts for Operations Management*. New York: Wiley. A detailed treatment (with examples and cases) of the ideas and concepts introduced in this chapter.
Wild, R. (1983) Decision making in operations management, *Management Decision*, **21**, pp. 9–21.

## QUESTIONS

**1.1** How far is it possible for the operations function within the firm to operate independently of the other main functional areas? Which functions, in particular, experience interlocking problems?

**1.2** Describe the principal types or classes of manufacture. What are the prerequisites for each of these types of manufacture and what are the principal operations management problems associated with each type? Illustrate your answers by describing actual industrial situations with which you are familiar.

**1.3** Identify seven basic operating system structures and give examples of each, making the simplifying assumption, if necessary, of single-channel inputs and outputs.

**1.4** Using the basic operating structures in series and/or in parallel, with multiple input and output channels if necessary, describe (i.e. model) the following operating systems:

(a)  a typical 'take-away' or 'fast food' shop (e.g. a hamburger house);
(b)  a restaurant;
(c)  a taxi service.

Identify and explain any assumptions you make.

# PART 2

# THE CONTEXT OF OPERATIONS MANAGEMENT

# INTRODUCTION TO PART 2

*Here we consider the business context of operations management. If we take the view that the operating system and operations management are the heart of any enterprise, we must recognize that there must be relationships with other functions in the business. Here we look at business policy decision-making, the nature of its influence on operations management, and the nature of the influence of operations management on it. We then consider the nature of the relationships between operations management and marketing. Throughout we shall concentrate on basic concepts and ideas, so that the nature of and reasons for these relationships are clear. Similarly in Chapter 4 we shall look at some basic aspects of operations economics and costs.*

# CHAPTER 2

# Business Policy and Operations Management

Although operations managers will have a considerable degree of control over decisions within their own area of responsibility, they will not, in general, be able to ignore the actions of others. Viewed from the position of operations managers there exists an external 'framework' for their actions. Marketing, financial, personnel and other decisions are the components of this framework. In fact, each component will perceive all others as providing their own particular external framework. In effect, therefore, there is a network of interrelated and interdependent decision-making areas. In a small organization most of these areas will be the sole and direct responsibility of one person. In such cases co-ordination is easy. In larger organizations some formal co-ordination is necessary. Procedurally this is provided through the hierarchical or pyramid-type structure of most organizations; thus, ultimately, at the apex of the pyramid someone has some knowledge of, and responsibility for, all areas. At this level, decision-making will be long-term, strategic, and concerned with the business as a whole. This business strategy or policy decision-making provides purpose and co-ordination throughout the organization and therefore largely creates the framework within which each function works. Before considering operations management decision-making we must consider the manner in which this policy mechanism works, for it is essential that we are aware of those factors which influence operations decisions and the manner in which this influence is exerted.

## THE NATURE OF BUSINESS POLICY

Planning occurs in all functions of an organization, but alone such plans are an inadequate basis for decisions concerning the future of that organization. The effectiveness of each function within the organization is dependent on effective planning, but all such planning must start and end with business policy, which is long-term, takes an organization-wide perspective and is concerned with the role, purpose and success of the business as a whole, and thus with the *total* resources of the organization.

Business policy planning is a continuous and systematic activity aimed not only at identifying purposes for the organization but also at defining procedures and organizing efforts to achieve these purposes and measuring results against expectations through systematic feedback of information. It is a systematic approach to both the formulation and the implementation of total business plans.

Formal systematic planning is essential, since detailed forecasts and action plans are required to allow co-ordinated action throughout the organization and adequate evaluation of performance. Such planning necessitates co-operation between functional specialists, sub-divisions, etc., and therefore brings about a degree of co-ordination and a perspective which might not otherwise have existed within the organization. The existence of detailed plans facilitates delegation and permits the establishment of relatively autonomous divisions, while ensuring that overall control remains. It provides a set of goals and criteria for assessing the merits of new opportunities and proposals, whether for concentration or diversification of the business.

## The business policy process

Two important and interrelated aspects are evident in the business policy process: formulation and implementation.

*Formulation* will involve:

1. the identification of opportunities for, and threats to, the organization, together with the estimation of the degree of risk associated with each;
2. the assessment of the organization's present and potential strengths and weaknesses, particularly in respect of its material, financial, technical and personnel resources, i.e. its potential capacity to pursue identified opportunities and/or to deal with threats;
3. consideration of the personal values and aspirations of the organization's major influential internal stakeholders, in particular its managers;
4. clarification and acknowledgement of the major social responsibilities and objectives of the organization.

Consideration of (1) and (2) above can give rise to the development of a rational *economic policy* for an organization through the matching of opportunities to capabilities. This is rarely the total perspective for the development of business policy, for it will often be necessary to consider personal aspirations and preferences (3). It will be necessary to identify what an organization will 'want to do' as distinct from, or as a sub-set of, what it 'can or might do'. Finally, the inclusion of (4) above—a largely non-economic dimension—raises the question of what the organization 'should do', i.e. having regard to its responsibilities and social objectives. This four-part perspective is illustrated in Figure 2.1, which identifies the economic and non-economic aspects of action.

The culmination of this policy formulation stage is the statement of policies on:

(a) the nature of the goods or services to be provided by the organization;
(b) the nature of the markets/demand to be served;
(c) the manner in which these markets are to be served.

These are all aspects of considerable direct significance to operations management.

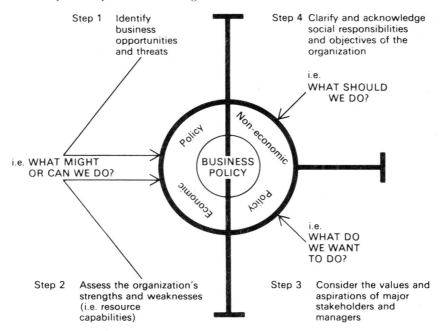

**Figure 2.1** *The formulation of business policy. From Wild, R. (1979)* Operations Management—A Policy Framework. *Oxford: Pergamon. Reproduced with permission.*

*Implementation* of an agreed policy is concerned with the acquisition and mobilization of resources, the creation of appropriate structures and processes, and monitoring and control. Again, four aspects can be identified:

(a) use of physical resources, e.g. equipment, machinery and labour, and the development of appropriate technology;

(b) the creation of appropriate organization structures and relationships, e.g. the roles and responsibilities of individuals, departments and functions, and the use of appropriate information systems, etc;

(c) organizational processes and behaviour, e.g. the development of individuals, their motivation and rewards, performance measurement, and the establishment of standards;

(d) top leadership, i.e. the provision, monitoring and updating of overall objectives, inter-function and inter-division co-ordination, overall resource allocation, etc.

## RELATIONSHIP OF BUSINESS POLICY AND OPERATIONS MANAGEMENT

Given that business policy decisions largely determine: (a) the nature of the goods or services to be provided; (b) the nature of the markets/demand to be served; (c) the manner in which these markets are to be served, their significance for operations management is clear. It will, however, be appropriate for us to look more closely at the mechanism of this relationship, and to this end we must consider: (a) the nature and manner of the influence of business policy decisions on operations management decisions; and (b) the contribution and manner of the contribution of operations management to business policy decisions.

## Influence of business policy decisions on operations management

Figures 1.5 and 1.6 in fact suggest means by which business policy decisions influence operations management. Policy decisions on the nature of the market/demand to be served and hence the predictability of the nature of demand will influence system structure feasibility (Figure 1.6). The manner in which markets are to be served influences the objectives pursued by operations management, which in turn must influence the choice or desirability of system structure (Figure 1.6) and the choice of management strategies (Figure 1.5).

Thus policy decisions on the nature of the goods or services to be provided, the nature of the markets/demand to be served and the manner in which these markets are to be served will influence operations management's choice of operating system structure, their choice of strategies and the formulation of operations management objectives. The influence on the formulation of objectives is direct, while as regards systems structure and strategies the business policy influence is indirect. These influences are shown diagrammatically in Figure 2.2 and discussed below.

### *System structure decisions and formulation of objectives*

The structure of the operating system influences the role and problems of operations management; however, operations managers are unlikely to have a free choice of system structure, since the nature of the function and the customers' influence on the system are major external factors influencing the appropriateness of a system structure (Figure 1.6). For example, we have indicated that one fundamental feature of transport and service systems is their dependence on inputs controlled by the customer. In practice an organization may have some scope for influencing the customer, and thus the 'pull' or 'push' on the operating system. Such influence may derive from advertising and marketing activities, pricing, product policies, etc. An organization may therefore have some influence on the structure of the operating system, but such influence will normally be external to the operations manager. From the operation manager's point of view the nature of the function and the customer influence on the system are constraints, deriving in part from decisions relating to the nature of the product or service and the nature of the market, i.e. the goods/service and market/demand characteristics determined through business policy decisions. Taking a slightly different viewpoint, the operations manager will recognize that in some circumstances certain system structures cannot be adopted, i.e. they are infeasible, since the factors which permit their existence are absent. There are certain prerequisites for the existence of an operating system structure. Certain factors will permit, and in exceptional conditions cause, one or more of the structures to exist. Such prerequisites or enabling factors are essentially of an external nature and, as we saw in Chapter 1, are mainly related to the predictability of the nature of demand. The feasibility of system structures is dependent on the predictability of the nature of the demands of the customer on the system. Such predictability is an enabling factor, hence it does not follow that the existence of predictable customer demand will necessarily give rise to the existence of a certain structure. For example, the nature of the demand for the output of a power station is known, yet output is not stocked. This condition is, however, one prerequisite—a further external factor—without which certain structures will not in reality exist. It will limit the extent to which operations management can choose, or change, structures, and again this constraint will be

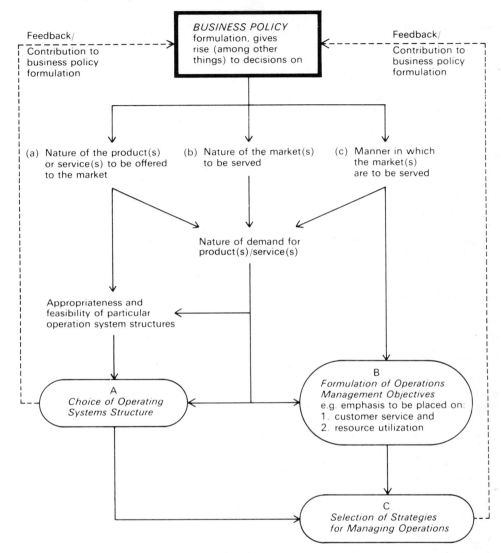

**Figure 2.2** *The principal influences of business policy on operations management decisions.*

largely influenced by decisions relating to the nature of the product or service and the nature of the market, i.e. the goods/market and market/demand characteristics determined through business policy decisions.

Given the feasibility of certain operating system structures, the choice between them will be influenced by the objectives of operations management. These will reflect management's view of what the customer wants or will be prepared to accept by way of service, and the need within this constraint to maximize resource productivity. While the general objectives of operations management are clear, the manner in which those objectives are pursued, and certainly the emphasis placed on each, may be influenced by broader business policy decisions. To some extent, therefore, operations management will be required to pursue a stipulated policy as effectively as possible. Policy on customer service may be influenced to some considerable degree by broader business policy considerations. Although a mail order firm, a luxury store and a supermarket are all concerned with the function of supply, they each have a different approach to the objective of customer service, hence operations management will not be required to achieve the same standards of service in each case. Often standards or objectives for customer service will be influenced by other functions in the organization.

Management can change structures by changing capacity, can allow changes to occur by not adjusting capacity to balance demand level changes, or can avoid structure changes by manipulating capacity to maintain a balance with a changing demand level. Such changes may result from changed objectives.

There are therefore both indirect and direct influences of business policy on operating system structure. Goods/service characteristics determine the nature of the function and the influence of the customer, which in turn determine which of the seven basic structures are appropriate. Both goods/service and market/demand characteristics determine the predictability of the nature of demand, which in turn influences system structure feasibility. Business policy will also influence the importance to be attached to customer service and resource productivity objectives, which affects the choice from among feasible structures.

### Operations management strategies

In Chapter 1 we considered how system structure and operations management objectives influence the strategies and role of operations management (see Figure 1.5). Each system structure is likely to have different problem characteristics in each of the three principal problem areas. The nature of the problems to be tackled by operations management is therefore influenced by system structure. The manner in which these and other problems are tackled will also be influenced by the objectives which exist. In other words, a problem may be tackled in a particular manner in order to achieve a particular outcome given one set of objectives, and in a different manner for a different end given a different set of objectives. Thus the strategies adopted for the management of a given system, i.e. the general approaches employed, will be influenced by the nature of the problems which exist and the objectives which are to be pursued. The selection of strategies is therefore influenced by business policy decisions in two ways: through the influences on the selection of system structure in the manner discussed above, and through the influence on operations management objectives.

### Contribution of operations management to business policy decisions

The principal means by which operations management contributes to or influences business policy decisions is through the provision of information on:

(a) the existing operating system structure, objectives and strategy;
(b) the implications for operations management of proposed or alternative goods/service and market/demand characteristics.

In possible 'change' situations, both (a) and (b) are relevant, whereas in the establishment of entirely 'new' systems only (b) is appropriate. Change situations may occur when a change or modification of the existing goods or service(s) is under consideration and/or when new markets are being investigated. In such situations an operating system is in existence and changes are being considered which might affect or necessitate a change of system objectives and strategies. Clearly some knowledge of the nature of the existing system, its characteristics and performance will be of value in making business policy decisions in such circumstances. The alternative is the 'greenfield' situation, in which business policy decisions will lead to the establishment of new operating systems. Here operations management must interpret alternative goods/services and market/demand strategies into implications for operations management, since the nature of the system structure, operations management objectives and strategies required to meet given goods/service and market/demand characteristics will influence the choice between alternatives.

Whatever the situation, operations management is, in effect, using the same type of information in seeking to influence business policy decisions. The main factor in both cases is the need to match operating system structures, operations management objectives and strategies to given goods/service and market/demand conditions, or vice versa. If it is intended to change goods/service and/or market/demand specifications, then a knowledge of the characteristics and capabilities of the existing operating system, existing operations management objectives and strategies, and the effectiveness of existing systems and strategies is important. Equally, it is important when considering alternative goods/service and/or market/demand specifications to know what system structures, objectives and strategies will be required for effective operation.

## Operations management policy decisions

We have seen that three operations management decisions are influenced by prior business policy decisions, i.e.

(a) selection/formulation of operations management objectives;
(b) selection/choice of system structure;
(c) selection/formulation of strategies for the management of the operating system.

These are key operations management decision areas. They are all concerned with planning. Operations management must determine system structure and objectives and contribute to the determination of objectives before anything can be manufactured, supplied, transported or serviced. They are key decisions, since wrong decisions in these areas will inevitably affect the performance of the system and the organization. Together they will determine the nature and character of the operating system. They are in fact operations management *policy* decision areas. The choice of operating system structure, the objectives of the system, and the strategies which will be employed in the management of the system are the principal ingredients in the formulation of an operations management policy.

We have seen that operations management contributes to business policy decisions by providing information on:

(a) the existing system structure, objectives and strategy, in order that the characteristics and capabilities of the system might be considered in the selection/change of goods/service and market/demand characteristics; or
(b) the implications of proposed or alternative goods/service and market/demand characteristics for system structure, objectives and strategy.

This contribution of operations management to business policy decisions therefore focuses on the three operations management policy decision areas. In fact, as might have been expected, it is principally the policy decisions of operations management which are both influenced by and contribute to business policy decisions.

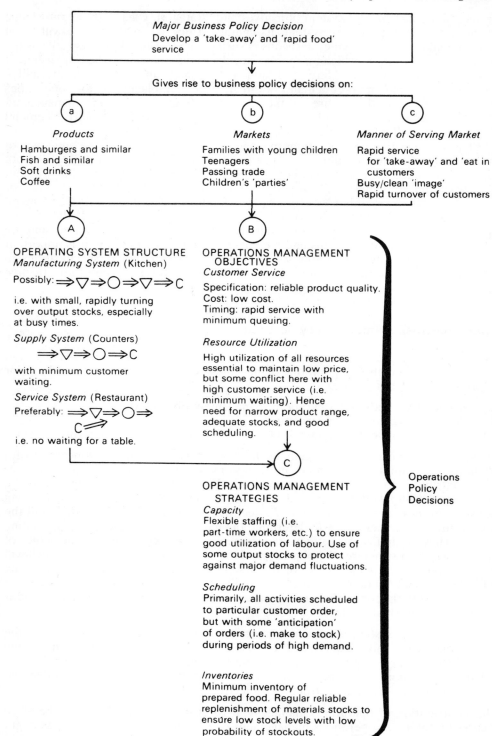

**Figure 2.3**  *An example of the major influences of business policy on operations management decisions: a restaurant.*

## EXAMPLE: A RESTAURANT

An example of the manner and nature of the influence of business policy decisions on operations management is shown in Figure 2.3. Here the major policy decision—to establish a 'take-away' and 'rapid food' restaurant—gives rise to decisions on the nature of the product, the markets to be served and the manner in which the organization is to deal with its customers. These decisions, in turn, give rise to the need for operations management decisions in the three key operations policy areas, which in turn will give rise to decisions on labour and staffing, the layout of the system, quality control, the maintenance of equipment, etc. Any problems anticipated in the implementation of the operations policies will encourage operations managers to feed back views to the business policy decision-makers with the intention if necessary, of modifying the business policy and/or modifying objectives of the operations function.

## FURTHER READING

Ansoff, H. I. (1970) *Corporate Strategy*. Harmondsworth: Penguin. A management science modelling approach to business policies focusing largely on market factors.

Hayes, R. H. and Schmenner, R. W. (1978) How should you organise manufacturing?, *Harvard Business Review*, Jan.–Feb., pp. 108–118. Concerned solely with manufacture.

Wild, R. (1979) *Operations Management—A Policy Framework*. Oxford: Pergamon. A conceptual/ theoretical treatment of operating systems and operations management in a business policy context. The text develops in detail many of the points raised in this chapter.

## QUESTIONS

**2.1** How might business policy decisions influence operations management decision-making? How might operations management contribute to the formulation of business policy?

**2.2** Discuss the relationship of operating system structure and (a) the characteristics of the goods or services provided by the system, and (b) the nature of the market(s) and demand(s) for the goods or services.

**2.3** What are the main policy decision areas of operations management? How are these related to business policy decisions?

# CHAPTER 3

# The Market Context of Operations Management

Chapter 2 showed that certain decisions which are largely 'external' to the operations function have a considerable influence on decisions within the function. These external policy-related decisions are largely concerned with the organization's relationship with its market(s).

Three market-related policy decisions have been shown to be of particular importance:

(a) the decision on the nature of the goods or services to be provided by the organization, i.e. the *goods/service(s) characteristics*;
(b) the decision on the nature of the markets to be served, i.e. the *market/demand characteristics*;
(c) the manner in which these markets are to be served.

Operations management must therefore recognize a close relationship with the marketing function in the business. This chapter will focus initially on the nature of the marketing function and its relationship with operations management. The three market-related policy decisions above will be examined, largely from the operations manager's viewpoint and we shall then consider some aspects of product design.

## THE MARKETING FUNCTION

The marketing function of the business is concerned primarily with the nature of the 'offering' (the goods/service characteristics) and the methods by which the 'offering' is made (the advertising and distribution methods, etc.). Conventionally such decisions are considered to comprise the elements of the *marketing mix* of goods or services, cost, distribution, and promotion. While all businesses must make decisions on each of these four elements of the marketing mix, different types of business will employ different mixes, since they will attach different relative importance to each element.

For example, companies involved in providing consumer goods might emphasize promotion (e.g. advertising), while companies providing a specialist service might emphasize cost or price. Decisions on these four elements, outlined below, may be considered to be the deliberate market decisions of the organization.

(a) *goods/service,* i.e. goods/service characteristics—the actual item, transport or service provided to the customer, its attributes and characteristics, the features and provisions surrounding it and the essential benefits it provides;

(b) *cost,* i.e. the purchase price of the goods or service and any additional costs or allowances;

(c) *distribution,* i.e. the location of the market, channels of distribution, outlets, territories, etc., involved in the provision of the offering to the customer;

(d) *promotion,* i.e. the publicity, selling and advertising practices employed to bring the goods or services to the notice of the intended customer.

These market decisions influence, but do not determine, the nature of the demand faced by the organization, i.e. the demand felt by the operating system. In addition, other factors only partially influenced by the organization will influence demand, i.e.

(a) environmental variables—factors (largely beyond the control of the enterprise) that have broad effects on demand, e.g. the economic situation, public policy and culture;

(b) competitive variables: factors under the control of competitors.

Figure 3.1 indicates the manner in which environmental, competitive and market decision variables influence demand. The introduction of a new product or service may affect the total actual demand for products or services of that type and will also attract a part of that total. Environmental variables, the action of competitors and the market decisions of the enterprise may all affect the size of the total potential and actual market. Certain actions of competitors, e.g. advertising or price changes, may affect the size of the actual market, and of course market decisions by an organization, particularly promotion decisions, will directly affect actual market share. The nature of the environment will be known and may therefore influence market decisions. The actions of competitors will be uncertain but nevertheless may be considered by an enterprise when making decisions on goods/services, cost, promotion and distribution.

   Within this framework we shall focus on market decision variables, i.e. those decisions required of the business. In so doing we shall look more closely at the market-related policy decisions identified at the beginning of this chapter in order to try to identify how these decisions, which directly influence operations management, are made, and thus to identify the means by which operations managers might influence them.

## FACTORS INFLUENCING DECISIONS ON GOODS/SERVICE CHARACTERISTICS

Here we are dealing with one market decision variable (1 in Figure 3.1). The nature of the offering (i.e. the product or service) is, from the operations manager's viewpoint, perhaps the most important market decision. We shall identify some of the factors that influence this decision.

   Growth is a common, if not universal, corporate objective. Goods/service(s)

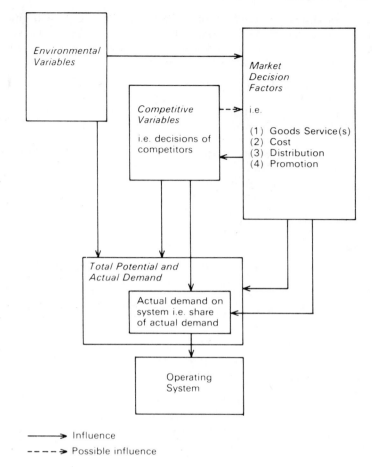

**Figure 3.1** *Factors influencing demand and operations management.*

decisions are an important ingredient in the formulation and implementation of each of the four policies for growth identified by Ansoff,[1] i.e.

1. *Market penetration* is the expansion of sales of existing offerings in existing markets by selling more to existing customers, and/or gaining new customers in existing markets.
2. *Market development* is the creation of new markets by discovering new applications for existing offerings.
3. *Product development* is the launching of new offerings onto existing markets.
4. *Diversification* or lateral integration is the development of new offerings for new markets.

For reasons of diversification and goods/service development, most enterprises will offer a range of goods and/or services. This market decision may therefore require consideration of the characteristics of a particular offering or the number and mix of the whole range of offerings. It may be concerned with the addition, change or abandonment of one offering or one group of offerings from the whole range, and/or

[1] Ansoff, H. I. (1968) A model for diversification, *Management Service*, **4** (4), pp. 391–414.

the nature, consistency and mix of the whole range. The following will be of relevance in this respect.

## Life-cycles

It has been found that products and services have a life-cycle during which demand increases, stabilizes and falls.

Four stages in the life-cycle of offerings can be identified: incubation, growth, maturity and decline. Life-cycles may be practically unnoticeable for some offerings and very obvious for others, such as consumer durables. The span of the life-cycle may be determined by such factors as:

(a) the degree of technological progress;
(b) changes in customer habits;
(c) ease of entry to the market.

Different actions or market decisions may be required at each stage of a life-cycle. Price decisions will be required before or at the launch time, while during the incubation period the emphasis will be on promotion. Distribution is all-important during the growth period. The maturity period may see the introduction of price changes or changes in specifications to prevent decline, and/or the introduction of new offerings.

## The development process

Goods/service development involves the search for new offerings as well as the improvement of the existing. Since the number of entirely new offerings is normally small, development is concerned largely with the introduction of variants through adaptations and improvements.

At least six stages of development can be identified. These are:

1. Exploration, including research, i.e. the continual search for new ideas.
2. Systematic, rapid screening to eliminate less promising ideas.
3. Business analysis, including market research and cost analysis.
4. Development of the remaining possibilities.
5. Testing the offerings developed.
6. Launching on a commercial scale.

Development, testing and launching (4, 5 and 6) are the most time consuming and most costly stages. Few new ideas are eventually launched, and of these only a small proportion succeed. For these reasons enterprises may adopt contrasting *philosophies on development,* resulting in:

(a) some enterprises assuming market leadership because of their strong research and development base; or
(b) some enterprises seeking to react quickly to the innovations of others and therefore joining the competition during the growth stage; or
(c) some enterprises joining in at a later stage, just before market saturation sets in, by adapting the offerings to the needs of special market segments; or
(d) some enterprises not wishing to be excluded from new markets but relying on their ability to produce on a mass scale and offer very competitive prices.

## Market policies

Three main methods are available to the enterprise to exploit the market: market aggregation, market segmentation and production differentiation.

*Market aggregation* is the penetration of the market to the greatest possible width and depth with a single offering or a very limited range. This approach relies on a uniform pattern of consumption and an appeal to the needs which customers have in common in order to win sales.

*Market segmentation* is concerned with placing an extensive range of offerings each of which is suited to the needs of a different submarket or market segment. Here a conscious search is made to determine the essential differences between buyer groups in order that they can be clearly separated into different segments, each varying in size, buying power and buyer behaviour.

*Product differentiation* is the deliberate attempt to encourage demand to adjust itself to the manner in which supply has been segmented. Unlike market segmentation, product differentiation may be employed where segments are not clearly defined and where segments must therefore be *created* by emphasizing the presence of product differences between the enterprise's own offerings and those of competitors, in particular by emphasizing product differences which promote a social—psychological segmentation of the market, favouring the product concerned.

## Quality, brand and brand policy

Quality is the extent to which an offering satisfies a need. Improving the quality of an offering or a line is known as 'trading up', and the reverse as 'trading down'. Quality may be changed. For example, it may be appropriate to adjust the range in response to economic developments such as the trade cycle, and/or to raise or lower both the quality and the price of offerings in the range. Trading up or down in the long term may help the enterprise to gain access, from its traditional market position, to other higher or lower segments of the market.

A brand is used to identify offerings and distinguish them from those of competitors. For brand policy to be successful the offering must lend itself to differentiation, to facilitate advertising and promotion. The aim of branding is to facilitate, improve and simplify control of the market process. A successful brand image will help secure a market. A·brand suggests consistency in the quality and origin of the offering.

## FACTORS INFLUENCING DECISIONS ON MARKET/DEMAND CHARACTERISTICS

Here, in effect, we are concerned with three market decision variables (2, 3 and 4 in Figure 3.1). Two aspects are of particular importance to the operations manager. First, there are those decisions which influence or determine the nature of the market for the offering and the nature of the demand felt by the organization. The operations manager will, of course, have some interest in these decisions and will wish to make some contribution to them. Second, given these decisions, the operations manager will be particularly concerned with the nature of the demand which is to be met. He or she will wish to measure or estimate demand, and may seek to predict future demand, all as a means to facilitate his or her own decision-making on capacity, schedules and inventories.

Here we shall consider the three remaining market decision variables—cost, distribution and promotion—all of which will influence market/demand characteristics.

## Cost

We shall concentrate on the price of the product or service—normally the most important, but not the only, cost factor.

Price is clearly important as a regulator of demand and a component of customer service. It:

(a) regulates sales volume;
(b) determines revenue;
(c) influences the rate of return on investment through its influence on sales profitability;
(d) has an impact on unit costs.

The principal decisions in pricing derive from four main problems:

1. How should the relative importance and the relative emphasis of price and non-price variables within marketing decisions be determined?
2. To which pricing policy is a particular price geared? Pricing policy, in a broad sense, should answer two questions:
   (a) What are the objectives for pricing?
   (b) How will these objectives be attained?
3. How should prices (i.e. price levels) for offerings be determined (and redetermined)?
4. How should pricing policy be implemented, e.g. the timing and extent of price changes and deviations such as discounts?

## Distribution

As the purpose of distribution is to move items from the point of provision to the point of consumption, market decisions on the nature of distribution are primarily the concern of *manufacture* and *supply* systems. Manufacture must rely upon a distribution system to ensure that goods reach the final customers or users. A supply system will form part of the distribution system for a manufacturer and may itself rely on subsequent distribution to the final user. For example, wholesalers will form part of the chain of distribution for a manufacturer and will themselves supply retailers.

Two aspects of decision-making for distribution can be identified: (a) distribution channel decisions, and (b) physical distribution management decisions. The latter, involving decisions on stock levels, etc., are more likely to influence operations management directly.

## Promotion

Promotion is concerned primarily with persuasion, aimed largely at securing and increasing the share of the actual market. Four promotional activities can be identified:

(a) *advertising*—any paid form of non-personal presentation and promotion of products or services by an identified sponsor;

(b) *personal selling*—oral presentation with one or more prospective purchasers for the purpose of making sales;

(c) *publicity*—non-personal stimulation of demand for a product or service, by planting commercially significant news about it in a published medium or obtaining favourable presentation of it that is not paid for by the sponsor;

(d) *sales promotion*—those marketing activities, other than personal selling, advertising and publicity, that stimulate consumer purchasing and dealer effectiveness, such as displays, shows and exhibitions, demonstrations, and various non-recurrent selling efforts not in the ordinary routine.

An enterprise must decide how much promotional effort to make, and the relative mix or importance of each of the above within that total effort. The importance of promotion will, among other things, depend on the merits of alternative non-promotional expenditure, the nature of the product or service offered by the enterprise and its competitors, and the stage in the product or service life-cycle.

Promotion is one way to secure and stimulate demand. Given limited resources, promotion competes for funds with the other three market decision variables. The more impersonal the method of distribution and the greater the similarity to the products or services offered by competitors, the greater is the need for promotional effort. Products and services which are at an early stage in their life-cycle, where exposure and customer awareness are important, may also need relatively high promotion.

## THE RELATIONSHIPS OF OPERATIONS MANAGEMENT AND MARKETING DECISIONS

Marketing managers are primarily responsible for the four 'marketing mix' decisions discussed above. These decisions are of substantial interest to operations managers, for they will determine the products/services to be provided by the operating system and the nature of demand for those outputs. Operations managers will, at least, wish to monitor all the decisions which influence them. In most cases they will wish to exercise some influence on these decisions, and in some cases they may need to ensure that marketing managers do not make decisions which give rise to circumstances which operations managers cannot adequately accommodate. For example, they will wish to avoid situations in which, as a result of decisions over which they had no influence, they feel obliged to deal with a great diversity of products/services, each with too small quantities, with unacceptable deadlines or delivery dates, too high a quality and too low a cost. This is an extreme situation, but operations managers must seek to avoid the impossible by emphasizing the feasible. It would be appropriate for them, therefore, to have in mind a 'checklist' of those decisions which influence the nature of the product/service, the market for that 'offering' and the manner in which that market is to be satisfied. Table 3.1 provides such a checklist.

**Table 3.1**  *A checklist of some marketing decisions which influence operations management.*

---

Product/service characteristics
    the development philosophy
    market policy
    the nature and quality of the product/service

Cost
    pricing policy
    the price of the offering
    price variations

Distribution
    level of service
    inventory decisions

Promotion
    advertising—amount
              —scheduling
    selling—size of sales force

---

Operations managers will also need to measure, estimate or forecast demand. We saw in Chapter 1 that, in certain types of operating systems, resources are stocked in anticipation of their being needed at a future date. Similarly, some systems rely on the provision of output stocks from which customers are supplied direct.

In all such systems the level of both resource and output stocks provided must be influenced by the level of demand which is expected to exist at some future date. In such cases, therefore, the estimation or prediction of demand is of importance.

Existing demand levels can be measured, and this is of significance in the management of operating systems which require resources to be obtained directly to meet demand from particular customers. It should be noted, however, that even given this need, and given the ability to measure demand levels. errors may be introduced. Rarely is it possible to measure directly the amount of resources required to satisfy particular customer orders. Normally, since orders will probably differ (otherwise resources will probably have been stocked), it will be necessary to estimate the resource requirements of a particular customer order. Thus for all types of operating systems the translation of either known or expected demand into required resources will be susceptible to error through:

(a) demand estimation/forecasting errors; and/or
(b) errors in the estimation of the resource requirements associated with customer orders/demand.

Operations management must employ such procedures in order adequately to accommodate this externally influenced factor and ensure realistic internal decision-making on problems such as capacity and inventory management and activity scheduling.

In demand forecasting, the length of the forecast period will depend largely on the nature of system resources and the nature of the market. For example, capacity planning may involve periods in excess of five years where there is sufficient stability or predictability of the nature of demand. A long-term view may be essential where there is a long lead time on the provision or replacement of resources. Examples might include:

(a) manufacture—steel manufacture, electricity generation and supply, oil production;

(b) transport—airlines, rail systems;
(c) service—hospitals, telephone service.

In contrast, a shorter-term view would be appropriate where the nature of demand is less stable or less predictable, and where resources are more readily provided or replaced, or where the manner in which the function is accomplished may change, for example through technological change. Examples might include:

(a) manufacture—fashion goods, consumer durables;
(b) supply—retail shops, mail order;
(c) transport—bus service, taxi service, road delivery service;
(d) service—secretarial services, security service.


## PRODUCT DESIGN


We shall now outline some aspects and procedures which relate specifically to product design, and which will therefore be of relevance primarily in respect of manufacture and supply systems.

Figure 3.2 outlines the various steps involved in product design, and the following brief discussion relates to some of these steps and certain other important considerations and constraints.


### Research and development


Product research is seldom begun only in response to consumer demand. Indeed a great deal of research is conducted in most industries, the purpose of which is to make discoveries, establish new applications and interpret new findings, in the hope or anticipation that these will lead eventually to commercial application. Pure or fundamental research is not specifically oriented to commercial application or product design, but is encouraged by companies in anticipation of its future commercial worth. The same justification and motivation applies, but to a lesser extent, to fundamental research conducted on behalf of companies by co-operative research establishments or universities. Applied research is of more immediate worth and is often undertaken in order to provide answers to specific problems relating to either existing or proposed products.

It is often difficult to distinguish clearly between research and development; however, development is concerned with either a prototype pre-production product or a specified design for a product or part of a product.


### Quality


In Chapter 19 we shall show that quality, and hence reliability, is invested in a product during two stages: design and manufacture. During the design stage quality is determined by the specification of appropriate standards and tolerances on dimensions, content, etc.

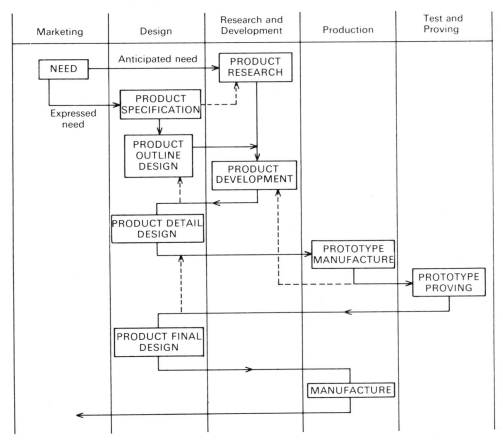

**Figure 3.2** *Product design, development and manufacture.*

The quality level obtained is, of course, a function of cost. While no product can be designed to have perfect quality or perfect maintainability and reliability, the expenditure of more money on materials, testing, manufacture and control will naturally improve quality levels. In practice, product quality will be determined not by the availability of suitable materials or production equipment, but by the quality of competitors' products, the elasticity of demand, and the planned product price. In many cases the use of standards, such as those formulated by the British Standards Institution or the American Society for the Testing of Materials, is obligatory or advisable.

## Purchasing

Since no manufacturer is completely independent of suppliers, for direct materials, indirect materials, components or sub-assemblies, the purchasing function will influence product design. Not only will the design of a new product depend on the ready availability of certain purchased items, but in the redesign, i.e. modification, replacement or improvement, of existing products, the purchasing department will play an important part because of its knowledge of such factors as the development of new materials and improved components.

## Make-or-buy decision

Theoretically, every item which is currently purchased from an outside supplier is a candidate for internal manufacture. Conversely, every item currently manufactured is a potential candidate for purchase. In reality the problem is not quite so extensive as this, since there will always be a good many items which it would just not be in our interest to make, such as raw materials, specialist parts and indirect items like stationery and ink. Similarly, there will always be many items which it would not be in our interest to purchase.

By making an item we reduce our dependence on other companies and avoid the consequences of their labour disputes; we are able to determine our own quality levels and we preserve our trade secrets. Conversely, to purchase items rather than make them ourselves may enable us to obtain them more quickly and obtain the benefits from a continual development programme which we ourselves could not sustain. Additionally, purchase instead of manufacture may reduce costs such as those associated with storage, handling, paperwork, etc., as well as releasing our facilities for jobs on which they might be more suitably and profitably employed. We can usefully consider the make-or-buy decision as falling into two categories: first, as above, decisions about items already being manufactured or purchased, and second, decisions about new items.

## Value analysis and value engineering

Value analysis has been defined as follows: '. . .an organized approach to get the same performance at lower cost without affecting quality'; '. . .an organized and systematic effort to provide the required function at the lowest cost consistent with specified performance and reliability'; and '. . .a functionally oriented scientific method for improving product value by relating the elements of product worth to their corresponding elements of product cost in order to accomplish the required function at least cost in resources'.

Often the title 'value engineering' is used synonymously with 'value analysis'. We shall use the latter title only, but it is perhaps worth noting that 'value engineering' is normally used in relation to the design of new products and 'value analysis' in relation to existing products.

How does value analysis differ from conventional cost reduction techniques? Cost reduction generally relates to existing products and is concerned with attempts to manufacture them at a lower cost by minimizing the material used, changing the design to facilitate manufacture, changing tolerances, methods, and so on. Value analysis, however, is more comprehensive, since it begins with an examination of the purpose of functions of the product and is concerned with establishing the means by which such a purpose or function can best be fulfilled.

The principal objective of value analysis is to increase profit by means of a critical examination of areas of high cost, with the purpose of eliminating unnecessary costs. Such an objective can, of course, be pursued retrospectively by an examination of existing products and parts, or currently by involvement in the design of future products or parts. We shall see later that the objectives of value analysis—indeed the methods of value analysis—are conceptually similar to those of method study.

Whereas the latter is concerned solely with the minimization of labour costs, value analysis is concerned primarily with material costs, which usually contribute substantially to the total manufacturing cost of any product. Although the cost breakdown varies between industries, it is common for direct materials to represent about 50 per cent of total product cost.

Hence value is maximized when the cost associated with achieving the necessary function is minimized. Alternatively 'value' can be defined as the 'lowest cost to accomplish the essential function reliably'.

Two types of value can be identified: *esteem* value and *use* value. Use value is related entirely to function, i.e. the ability of an item to perform its specific purpose. Esteem value is not directly concerned with function but with the status or regard associated with ownership. Value, for our purpose, is the sum of these two, use value normally being the principal component.

The result of properly applied value analysis is not, as is sometimes claimed, an inferior product but rather a product whose value/cost relationship is improved, a product which provides the necessary function with the essential qualities, at a minimum cost.

Although other methods of conducting value analysis are available, it is usually found that the team approach is most appropriate and successful. Value analysis teams should consist of members with complementary skills drawn from the following departments within a company.

Design
Purchasing
Marketing
Production
Accounts

Such an approach is desirable, since value can be determined at any or all of the stages between initial conception and final delivery. Furthermore, since maximum cost savings are often associated with purchased items, it is usual to draw upon the specialized knowledge of the supplier.

Value analysis is therefore a common-sense approach to product design or redesign, which involves the following steps:

1. Determine the function of the product.
2. Develop alternative designs.
3. Ascertain the costs.
4. Evaluate alternatives.

The relative importance placed by the customer upon the following will determine design or redesign objectives:

(a) function;
(b) appearance;
(c) esteem associated with possession;
(d) intrinsic cost of materials or labour;
(e) replacement, exchange or disposal value.

As regards existing products, the following questions will help to identify potential value improvements:

1. Which areas appear to offer largest savings?
2. What percentage of total cost is associated with bought-out items?
3. What percentage of total cost is associated with labour?
4. What percentage of total cost is associated with materials?

Often the maximum cost saving associated with existing products relates to bought-out parts or materials. The value of purchased parts and materials can be investigated with a view to material or design changes by asking questions such as the following:

1. How does it contribute to the value of the product?
2. How much does it contribute to the total cost of the product?
3. Are all its features and its specification necessary?
4. Is it similar to any other part?
5. Can a standard part be used?
6. Will an alternative design provide the same function?

Generally six main steps are involved in a value analysis investigation, whether in relation to a new or an existing product.

The first step involves the collection of information. Information should be collected about costs, function, customer requirements, the history and possible future development of the product design, the manufacturing methods, and so on.

The second stage covers the development of alternative designs, i.e. alternative methods of achieving the required function. This is the creative, speculative stage during which use may be made of 'brainstorming' sessions, etc.

No reasonable alternative or suggestion should be rejected during this stage, irrespective of apparent cost or practical disadvantages.

It should be the objective during this stage to:

(a) eliminate parts or operations;
(b) simplify parts or operations;
(c) substitute alternative materials;
(d) use standard parts or materials;
(e) relax manufacturing tolerances;
(f) use standard manufacturing methods;
(g) eliminate unnecessary design features;
(h) change design to facilitate manufacture;
(i) buy rather than manufacture parts if cheaper;
(j) use prefinished materials;
(k) use prefabricated parts;
(l) rationalize product ranges;
(m) substitute low-cost manufacturing processes;
(n) rationalize range of purchased parts;
(o) eliminate material waste.

Use of checklists such as that shown in Table 3.2 may be of value during this stage.

The third stage involves the *evaluation of alternatives*. Alternative designs must be compared on a cost basis, cost information relating to all aspects of the designs being obtained from the purchasing, production and accounts departments. The temptation to dismiss alternatives perfunctorily should be resisted. Furthermore, whenever possible, ideas should be salvaged from eliminated alternatives.

The final stage is *recommendation* and *implementation*.

## Classification, coding and standardization

Specifications provide details of product or component requirements in terms of materials, composition, dimensions, performance, and so on, while a standard can be

**Table 3.2**   *Value analysis checklist.*

| Area | Questions |
|---|---|
| Production function | 1. What are basic functions? |
| | 2. What are secondary functions? |
| | 3. Are all the functions necessary? |
| | 4. What else will perform the same function? |
| | 5. Can any of the functions be incorporated in other components? |
| Materials | 1. What material is used? |
| | 2. What is the material specification? |
| | 3. Can any other material be used? |
| | 4. Can any other specification of the same material be used? |
| | 5. Can waste material be reduced? |
| | 6. Can raw material be standardized? |
| | 7. Can raw material be obtained in a different form? |
| | 8. What is the price of the material? |
| | 9. What indirect materials are used (e.g. packing, lubrication)? |
| | 10. Can pre-finished materials be used? |
| Size and specification | 1. Can dimensions be reduced? |
| | 2. Is the part oversize? |
| | 3. If less expensive material is used can size be increased? |
| | 4. What tolerances are specified? |
| | 5. Which tolerances are not critical? |
| | 6. Can tolerances be increased? |
| | 7. Can a standard part be used? |
| | 8. What finish is required? |
| | 9. Are the finish standards essential? |
| | 10. Can an alternative method of applying the finish be used? |
| Manufacture | 1. Can any operations be eliminated? |
| | 2. Can any operations be combined? |
| | 3. Can any operations be simplified? |
| | 4. Would a different material simplify manufacture? |
| | 5. Can standard processes be used? |
| | 6. Can standard tools and jigs be used? |
| | 7. Can assembly operations be reduced? |
| | 8. Can prefabricated parts be used? |
| | 9. Would it be cheaper to buy the parts? |

defined as any accepted or established rule, model or criterion against which comparisons can be made. *Standardization* is therefore concerned with the concept of variety, and, more specifically, with the control of *necessary* variety. Company standardization begins to operate once unnecessary variety has been eliminated. The elimination of unnecessary variety (variety reduction) can be defined as 'the process of eliminating the unnecessary diversity which frequently exists in the various stages from design to manufacture or selling' and is undertaken in anticipation of obtaining some or all of the following advantages:

1. There is increased interchangeability of parts, simpler stock-keeping and improved customer service.
2. Production of parts in larger quantities enables better machine utilization.
3. Production planning and control are facilitated.
4. Operator training is simplified.
5. Drawing office, sales and service records are simplified.
6. There are lower stocks of raw materials, work in progress, and finished products.
7. There are fewer jigs, tools and fixtures.
8. There are fewer set-ups and change-overs of machinery.

The principal prerequisite for successful standardization is an effective system of coding and classification which will enable component or part variety to be identified and controlled. An appropriate classification and coding method is invaluable during variety reduction, as well as during the design of new products, and such a coding and classification method should satisfy the following requirements:

1. It should enable items identical or similar to others to be identified and located.
2. It should enable existing items to be used in new designs where possible.
3. It should facilitate the reduction of necessary variety.
4. It should enable substitutes for 'out of stock' items to be identified.
5. It should enable groups of similar items to be located for production planning and production purposes.

Clearly an adequate coding and classification system is beneficial to many departments in the company; indeed, one of the principal benefits of such a system is contained in requirement 5 above. The manufacture of parts in groups or families rather than in small quantities makes increased machine utilization possible and often results in an entirely different plant layout. This method of manufacture, normally called *group technology,* depends entirely on effective coding and classification methods and will be discussed in more detail in Chapter 14.

Here we are concerned primarily with the design of products, and hence the principal benefit of an effective coding system is that it enables similar items to be classified together and thus facilitates the control of variety during design. In many cases, because of the lack of such a system, a great deal of time is wasted in designing items similar (often identical) to designs already in existence.

## Methods of coding

Parts or components are frequently coded by one of the following methods.

### Sequential coding

When drawings for new parts are coded sequentially, with numbers taken from a register, no useful classification results. Occasionally code letters are used in conjunction with sequential numbering, but even so little useful classification is obtained.

### Product coding

Parts are often coded in such a way as to indicate the product for which the part was originally designed. Alpha numerical codes are often used, the numerical portion giving a unique identity to the part, while the alphabetical part identifies the original product or even the original contract or customer.

### Production process code

Less frequently, parts are coded according to their method of manufacture or their sequence of operations. For example, differing codes will be used for cast, forged and welded items, for items produced from stock bar, plate, etc.

*Design code*

Often, where there is an effort to maintain variety control and standardization, parts coding is mainly on a design basis. Products of similar appearance or purpose are coded in a similar manner, thus facilitating the selection and adoption of suitable existing parts rather than the design of new ones.

Clearly, if any useful classification of products or components is to result, some form of design coding must be adopted. There have been basically two approaches to the problem: the overall or macro approach and the specific or micro approach.

Several research workers, adopting the macro approach, have attempted to develop universal component classification systems as a result of studies of statistics of the components most commonly found in certain industries. The first of these research projects was begun at the Aachen Machine Tool Laboratory in Germany in the early 1950s and resulted in the Opitz method of coding and classification. The object of this research was to determine the statistics of the components commonly manufactured in the engineering industries. The Opitz method of classification, which is used for machined parts only, uses a five-digit form code to describe the shape of the component, and a four-digit supplementary code to specify the component size, material, raw material and accuracy.

Depite the relative popularity of universal classification systems, particularly the Opitz system, macro systems have recently been subject to a good deal of criticism. It is argued that the proportion of certain types of component, e.g. rotational components, found in industry is likely to vary with the nature of the industry concerned, and that the statistics or features of a particular class of components are likely to vary according to the type of industry concerned.

Several researchers have concluded, therefore, that there is no fixed pattern of components throughout industry and that the concept of a universal classification system is at worst mistaken and at best of very limited value.

In contrast to the overall or macro approach, the micro approach concentrates on the particular requirements and characteristics of an individual company. Perhaps the best example of this approach is the Brisch classification system. The Brisch system is designed for the needs of each particular company, needs which can be established only after a survey of the types of component and methods of production. The method of coding is mainly design-oriented, but additional 'production' information can be added by means of a second code. The design information is contained in a *monocode,* e.g. shape, design, size, features, while a *polycode* contains information relevant to during-production planning. The micro system can therefore be designed specifically according to the requirement of the drawing office concerned and is therefore considered by many to be a superior approach to company standardization.

## Computer-aided design (CAD) and manufacture

The designer provides product specifications. Production engineers convert these specifications into manufacturing instructions. Traditionally, all such information is contained on product drawings and production process sheets, but this structure is now changing with the use of computer-based design methodology and computer-controlled manufacture. The use of computers in manufacture has required the solution of some complex problems, but soon the batch manufacture of discrete items—which is the major portion of engineering manufacture in most industrialized countries—will be transformed by the use of computers. Already computer-aided design in such industries is well established. Computer-aided manufacture is now emerging.

### Computer-aided design

The designer, working with a CAD system, operates from a design terminal or work station, typically comprising a VDU screen, keyboard, graphics tablet, light pen and printer. Here the designer interacts with the computer system to develop a product design in detail, monitoring his or her work constantly on the VDU display. By issuing commands to the computer system the designer creates a design, manipulating, modifying and refining it, all without putting pen to paper. To facilitate this design process, the computer can manipulate the designer's 'drawing' by enlarging, rotating, sectioning, etc. any part of it. This software can be used for design calculations, to insert dimensions, to work out tolerances, etc. All such information can then be retained in the computer file and printed out as a drawing of the detailed product design.

A computer can file this design using an appropriate coding/classification system. It can be accessed by other designers at a later stage so that parts can be used for other designs and to ensure adequate product standardization. The CAD system considerably facilitates the design process and greatly increases design productivity. The use of such a facility also enables a comprehensive design database to be generated. The sophistication of such a database and the ease of access to it encourage product standardization and provide an interface with a system of computer-aided manufacture (CAM).

### Computer-aided manufacture

The design specification largely comprises dimensional and shape details together with the materials specifications of products. Traditionally, such information was used by production engineers to produce manufacturing process instructions comprising operations lists, lists of tools and machinery requirements, operations routeing details, details of jigs, fixtures, etc. Now this information can be added to the computer database for each product. Indeed, to some extent, the determination of these details can be undertaken automatically, e.g. process routeing. Further, it is possible through a CAM system to produce information for computer-controlled manufacturing processes; for example, a computer-controlled machining centre will require data to enable it to make the necessary cuts in the material to produce an item to correspond to dimensional specifications. This sequence of operations can be produced from the database as a magnetic tape for transfer to the machining centre, or can be 'downloaded' directly to the machining centre through the CAD/CAM system. In addition, tooling requirements, tool change requirements for machines, and production schedules can be produced from the CAD/CAM database, given information on available capacity, delivery requirements, etc.

Therefore an adequate design/manufacturing database is a prerequisite for the effective use of CAD/CAM and the use of computer-controlled integrated manufacture. The existence of an adequate database, the adoption of particular design principles and the existence of computer-controlled manufacturing facilities will also enable other advantages to be gained. For example, in batch production, similar items can be identified to facilitate machine set-up, etc. (see Chapter 4).

## FURTHER READING

Crum, L. W. (1971) *Value Engineering: Organized Search for Value*. Harlow: Longman. Value engineering and analysis briefly described, with examples.

Grooves, M. P. and Zimmers, E. W. Jr (1984) *CAD/CAM—Computer Aided Design and Manufacturing*. Englewood Cliffs, NJ: Prentice Hall.

Holt, R. (1977) *Product Innovation*. Sevenoaks: Newnes-Butterworth. Covers all decisions from conception to product launch.

Kotler, P. (1976) *Marketing Management—Analysis, Planning and Control*, 3rd edition. Englewood Cliffs, NJ: Prentice-Hall. A comprehensive treatment of marketing. Chapters 12 to 17 will be of particular relevance.

Kuhlmeijer, H. J. (1975) *Managerial Marketing*. Leiden: Stenfert Kroese.

## QUESTIONS

**3.1** How do marketing mix decisions influence the customer demand on the operating system?

**3.2** How does the performance of the operating system influence decisions on the 'market decision variables'?

**3.3** Identify and discuss the principal considerations and factors which will be taken into account in determining the nature of the goods or services to be provided by the organization.

**3.4** What factors or variables can be manipulated in order to create particular market/demand conditions and how might decisions about these factors/variables be made?

**3.5** (a) What is value analysis?
(b) What is value engineering?
(c) How does value analysis differ from conventional cost reduction?
(d) 'Value analysis is merely the application of the techniques of method study to the problems of product design.' Discuss.
(e) 'There is no need for the existence of a value analysis department in a company which employs competent product designers.' Discuss.

**3.6** You are required to conduct a value analysis exercise on the product shown below, which is a domestic five-amp unfused electric plug. Enumerate the principal steps involved in such an exercise and at each step provide the appropriate information or answers from your knowledge of this particular product, its use and its specification. As a result of this exercise suggest an alternative design if possible.

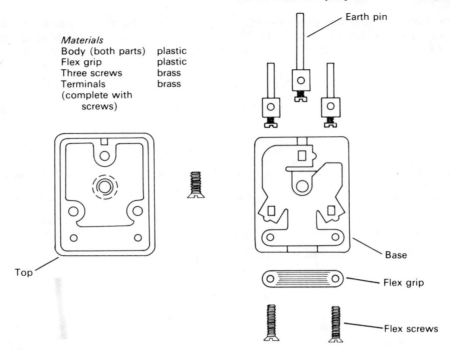

*Materials*
Body (both parts)   plastic
Flex grip           plastic
Three screws        brass
Terminals           brass
(complete with
    screws)

**3.7** Discuss the advantages and disadvantages of employing a value analysis engineer working alone against the use of an organized value analysis team. What would you consider to be the best composition of the value analysis team, and to whom should the team leader report?

**3.8** What are the requirements of an effective method of coding and classification? What are the benefits to a small jobbing engineering company of adopting such a method of coding and classification?

# CHAPTER 4

# Operations Economics

The transformation process within any business adds value and cost to the goods or service output from the system. In a manufacturing system the cost of physical conversion, e.g. materials processing, will often represent a major part of the total cost of the products produced. In transport, the cost of moving the customer, comprising the cost of the equipment used (e.g. the vehicles and service equipment) and the cost of the labour employed, as well as any overheads, will often be a major ingredient determining the total cost of the transport to the customer. Similarly, in supply and service systems the operations function, the responsibility of the operations manager, will contribute significantly to the total cost of the items or service provided for the eventual customer. Given this responsibility for 'cost contribution', the operations manager must be familiar with the factors contributing to the cost of operations, the factors influencing these costs, and the means available for the measurement and control of the cost of operations.

Without venturing into a detailed discussion of either microeconomics or cost accounting, we must here devote some time to a consideration of the nature of the costs associated with operations and the means available for the control of such costs.

## OPERATIONS COSTS

The components of cost may be direct or indirect. Direct costs comprise those which may be separately identified for each good or service produced, e.g. the cost of the direct materials consumed or incorporated and the cost of the direct labour involved in the provision of output items or services. Indirect costs are all other expenses which cannot be specifically charged to particular output items, services or transports. Indirect costs include the cost of indirect materials, indirect labour and all other charges involved in operating the system where such charges cannot realistically or accurately be allocated to particular goods or services, e.g. administration costs.

Together these costs might be seen, sequentially, to build up to the total cost of the operation and thus, with the profit, to the total cost to the customer, i.e. the selling or purchase price, in the manner shown in Figure 4.1. It will be noticed that, while the prime cost is normally considered to comprise the sum of direct labour and materials, no provision is made for direct costs associated with the third of our major resource inputs to the operating system, i.e. the machinery employed. The assumption here, as is usually the case in practice, is that machinery is used for multiple purposes and its costs therefore cannot normally be seen as a direct charge; they must be allocated as part of the overheads associated with the operation. While in some cases expenses other than those associated with labour and materials can be charged directly to particular outputs, other expenses are normally seen as part of the operations overhead. The operations overhead can, in turn, be subdivided into material, labour and other expenses in the manner outlined in Table 4.1.

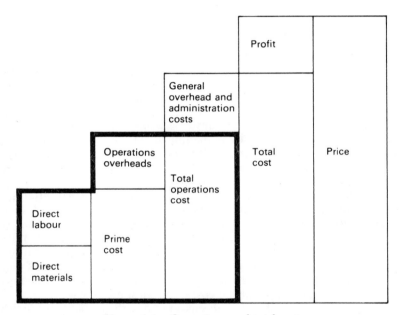

**Figure 4.1** *Operations and total costs.*

**Table 4.1** *Operations overheads.*

| Indirect materials | Indirect labour | Other expenses | |
|---|---|---|---|
| | | Standing costs | General costs |
| Tools | Supervision | Rent | Management |
| Consumed materials | Technical services | Depreciation | Welfare costs |
| | Transport | Insurance | Planning |
| | Quality control | Rates | Services |
| | Operations control | | Power |
| | | | Maintenance |

Together the operations overhead and the direct costs, i.e. the prime cost of the operation, constitute the total operations cost. These costs will be of particular interest to and will often be the ultimate responsibility of the operations manager. Other administrative and overhead costs, when added to the total operations cost, give the total cost associated with the item, transport or service provided. This total cost plus profit will give the total price or charge to the customer.

Operations managers will also be interested in the distinction between fixed and variable costs. Over a fairly short period of time certain of the organization's costs, in particular those associated with the operating system, can be seen to be fixed; they will not be affected by changes in the scale of the operation, i.e. changes in the throughput rate or output rate. These fixed costs will include many of the operations overheads, e.g. rent and rates on premises, depreciation on significant items of equipment, and insurance. Certain other costs, e.g. direct costs, in particular wages and the cost of consumer materials, will vary in the short term in that they will increase roughly in proportion to increased throughput or output, and vice versa.

## Factors influencing operations costs

Clearly the objectives established for the operating system will have fairly substantial cost implications. For example, in a manufacturing system the need to produce high-quality items may necessitate different manufacturing methods, the use of different materials and indeed the use of different labour from what would have been the case in the manufacture of a similar item of lower quality. The cost of manufacturing to this higher quality, other things being equal, will therefore be higher. It follows that the specification of the item to be produced, or in the case of non-manufacturing systems the specification of the service or transport to be provided, has significant implications for the cost of operations. The manner in which the operating system is managed, e.g. the choice of batch sizes and the scheduling of operations, must also have cost implications. The productivity of the resources employed will clearly affect unit operations costs. Indeed, taking an economist's view of operations and considering the principal prerequisites to be 'land', 'capital' and 'labour', the costs of operations may depend on the nature of the mix of these ingredients. In certain industries the value added to inputs is very much greater. Such differences cannot be attributed solely to the productivity of the various operations resources, but rather to the nature and mixture of these resources. For example, the greater the quantity of machinery the lower the labour charges per unit of output. Thus, where labour charges are high, there will be some benefit in substituting machinery for labour, despite the fact that the additional machinery incurs depreciation, maintenance and other costs. Comparisons between industries will provide the opportunity only for long-term control, and insufficient opportunity for day-to-day control of costs within the operations function. For this reason certain budgeting and cost control systems must be employed (see p. 57).

It should also be noted that certain scale factors are associated with the cost of operations, such that with increasing throughput or output rates unit costs might reduce. These are discussed in the following section.

## OPERATIONS ECONOMICS

Figure 4.2 illustrates some aspects of the relationship between operations cost and output (or throughput) rate. Over a short period certain of the operations costs can be

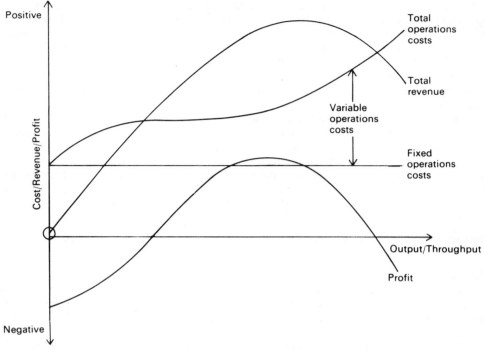

**Figure 4.2** *Costs* v. *output.*

seen to be fixed while others, the variable costs, will increase as output or the scale of operations increases. Initially this increase will be fairly rapid, then become more stable, and eventually become rapid as the maximum possible output or throughput rate is reached, and as bottlenecks are experienced and overtime working/subcontracting, etc. become necessary. The sum of the fixed and variable costs is shown in Figure 4.2 as the total operations costs.

Also shown in Figure 4.2 are curves representing revenue, i.e. the income generated from customers in payment for the goods or services provided by the operating system, and a curve representing the profit associated with that output, i.e. revenue less total costs. Total revenue rises as the organization is able to expand its scale of operations and thus its sales, although eventually revenue will reach a maximum point as price is lowered in order to stimulate further sales. The profits are maximized at a point where the difference between the total revenue and total cost curve is greatest. Notice that in most cases this profit maximization point occurs at a lower level than the point of maximum revenue, which in turn occurs at less than maximum output/sales.

The relationship which will be of particular interest to the operations manager is that between the cost per unit throughput or output and the level or scale of throughput or output. In the short term the operations manager might seek to alter output by varying the amount of variable factors employed, e.g. materials and labour, whereas in the longer term all factors can be varied. In the short term the unit cost structure might appear as in Figure 4.3. As fixed costs remain the same the fixed cost per unit will fall as output or throughput increases. The variable cost per unit will at first fall and then rise as further variable factors are employed in order to expand output or throughput. Figure 4.4 shows the long-run average total cost/output relationship. Superimposed on this long-run average total cost curve is an average

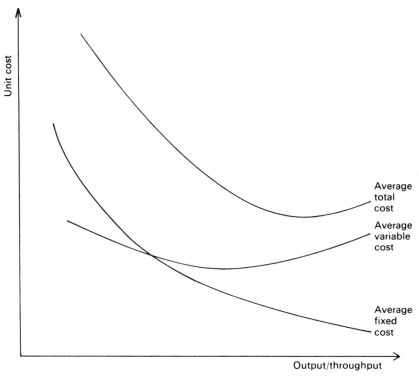

**Figure 4.3**  *Short-term unit cost/output relationship.*

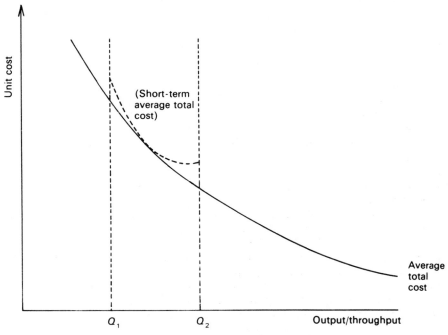

**Figure 4.4**  *Long-term unit cost/output relationship.*

total cost curve for a short-run period. Thus while in the short term increasing output or throughput from $Q_1$ to $Q_2$ will give rise to a U-shaped curve representing falling unit total cost followed by increasing total costs, in the long run, since the 'fixed' factors can also be varied, the unit total cost curve should continue to fall. Thus in the long term, since all the factors can be considered variable, increasing output should result in economies of scale reflected in reduced unit costs.

It follows that while the operations manager might, by clever combination of the resources at his or her disposal, effect a reduction in unit cost in the short term, continued increase in the scale of operations can be undertaken economically only by the manipulation of the mix of all of the factors involved, including those which in the short term are fixed.

**Break-even point**

A break-even point chart also shows the relationship between output or throughput on the one hand, and cost on the other. Figure 4.5 shows two break-even charts. A chart for operating system A shows relatively low fixed costs but fairly substantial variable costs and thus a fairly steeply rising total cost curve, albeit one starting from a relatively low point. The cost structure for operating system B shows higher fixed costs

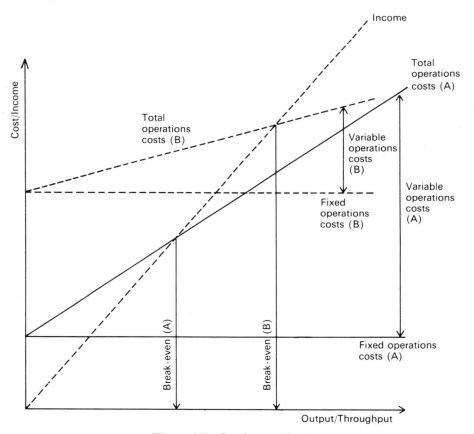

**Figure 4.5** *Break-even charts.*

with relatively low variable costs, thus a less steeply rising total cost curve, albeit one starting from a substantially higher initial total cost point than in system A. The cost structure for operating system B might reflect the higher capital investment of that system, whereas operating system A may be more dependent on the use of overtime work, double staffing, etc. to achieve increased outputs. Notice that because of the differing cost structures the break-even point, i.e. the point at which income begins to exceed total costs, is lower for operating system A than it is for B but that the excess of income over total cost increases more rapidly beyond the break-even point in the case of operating system B. A point worth noting, therefore, is that for systems dependent on greater fixed costs, greater output must be achieved before a break-even point is reached but that thereafter rewards are likely to increase at a greater rate.

## COST CONTROL SYSTEMS

Some form of cost accounting or cost control system will be essential within an organization and will be of considerable importance to the operations manager. As with all such managerial control systems, the operations manager will seek to employ the cost control mechanisms to sustain and improve the efficiency of the operating system, whereas his or her superiors will use the same cost information, albeit analysed somewhat differently, as a means to establish objectives for and maintain control over the operations manager.

From the operation manager's viewpoint, therefore, the cost control mechanism provides a means of assessing the efficiency of the operating system, noting significant variations from normal or budgeted performance, assessing the efficiency of new operating methods, determining the relative allocation of resources, determining the capacity required, etc. The cost control or cost accounting system adopted by an organization, and thus by the operations manager, will depend largely on the scale and nature of the organization, in particular on the type of operating system employed and the type of goods/service provided. Basically, two types of costing system can be identified: job costing and process costing.

### Job costing

Job costing is often employed by organizations which produce goods or provide services, transport, etc. to the specific requirements of the customer. In job costing, items or customers passing through the system remain identifiable and are associated with particular costs. All costs specific to particular jobs, items or customers will be accumulated, while all indirect costs will be apportioned or allocated to jobs such that on completion the total cost of each job is ascertained.

### Process costing

Process costing is used by organizations engaged in more repetitive activities, i.e. where the operating system is devoted to the provision of a relatively small variety of goods, services or transports on a fairly repetitive basis. Since in such situations it is not practical to identify separate items of throughput, unit costs are determined by dividing the total costs of each process by the number of units, i.e. goods or customers, output or throughput, making allowances for items partially completed or customers partially serviced at the beginning and the end of the costing period.

## Budgeting

The long-range plans formulated for the organization must be translated into detailed short-term plans or budgets for individual departments. The performance of departments, including the operating system, will be evaluated against these departmental budgets. The operations budget will specify the output or throughput required as well as the planned direct and indirect costs, broken down into appropriate detail. Preparation of this budget will involve apportioning or allocating operations overheads on some equitable basis between departments and/or 'jobs'. Overheads might be apportioned in proportion to the direct wages or direct materials costs, etc. The budget will make a distinction between current costs and revenue items and capital expenditure items. The former comprises such things as wages, salaries and material costs. The latter group includes expenditure on equipment and building.

   Once budgets have been established and the periods to which they relate have commenced, the actual costs incurred during each period must be collected for subsequent comparison.

## Standard costing

Standard costing is widely used in industries where rapid cost feedback information is required, i.e. where operations take place on a relatively short cycle time. In such circumstances costs are estimated and compared with actual costs on a month-by-month basis. The estimate is referred to as the 'standard cost'. Standard costs for items or services are established by category, e.g. labour, materials and overheads, based on predicted prices, labour rates and other expenses for the given period. Variations from predicted costs can be assessed and the necessary action taken to prevent their recurrence without the need to wait for the end of the costing period, e.g. one year, before the necessary cost control information is available.

## Marginal costing

Accurate standard costs necessitate the use of realistic means and bases for the apportionment of overhead costs to departments, cost centres, jobs, etc. and accurate estimation of throughput or output volumes as bases for establishing cost rates. The use of marginal costing avoids these problems. After distinguishing direct from overhead costs, marginal costing divides overheads into those which vary with output and those which are fixed. Direct costs are also divided into the categories 'variable' and 'fixed'. All variable costs are then related to units of throughput/output while fixed costs are not charged to separate units but are kept as a single block to be set against revenues earned by the throughputs of the system. Thus with marginal costing the cost of unit throughput or output is considered to comprise direct material, direct labour and direct expenses plus their variable overheads only, the total being the variable cost per unit output/throughput. This variable cost is in fact the marginal cost, since it is the amount by which total cost would increase as a result of the processing of one extra unit. Marginal costing provides a convenient way of assessing the effects of volume on profits and can be used in conjunction with the break-even chart approach (Figure 4.5).

## FURTHER READING

Sizer, J. (1979) *An Insight into Management Accounting*. Harmondsworth: Penguin.

## QUESTIONS

**4.1** Within organizations overheads are usually divided between operations overheads and general and administrative overheads and costs (including administrative overheads and selling and distribution overheads). Explain why this distinction is made and suggest methods by which each class of overhead can be absorbed or allocated to units of throughput/output.

**4.2** The following data relate to a manufacturing company:

Total capacity, 75 000 units
Fixed costs, £12,000 per annum
Variable expenses, 75p per unit
Sales prices, up to 4000 units £1.5 per unit and then over 4000 units £1.0 per unit

Draft a break-even chart incorporating these data.

**4.3** Throughput volumes (or output volumes) can affect unit operating costs. In addition, batch volumes can affect unit costs. Both output/throughput volumes and costs are related to profits. Outline the nature of these relationships, illustrating your answer with simple graphs.

**4.4** How, in the long term, might a transport organization seek to reduce unit total operations costs beyond the level available in the short term?

# PART 3

# THE ARRANGEMENT OF FACILITIES

# INTRODUCTION TO PART 3

*This section deals with locational and layout decisions. We deal with the relatively rare problem of locating internationally an entirely new facility. We also deal with the problem of locating an additional new facility for an organization, to provide access to existing facilities, suppliers and markets. In Chapter 6 we look at layout decisions—themselves a form of layout problem. We look at the fairly uncommon problem of arranging an entirely new layout for a facility, and consider also the modification of existing facilities and the addition of new departments or items of equipment to existing facilities. Throughout we consider the nature of the problems involved and introduce some relevant procedures and techniques. We emphasize computer-based techniques, for this is an area in which numerous alternative solutions exist and where there is considerable merit in obtaining some alternative solutions quickly and economically.*

# CHAPTER 5

# Location of Facilities

The facilities location problem is of major importance in all types of business. Whether we are concerned with manufacture, supply, transport or service we must consider the location problem, i.e. where to base our operation. Certainly the location problem for a transport operation is slightly different, since, by definition, transport moves. However, even in such cases there will normally be a 'home base' or centre of operations at which certain facilities are provided. Throughout this chapter, when referring to facilities we mean that collection of *static resources* required for the operation.

Having decided the nature and specification of the goods/services to be provided, the location of the business facilities is the next major problem to be considered. In most cases this will be the logical order of decisions, i.e. 'What?' and then 'Where?', since often the nature of the offering will suggest suitable locations and preclude others. At times, however, these decisions may occur in the reverse order, or the two decisions may even be quite unconnected. For example, a company intending to manufacture ships will be restricted to comparatively few locations, unlike a company intending to manufacture scientific electronic instruments, and the location of ferry services will be relatively restricted compared with the location of furniture removers.

We can consider the facility location problem as applying in two basic situations, i.e. the case of the entirely new business and the case of the existing business.

The choice of location is a vital decision for any new business; indeed, there are numerous examples of new businesses which have enjoyed brief and troubled lives, solely because of their disadvantageous location. Theoretically the new business has a vast choice of possible locations from which to choose. The problem will involve the selection of an appropriate part of the world and part of the country, and the selection of an appropriate site within a locality. In practice the company is not entirely free to take an open decision, since governments, anxious that the choice of location shall be to the national benefit, will often seek to influence the decision.

The existing firm will seek facility locations either in order to expand capacity or to replace existing facilities. An increase in demand, if it is to be satisfied by the organization, gives rise to one or more of three decisions:

(a)  whether to expand the present capacity and facilities;
(b)  whether to seek locations for additional facilities;
(c)  whether to close down existing facilities in favour of larger premises elsewhere.

Replacement of existing facilities may be occasioned by one or more of the following occurrences:

(a)  the movement of markets, i.e. changes in the location of demand;
(b)  changes in the cost or availability of local labour;
(c)  changes in the availability of materials;
(d)  demolition or compulsory purchase of premises;
(e)  changes in the availability or effectiveness of transport;
(f)  relocation of associated industries or plants;
(g)  national legislation

For our purposes in discussing the facility location problem, it makes little difference whether we consider the problem as applying to a new business or to an existing one. However, since the latter tends to be the more complex case, our discussion will relate largely to the problems of the existing business. An increase in demand will, unless

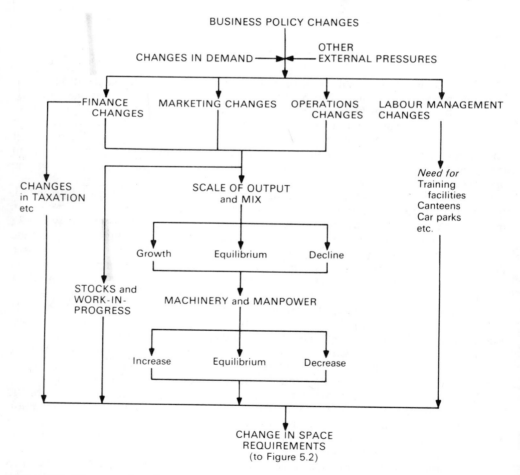

**Figure 5.1**  *Pressures for change in space (which must give rise to the need to select a facility location).*

associated with increased productivity, inevitably result in pressure for additional capacity; the only alternatives to an expansion of the existing facilities or the acquisition of additional facilities are a reduced share of the market or an increased amount of subcontracting. On the other hand, a reduction in demand will often result in the under-utilization of existing capacity and encourage a move to smaller premises. Figure 5.1 describes the forces within a company which give rise to the pressure for either an increase or a decrease in the amount of space available. Although the main forces are associated with demand, and hence with the operations and marketing functions, it is worth noting that both finance and labour management might also be instrumental. Changes in interest rates may affect the cost of holding stock and cause a change in stock-holding policy, which in turn may affect space requirements.

Legislation relating to investment allowances, depreciation, etc. may influence company financial policy enough to affect the scale or the nature of the undertaking; similarly, legislation relating to labour may necessitate a change in the nature or extent of facilities, e.g. the addition of extensive training facilities and welfare facilities. Scientific discoveries or developments, new fields of technology, increasing competition and licensing or patent arrangements all may affect company research and development effort, which in turn will influence space requirements. Likewise,

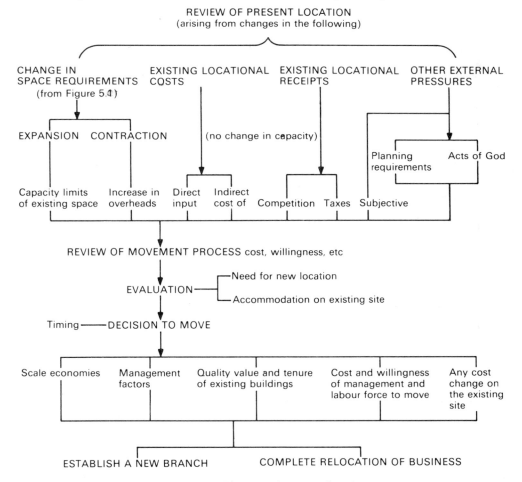

**Figure 5.2** *Pressures for a new location.*

changes in operations technology, the obsolescence of equipment, etc. will influence space requirements.

A change in space requirements is only one of several possible reasons for the need to consider the acquisition of an additional facility location. Figure 5.2 identifies other forces which may give rise to such a decision. The need to seek smaller or larger premises may arise without the occurrence of a change in demand and thus capacity. For example, the costs associated with the present location may change through increases in the cost of labour, caused, perhaps, by increasing employment opportunities in the area. The price of raw materials or indirect materials may change through changes in the cost of transport or changes within associated industries. Indirect costs such as those associated with communications, education, housing etc. may change. Also, new competition or changes in local taxation may prompt the decision to seek alternative premises, as may other external pressures such as labour disputes. Such forces may prompt the consideration of a complete move or the acquisition of an additional site(s).

Now let us consider the actual choice of plant location or site. Three general considerations will influence the location decision: the variable costs involved, the fixed costs involved, and subjective assessments (see Figure 5.3).

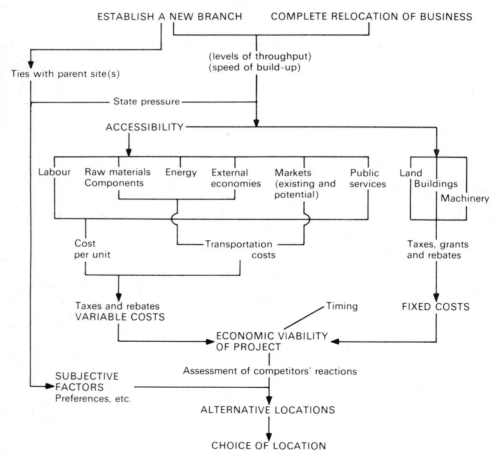

**Figure 5.3** *The choice of a new site. (Figures 5.1, 5.2 and 5.3 adapted with permission from Townroe, P.M. (1969) Locational choice and the individual firm,* Regional Studies, **3***(1), pp. 15–24.)*

*Variable costs*

Perhaps the main factor here is the 'accessibility' of the proposed location in terms of both inputs and outputs. As regards input, accessibility to labour is important—not merely sufficient labour of course, but labour of the correct type and at a correct price. Accessibility of raw materials, sub-assemblies and components is important, the cost of such input being mainly a function of transport. Access to technical advice and to other services such as warehousing and maintenance is often essential. With regard to output, a location must clearly have easy access to adequate markets, as well as public services and associated industries.

*Fixed costs*

These are associated with the provision and maintenance of facilities. The design of buildings and the layout of facilities will influence such costs. The cost of erecting and maintaining buildings, the cost of access roads, the cost of transportation of machinery, rates, rent, and so on will all influence the choice of location. We should also consider as fixed costs the cost of inventories of materials and finished items which may depend on the plant location.

A further factor which will influence the choice of location is the time factor, i.e. the urgency of acquiring the facility compared with the time required to make it available, the latter being influenced by the necessity for planning permission, construction of plans, purchase of land, availability of building labour, provision of services, electricity, water, roads, etc.

*Subjective or non-quantitative assessments*

These may also influence the decision. Individual preferences, congeniality of the district, attitudes of present employees, etc., will all be important. National and regional data relating to the various factors influencing the facility location decision are available from a variety of sources. Data on population change, average wage levels, unemployment, industrial disputes, absenteeism, labour turnover levels, etc. may be of relevance and will often be available.

The role of central and local governments and the influence of legislation and incentives are of considerable importance in locational choice. Legislation such as the Special Areas (Development and Improvement) Acts 1934 and 1937, the Distribution of Industry Act 1945, the Town and Country Planning Acts 1947 onwards, the Distribution of Industry (Industrial Finance) Act 1958 and the Local Employment Act 1960 was but the forerunner of a great deal of direct and indirect effort by the government to influence the location of manufacturing industry, offices, etc. In the present situation, very substantial incentives exist to encourage companies to establish plants in certain parts of the country designated for industrial and economic development. All this has tended to reduce but not, of course, to eliminate the influence of the factors discussed in the previous section.

Similarly, factors exist in other countries where legislation and other devices provide incentives and obstacles in locational choice. Furthermore, with the growth of multinational firms and the increasing importance of the international dimension in locational choice, for example in industries such as motor vehicles and chemicals, similar factors at an international level (e.g. with the EEC), the 'competitive' bidding of national governments, etc., are of considerable significance.

# THE SINGLE-FACILITY LOCATION PROBLEM

Here we are concerned largely with the single-facility business, e.g. the single-plant firm, single-facility service organization, etc. The problem of selecting the location of this single facility will arise when the business is first established and will subsequently occur should a change of location be necessary or desirable. In such cases the locational choice may be influenced by factors such as:

(a)  the availability of resources;
(b)  location of and access to markets/customers;
(c)  location of and access to supplies;
(d)  costs of establishing/creating the facility (e.g. building costs);
(e)  community factors.

Unlike the multi-facility location problem, the existing or future locations of other facilities within the business will be of little relevance. Here, therefore, we are *not* concerned with the type of locational problems encountered in businesses with interdependent facilities (as in the motor industry, in which different parts of final products are made in different facilities, or specialized hospitals and clinics in a regional health service). Procedures for tackling the single-facility location problem may be of relevance, however, in multi-facility organizations in which there is no specialization or interdependence of facilities, e.g. supply organizations comprising several similar outlets servicing different areas.

## Checklists

Given a choice of possible locations, perhaps the simplest but least rigorous means for decision-making involves their comparison against a checklist of relevant factors. Such a checklist is shown in Table 5.1, which also gives some indication of the relevance of each factor at each of four 'levels' of decision-making, i.e. selection of region (internationally), selection of area (national), selection of community (city), and selection of actual site. If not an adequate means of decision-making, such a checklist at least provides a means of initially narrowing down the range of alternative regions and/or areas and/or communities and/or sites.

## Location factor comparisons

Most locational decisions will at some stage involve the preparation of list or tabular comparisons of the type shown in Table 5.2. In some cases it will be possible and appropriate to draw up such comparisons entirely in cost terms, in which case addition of columns provides a means for comparison of alternatives and therefore for the choice of location. Frequently, however, it will be necessary to consider cost and non-cost factors and some of the latter may be represented only by 'yes' or 'no'. This ensures that the use of this type of approach, while providing a means of summarizing the factors to be considered, or providing a checklist against which to assess alternatives, must normally be employed alongside more rigorous procedures of the type discussed below.

**Table 5.1** *Checklist: some factors influencing locational choice.*

| | Of region (international) | Of area (national) | Of community (city) | Of site |
|---|---|---|---|---|
| Political stability | √ | | | |
| Relevant legislation, e.g. industrial relations | √ | | | |
| Unionization of labour | √ | | | |
| Industrial relations 'climate' | √ | | | |
| Feasibility of joint operations | √ | | | |
| Capital restrictions | √ | | | |
| Transfer of earnings restrictions | √ | | | |
| Taxation for foreign firms | √ | | | |
| Currency restrictions | √ | | | |
| GNP trends | √ | | | |
| Foreign investment trends | √ | | | |
| Restrictions on foreign labour/staff | √ | | | |
| Climate | √ | | | |
| Language | √ | | | |
| Management preference | √ | √ | √ | ? |
| Location of company's existing facilities | √ | √ | √ | ? |
| Availability of 'suitable' areas | √ | | | |
| Cost of living | √ | | | |
| Standard of living | √ | | | |
| Location of markets | √ | √ | √ | |
| Location of suppliers | √ | √ | √ | |
| Proximity to related industries | √ | √ | √ | |
| Labour/staff availability and skills | √ | √ | √ | |
| Unemployment, turnover and absenteeism | ? | √ | √ | |
| Pay levels and scales | ? | √ | √ | |
| Planning and development restrictions | ? | √ | √ | ? |
| Tax structures and incentives | ? | √ | ? | |
| Environmental (e.g. pollution) controls | ? | √ | ? | |
| Communications: international | √ | | | |
| national | | √ | | |
| local | | | √ | |
| Transport; air | √ | √ | √ | |
| rail | √ | √ | √ | |
| road | √ | √ | √ | |
| other | √ | √ | √ | |
| Availability of suitable communities | | √ | | |
| Land availability and costs | | √ | √ | |
| Availability of premises | | √ | √ | |
| Cost of land | | √ | √ | |
| Cost of building | | | √ | |
| Rents for premises | | | √ | |
| Cost of services | | | √ | |
| Zoning and planning restrictions | | √ | √ | |
| Availability of utilities | | √ | √ | |
| Availability of amenities | | | √ | |
| Availability of education and training | | √ | √ | |
| Community attitudes and culture | | | √ | |
| Energy availability | | √ | √ | |
| Energy costs | | √ | √ | |
| Impact on environment | | | √ | |
| Development plans | | | √ | |
| Availability of subcontractors | | | √ | |
| Availability of suitable sites | | | √ | |
| Site characteristics | | | | √ |
| Availability of adjacent space | | | | √ |
| Transport access | | | | √ |
| Parking space | | | | √ |
| Local transport provisions | | | | √ |
| Facilities for waste disposal | | | | √ |

**Table 5.2**  *Comparison of factors for three possible locations for a retail shop.*

| Location factor | Location A | Location B | Location C |
|---|---|---|---|
| Site rental p.a. | £1000 | £1200 | £800 |
| Car parking spaces | | | |
|     within ½ km | 110 | 30 | 205 |
| Shop frontage | 4m | 3m | 4m |
| Cost of services p.a. | £750 | £275 | £800 |

## Dimensional analysis

Even if we are able to identify the various factors influencing locational choice, the problem of quantification remains. How, for example, do we determine, for various potential locations, the cost of moving or the cost of labour? Furthermore, having quantified such factors, what weight or importance do we attach to each? Do we, for example, consider the subjective factors as being of equal importance to the fixed-cost factors? Do we consider the cost of labour as being of more or less importance than transport costs? Indeed, we may even find that we are unable to attach actual cost figures to some of the important factors. For example, regarding the cost of moving, we may be able to rank the potential locations or evaluate them only in terms of high, medium or low cost.

Consider a simple example in which we are faced with two possible locations. We have decided that the choice between these locations will be made on a basis of the following factors:

(a) the cost of land;
(b) the cost of buildings;
(c) the cost of labour (fixed cost for the total required labour force for a location).

We have further found that the cost associated with each of these three factors for each of the possible locations is as shown in Table 5.3.

**Table 5.3**

| Factor | Location A £ | Location B £ |
|---|---|---|
| Land | 10 000 | 15 000 |
| Buildings | 25 000 | 30 000 |
| Labour | 15 000 | 10 000 |

We might compare the relative merits of the two locations merely by summing the relevant costs:

$$\text{Total for A} = \pounds 50\ 000$$
$$\text{Total for B} = \pounds 55\ 000$$

Using this method of comparison we would choose location A, since it is the cheaper of the two. This method assumes that each of the factors is of equal importance, a situation which may be far from true. For example, suppose we decide that, while the costs of land and buildings are equally important to our decisions, the cost associated with labour is twice as important as the two other costs. Then we may assess the alternatives by introducing this weighting factor:

$$
\begin{array}{ll}
\text{Location A:} & \begin{array}{r} \text{£} \\ 10\ 000 \\ 25\ 000 \\ +2(15\ 000) \\ \hline =\text{£65 000} \\ \hline \end{array}
\end{array}
$$

$$
\begin{array}{ll}
\text{Location B:} & \begin{array}{r} \text{£} \\ 15\ 000 \\ 30\ 000 \\ +2(10\ 000) \\ \hline =\text{£65 000} \\ \hline \end{array}
\end{array}
$$

Now it appears that the locations are equally attractive.

Let us take this type of argument a little further by introducing two more factors into our examination of the two locations. Now, as well as the costs associated with land, buildings and labour, we need to consider the influence of community relations and the cost of moving. Because of the subjective nature of the former and the rather complex nature of the latter, we find it extremely difficult to place an accurate cost on either of these factors for the two locations concerned; consequently we settle for a system of rating using a scale of 1 to 100. A rating of 1 indicates that a location scores very highly, i.e. it is the best possible result, whereas a rating of 100 is the worst possible result. In other words, in terms of costs, 1 is equivalent to a low cost whereas 100 is equivalent to a high cost.

Because we are no longer dealing solely with cost, we have a dimensional problem. In fact in this case we are dealing with two separate dimensions, a fact which should influence our analysis.

Suppose that the five factors for the two locations are quantified as shown in Table 5.4, then we might again compare locations by adding together the figures to obtain the totals shown in Table 5.4. This comparison would lead us to select location A.

**Table 5.4**

|  | Location A | Location B |
|---|---|---|
| Land (cost) | 10 000 | 15 000 |
| Buildings (cost) | 25 000 | 30 000 |
| Labour (cost) | 15 000 | 10 000 |
| Community relations (score) | 60 | 30 |
| Cost of moving (score) | 80 | 40 |
| Total | 50 140 | 55 070 |

However, this type of analysis is quite wrong, because we have indiscriminately mixed together two dimensions. To illustrate the inadequacies of the procedure, suppose that we alter the scale of the first three factors and perform our calculations in £'000s rather than £s, i.e.

$$
\begin{array}{llcll}
\text{Location A} & \begin{array}{r} 10' \\ 25' \\ 15' \\ 60 \\ 80 \\ \hline 190 \\ \hline \end{array}
& \qquad &
\text{Location B} & \begin{array}{r} 15' \\ 30' \\ 10' \\ 30 \\ 40 \\ \hline 125 \\ \hline \end{array}
\end{array}
$$

Such an analysis would lead us to select location B, since the change of scale has distorted our analysis.

So that such an anomaly does not occur, we must take care to treat such multi-dimensional analysis in a more satisfactory manner. Such a method was developed by Bridgeman,[1] and is referred to as dimensional analysis.

Using the following notation:

$$O_{i_1}, O_{i_2}, O_{i_3}, \ldots O_{i_n} = \text{costs, scores, etc., associated with factors } 1, 2, 3, \ldots n \text{ for location } i$$

$$W_1, W_2, W_3, \ldots W_n = \text{the weight to be attached to factors } 1, 2, 3, \ldots n$$

the merit of the various locations should be assessed as follows:

$$\text{For location } i, \text{ merit} = (O_{i_1})^{W_1} \times (O_{i_2})^{W_2} \times (O_{i_3})^{W_3} \ldots \times (O_{i_n})^{W_n}$$

In the case of two possible locations the merit might be compared as follows:

$$\frac{\text{Merit of A}}{\text{Merit of B}} = \left(\frac{O_{A_1}}{O_{B_1}}\right)^{W_1} \times \left(\frac{O_{A_2}}{O_{B_2}}\right)^{W_2} \ldots \times \left(\frac{O_{A_n}}{O_{B_n}}\right)^{W_n}$$

If $> 1$, select B.
If $< 1$, select A.

---

### EXAMPLE: A RETAIL SHOP

Several factors are identified as being important in choosing one of two available locations for a new retail shop. Wherever possible the factors have been costed; otherwise a score from 1 to 10 has been given, 1 representing the best possible result and 10 the worst possible. The factors are considered as being of varying importance, so they have been weighted from 1 to 10 (weight of 1 indicating least importance and 10 most importance) (Table 5.5).

**Table 5.5**

| Factor | Location A | Location B | Weight |
|--------|-----------|-----------|--------|
| Cost | £10 000 | £15 000 | 1 |
| Score | 3 | 7 | 2 |
| Score | 6 | 2 | 3 |
| Cost | £1 500 000 | £1 000 000 | 4 |
| Score | 4 | 7 | 4 |
| Score | 5 | 5 | 3 |

The merit of location A is represented by:

$$(10\ 000)^1 \times (3)^2 \times (6)^3 \times (1\ 500\ 000)^4 \times (4)^4 \times (5)^3$$

and that of location B by:

$$(15\ 000)^1 \times (7)^2 \times (2)^3 \times (1\ 000\ 000)^4 \times (7)^4 \times (5)^3$$

To assist the calculations we can change the scales as and where convenient, i.e. changing the scale of the cost dimension gives:

---

[1]Bridgeman, P. W. (1963) *Dimensional Analysis*. New Haven, Connecticut: Yale University Press.

$$A: \quad (1)^1 \times (3)^2 \times (6)^3 \times (150)^4 \times (4)^4 \times (5)^3$$
$$B: \quad (1.5)^1 \times (7)^2 \times (2)^3 \times (100)^4 \times (7)^4 \times (5)^3$$

$$\therefore \frac{\text{Merit of A}}{\text{Merit of B}} = 1.79$$

Such an analysis indicates that location B is superior on a basis of the six factors considered.

In this example we have considered only factors which should be minimized, i.e. costs. Such an analysis might also be undertaken even where some factors are to be maximized (e.g. profits, revenue) while others are to be minimized. In such a case the powers would be positive for factors to be minimized and negative for factors to be maximized.

## EXAMPLE: A CINEMA

Compare the merit of two locations X and Y on the basis of factors with different weights, i.e.

| | Location X | Location Y | Weight |
|---|---|---|---|
| Costs (£) | 10 000 | 12 000 | 4 |
| Benefits (score) | 8 | 6 | 3 |

$$\frac{\text{Merit of X}}{\text{Merit of Y}} = \frac{(10\ 000)^4 (8)^{-3}}{(12\ 000)^4 (6)^{-3}}$$
$$= \frac{(10)^4 (8)^{-3}}{(12)^4 (6)^{-3}}$$
$$= 0.203$$

$$\therefore \text{Select location X}$$

## Minimization of transport costs

It is clear from our previous discussion that many factors other than transport cost are likely to affect locational choice. Nevertheless, minimization of transport costs may provide a suitable first solution which might then form a basis for further discussion, analysis and modifications. Such an approach might be relevant in selecting the location of a warehouse relative to its principal customers or markets, or a manufacturing plant relative to its supplies and customers. At a different level, considered in detail in Chapter 6, this approach to the location problem resembles an approach employed in determining the layout of facilities within an area (e.g. a factory or office) where movement and travel is also an important criterion for efficient layout.

## THE MULTI-FACILITY LOCATION PROBLEM

Whereas in the case of the single-facility location problem we have been concerned with selecting the minimum-cost location, in the multi-facility location problem we must select the location which, when added to existing locations, minimizes the cost of the entire system. Each of the potential locations must be assessed not on its own merits alone, as was the case previously, but in the context of a multi-facility situation. Multi-facility location problems are considerably more complex than the single-facility problem not only because the entire system must be considered but also because, since more than one facility is to be considered, the question of size arises. Thus there are in fact two basic factors in the general multi-facility location problem:

(a) the need to identify locations for facilities relative to suppliers and customers;
(b) the need to determine the appropriate size or capacity of each such facility.

To deal with both aspects simultaneously would necessitate the use of extremely complex procedures. In many cases, therefore, the two aspects are treated separately. Again the procedures which are available apply equally to problems involving the location of manufacturing facilities, supply establishments, etc. One of the better-known approaches involves the use of the transportation method of linear programming.

It should also be noted that the factors influencing location decisions are liable to change. The logical location at the present time may, at a later date, appear inferior because of change in one of the many factors which influenced the original choice.

Conceptually, the problem of the location of facilities abroad does not differ from the problems discussed in this chapter. In practice, such a problem will often be more complex and will assume greater proportions, if only because more investment may be involved. In such situations the identification and quantification of factors may be more difficult; nevertheless, the decision is amenable to the type of technique discussed earlier.

### FURTHER READING

Bridgeman, P. W. (1963) *Dimensional Analysis*. New Haven, Connecticut: Yale University Press. Describes dimensional analysis.

Greenhut, M. (1956) *Plant Location in Theory and Practice*. Chapel Hill, North Carolina: University of North Carolina Press. Most textbooks devoted to this subject treat the problem from an economist's point of view; this book reviews economic location theory as well as plant location practice (although it is now rather dated).

Karaska, G. J. and Bramhall, D. F. (1969) *Location Analysis for Manufacturing*. Cambridge, Massachusetts: MIT Press. This book and the following one deal with the plant location problem in the broader context.

Townroe, P. M. (1969) *Location Analysis for Manufacturing*. Cambridge, Massachusetts: MIT Press.

### QUESTIONS

**5.1** Briefly, what changes might result in the need for additional space for a service operation (of your own choice)? Under what circumstances might such changes lead to the need for an entirely new site, and what would influence the choice of such a site?

**5.2** The following information is available on two possible locations for a new office. Which location would you choose? What assumptions have you made?

|  | Location A | Location B |
|---|---|---|
| Site rental/year (£) | 7000 | 6500 |
| Cost of services/year (£) | 500 | 950 |
| Cost of modifying buildings (£) | 2400 | 1900 |
| Local housing cost index (%)[a] | 50 | 75 |

[a] Average cost of a four-bedroom house as a percentage of national average cost.

**5.3** 'The locational choice problem is complex mainly because multiple objectives and criteria are normally evident.' Discuss and illustrate.

**5.4** Show, using numerical examples, that the simple addition of costs in the evaluation of alternative locations might lead to different decisions in different circumstances.

# CHAPTER 6

# Facilities Layout and Materials Handling

The facilities layout problem is common to every type of enterprise. Cooks must arrange their kitchens, not only the cupboards, shelves and appliances, but also the utensils, crockery, food, etc. Retailers must arrange their counters, shelves, cashdesks, etc., to utilize available space, facilitate movement and attract custom. Manufacturers must arrange their facilities, not only the departments within the factory, but also the plant, stores and services within those departments. The problems of layout are fundamental to every type of undertaking, and the adequacy of the layout affects the efficiency of subsequent operations.

Here we have an absolutely fundamental and common problem but, unfortunately, there is no single meaningful goal, since objectives will vary from one situation to the next. Furthermore, there is no single acceptable and rigorous procedure by which to achieve our objectives. In arranging their kitchens cooks will aim to minimize the amount of walking, bending and reaching they have to do, but since they will be dealing with a comparatively small problem they may achieve these objectives quite quickly by trial and error. Objectives in one industrial situation may differ substantially from those in another. In a steel mill dealing with hot metal the speed of movements will be of paramount importance, whereas in a small engineering shop, utilization of equipment and labour may be the primary concerns. Even in seemingly straightforward situations, where comparatively few items are to be arranged, a vast number of alternative acceptable solutions are available.

## FACILITIES LAYOUT PROBLEMS

Facilities layout begins with facilities location and continues through three further levels:

(a) the layout of departments within the site (e.g. departments in a retail store);

(b) the layout of items within the departments (e.g. counters in a department);
(c) the layout of individual areas (e.g. of each counter).

In this chapter we are explicitly concerned with level (a), but implicitly the discussion relates to level (b) also, since they are the large- and small-scale levels of the same problem. Level (c), being concerned with ergonomics and work study, is dealt with in Chapters 7 and 9.

Why do layout problems occur? In manufacture the need to produce a new or redesigned product may result in a need to reorganize the existing plant or to provide an additional plant. Changes in the level of demand or the location of markets for existing products may have similar results. Obsolescence or failure of existing equipment may result in the decision to install equipment whose characteristics provoke some rearrangement. The need for cost reductions may promote a reappraisal of layouts, as may factory legislation, accidents, and so on. Similar factors may give rise to layout or relayout problems in supply, service and transport operations. Increased demand and/or the introduction of a new line of goods may necessitate the relayout and possibly the extension of supply facilities and stores. The addition of facilities, in turn necessitating the rearrangement of existing facilities, may result from an increase in demand for a service or transport; and in all cases, the desire for cost reduction, the improvement of facilities and amenities, etc., may give rise to some rearrangement of existing facilities.

We often tend to think in terms of planning complete layouts and designing entirely new factories, but although such occasions undoubtedly do arise the following are the types of problem we are much more likely to encounter.

## Enlarging or reducing existing departments

The addition or removal of facilities, the trading of areas between departments, or a complete relayout may be necessary because of increases or decreases in demand for goods or services or changes in the scope or capability of processes.

## Movement of a department

The need to move a department because of a change in the specification or nature of the goods or service, or because of changes in demand or operating processes, may constitute a simple exercise. Alternatively, if the existing layout is inadequate, it may present the opportunity for a major change, the extent of which bears little relationship to the primary cause.

## Adding a department

This may result from the desire to undertake work never before done on the site, or the desire to centralize work previously undertaken in several separate departments.

## Replacing equipment and adding new equipment

Frequently, even equipment designed to perform exactly the same function as its predecessors is physically different and its installation necessitates a certain amount of reorganization. Occasionally new machines may be installed to replace or supplement existing machines: a numerically controlled machining centre may be installed to replace existing milling and drilling machines, an electron beam welder installed in addition to existing welding equipment, to undertake work previously done with difficulty on conventional machines. Smaller computers may replace earlier generation equipment. Electronic equipment may replace larger electro-mechanical devices such as cash registers and office equipment.

## FACILITIES LAYOUT OBJECTIVES

What are the objectives of facilities layout, and what criteria should be adopted to assess and compare alternative layouts? A general definition of facilities layout is 'the arrangement of physical facilities to provide efficient operation'. However, 'efficient operation' is too general a concept and more specific objectives are necessary. Some of the advantages of good facilities layouts and hence some possible objectives while planning layouts are as follows.

## Cost of materials handling and movement

In most operating systems there will be physical flows. The extent and cost of these flows will be affected by the layout of facilities. In manufacturing, the handling and movement of materials, components and the finished product, as well as the movement of labour, are dependent primarily upon the location of the production and service facilities. The movement of customers in a retail store or in a service system such as a hotel or restaurant will be influenced by the layout of facilities. Improved layout will result in a reduction in the distance moved by items and/or customers, the time consumed and, hence, the cost of such movement whether to the organization or to the customer.

## Turnover

The objective of most operations is to add to the value of inputs. This is achieved by subjecting inputs to some form of processing. No value is added and nothing is contributed to profits by delays or storage during operations. Although the extent of work in progress is also determined by the effectiveness of operations scheduling and the nature of the production process, poor facilities layout may necessitate high work in progress and hence increase throughput time. Time spent by the customer waiting in a system generates no turnover; the turnover of a supply system is adversely affected by delays in obtaining items for customers, hence in all such cases an objective will be to minimize congestion and delay and thus provide for the more intensive use of facilities and the more efficient use of capacity.

## Utilization of space, facilities and labour

The cost of space is high and wasted space may be eliminated and the total area necessary for an operating system minimized by adequate facilities layout. Effective arrangement of facilities may reduce idle time and cut down investment in both direct (e.g. plant) and indirect (e.g. support) equipment. Adequate layout also facilitates operation, maintenance, service and supervision, and therefore permits a better utilization of labour.

Our discussion above raises two issues which merit further comment at this stage. We have identified the importance of movement and flows and thus the handling of physical items and/or customers as factors or criteria in layout planning. Much of our discussion of layout planning techniques will reflect the importance of minimizing physical movement and handling. We have also referred to capacity, one objective of layout planning being the maximization of capacity utilization. When planning a new facilities layout we must know the extent or quantity of each type of facility to be provided. We must know what capacity is to be provided. Layout planning is therefore contingent upon capacity planning, which is discussed in Chapter 11.

## BASIC TYPES OF FACILITIES LAYOUT

### Manufacture

There are, classically, three main systems of manufacturing plant layout, each with individual characteristics and each appropriate to some form of manufacture, depending on the output rate and the range of products involved. Although each system is normally associated with a particular type of production, none is exclusive to any one industry. We shall examine each of these basic systems in turn, identifying the nature of production and the characteristics of each.

### *Layout by process or functional layout*

In a process or functional layout all operations of a similar nature are grouped together in the same department or part of the factory. For example, separate areas may exist for drilling operations, milling, grinding, fitting, and so on.

Layout by process is appropriate where small quantities of a large range of products are to be manufactured, perhaps the best example being jobbing production. The nature of the layout permits flexibility in production, i.e. complex products, requiring processing in every one of the functional departments, may be made alongside simple products requiring processing in only a few departments. Such a situation would be difficult to accommodate in either of the other two systems of layout. This flexibility, however, brings disadvantages. Process layouts normally operate with a comparatively high level of work in progress, and throughput time is high. Specialist supervision is possible, and the grouping of operatives of a similar type and skill within the same department promotes cohesiveness and enables individual bonus schemes to be used. The provision of services, e.g. water, power, removal of scrap, is simpler than in other forms of layout, but the cost of materials handling is high.

### Layout by product

Layout by product is appropriate for the production of a small range of products in very large quantities. Ideally, only one standardized product is involved and production should be continuous, as in mass production industries such as the motor industry. Facilities are arranged according to the needs of the product and in the same sequence as the operations necessary for manufacture. Because this is a specialized production layout, designed solely for the production of large quantities of one or a very small range of standardized products, it is relatively inflexible. Sufficient and stable demand to ensure high utilization of equipment is absolutely essential, as is a regular supply of the right quantities of raw materials and components. Failure in the supply of a piece of equipment results in the entire production line stopping, and apparently quite remote failures can result in disproportionately high losses.

The provision of services is difficult, since where particularly elaborate machinery is used quite different pieces of equipment with different characteristics and requirements may be located adjacent to one another. A mixture of skills and operations frequently occurs, resulting in difficulties in payment and supervision, but usually little specialized supervision is required since the work performed is often highly rationalized. Minimum floor space is required, work in progress is minimized and throughput is high. The requirements for handling materials are small and machine utilization is high.

### Layout by fixed position

In the two previous layout systems the product moves past stationary production equipment. In this case the reverse applies. In the extreme case, e.g. civil engineering, neither the partly completed nor the finished product moves. Alternatively, as in ship building, the product remains stationary only until it is completed.

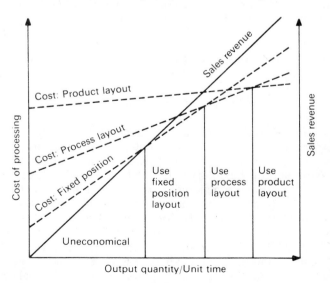

**Figure 6.1**  *Break-even analysis showing economic advantage of various types of layout for the same product at different output levels.*

Unlike in the period prior to the Industrial Revolution, when a large proportion of production was undertaken by artisans in their own homes, layout by fixed position is now comparatively unimportant, except where civil engineering or large items such as ships and aircraft are concerned.

Figure 6.1 shows a break-even point analysis of three types of production, indicating the relative cost benefits first of process layout, then of product layout as output increases.

### Group layout

Process, product and fixed-position layouts are the traditional forms in manufacturing industry. Recently, however, in batch production, configurations known as group or 'family' layouts have begun to emerge as a distinctive facilities arrangement. In effect, group layout is a hybrid form which provides a type of product arrangement of facilities for the manufacture of similar items, each of which, if taken individually, would normally be manufactured through a process or functional configuration. This approach is used as a means of achieving some of the benefits of layout by product (e.g. low work in progress, low space requirement) in the batch manufacture of products. Groups or families of similar items, or parts of products, are formed using group technology classification procedures of the type described in Chapter 3. Given a large enough group of sufficiently similar items it is practical to arrange in one area those facilities required for their production, and in this way a 'product type' layout is formed. Group layouts differ from layouts by product, therefore, in that they are used for the manufacture of similar (but not the same) items required for the batch manufacture of final products. In most cases, all items passing through a group layout will not require the use of all facilities, thus flow patterns will differ, yet because of the similarity of items utilization will be high. The merits of group manufacture are shown by the comparison of Figures 6.2 and 6.3, which show flow patterns for alternative arrangements.

Most practical manufacturing layouts are combinations of process and product layout. Rarely are companies in the enviable situation where they are able to produce continuously large quantities of an absolutely standard product. Similarly, even the largest range of products normally uses certain common components, and firms obliged to concentrate on process layouts are normally able to support some product layouts as well.

### Supply and service

Similar configurations can be identified in supply and service systems. In supply the principal flows and movements will resemble those of manufacturing systems, since goods are again involved. In service systems the principal flows may involve people, often customers. In a warehouse, for example, a functional layout may be employed in which particular areas are used for the storage of particular product lines or goods. In such situations flow patterns will be relatively simple in that goods will be received into the warehouse and placed into storage, from where they will be transferred to eventual customers. In such cases therefore there will be little flow or movement between areas, and thus the layout problem is considerably simplified. A similar situation may exist in a retail store. In these situations, however, the 'picking' problem

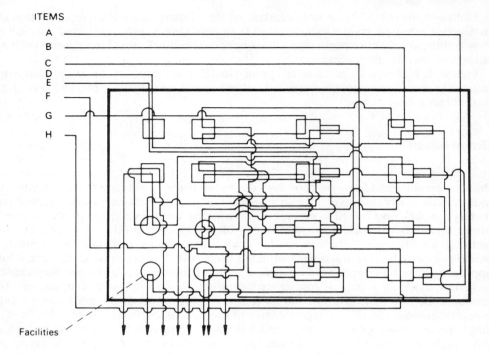

**Figure 6.2**   *Work flow in a functional layout.*

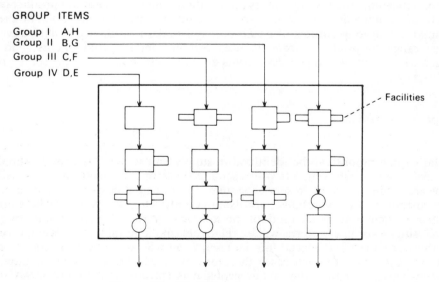

**Figure 6.3**   *Work flow in a group layout.*

will exist in that warehouse or counter staff may be required to collect together all items required for a particular customer by travelling between the appropriate areas within the facility. Thus movement problems are of importance and minimization of movement becomes a relevant criterion for layout planning. In service systems such as hospitals, the process or functional layout will often be found, since particular wards and particular parts of the hospital will be devoted to particular types of activity, e.g. general surgery, medicine, geriatrics. Here there may again be substantial movement between areas, since customers, i.e. patients, may need attention from several areas, and staff will have to move between and work in several of these areas. In certain medical facilities the layout by product or flow type layout may be used. For example, in certain cases a series of fairly elaborate medical tests will be made on patients as part of a screening or diagnosis procedure. These tests may be arranged sequentially and facilities provided to minimize throughput time and maximize resource utilization. In both of these functions it is possible to envisage a layout by fixed position, in particular in the service sector, where facilities might be brought to a customer, e.g. in the case of a road accident medical facilities would be brought to the injured patient.

Thus the three traditional layouts and also the group layout may exist in supply and service organizations and the movement and flows of items and people between areas within the layout may be a principal feature in determining the configuration.

## Transport

The essential feature of transport systems is movement. In many such systems the principal facilities employed are mobile. In this chapter we are concerned with the arrangement of essentially static facilities, so a somewhat different situation applies as regards facilities layout for transport systems, since in this context we are concerned only with the arrangement of a portion—perhaps in a way the least important portion—of the facilities of the system, namely the fixed facilities, e.g. garage, service bays. Given this, however, much the same situation might be found and again it will be possible to identify at least two of the three traditional configurations, namely layout by process and by product. As with manufacture, supply and service, movement and physical flows may again be seen to be the principal criteria in establishing the layout.

## FACILITIES LAYOUT PROCEDURES

We are proposing to establish a new set of facilities in one location. It is assumed that the precise nature of the goods or service to be provided from the facilities and the demand for them either are known or may be determined by appropriate market research. Given this information, the required capacity and hence the number and nature of facilities can be determined (see Chapter 11).

In addition to the principal facilities required other equipment will be needed, hence additional space must be provided. Storage space will be required, depending on such factors as fluctuations in demand for goods or services and the supply of raw materials. Departments such as personnel must be accommodated.

Plant layout planning procedure therefore involves consideration of the following stages: demand, capacity, work methods and standards, resource requirements, handling and movement, and space requirements, among other factors.

## Demand

Normally an operation will be established to meet an existing demand. If we are building a new factory to increase the output of an existing product, then the extent of the demand for the product will be known. If we are building a new warehouse to supply a particular area with existing items we will again know something of expected demand. Otherwise we will rely on market research to establish the following:

(a) specification of the goods/service;
(b) selling price;
(c) demand for each good/service;
(d) expected fluctuations in demand.

This information will help in the determination of the capacity required.

## Capacity

The determination of capacity requires not only the estimation of steady state or average demand levels but also decisions on how best to deal with demand level fluctuations. In Chapter 11 it will be seen that the accommodation of demand fluctuations may necessitate the provision of storage space, over-capacity, etc.; thus detailed capacity planning is essential before facilities layout planning is begun.

## Work methods and standards

Work study data should exist or be generated for each operation required in the manufacture and supply of goods and/or provision of services. Method study (see Chapter 7) will establish the sequence of operations to be performed and the types of equipment to be used. Given standard work methods, work measurement (see Chapter 8) will be used to establish operation times. Such information, which is a prerequisite for all operations planning, will be of relevance in determining the configuration of facilities.

## Resource requirements

Given an estimate of the required capacity in terms of output and work standards, it will be possible to calculate resource requirements in terms of both labour and equipment. Some allowance must be made for breakdowns, holidays, stoppages, etc.

## Handling and movement

Although in many cases the layout planning procedure will seek to minimize movement, distance or time, and/or handling cost, some knowledge of the nature of the movement and the manner in which it is to be achieved, i.e. the nature of any handling equipment, will be essential in planning the layout. The equipment required to provide movement and handling will itself require space both for operation and for maintenance, repair, etc. Furthermore, in certain industries movement and handling may be achieved only in particular ways because of the particular requirements of the process.

## Space requirements

In addition to the space necessary to accommodate the machinery and materials required in the operation, allowances must be made for the movement of personnel and for service and repair, etc.

## Other factors affecting layout

Normally additional, often obscure, factors affect layout. For example the removal, reprocessing or use of scrap and waste materials, the characteristics of the materials used, e.g. stability, value, etc. noise, safety legislation, customer areas, anticipated developments and the necessity for change may all be important. Consequently, the stages above can be considered only as a general procedure for the generation and collection of basic data which, along with other considerations peculiar to the particular circumstances, enables us to begin to plan the layout. Some of these considerations will be outlined later, with particular reference to supply and storage layouts.

## PLANNING NEW LAYOUTS

Visual aids play an important part in layout planning. Some form of scale representation is invariably used, e.g. scale drawing, templates, three-dimensional models. Frequently movement patterns are shown on the drawings or models. String diagrams are a familiar method of showing movement, coloured cord being attached to diagrams or models to indicate the paths taken by different products.

The main criticism of these methods, about which little more need be said here, is that they are completely unstructured and depend entirely on the knowledge, experience and insight of the planner. This same fact, however, can be interpreted as their main advantage. If they are completely unstructured it is theoretically possible, while planning the layout, to take into account all relevant constraints. Their merit, therefore, is the breadth of their approach rather than their rigour.

If we attempt to develop analytical methods of layout planning we must determine precisely what our objective is, e.g. to maximize facilities utilization or to minimize movement, congestion, etc. Undoubtedly, the lowest common denominator of all layouts, whether in manufacturing, supply, service or transport, is the need for movement. Even in visual planning procedures the need to minimize movement is usually the first consideration, and only after an initial layout has been obtained are additional objectives allowed to intervene. In most situations there will be some need for movement, and the type of equipment used, the distance travelled and the time involved will affect the total cost. However, in planning layouts, particularly new layouts which exist only on paper, it is often possible to measure only the distance involved in movement. Each movement operation normally involves pick-up, movement, put-down, but the distance is the main variable factor.

It is reasonable, therefore, to adopt as our primary objective the minimization of the total movement cost for items or people, and as our main criterion the total distance moved. This approach will be taken in this and the following section. Other factors will then be considered, with particular reference to service and supply systems.

## Cross and relationship charts

The pattern and extent of movement or handling which is known to take place, or expected to exist, are often summarized on some form of chart, which can then be used to assist in layout planning.

| FROM \ TO — Dept no. | 1 | 2 | 3 | 4 | 5 | 6 | 7 | 8 | 9 | 10 | TOTAL |
|---|---|---|---|---|---|---|---|---|---|---|---|
| 1 | | 15 | | | | 12 | 8 | 5 | | | 40 |
| 2 | | | 10 | 5 | | | | | | | 15 |
| 3 | | | | 10 | | | | | | | 10 |
| 4 | | | | | 5 | 7 | | 3 | | | 15 |
| 5 | | | | | | 5 | | | | | 5 |
| 6 | | | | | | | 12 | | | | 12 |
| 7 | | | | | | | | 12 | 8 | | 20 |
| 8 | | | | | | | | | 12 | 8 | 20 |
| 9 | | | | | | | | | | 20 | 20 |
| 10 | | | | | | | | | | | |
| TOTAL | | 15 | 10 | 15 | 5 | 24 | 20 | 20 | 20 | 28 | |

Figure 6.4 Cross chart showing the nature and extent of the movement of items among departments over a given period of time.

The cross chart shown in Figure 6.4 indicates the pattern and the amount of movement of items among ten departments in a small factory. In the case of a new layout the routeing will have been obtained from routeing instructions, e.g. flow process charts, and the quantities from production requirements. The figures in the matrix are the number of items or loads which in a given period of time must move from department $i$ to department $j$. In the case of the existing layouts this information may be obtained by sampling of the activity taking place within the factory.

Notice that the row and the column totals are not necessarily equal. Where some of the items are consumed or assembled during production, row totals may be less than column totals. For example, in this particular case 12 items were sent from department 1 directly to department 6, i.e. a total of 24 items were sent to department 6. However, only 12 items left department 6 for department 7, since the two groups of 12 had been assembled in pairs.

The movement pattern shown in this chart is associated with a process-type layout. Absence of any figures below the diagonal means that none of the items backtracks between departments, but the scatter above the diagonal indicates a varied movement pattern characteristic of the production of several products. Some of the items follow a path through from department 1 to department 10, but, judging from this information alone, a 'product layout' seems impractical.

Cross charts are a means of collecting and presenting information from which preferable departmental relationships can be obtained. This information can then be summarized on a *relationship chart*. For example, the relationship chart shown in Figure 6.5 is derived partly from the previous cross chart (Figure 6.4). Most of the preferable relationships between departments 1 to 10 result from a desire to minimize the materials movement given on the cross chart.

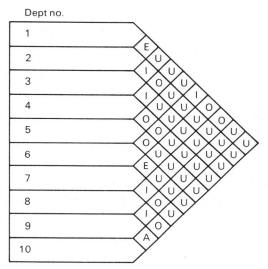

**Figure 6.5** *A relationship chart (derived partly from the cross chart in Figure 6.4).*

## General requirements of a layout planning procedure

To be of value, any procedure must:

1. take as its objective(s) something that we believe to be of overriding, if not sole, importance;
2. (a) be capable of producing several good layouts, from which we might choose the best or most appropriate, or which can be modified to take into account additional objectives and/or constraints; *or*
   (b) work in such a way that the development of one layout, or a set of alternative layouts, is undertaken interactively, with the layout designer being given the opportunity to modify, adapt or select alternatives at each stage in the development of the layout(s);
3. (a) be capable of dealing with the situation in which an entirely new layout, or a set of alternative layouts, are to be developed from a set of data; *or*
   (b) cope with the situation in which an existing layout is to be improved, modified or changed in some way.

Taking point 1 above, we have previously agreed that our primary objective will often be that of minimizing total movement cost. Additionally, we also often need a procedure which can accommodate:

(a)  different floor areas for departments;
(b)  a wide variety of flow patterns among departments;
(c)  different costs of movement;
(d)  the fact that certain departments may need to remain in a given position;
(e)  the fact that, in certain circumstances, certain departments must have a given relationship with one another;
(f)  the use of more than one floor.

In respect of 2(a) above, it will be appreciated that no procedure which satisfies the above requirements is likely to be optimal. In practice a heuristic procedure will be used, and in these circumstances the procedure should, preferably, develop several alternative layouts, since the designer is more likely to want to choose between alternatives, and perhaps modify these alternatives, than simply take one layout as being the most appropriate.

In respect of 2(b) above it may, alternatively, be appropriate to develop layouts interactively, i.e. to employ a method which does not simply produce one or more given layouts for a set of data, but which provides a procedure for moving towards a solution, with the opportunity to input additional information or modify the layout at various stages.

In respect of 3(a) and (b) above, any layout planning procedure which is to be of value in practice must be able to cope with the situation in which a new layout is to be planned and/or the situation in which improvements or modifications are to be made to an existing layout.

**Computer programs**

It was not until 1963 that procedures were developed which began to comply with at least some of the above requirements. In 1963 the first of many computer programs for layout planning became available. From that date there has been considerable interest in the use of computers in layout planning, and at the present time twenty or more such programs are available commercially. These programs have in some cases been developed to deal with specific situations. For example, some are 'complete design' programs in that they are capable of providing a complete layout from a set of input data, while others are 'improvement' or 'modification' programs which in effect seek to modify, improve or change an existing layout in order to satisfy certain new or additional requirements. The majority of the programs which have been developed to date would satisfy 1, 2(a) and 3 above, but only recently have programs been developed which will satisfy requirements 1, 2(b) and 3. The early programs, which were designed for batch processing on mainframe computers with line printer output, were not interactive. More recently, however, there has been an emphasis on the development of interactive programs, and in particular on the use of computer graphics in facilities layouts, possibly as part of a comprehensive computer-aided design/computer-aided manufacturing approach.

So far computer programs for layout planning have not found widespread use. Where used they have tended to provide only marginally better layouts than might have been achieved by using a systematic manual method. There are several problems, the difficulty of preparing data and the restricted number of factors which can be taken into account being perhaps the most important. However, rapid progress is being made, and such methods, particularly interactive and graphics-based methods, will find widespread application.

## Non-interactive programs

In this section we shall describe the *original* versions of three programs. They were the first to become widely available and are described here not because they are the best or the most useful, but because they are indicative of the *type* of approach which can be employed when using a computer-based layout planning procedure.

### CRAFT (Computerized Relative Allocation of Facilities Technique) (Armour and Buffa (1963))

CRAFT was developed in order to satisfy requirements 1, 2(a), 3(a) and 3(b) above and has as its objectives the minimization of total materials handling costs. The program requires an initial layout to be input at the beginning. It can therefore be considered as an 'improvement' or 'modification' *procedure*; however, it is in fact intended for the design of new layouts, since the initial layout can be an arbitrary one.

A simplified flow diagram for the program is shown in Figure 6.6.

The necessary input is:

(a) interdepartmental flow matrix, which gives the number of unit loads moving between all departments over a given period of time (this matrix need not be symmetrical);
(b) interdepartmental movement cost matrix, giving the cost per unit distance of movement between all departments (this matrix need not be symmetrical);
(c) initial layout configuration showing the size of departments, arranged so that one line can be represented by an 80-column punch card (it may be an arbitrary or an existing layout);
(d) any restrictions, i.e. fixed departments which cannot be moved.

The program then attempts to improve on the initial layout by interchanging pairs of departments. Every pair of departments is examined and the effect of their interchange on the total movement cost for the layout is calculated. The pair change giving the greatest reduction in total movement cost is effected and the process is repeated until no further interchange of departments will provide any additional reduction in the total movement cost associated with the layout.

The algorithm by which the program operates is as follows:

1. Determine which pairs of departments may be interchanged. Departments are considered for interchange when they are adjacent, of equal area, or bordering on a common third department.
2. Calculate the distance between departments, the distances being taken as those between the centres of the departments.
3. Calculate the reduction in total movement costs resulting from the interchange of all possible pairs of departments.
4. Interchange the two departments which provide the greatest saving in total movement costs.
5. Calculate the total movement cost and print out the revised layout.

This procedure is repeated until no further cost saving is possible, and then the final layout is printed.

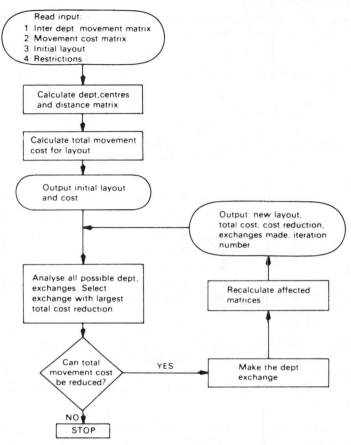

**Figure 6.6**  *Simplified flow chart for CRAFT program. From Armour, G.C. and Buffa, E.S. (1963) A heuristic algorithm and simulation approach to the relative location of facilities,* Management Science, **9***(2). Reproduced with permission.*

## CORELAP (Computerized Relationship Layout Planning (Lee and Moore (1967))

CORELAP was developed about 1967 and adopts a quite different approach to layout planning. It satisfies requirements, 1, 2(a) and 3(a) and is intended for use in the design of new layouts. Unlike CRAFT, CORELAP concerns itself only with the latter part of the layout problem, i.e. developing an acceptable layout from given preferable departmental relationships. In fact a relationship chart of the type described previously (Figure 6.5) forms part of the input to this program, the rest of the input being: (a) departments and their required areas; and (b) a maximum building length to width ratio.

The advantage of this type of approach is that, since layouts are developed from stated, preferred relationships, all the necessary reasons for a desired relationship between departments can be taken into account in developing the layouts, unlike CRAFT, which depends solely on product flow.

A further advantage of CORELAP is that an initial layout is not required, the only constraint being the maximum building length to width ratio. This ratio is necessary to ensure that the program does not develop unrealistic layout configurations, e.g. very long, thin layouts.

*ALDEP (Automated Layout Design Program (Seehof and Evans (1967))*

ALDEP is similar to CORELAP in that it employs a preference ratings approach. The program either generates a series of random layouts and selects that with the best total performance score, or generates one random layout and then makes comparisons and exchanges between pairs of areas until no further improvement of the total preference score is possible.

## Interactive programs and computer graphics

*Interactive CORELAP (Moore (1971))*

Interactive CORELAP was introduced around 1971, since when it has been further developed. The program is able to handle both new plant and existing plant problems. It permits certain departments to be placed in a fixed location, and scores any alternative layout. The program is designed to be run in an interactive manner from a terminal on a time-sharing computer. The designer, at the terminal, can interrupt the program to make adjustments, or the program might interrupt itself when it gets into a particularly difficult situation in order to seek further information and/or assistance from the designer. At any stage the designer can ask the program to cost alternative layouts, and he or she may move departments around in much the same way as moving templates around on a drawing board. The more recent developments of interactive CORELAP provide for graphical input and output of information. Data can be input through a keyboard, but in addition can be generated directly by the designer on the terminal screen, and alternative layouts can be displayed there for inspection and modification.

Other interactive programs are available specifically for use in non-manufacturing situations. For example, that described by Jacobs et al (1980) provides an interactive improvement procedure.

*Computer-aided design (CAD)*

The availability of powerful interactive computer *graphics* facilities has opened new possibilities for computer-aided facilities layout planning. In particular the introduction of Computer Aided Design (CAD) permits the development of layouts in an interactive fashion, with the possibility of storing layout information, modifying layouts, and printing out departmental and plant layouts using high speed plotters. In considering the use of CAD it is important to distinguish two applications. At the simplest level CAD provides for computer-assisted drafting. This is of some relevance in facilities layout planning, in that it provides an alternative to the use of the drawing board or the use of templates on a scale model, but it does not itself provide a procedure for the development of layout plans and therefore does not satisfy the requirements listed earlier. At a more sophisticated level, CAD also provides a procedure or algorithm for the design of layouts from certain input data, whether for an existing or for a modified layout, with the opportunity for the designer, seated at a graphics terminal, to interact directly with the computer. The computer develops a layout plan which is shown at each stage on the terminal screen. The designer may interrupt the program as required to impose particular requirements on the layout or to try out alternatives. This interruption can take the form of direct manipulation of the layout on the screen using either digitizing tablet and/or light pens, and may also involve the input of additional information through the terminal keyboard. Through this 'on-line interactive' procedure many alternative layouts will be developed for subsequent modification or choice, and ultimately the chosen layout will be printed out in full or in part, in detail. The CAD facility can be used in preparing details, e.g. for the location of services, pipe lines, services to the buildings, etc., all of which can be stored for subsequent reference or modification and provided as detailed drawings through a line plotter. At the time of writing such programs are becoming available and are of use in facilities layout planning in engineering, manufacture, architecture, the health services, etc.

## MODIFYING EXISTING LAYOUTS

Many of the computer-based procedures described above will be of relevance when modifying existing layouts. For example, the CRAFT procedure requires the input of an initial layout which it then seeks to improve, given certain traffic information and movement cost. CRAFT is in effect an 'improvement' program. Other 'improvement' programs include COFAD, HC.66, COL and FRAT. The use of these programs may be of relevance where an existing layout is to be modified, e.g. the addition of a new department, the redistribution of space in existing departments, or the relocation of one of the existing departments.

## LAYOUT BY PRODUCT AND FIXED POSITION

Many of the procedures discussed above are of particular relevance for the planning of functional or process layouts. While they may be used in planning product or group-type layouts where a predominant directional flow is required (e.g. manufacturing flow lines or flow-type service systems), other approaches are of particular relevance in these cases. Some of these procedures are introduced in Chapter 15, which deals specifically with the design of flow-type systems.

A somewhat different situation exists in planning fixed-position layouts. Here the principal item or customer does not move, but all necessary parts and facilities move to and from it. Such a situation might be visualized as several fixed departments or areas within a site, one of which is the customer for all the others. This 'customer' area is the fixed location of the item being manufactured or the customer being serviced, while all other areas are the permanent locations of the facilities required in this process. For example, in building a ship the construction area is fixed, and around it are located areas in which plating work is undertaken, stern gear is manufactured, engines are prepared, etc. The location problem therefore involves the arrangement of these areas around the main construction area. Again, movement cost can be important; thus it will be desirable to place close to the construction area those departments which must supply heavy items and/or large quantities of items, while areas providing smaller quantities of smaller or lighter items might be located further away. Taking this approach the problem may be tackled by one of the procedures outlined above, since in effect we are planning a process-type layout in which the material flow pattern is largely one in which all departments communicate with a supply department.

## SUPPLY AND STORAGE LAYOUTS

While the above procedures, which focus primarily upon movement, may be relevant in planning the layout of supply and storage systems, it is appropriate to consider such systems separately, since in these cases other factors may also be of some importance.

The facilities layout problem in supply systems often involves the location of display and/or storage areas to which customers have direct access. The arrangement of display and shelving areas in a supermarket is a good example of the type of problem often encountered. In such cases there will be a need to minimize total movement for most customers. Thus the procedures referred to above will be of relevance providing that those responsible for layout planning have some data concerning the average or typical customer's needs in terms of goods or items to be acquired. Given this information, shelving and passageways can be arranged so that, with a knowledge of the layout, customers may collect their goods with the minimum of movement. Other factors, however, are of relevance in the planning of layouts and should be introduced at this point. For example, the arrangement of displays and storage in supply systems such as supermarkets is also a function of display-type considerations. For example it is well known that 'traffic' patterns in supermarkets follow a particular form, with most customers preferring, initially at least, to travel around the edges of the area rather than along intermediate aisles and passageways. It is known that goods displayed at the end of the aisle tend to sell better than those placed in the middle of an aisle and that goods stored in such a way that they can be seen from the entrance or through windows attract the customer to the store. Thus it might be argued that the arrangement of such facilities must take account of certain customer-oriented factors rather than simply concentrating on retailer-oriented factors such as maximum use of space and minimum transport.

The arrangement of storage areas such as warehouses also necessitates the consideration of factors other than movement. In such cases there is often a conflict between the need to obtain maximum space utilization and the need to minimize the cost of movement. For example, maximum space utilization often involves high stacking, whereas the storage of items in this manner often necessitates the use of expensive materials handling equipment and therefore gives rise to high movement costs. The arrangement of passageways is also of considerable importance, while the possibility of future expansion, the need to accommodate new items which may have different dimensions or different weight, the need to locate items associated with one another in the same area, the need to provide secure areas for other items, etc., are all of some importance in layout planning.

## EVALUATION OF ALTERNATIVE LAYOUTS

Determining which of many alternative layouts to adopt is often a very difficult problem. If we consider all the possible features and characteristics then our list is likely to be very long indeed. If, on the other hand, we consider only the problem of movement and evaluate the alternative layouts only in this light, we shall very probably neglect certain quite important considerations and be guilty of sub-optimization. One factor should be common to whatever considerations we adopt: cost. We must, as a rule, aim to minimize the total cost involved in establishing and using the layout. Muther, referring specifically to manufacturing systems, has suggested that layouts should be evaluated on the basis of the following costs.

1. Investment
   (a) Initial cost of new facilities of all kinds:
       (i)     *buildings
       (ii)    *construction
       (iii)   *machinery
       (iv)    *equipment

   (b) Accessory costs:
       (i)     tools, jigs, fixtures
       (ii)    *handling equipment
       (iii)   *containers
       (iv)    benches and chairs
       (v)     timeclocks, water coolers, etc.
       (vi)    *shelves, bins, racks
       (vii)   wiring and lighting
       (viii)  piping and ducting

   (c) Installation costs:
       (i)     *building changes
       (ii)    *machinery and equipment
       (iii)   *services and supporting facilities
       (iv)    *auxiliary service lines

   (d) Depreciation and obsolescence costs

2. Operating costs
   (a) Material:
       (i)     production
       (ii)    scrap and waste
       (iii)   supplies and packing
       (iv)    maintenance parts and materials

   (b) Labour:
       (i)     direct
       (ii)    overtime or extra-shift premium
       (iii)   idle or waiting time
       (iv)    efficiency variation
       (v)     clerical
       (vi)    maintenance
       (vii)   inspection
       (viii)  *handling and storerooms
       (ix)    other indirect labour
       (x)     supervision

   (c) General:
       (i)     *floor space
       (ii)    power
       (iii)   fuel
       (iv)    taxes
       (v)     insurance
       (vi)    rentals
       (vii)   interest on investment

This is not the most comprehensive list that could be suggested, but even so it is a little
difficult to appreciate how certain of these items will vary with different layouts, or to

understand how some depend on layout at all. We would suggest that in the majority of cases cost items marked with an asterisk will be the most important. Nevertheless, in certain circumstances many of the other costs will merit consideration. The comparison and evaluation of designs for completely new layouts is a difficult problem, and, while such factors as movement, cost of equipment and space required are normally the principal components of comparison, they are by no means the only components.

The evaluation or rearrangement of parts of factories or departments constitutes an easier problem only because of the size of the layouts, and not because fewer factors need be considered.

## MATERIALS HANDLING

The fact that we have considered the minimization of total movement cost as a principal objective in planning facilities layout is sufficient evidence of the importance of efficient handling and the efficient management of movement in most operating systems. Although we have adopted the title 'Materials Handling' we should emphasize that the management, i.e. the efficient planning and control, of movement in all types of systems is of considerable importance, whether that movement relates to raw materials, finished goods, customers or indirect materials. Movement of materials, work in progress and finished goods is of crucial importance in all manufacturing operations. The movement of customers and goods is clearly of ultimate importance in transport systems, while the handling, i.e. the organization of the movement of customers and items, is of considerable importance also in supply and service systems. Here, therefore, we are concerned with the movement of customers or items (whether materials or finished goods) into or out of stores, during processing, into the operating system, and from the operating system to the final customer.

Efficient materials handling (i.e. the movement of items or customers) can bring considerable cost benefit to operating systems. Work in progress might be reduced; accidents or losses might be reduced: the capacity of the operating system might be increased; speed of processing, i.e. the throughput time, might be improved; level of service to the customer, e.g. the waiting time and the number of stock-out situations, might be improved; total space required by the operation might be reduced; etc. Naturally there are equally substantial costs involved in designing, installing, staffing and maintaining an efficient system, including both recurrent and capital costs, so the design and planning of the system must be undertaken with a full awareness of, and therefore after detailed analysis of, movement needs, conditions, requirements and constraints, both present and future.

The principles of efficient materials handling are listed in Table 6.1, from which it will be seen that an early objective should be the elimination of the need for handling or movement, or, failing that, a reduction in the need for such handling or movement. This might be achieved by more appropriate layout of the operating facilities, by combining operations with movement, etc. The *necessary* handling/movement should be organized in as efficient a manner as possible. This will often involve the minimization of 'pick-up/put-down' movements, the use of unit loads and pallets, the use of straight-line movement, the use of mechanical rather than manual movement, and the separation of items which require subsequent separate processing.

Table 6.2 identifies the principal classes of materials handling equipment and suggests some of the normal applications for such equipment. In this table the applications are considered in terms of the type of movement required, i.e. whether predominantly overhead, vertical, a combination of vertical or horizontal, or largely horizontal (having a fixed route, or with a variable, i.e. non-fixed, route). Certain types of equipment conventionally operate at a constant speed, although often on an intermittent basis. Conveyors normally fall into this category. Other equipment, e.g. trucks and cranes, is able to operate at variable speeds.

**Table 6.1** *Principles of efficient materials handling.*

1. Eliminate need for handling/movement (e.g. by eliminating unnecessary movement and by suitable arrangement of processes)
2. Combine processing and movement
3. Plan layout of operations together with planning of materials handling to minimize handling/movement
4. (In general) use mechanical handling where regular high-volume movement is required or where safety hazards exist
5. Arrange handling/movement to minimize number of 'pick-up/put-down' movements
6. Use unit loads and use pallets and containers to avoid damage, reduce subsequent handling, etc.
7. Avoid mixing items/materials which subsequently need to be separated
8. Use straight-line movement

**Table 6.2** *Methods for materials handling and applications.*

| Class of equipment | Type of equipment | Speed (v = variable; c = constant) | Normal applications (type of movement) | | | | |
|---|---|---|---|---|---|---|---|
| | | | Overhead | Vertical | Vertical/horizontal | Horizontal fixed route | Horizontal non-fixed route |
| Cranes | Gantry | v | ✓ | ✓ | ✓ | | |
| | Mobile (e.g. truck) | v | ✓ | ✓ | ✓ | | |
| | Revolving | v | ✓ | ✓ | ✓ | | |
| Lifts | Elevator | v | | ✓ | | | |
| | Escalator | v | | ✓ | | | |
| | Bucket | c | | ✓ | | | |
| Trucks | Fork | v | | | | | ✓ |
| | Hand | v | | | | | ✓ |
| | Tractor | v | | | | | ✓ |
| | Sideloader | v | | | | | ✓ |
| | Platform | v | | | | | ✓ |
| | Pallet | v | | | | | ✓ |
| | Straddle | v | | | | | ✓ |
| Conveyor | Belt | c | | | | ✓ | |
| | Roller | c | | | | ✓ | |
| | Flight | c | | | ✓ | ✓ | |
| | Pneumatic | c | | | ✓ | ✓ | |
| | Screw | c | | | | ✓ | |
| | Slatted | c | | | | ✓ | |
| | Vibrating | c | | | | ✓ | |
| | Drag chain | c | ✓ | | | ✓ | |
| Towing | Overhead chain | c | ✓ | | | ✓ | |
| | Overhead monorail | v | ✓ | | | ✓ | |
| | Floor | c | | | | ✓ | ✓ |
| Chute | Gravity | c | | | ✓ | ✓ | |
| | Spiral lift | c | | | ✓ | | |

The selection of appropriate materials handling equipment will be determined by the type of applications required as well as by factors of the type listed in Table 6.2. Principal among these (see Table 6.3) are the types of materials/items/customers to be moved, their volume or weight, the frequency and regularity of movement and of course the extent to which this movement requirement is temporary or 'permanent'. The movement route, particularly whether fixed or variable, and the extent to which this route is influenced by existing constraints such as the location of equipment and the shape of buildings, will be of considerable importance. In certain cases the speed of movement is determined, e.g. the handling of hot items may require a speed of movement differing from that needed for the handling of fragile items. In certain cases the speed of movement required is low, since some form of processing is associated with the movement; for example in the brewing industry, movement, storage and maturing often occur simultaneously. The type of storage employed, both before and after movement, will influence the type of materials handling equipment envisaged, as will considerations of safety and the needs of concurrent and subsequent processes.

A recent development in materials handling in industry is the use of 'unit load procedures'. The use of pallets, containers and other unit load handling is often associated with unit load storage procedures. Such an approach might be considered as a form of batch materials handling in situations in which larger quantities of identical or similar items are collected together into a container, pallet or other device for convenience in storing and handling. Alternatively, unit load procedures are used as a form of 'kit' handling and storage where a variety of different yet complementary items are collected together such that the entire unit or 'kit' contains all necessary items for a particular purpose, e.g. for the manufacture or assembly of a particular item.

**Table 6.3** *Factors influencing selection of materials handling equipment.*

| | |
|---|---|
| Materials/items | to be moved<br>i.e. size, weight, nature (e.g. fragility or hazards) |
| Volume/rate | of movement<br>i.e. frequency of movement<br>volumes to be moved<br>regularity of movement<br>temporary or 'permanent' need |
| Route of movement | i.e. whether fixed or variable, or complex (or straight line) and whether influenced by building layouts, etc. |
| Speed of movement required | i.e. speed required/necessary (e.g. fast for hot items, slow for fragile items) |
| Storage | method employed (for storage before and after movement)<br>i.e. how and where stored (e.g. pallets, unit loads, loose, packed, etc.) |
| Safety/hazards | involved<br>e.g. fire hazards, spillage risk |
| Concurrent processing | involved or possible<br>e.g. whether movement can be combined with processing |

## FURTHER READING

Armour, G. C. and Buffa, E. S. (1963) A heuristic algorithm and computer simulation approach to the relative location of facilities, *Management Science,* **9**(1), pp. 294–309.
Lee, R. C. and Moore, J. M. (1967) CORELAP—Computerized relationship layout planning, *Journal of Industrial Engineering,* **18**(3), pp. 195–200.

Moore, J. M. (1971) Computer program evaluates plant layout alternatives, *Industrial Engineering*, **3**(19).

Muther, R. and McPherson, K. (1970) Four approaches to computerized layout planning, *Journal of Industrial Engineering*, **2**(2), pp. 39–42.

Seehof, J. M. and Evans, W. O. (1967) Automated layout design programme, *Journal of Industrial Engineering*, **18**(12), pp. 690–695.

Woodley, D. R. (1964) *Encyclopaedia of Materials Handling*. Oxford: Pergamon.

# QUESTIONS

**6.1** The following cross chart has been constructed by means of observations of all movement between the seven production departments of a factory over a typical one-month period. In addition to these seven production departments, there are three other departments: the general office, the drawing office and the personnel department. The general office should preferably be close to the assembly department but not close to the test department. The drawing office should preferably be close to assembly, stores and the general office, but must not be close to the test area. The location of the personnel department is comparatively unimportant; however, it should not be too far away from any of the production departments. The relative location of the production departments depends on materials flow only, as shown in the figure below.

| | R | S | T | M | G | A | T |
|---|---|---|---|---|---|---|---|
| Receiving | | 40 | | | | 3 | 3 |
| Stores | | | 20 | 20 | | | |
| Turning | | | | 18 | 2 | | |
| Milling | | | | | 18 | 20 | |
| Grinding | | | | | | 10 | 10 |
| Assembly | | | | | | | 38 |
| Testing | | | | | 5 | | |

Construct a relationship chart showing the desirable relative locations of these ten departments. Use an appropriate notation to indicate the desired proximities.

**6.2** 'Visual or graphical minimization is the only satisfactory and practical method of designing facility layouts, and the minimization of total movement costs is the most appropriate objective function during layout planning.' Discuss.

**6.3** Determine a rectangular plant layout consisting of the eleven departments included in the table below.

| Department | Part | | | | | Department area (m²) |
| | A | B | C | D | E | |
| --- | --- | --- | --- | --- | --- | --- |
| 1 | 2 | 2 | 2 | 2 | 2 | 500 |
| 2 | 3 | 7 | 3 | 4 | 3 | 400 |
| 3 | 5 | | 4 | | 4 | 200 |
| 4 | | | 7 | 6 | 7, 7 | 600 |
| 5 | 7 | | | | | 200 |
| 6 | 9 | 9 | | 10 | 4 | 500 |
| 7 | 6 | 8 | 8 | | 8, 9 | 1000 |
| 8 | | 6 | 9 | | 6 | 500 |
| 9 | 10 | 10 | 10 | | 10 | 800 |
| 10 | 11 | 11 | 11 | 11 | 11 | 500 |
| 11 | | | | | | 500 |

| | A | B | C | D | E |
| --- | --- | --- | --- | --- | --- |
| Loads/month | 50 | 100 | 250 | 100 | 100 |

**6.4** What factors, other than the cost of movement, need to be considered during the planning of a new layout, and how is the consideration of these factors included in the whole layout planning procedure?

**6.5** Discuss the requirements of the handling systems and identify appropriate types of handling equipment for the following applications:

(a) the handling of customers' baggage (other than hand baggage) in an airport terminal;
(b) the movement of metal waste from the machine shop of a mass-production engineering company;
(c) the movement of goods from the goods receiving department through stores, onto shelves and to customers in a large supermarket.

# WORK AND WORK SYSTEMS

# INTRODUCTION TO PART 4

*In this part of the book we shall concentrate on work systems. We shall focus on human work, i.e. the execution of tasks by people within the operating system, and in so doing we shall look at some traditional and established areas of responsibility of operations management as well as at some newer topics. We shall look at work methods, work standards, the rewards for work, the problems of learning, people's attitudes to work, the design of the workplace, health and safety considerations, etc. All these topics are interrelated. For our purposes we can perhaps identify four sets of considerations which must be taken into account in the design of work systems. We might take as our focus the design of the work itself, i.e. the specification of the tasks to be performed—the work content, the determination of appropriate methods of executing these tasks and the establishment of standards of performance for this work. This* work focus *is a necessary but insufficient consideration in the design of work systems. We might take as our focus the* conditions *in which people work, that is the design of the workplace, the ergonomics of the workplace, and health and safety considerations. Again, this is a necessary but insufficient consideration. An important aspect to consider is the workers themselves: workers' needs, motives, expectations and attitudes, their skills, abilities, the need to learn, etc. This* worker focus *is a necessary but insufficient consideration. We might take an* organizational focus *and consider the nature and design of the organization in which the work is to be undertaken, the reward or payment system for such work, etc. Again this is a necessary but insufficient consideration. These four sets of considerations are each examined in the following chapters. No one set of considerations is more important than any other. All must be taken together.*

# CHAPTER 7

# Work and Work Methods

In this and the next chapter we shall concentrate on physical work and use the term 'work study' to cover all aspects of the design of work methods and the establishment of work standards.

Work study is concerned primarily with human manual work and is therefore relevant in all types of operating systems. Although traditionally associated with manufacture, work study practitioners are now employed in manufacturing, supply, service and transport systems. Specifically it is concerned with the efficient design of work, and with the establishment of standards of performance.

## THE STRUCTURE AND PURPOSES OF WORK STUDY

Throughout these two chapters we shall use the British terminology and, where possible, the British Standards definitions (*Glossary of Terms in Work Study*, BS 3138, 1959). The British Standards Institution defines work study as 'a generic term for those techniques, particularly method study and work measurement, which are used in the examination of human work in all its contexts, and which lead systematically to the investigation of all the factors which affect the efficiency and economy of the situations being reviewed, in order to effect improvements'.

The aims of work study are, by analysis of work methods and the materials and equipment used, to:

(a) establish the most economical way of doing the work;
(b) standardize this method, and the materials and equipment involved;
(c) establish the time required by a qualified and adequately trained worker to do the job, while working at a defined level of performance;
(d) install this work method as standard practice.

Work study, then, is a comparatively low-cost way of either designing work for high productivity or improving productivity in existing work by improving current work methods and by reducing ineffective or wasted time. In each case the design or improvement is sought within the context of existing resources and equipment; consequently work study is an immediate tool and is not dependent on redesign of goods or services, research and development of operating processes, or extensive rearrangement of facilities.

As with any other procedure it is particularly important that it should be applied in circumstances where it is likely to achieve maximum benefit. There is little point in conducting an extensive work-study investigation of jobs in which there is little manual work, since operations will be dependent largely on the design of the machines, and basic redesign of machinery is neither a short-term nor an inexpensive method of improving productivity. Similarly, there is little benefit in applying work study to manual work which is temporary or which, for some other reason, is expected to be short-lived. We must apply the technique in circumstances from which we expect maximum returns. The economic results of the study, whether they are increases in output, reduction in scrap, improved safety, reduction in training time, or better use of equipment or labour, should always outweigh the cost of the investigation, and to attempt to ensure this we should consider:

(a) the anticipated life of the job;
(b) whether manual work is an important part of the job, e.g. the wage rate for the job and the ratio of machine time to manual time in the work cycle;
(c) utilization of equipment, machines, tools, etc., the cost of such equipment, and whether the utilization is dependent on the work method;
(d) the importance of the job to the company, e.g. the output quantity, profit margin, and so on.

We should distinguish between work study of existing jobs and that of proposed or anticipated jobs. Whenever new products are to be made or new equipment used, jobs must be designed. Consequently the question is to what extent shall we use work study, and how much effort is justified by the importance of the job? Some investigation may be necessary on existing jobs, not necessarily because they were inadequately designed in the first place, but perhaps because there has been a slight change in the product, new equipment is being used, or wage rates or incentives are to be altered. Examinations of existing work methods could also result from low machine utilization, excessive labour overtime or idle time, complaints from the workers, inadequate quality, high scrap or wastage rate, etc.

Figure 7.1 shows the structure of work study. Two aspects exist: first, method study, concerned with establishing optimum work methods; and second, work measurement, concerned with establishing time standards for those methods. One can consider methods without considering time, although in practice this rarely occurs. Occasionally the reverse applies, i.e. work measurement is conducted without prior method study.

## METHOD STUDY

'Method study is the systematic recording and critical examination of existing and proposed ways of doing work, as a means of developing and applying easier and more effective methods and reducing costs' (BS 3138). The procedure consists of a maximum of seven steps:

1. Select the work to be studied.
2. Record the existing work method and all other relevant facts.

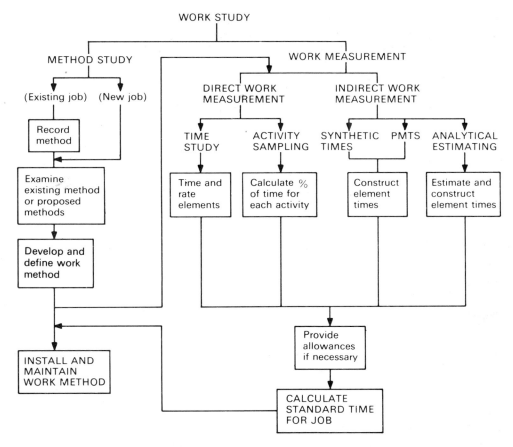

**Figure 7.1** *The structure of work study.*

3. Examine the record.
4. Develop the most efficient or optimum method of doing the work.
5. Define the method.
6. Install this method as standard practice.
7. Maintain this practice.

These seven steps constitute method study procedure when applied to an existing job. Step 1 will not apply in the case of new jobs. Productivity may be increased by eliminating inefficiencies from existing work, but a greater contribution can be made by ensuring that these inefficiencies never arise in the first place.

Nevertheless, the case of existing work is the most comprehensive problem, and this is what we shall use as our example throughout the chapter. The steps are discussed in more detail below.

## Step 1: Select

The problem of selecting the work to be studied has been mentioned above. Maximum cost benefit is the normal objective, but here we should perhaps define what we mean by cost. We ought to be concerned with the total cost of production, and ostensibly we are. Direct cost of labour, materials and equipment is certainly the main component of total cost, but indirect cost, such as the cost of supervision, training, recruitment and welfare, is also relevant. Although work methods may affect each of these costs there is an understandable tendency to restrict one's consideration to direct costs, and to develop work methods which minimize the cost of labour, machinery and materials. This practice has been the subject recently of a consolidated attack by managers, researchers, theorists and academics who are concerned with the human or behavioural implications of work design (Chapter 9). They rightly point out that factors such as absenteeism and labour turnover may result from the nature of the work, and that work design should be evaluated in a far broader manner than has hitherto been the practice.

### Step 2: Record

 We shall begin by considering records which provide relatively little detail of the work method: such records might be appropriate for a preliminary investigation of a work method. Later we shall look at more detailed records which might be appropriate for detailed critical examination of existing work methods with a view to improvement and/or where a subsequent objective is to establish a work standard for the method. In the latter context it is worth noting that the subsequent use of the record may determine the type of record and the type of notation which will be employed. For example, if a work standard is to be developed using a predetermined motion time system (PMTS) (e.g. MTM, see Chapter 8), then the record of the method must be in sufficient detail, and must employ the same terminology as the appropriate PMTS system.

The principal types of records are listed in Table 7.1.

### 1. Diary

This is usually a self-recording of the work method by the worker himself or herself. Usually fairly little detail is obtained, and often the record is in the form of a diary of activities or movements. This method of recording might be appropriate as a first means of establishing the amount of time devoted to particular jobs, etc.

### 2. Flow diagrams

Three types of flow diagram are in general use. *A flow diagram* shows the location and sequence of the activities carried out by workers and the routes followed by materials, components, etc. A *string diagram* is a scale diagram (or model) on which coloured thread wrapped around pins or pegs is used to indicate the paths taken by workers, materials or equipment during a sequence of activities. String diagrams are a useful means of recording when complex movement patterns are involved and/or when the objective is to record and illustrate the movement of numerous items or workers. They can, like flow diagrams, be used to record movements throughout large areas, such as entire departments or buildings, or movement throughout smaller areas, such as individual workplaces. The *travel chart,* sometimes called the cross chart, is a slightly more sophisticated instrument for recording patterns of movement and the extent, e.g. volume, of movement between areas. Further details are given in the discussion of facilities layout planning in Chapter 6.

## 3. Multiple activity charts

These are also referred to as *activity analysis* or *worker and machine charts*. This type of record is of value where the activities of one or more workers and/or pieces of equipment are to be examined. The activities and their duration are represented by blocks or lines drawn against a timescale in the manner of a bar chart. It is not usually possible to include much detail on such charts, but colour or shading is often used to distinguish between:

(a) independent work (worker working independently of equipment, e.g. reading instructions or preparing material, or equipment working independently of worker);
(b) combined work, where both worker and equipment work together, e.g. setting up, adjusting;
(c) waiting time, by either worker or equipment.

## 4. Process charts

The three types of process charts are certainly the most familiar of the method study recording procedures. The sequence of events is represented by a series of symbols which are basically the same for each type of chart. The (American Society of Mechanical Engineers) symbols shown in Table 7.2 differ slightly from those originally developed by Gilbreth, but these are the ones currently used. The definitions are based on those suggested by the British Standards Institution.

An *outline process chart* is a record of the main parts of the process only (i.e. the operations and the inspections). It is often used as a preliminary step in a method study investigation, prior to a more detailed study. Alternatively, outline process charts are often used to record basic information for use during the arrangement or layout of plant, during the design of the product, or even during the design of machinery for manufacturing the product. It is a simple record of the important 'constructive' and essential steps in a process, omitting all ancillary activities.

A *flow process chart* may be concerned with either materials (material flow process chart) or workers (worker flow process chart), or both. It is an amplification of the outline process chart and shows, in addition, the *transportations, storages* and *delays* which occur. In material flow process charts, *operations* occur when an object is intentionally changed in any way; *transportations* when an object is moved, except where such movement forms part of the operation; *inspections* when an object is examined; *storage* when an object is deliberately kept or protected against unauthorized removal; and *delay* when conditions do not permit the performance of the next activity. There is no storage symbol for worker flow process charts since it is assumed that the worker will never have cause deliberately to place himself or herself in confinement; otherwise the symbols for the two types of charts are the same. Figure 7.2 shows a simple worker-and-material flow process chart.

**Table 7.1** *Principal types of recording* (Based on Wild, R. (1980) *Management and Production*, 2nd edition. Harmondsworth: Penguin. Reproduced with permission.)

| Type of record | Definition (where appropriate from BS 3138) | Amount of detail | Applications |
| --- | --- | --- | --- |
| 1. Diary | A record of a work method, normally constructed by the worker himself or herself, in the form of a diary or list of activities | Usually very little, e.g. often just a diary of activities or movements | To establish amount of time devoted to particular jobs, etc. |
| 2. Flow diagrams (a) Flow diagram | A diagram or model substantially to scale which shows the location of specific activities carried out and the routes followed by workers, materials or equipment in their execution | Shows location with respect to departments, etc. and sequence of principal activities | Particularly useful as a means of studying layout |
| (b) String diagram | A scale plan or model on which a thread is used to trace and measure the paths of workers, materials or equipment during a specified sequence of events | Shows only extent and nature of movement between areas | Particularly useful as a means of studying layout |
| (c) Travel chart | A tabular record for presenting quantitative data about the movement of workers, materials or equipment between any number of places over any given period of time | Gives in quantitative terms extent of movement between areas | Particularly useful as a means of studying layout |
| 3. Multiple activity charts (activity analysis) | A chart on which the activities of more than one subject (worker, machine or equipment) are each recorded on a common timescale to show their interrelationship | Difficult to record more than a limited number of types of activity, e.g. working, idle, delay, etc. | As a preliminary investigation, or to study extent of occurrence of particular activities |
| 4. Process charts (a) Outline | A process chart giving an overall picture by recording in sequence only the main operations and inspections | Shows principal elements only, i.e. operations and inspections | As a preliminary investigation |
| (b) Flow process chart for worker | A process chart setting out the sequence of the flow of a product or a procedure by recording all events under review using the appropriate process chart symbols. This chart gives a record of all events associated with the worker | Operations, inspections, movements and delays associated with the worker | Normally used as the principal means of recording work methods |
| (c) Flow process | A process chart setting out the sequence of the flow of a product or a procedure by | Operations, inspections, movements, delays and storage of | ditto |

| | | | |
|---|---|---|---|
| chart for material | recording all events under review using the appropriate process chart symbols. This chart gives a record of all events associated with the material | material | ditto |
| (d) Flow process chart for worker and material | A process chart setting out the sequence of the flow of a product or a procedure by recording all events under review using the appropriate process chart symbols. This chart gives a record of all events associated with worker and material | Operations, inspections, movements, delays and storage | ditto |
| (e) Flow process chart for equipment | A process chart setting out the sequence of the flow of a product or a procedure by recording all events under review using the appropriate process chart symbols. This chart shows how equipment is used | ditto | |
| (f) Two-handed (or operator) | A process chart in which the activities of a worker's hands (or limbs) are recorded in relationship to one another | Shows work method in same detail as above for each hand of operator at a given workplace | Operations at a workplace. To provide greater detail than other types of process chart. |
| 5. SIMO (simultaneous motion chart) | A chart, often based on film analysis, used to record simultaneously on a common timescale the Therbligs or groups of Therbligs performed by different parts of the body of one or more workers | Equivalent to above but gives much more detail, i.e. in terms of 'work elements' | Where considerable detail is required, or as convenient record of film analysis |
| 6. Memomotion | A form of time lapse filming which records activity frame by frame at longer intervals than normal. The time intervals usually lie between 1/2 second and 4 seconds | Little detail but compacts activities occurring over a long period of time into shorter periods | For studying jobs with long cycle times, or jobs involving many people and movement over a large area |
| 7. Cyclegraphic (a) Cyclegraph | A record of a path of movement, usually traced by a continuous source of light on a photograph, preferably stereoscopic | Paths of movement of limbs within a fixed area | Movement of limbs at workplace (infrequently used) |
| (a) Chrono-cyclegraph | A cyclegraph in which the light source is suitably interrupted so that the path appears as a series of pear-shaped spots, the pointed end indicating the direction of movement and the spacing indicating the speed of movement | Details of direction and speed of movement of limbs within a fixed area | Movement of limbs at a workplace with added timescale |

**Table 7.2**   *Process chart symbols.*

| Symbol | Process chart | | | |
|---|---|---|---|---|
| | Outline | Flow process chart | | Two-handed (or operator) |
| | | Worker type | Material type | |
| ○ | Operation | Operation | Operation | Operation |
| ◊ | — | Transportation | Transportation | Transportation |
| □ | Inspection | Inspection | Inspection | — |
| ▽ | — | — | Storage | Hold |
| D | — | Delay | Delay | Delay |

*Note:* Operation indicates the main steps in a process method or procedure. Usually the part, material or product concerned is modified or changed during the operation

Transportation indicates the movement of workers, materials or equipment from place to place

Storage indicates a controlled storage in which material is received into or issued from stores under some form of authorization, or an item is retained for reference purposes

Delay indicates a delay in the sequence of events, for example work waiting between consecutive operations. or any object laid aside temporarily without record until required

Inspection indicates an inspection for quality and/or a check for quantity

Hold indicates the retention of an object in one hand, normally so that the other hand may do something to it

A *two-handed or operator process chart* is the most detailed type of flow process chart, in which the activities of the worker's hands are recorded in relation to one another. Unlike the previous recording methods, the two-handed process chart is normally confined to work carried out at a single place. The ordinary symbols are used, except *inspection* is omitted since this can be represented by movements of the hands, and the *storage* symbol is now taken to mean *hold*.

Pre-printed charts are normally used, and the necessary comments, descriptions and explanations of activities are usually included in the record. The value of the chart is restricted by the rather broad meaning of the symbols, which prevent detailed descriptions of the movement of hands and arms from being shown. Furthermore, the paths and directions of movement are not shown on the chart. Nevertheless, this is certainly the most popular chart used to record movement when studying methods at a single location, and, while even more detailed recording methods are available, the occasions when the extra work involved is justified are infrequent. A two-handed process chart for a simple job is shown in Figure 7.3.

### 5. SIMO (simultaneous motion cycle) charts

When it is necessary to study work in more detail than is possible using two-handed or flow process charts, a different notation and a different type of record is required. The recording method most frequently used is the SIMO chart which shows in detail the work method, usually for the worker's left and right hands. Two types of notations are available: 'Therbligs' and 'PMTS' notation.

Frank Gilbreth was responsible for identifying and defining the 17 elementary or fundamental movements which together constitute all types of manual work. These Gilbreth called *Therbligs*. Since Gilbreth's work (about 1924), one additional element has been added to the original list of 17 and the symbols given to the movements have been altered.

This classification of elementary movements is based on an analysis of the purpose of the movement and not on physiological definitions. Because of the precise nature of

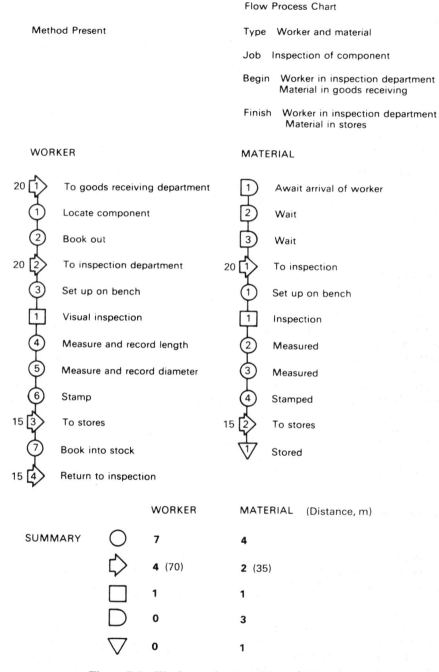

Flow Process Chart

Method Present

Type    Worker and material

Job    Inspection of component

Begin    Worker in inspection department
Material in goods receiving

Finish    Worker in inspection department
Material in stores

WORKER

20 ⟩1  To goods receiving department

1  Locate component

2  Book out

20 ⟩2  To inspection department

3  Set up on bench

1  Visual inspection

4  Measure and record length

5  Measure and record diameter

6  Stamp

15 ⟩3  To stores

7  Book into stock

15 ⟩4  Return to inspection

MATERIAL

1  Await arrival of worker

2  Wait

3  Wait

20 ⟩1  To inspection

1  Set up on bench

1  Inspection

2  Measured

3  Measured

4  Stamped

15 ⟩2  To stores

1  Stored

| | WORKER | MATERIAL (Distance, m) |
|---|---|---|
| SUMMARY ○ | 7 | 4 |
| ▷ | 4 (70) | 2 (35) |
| □ | 1 | 1 |
| D | 0 | 3 |
| ▽ | 0 | 1 |

**Figure 7.2**  *Worker-and-material flow process chart.*

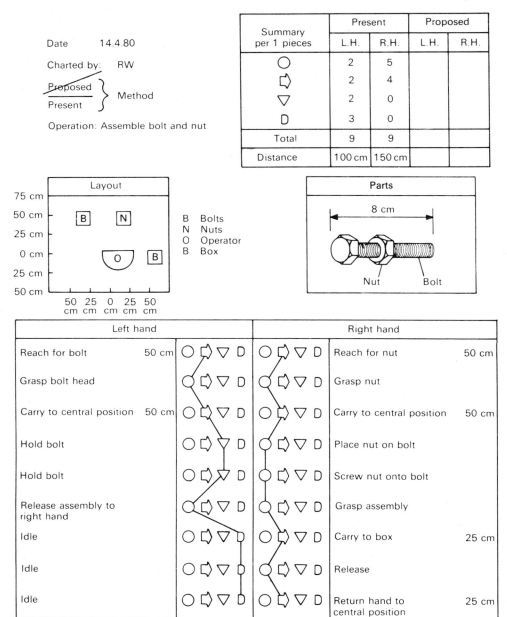

**Figure 7.3** *Two-handed process chart.*

Therbligs, their use facilitates a very detailed study of movements, this technique being referred to as micromotion study (Figure 7.4).

The construction of a SIMO micromotion analysis permits detailed study of the work method. As an alternative to the use of the Therblig notation various predetermined motion time system (PMTS) notations are available. PMT systems classify motions and provide codes to identify each type and class of motion. They are

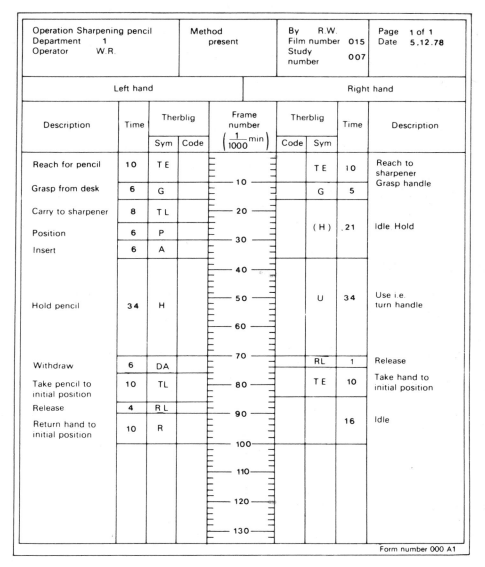

**Figure 7.4**  *SIMO (simultaneous motion) chart with Therblig notation.*

of particular value in developing work standards, since each type and class of motion has a known standard time. The PMTS notion can be used in recording and describing the method, especially where it is intended to use the record subsequently to determine a standard time for the job. (See Chapter 8.)

In the methods of recording referred to previously, visual observation has been enough to obtain the data necessary to construct the charts. By contrast, in micromotion study, visual observation is often inadequate for identifying the detail required and consequently movie or cine photography is normally used. In this way work methods can be filmed and played back at various speeds, or even frame by frame, and from this the SIMO chart can be constructed.

## 6. Memomotion filming and work sampling

Memomotion filming is a technique for recording movements using equipment designed to take pictures at longer-than-normal intervals. Traditionally cine equipment is used, but video-tape recording equipment is now available for this purpose.

A cine camera designed for memomotion photography can film at from 1 frame per second to 2 frames per minute. A similar approach is used with video equipment. Memomotion photography is thus a method of sampling or observing activities at regular intervals rather than continuously, and it is therefore particularly suitable where there are long or irregular work cycle times, or where method studies of groups of workers are to be undertaken. Frame-by-frame analysis of a memomotion film will indicate the nature of movement about an area, the utilization of equipment and space, the extent of idle time, the presence of bottlenecks, etc. Where work cycle times are regular it is inadvisable to adopt a sampling routine which also uses regular sampling intervals, since this may cause certain activities during the work cycle to be missed altogether. In such cases work sampling at irregular intervals is essential, and this will often be carried out manually.

## 7. Cyclegraphs and chronocyclegraphs

The Gilbreths were also responsible for developing this technique for recording movement at the workplace. It is used only in special situations. The cyclegraph is a record of the paths of movement obtained by attaching light sources to the moving objects and exposing them to a photographic plate. Usually small bulbs lit from a battery are attached to the wrists of the operator, who then performs his or her work cycle in front of a plate camera with an open shutter. The paths of movement are shown as continuous white lines on the photograph. The overall time for the cycle can be obtained using a stopwatch; otherwise no timescale is included on the record. The main defect of the cyclegraph is that it does not indicate either the speed or the direction of movement. A further development of this technique, therefore, was to arrange for the power to the bulbs to be pulsed at a known frequency which could be adjusted according to the speed of movement. The record then appears as a dotted line, the spacing of the dots corresponding to the speed of movement and the pointed end of the pear-shaped dots indicating the direction of movement.

### Recording procedure

The type of record to be obtained, in particular the level of detail to be incorporated, will in part determine the recording procedure to be used. For example, a 'self-recording' procedure will be feasible for obtaining a diary-type record. The construction of a record of a work method by the worker himself or herself may also be feasible for some of the less detailed flow diagrams or process charts, but in general work method records will be obtained by an independent 'observer' adopting one or more of the procedures outlined below.

Direct observation of a work method will permit the development of any one of the records listed in 2 and 4 above, but when more detail is to be obtained, e.g. in two-handed and SIMO charts, the observer will need to watch several repetitions of the task. It may, therefore, take some considerable time to develop a process chart for even a short cycle-time task. Similarly, in developing a multiple activity chart several complete work cycles must be observed. Direct visual methods can be used without too much difficulty in developing outline process charts etc.

For simple tasks and for the development of records with little detail, it may be possible to describe a task, i.e. to prepare a method record directly from memory. The extent to which the recorder is familiar with the task will, of course, affect the accuracy and the level of detail which can be obtained.

Video (and less frequently, cine) filming is of considerable use in method study. A film or video record of a work method permits a permanent record to be held and also facilitates method analysis 'away from the job'. Such an approach has been found to be time saving, up to 30 per cent time saving being claimed in many cases for methods analysis of a job or subsequent development of the time standard for a method. If a video film of a method is obtained, process charts can subsequently be developed in any level of detail, or 'frame-by-frame' analysis can be undertaken to develop a micromotion record.

Increasingly, electronic portable 'data capture' terminals are used in work study. These are of particular use in time study, where the objective is to record the times for the elements of a job in order to determine the time required. The terminals will store such information and then transmit it to a computer for analysis. Some such terminals allow the type of work elements to be recorded as well as the elapsed time. Using an alpha/numeric code the keys on the terminal can be used to record the sequence of (predefined) work elements in a job for subsequent examination. (See Chapter 8 'Computers in Work Study'.)

Techniques have also been developed to enable the observer to dictate information about the job to be recorded into a tape recorder. *Tape data analysis* provides a 'terminology' and set of codes for this purpose, the tape subsequently being transposed/interpreted to provide a detailed work method record.

## Step 3: Examine

The third stage of method study begins the constructive procedure. The purpose of recording the existing method is to enable subsequent examination and criticism. The recording method used should be sufficient to show all the relevant information, but of course not until we examine the record are we likely to know exactly how much information is needed. Therefore it may occasionally be necessary to repeat the second stage, either to obtain more detail of the entire work method or to enlarge upon certain areas.

Many procedures for examining and criticizing existing work methods have been suggested and adopted, but basically they simply involve asking six basic questions: Why? What? Where? When? Who? How?

*Examine the process as a whole.* The purpose of this is to define what is accomplished, how and why.

> Why was the process undertaken?
> What purpose does it serve?
> Where is it accomplished and why?
> When is it accomplished and why?
> Who is involved and why?
> How is it accomplished and why?

The answer to these primary questions will serve as a means of determining the effectiveness of the process as a whole, and should indicate whether or not any of the following major changes would be beneficial:

(a) changes in material used;
(b) changes in the design of the product;
(c) changes in the nature or design of the process.

*Examine aspects and parts of the process.* The various activities in the process belong in one of two categories. Activities in each category must be examined and considered for elimination or change. First are those in which something is happening to the material or the product, i.e. it is being moved, inspected or worked on. Second are those in which nothing constructive is happening to the material or the product, i.e. it is being delayed or stored.

The first category can be further divided into *make ready, do,* and *put away. Make ready* activities are required to prepare the material or workpiece and set it in position ready to be worked on; *do* activities occur whenever the material or product is changed in shape, condition or composition; and *put away* activities occur when the material or product is moved away from the machine or workshop. (This may also constitute the subsequent *make ready* activity.) It is obviously beneficial to have a high proportion of *do* activities during the process and a low proportion of the others, since it is only *do* activities which carry the product towards completion, and it is only during these activities that value is added to the raw material.

Examination of these activities will question purpose, place and sequence, the person undertaking the activity and the means by which it is performed, in order to establish useful alternatives which subsequently can be examined and perhaps incorporated in an improved work method.


## Step 4: Develop an improved work method

The device specifically designed for improving work methods is known as the *process improvement formula.* The formula, which consists of four steps—eliminate, combine, sequence, simplify—is applied to each separate activity in the job, i.e. to each meaningful group of work elements.

Complete *elimination* of unnecessary activities is clearly the most important step that can be taken in developing an improved work method. An activity may have been retained because of custom, history, inertia, inadequate communications, or even ignorance. Changes in materials, product design, process design, tools or the workplace may facilitate the elimination of activities. If elimination is not possible, then combination of activities should be considered. In many processes two or more activities may be usefully *combined,* e.g. drilling and facing holes, or drilling and countersinking holes. Changes in the *sequence* of activities is the next possibility, and this may then facilitate elimination or combination. Should none of these three steps succeed in eliminating or combining the activity then the last, more expensive step should be considered, i.e. attempting to *simplify* the activity by reducing the number of operations, reducing or eliminating delays and storage, or minimizing transportation. It may become necessary to conduct a more detailed motion study to obtain enough information to enable activities to be simplified, and again consideration should be given to changes in materials and to product and process design. The object of simplifying the activity is to permit the worker to complete the job more quickly and easily. The principles of motion economy shown in Table 7.3 provide a means of developing efficient work methods.

**Table 7.3**  *Principles of motion economy: use of the worker's body and design of the workplace, tools and equipment.*

*Use of the worker's body*

1.  It is easier and more natural to work with two hands rather than one.
2.  The two hands should begin and complete their movements at the same time.
3.  The motion of the arms should be in opposite directions and should be made simultaneously and symmetrically.
4.  Hands and arms naturally move smoothly in arcs, and this is preferable to straight-line movement.
5.  Hand, arm and body movements should be confined to the lowest classification with which it is possible to perform the work satisfactorily, e.g. Gilbreth's classification of hand movements:
    (a) fingers
    (b) fingers and wrists
    (c) fingers, wrists and forearm
    (d) fingers, wrists, forearm and upper arm
    (e) fingers, wrists, forearm, upper arm and shoulder.
6.  Work should be arranged to permit natural and habitual movements.
7.  Movements should be continuous and smooth with no sharp changes in direction or speed.
8.  The two hands should not, except during rest periods, be idle at the same time.
9.  Whenever possible, momentum should be employed to assist the work and minimized if it must be overcome by the worker.
10. Ballistic movements are faster, easier and more accurate than controlled (fixation) movements.
11. The need to fix and focus the eyes on an object should be minimized and, when this is necessary, the occasions should occur as close together as possible.

*Arrangement of the workplace*

1.  There should be a definite and fixed position for all tools, equipment and materials.
2.  All tools, equipment and materials should be located as near as possible to the workplace.
3.  Drop deliveries of materials (and even tools and equipment) should be used whenever possible.
4.  Tools, equipment and materials should be conveniently located in order to provide the best sequence of operations.
5.  Illumination levels and brightness ratios between objects and surroundings should be arranged to avoid or alleviate visual fatigue.
6.  The height of the workplace and the seating should enable comfortable sitting or standing during work.
7.  Seating should permit a good posture and adequate 'coverage' of the work area.
8.  The workplace should be clean and adequately ventilated and heated.
9.  Noise and vibration, both local and general, should be minimized.

*Design of tools and equipment*

1.  Wherever possible, clamps, jugs or fixtures rather than hands should be used to hold work.
2.  Wherever possible, two or more tools should be combined.
3.  Wherever possible, tools and equipment should be pre-positioned.
4.  The loads should be distributed among the limbs according to their capacities.
5.  Wheels, levers, switches, etc., should be positioned to enable manipulation with the minimum movement of the body.

## Step 5: Define the new method

It will be necessary to describe the work method to be adopted in sufficient detail for others to be able to install it or for subsequent use in training and instructions, etc. This definition comprises a statement of the nature of the work method and may be used subsequently in the case of any disputes or misunderstandings. It may be referred to when work method changes are contemplated or when changes are considered to have taken place.

## Steps 6 and 7: Install and maintain the new method

Clearly the first stage is to gain acceptance of the method from management, supervisors and workers. Then a programme for the installation of the method should be developed showing the main steps, those responsible for carrying them out, and the timetable involved. This will include time for training and the rearrangement of equipment, tools, workplaces, etc.

Finally, once the method is installed, a period of maintenance will be needed. Unless necessary or beneficial, deliberate or accidental alterations in the new work method should not be allowed, and periodic reviews should be conducted to ensure that the work method is satisfactory, that disputes do not arise, that earnings are maintained, and that complications in associated departments or with suppliers do not jeopardize the benefits of the new work method.

## Computers in method study

Increasingly, computers are being used in work study. They permit the rapid recording and analysis of data, storage of data for subsequent use, etc., and such applications benefit all aspects of work study, i.e. method study and work measurement. We shall look at some of these applications in the next chapter, but here we consider some uses of computers and computing *specifically related to method study*. Such applications can be seen to fall into one of three categories: methods development and analysis; methods description; and data storage and retrieval. In all cases the use of computers in method study will be justified more easily if computer-based work measurement is also to be employed. (See Chapter 8 'Computers in Work Study'.)

### *Methods development and analysis*

Several computer programs or suites of programs are available to the work study engineer to assist in the development or analysis of work methods. A brief description of one set of programs will illustrate the types of facilities which are available.

The AUTOMAT methods generator is available commercially as part of a broader range of programs for computer-aided work study.[1] Using the AUTOMAT programs the work study practitioner may input certain information relating to the work method, the layout of the workplace and the tools and equipment employed, from which the program determines the most appropriate work method and provides a detailed workplace layout with tool positions, etc. (The program will also produce a standard time for this method for subsequent use in the development of work standards; see Chapter 8.) The program uses the MTM notation for this purpose, so details of the work method must be input using the MTM notation, and the output is normally in the form of a type of SIMO chart (see above).

The system is quite flexible, so the work study practitioner can specify the work method in a variety of ways, and in different levels of detail, ranging from an outline

---

[1] Schofield, N. A. (1980) Computer aided work study using AUTOMAT and COMPUTE—practical tools for the industrial engineer, *International Journal of Production Research*, **18**(2), pp. 153–168. (Available as part of 'TIMELINK' system from Compeda, now part of Prime CAD/CAM Ltd.)

operation description to a more detailed analysis of the method. Similarly, the workplace layout input can be in as much detail as is considered appropriate. The computer automatically generates a detailed workplace layout with positions of parts, tools, equipment, etc., and generates and prints an MTM description of an appropriate work method together with the standard times for that method. The program uses a set of heuristic procedures to generate good work methods from the input information. If the initial input description of a method is in relatively little detail, i.e. if it is an outline description, then the computer program is capable of generating a detailed statement of an appropriate work method. The work method developed by the program takes into account the need to seek motion economies, etc. While developing the work method from the input data the program keeps and accumulates information to describe the operator's movements, idle time, distance travelled, number of body motions, etc. These measures can then be used to highlight bad methods of working, or as criteria for evaluating alternative methods. These measures of the 'efficiency' of the method can also be printed out together with the SIMO chart type description of a work method.

The type of program described above provides an opportunity not only for automatic development of work methods but also for rapid comparison of alternative work methods. For example, by varying the input slightly different methods will be developed and these can be compared against the criteria mentioned above, e.g. percentage idle time of each hand, distance travelled of each hand, percentage time spent in body movements, number of body movements, number of difficult motions. Other computer programs which are commercially available also provide such a facility. For example, the 4M DATA[2] computerized work measurement system (see also Chapter 8) also provides 'simulation capability'. This permits the work study engineer to try out several methods interactively with the computer before selecting the one to be used and requesting the computer program to develop a detailed statement of work standards etc. for that method.

## *Methods description*

Less ambitious than methods development programs are those which seek only to provide detailed methods descriptions. These (e.g. the MOST computer system; see Chapter 8) require as input a description of a work method in at least outline and coded form. Then, using stored information from which detailed element descriptions can be obtained, and using one of the PMTS notations, the computer prints out a description in, for example, SIMO chart format of the job (usually with element and operation times; see Chapter 8). In this type of application the computer is taking over the detailed, often time-consuming task of preparing printed work-method descriptions in a usable format, often also drawing upon filed data for standard or commonly used elements or sequences of elements.

## *Data storage and retrieval*

Most of the computerized work study programs provide a facility to store information on work elements, sequences of work elements and complete work methods together

---

[2] The 4M DATA MOD II computerized work measurement system. MTM Association for Standards and Research, 16-01 Broadway, Fairlawn, New Jersey 07410 USA.

with information on tools, equipment, layouts and time standards. Such data will be of particular relevance in the development of work standards for jobs, and this will be discussed in the following chapter. Additionally, in developing and specifying work methods for new jobs, it may be possible to 'build up' a method simply by fitting together appropriate sequences, etc., from the data file. With this type of facility it is possible to reduce considerably the time required to develop and specify the new work method. The method study analyst need only identify the major parts of the total job, and the computer program can then construct detailed methodology using the filed data.

## FURTHER READING

Barnes, R. M. (1969) *Motion and Time Study*, 6th edition. New York: Wiley. This is still one of the best books on work study, though slightly confusingly arranged.
BS 3138, *Glossary to Terms in Work Study*, British Standards Institute, London, 1969.
Nadler, G. (1967) *Work Systems Design: The 'Ideals' Concept*. Homewood, Illinois: Irwin. A description of the ideals concept (ideal design of effective and logical systems), i.e. the design of the work system which will be the most effective in achieving a necessary function.

## QUESTIONS

**7.1** Describe, with examples, the method study techniques you would use to investigate the work of:

(a)  a team of six workers in a hotel reception/cashier area;
(b)  a single worker on a short-cycle repetitive clerical task.

**7.2** The Gobust Co. packs 'nick-nacks'. They are imported and weighed out in lots of ½kg. There are 12 'nick-nacks' to the kg, on average. The 'nick-nacks' must be inserted in a jar, to which a portion of 'nick-nack' juice is added. The jar is then sealed with a twist cap.

(a)  Analyse the job. Develop a 'good' sequence of work elements.
(b)  Sketch the process flow and layout.
(c)  Use an operation chart to detail the work involved.

**7.3** The electrical plug shown in Question 3.6 is to be assembled manually in large quantities. Develop a method of assembling the nine components of the plug and sketch the workplace layout. Use a two-handed process chart to indicate your method. You may approximate the element times.

**7.4** Draw up a micromotion analysis of the two-handed operation shown in Figure 7.3, using a SIMO chart and Therbligs.

**7.5** What are the seven important steps involved in performing a method study? Describe very briefly the principal techniques available for the execution of the second of these steps, and describe also the logical sequence or 'formula' which constitutes step 4.

**7.6** Discuss the problems in human relations which are likely to occur during a method study exercise, and indicate how they might be minimized. In your answer show how the problems differ at various stages of the investigation.

# CHAPTER 8

# Work Measurement and Work Standards

Work measurement is defined in British Standard 3138 as the 'application of techniques designed to establish the time for a qualified worker to carry out a specified job at a defined level of performance'. In fact, there are two classes of work measurement: direct time study and indirect time study, both of which will be described below.

## USES OF WORK STANDARDS

Some of the uses of work time estimates and work standards are outlined in Figure 8.1. Times are necessary for the comparison of work methods, for operations

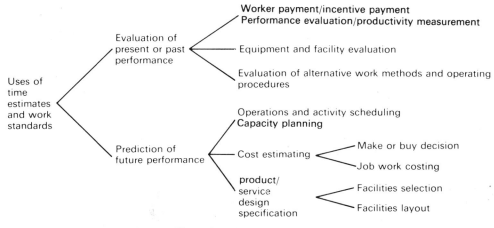

**Figure 8.1** *Uses of work time estimates and standards.*

scheduling and for capacity planning. The proper co-ordination of operations depends on the availability of accurate time estimates.

The allocation of facilities to a single worker and the even distribution of work among members of a team cannot be accomplished without estimates of the duration of all operations. The output of flow process systems depends, to a large extent, on the output of the workers with the longest work cycle; consequently the balanced allocation of work is essential.

Standard times for jobs, once established, may be used to set labour standards for payment purposes, to determine the operating effectiveness of equipment, workers, groups of workers, departments or factories, and to determine standard costs of operations for pricing or estimating purposes. (Payment systems are discussed in Chapter 10.)

## MEASUREMENT OF WHAT?

Work study is concerned primarily with manual work. To a lesser extent it is concerned with work performed by machines, but hardly ever directly with mental work.

There is normally little difficulty in measuring machine work, since machine times are usually a function of machine speeds, etc. However, even where human manual work is highly rationalized and repetitive, there is a need for most workers to exercise some mental ability. As far as work study and work management are concerned, mental work is often too difficult to measure directly. Part of the process of establishing standard times for a job involves the adoption of allowances, i.e. provision of additional time to compensate for atmospheric conditions, contingencies, etc. Mental effort is dealt with in precisely the same way, i.e.

1. Physical human work is measured.
2. Machine work is calculated.
3. Mental human work is allowed for.

## WORK MEASUREMENT PROCEDURES

There are two categories of work measurement procedures (see Figure 7.1). Direct time study is the traditional stopwatch procedure and accounts for the majority of the exercises conducted. Indirect methods are on occasion either desirable or necessary. In the case of a new job it is impossible to conduct direct studies and, where jobs are to be undertaken for a comparatively short period of time, there may not be enough time to conduct direct work measurement. With the exception of analytical estimating, the indirect methods are of more recent origin. They have many advantages in terms of consistency and accuracy, and possibly additional developments may increase their future scope and value.

Table 8.1 summarizes the conventional procedures for work measurement, which are discussed in more detail below.

**Direct work measurement**

*Time study*

As with method study, we can break down time study procedure into a series of simple, logical and important steps, as follows.

*Obtain all necessary information*

Our objective in conducting a work measurement exercise is to determine the time required for a job carried out under specified conditions. It is necessary, therefore, to have a record of these conditions in case the exercise is referred to or used at a later date. There is usually provision for recording information about the worker, machine, material, layout, output, method, quality standard etc., on one of the forms used during the study or, alternatively, it may be sufficient to refer to the appropriate method study for this information.

*Divide the job into elements*

This is necessary for the following reasons:

(a) to provide a better understanding of the nature of the job;
(b) to break a time study exercise up into manageably sized 'pieces';
(c) to permit a more accurate study;
(d) to distinguish different types of work;
(e) to enable 'machine' elements, i.e. machine-paced work, to be isolated from 'worker' elements;
(f) to enable detailed job descriptions to be produced;
(g) to enable time standards to be checked or modified;
(h) to enable times for certain common or important elements to be extracted and compared.

Jobs may consist of constant or variable elements, manual or machine elements, repetitive, occasional, or even 'foreign' elements. Constant elements are of identical specification and have the same duration whenever performed, unlike variable elements, the times of which vary according to characteristics such as weight, size, distance, etc. Machine elements are often constant while worker elements are often variable. Occasional elements do not occur in every cycle but nevertheless are an essential part of the job, whereas foreign elements are unnecessary.

The ease with which the study is conducted, as well as the data obtained, is very much dependent on the definition of the job elements; fortunately, there are some general and well-tried rules which can be used at this stage.

1. The elements selected will be timed separately and repeatedly; consequently it is essential that clearly defined beginning and ending points should be available to identify the element.
2. Elements should be as short as possible yet not too short to be conveniently timed.
3. Elements should be as unified as possible. Whenever possible, elements consisting of a logical sequence of basic motions should be used.
4. Worker and machine elements should be separated.
5. Regular and irregular elements should be separated.

**Table 8.1** *Procedures for work management* (From Wild, R. (1980) *Management and Production*, 2nd edition. Harmondsworth: Penguin. Reproduced with permission.)

| | Technique | Definition (BS 3138) | Steps involved | Accuracy detail | Applications |
|---|---|---|---|---|---|
| Direct work measurement | 1. Time study | A work measurement technique for recording the times and rates of working for the elements of a specified job carried out under specified conditions, and for analysing the data so as to obtain the time necessary for carrying out the job at a defined level of performance | 1 Get all information concerning job to be measured<br>2. Divide job into *elements*<br>3. Time and rate the elements<br>4. Determine number of cycles to time<br>5. Determine allowances<br>6. Calculate standard time for job | Amount of detail is determined by step 2 and accuracy is determined largely by the process of *rating* (step 3), which is largest subjective area of time study | Widely used, particularly for direct work. May be used as a preliminary to generating synthetic data |
| | 2. Activity sampling | A technique in which a large number of instantaneous observations are made over a period of time of a group of machines, processes or workers. Each observation records what is happening at that instant and the percentage of observations recorded for a particular activity or delay is a measure of the percentage of time during which that activity or delay occurs | 1. Get all details of job(s) to be measured<br>2. Divide job into activities<br>3. Conduct pilot study to:<br>  (a) determine number of observations<br>  (b) check method<br>4. Conduct study; make readings<br>5. Calculate proportion of time for each activity | Gives information about proportion of time spent on each activity only | Intermittent work. Long cycle times. As a preliminary investigation |

| | Technique | Definition | Procedure | Detail/accuracy | Remarks |
|---|---|---|---|---|---|
| Indirect work measurement | 1. Synthetic timing | A work measurement technique for building up the time for a job at a defined level of performance by totalling element times obtained previously from time studies on other jobs containing the elements concerned, or from synthetic data | 1. Get all details of job to be measured<br>2. Divide job into elements<br>3. Select times from synthetic data<br>4. Determine allowances<br>5. Calculate standard time for job | Usually as much detail as time study, since data have usually been obtained from prior time studies. Accuracy depends on amount of data available and care in application usually consistent | Where adequate data have been gathered usually provides a sufficiently accurate and rapid method of determining times, often without recourse to stopwatch, and prior to starting job |
| | 2. Pre-determined motion time systems | A work measurement technique whereby times established for basic human motions (classified according to the nature of the motion and the conditions under which it is made) are used to build up the time for a job at a defined level of performance | 1. Get all details of the job to be measured<br>2. Determine amount of detail required<br>3. Construct time for job<br>4. Determine allowances<br>5. Calculate standard time for job | Systems are available to provide various levels of detail. Consistency is ensured, and accuracy with many systems is greater than that of time study | Where consistency and accuracy are important. Detailed systems are time consuming to apply. Later systems forfeit detail for speed of application. Suitable for use on indirect workers and for intermittent work |
| | 3. Analytical estimating | A work measurement technique, being a development of estimating, whereby the time required to carry out elements of a job at a defined level of performance is estimated from knowledge and practical experience of the elements concerned | 1. Get all information concerning job to be measured<br>2. Divide job into elements<br>3. (a) Apply synthetic data where available<br>   (b) Estimate or time element durations<br>4. Determine allowances<br>5. Calculate standard time for job | Uses synthetic data supplemented by either time studies or estimates. Slightly less accurate and consistent than synthesis | Where insufficient synthetic data are available. Rapid method, suitable for intermittent work. e.g. maintenance |

6. Elements involving heavy or fatiguing work should be separated out.
7. Finally, constant elements should be separated from variable elements.

*Timing elements*

Conventionally, analogue or digital stopwatches are used for timing elements. More sophisticated electronic equipment is also available and is increasingly used in element timing. A variety of types of 'event recorder' are available which combine ease of use with accuracy and versatility. Electronic data capture terminals are also used, particularly where summary statistics and calculations are to be performed locally on the data, or where data are to be input directly to a computer for subsequent analysis. Such terminals are in effect alpha/numeric keyboard devices with some internal storage and a small LCD display. Such devices can be programmed to 'prompt' the observer with element descriptions in code form so that times can be recorded and then stored within the device. Summary calculations can be performed, and in some cases by interfacing the device directly with a typewriter a list of element times can be printed out for editing and for checking for missing observations, etc. In most cases such devices provide for interfacing with the computer so that the stored information can be 'down loaded' to the computer for subsequent analysis.

There are also available a variety of 'proprietary' devices to provide specific facilities. Electronic 'time study boards' are available with keys marked with work study terminology for recording information on a tape cassette carried in a shoulder pack by the observer. Other boards are available with 'built-in' electronic clocks and one or more displays. These are in effect sophisticated versions of the traditional clip board with paper and the analogue clock recording devices described above.

We shall look in more detail at electronic data capture terminals later in this chapter.

Some methods of timing elements involve filming. A cine or, more usually, video film can be made of the operation for subsequent analysis 'off the job'. In some cases the filmed record can incorporate a clock so that detailed timings can be obtained, or the film can be run at a known and constant speed so that a frame by frame or 'foot by foot' analysis can be undertaken.

*The number of cycles to be timed*

We must take enough readings to be reasonably confident of an accurate result. Direct time study is a sampling process, and the accuracy of the sample as a measure of the elements themselves is determined by the variability of the elements and the size of the sample. The number of observations to be taken depends on:

(a) the variation in the times of the element;
(b) the degree of accuracy required;
(c) the confidence level required.

A 95 per cent confidence level and an accuracy of ± 5 per cent or ± 10 per cent are usually adopted. This means that the chances are at least 95 out of 100 that the mean or average we obtain from the observations will be in error by ± 5 per cent or ± 10 per cent of the true element time.

Before the number of observations necessary to fulfil this requirement can be calculated, we must establish the variability of the element time by conducting a brief 'pilot' study. We can then use one of the following formulae to calculate the required number of observations.

95 per cent confidence $\pm 5$ per cent accuracy:

$$N^1 = \left( \frac{40\sqrt{N \Sigma x^2 - (\Sigma x)^2}}{\Sigma x} \right)^2$$

95 per cent confidence $\pm 10$ per cent accuracy:

$$N^1 = \left( \frac{20\sqrt{N \Sigma x^2 - (\Sigma x)^2}}{\Sigma x} \right)^2$$

where $N^1$ = required number of observations for given confidence and accuracy
$N$ = actual number of observations taken in pilot study
$x$ = each observed element time from the pilot study

## Rating the worker

So far we have been concerned only with the observed or actual times required by a worker to perform elements of work, but the object of work measurement and time study is to determine not how long it *did* take to perform a job or elements of a job, but how long it *should* take. It is necessary, therefore, to compare the actual rate of working of the worker with a standard rate of working so that the observed times can be converted to basic times, i.e. the time required to carry out an element of work at standard performance. In fact every observation we make must be rated and the appropriate rating factor recorded on the record chart before the observed time is recorded.

Performance rating is the comparison of an actual rate of working against a defined concept of a standard rate of working. The standard rate corresponds to 'the average rate at which qualified workers will naturally work at a job, provided they know and adhere to the specified method, and provided they are motivated to apply themselves to their work' (BS 3138). On the British Standard Performance Scale (which we shall use throughout this chapter) standard rating is equal to 100, i.e. a rating of 50 is equal to half the standard rate of working. In the USA the '60/80 scale', where standard performance is 80, is used.

Although standard rate is defined above, it is really only a concept. In practice the standard rate of working is a function of the situation, e.g. the physical conditions, the type of labour, company policy, and may differ greatly between companies. Consequently, the company must train the time study analyst to recognize what the company or industry regards as standard performance.

Several systems of rating have been developed. *Effort rating* is concerned primarily with work speed, the operator being rated according to the speed of his or her movement, adjustments being made to the rating according to the perceived difficulty of the job being done. *Objective rating* is a similar method depending on the consideration of two factors: speed and difficulty. The operator is rated first according to the speed of his or her movement, irrespective of the nature of the job. After this speed rating an adjustment is made depending on the nature of the job being performed, particularly:

(a) how much of the body is used;
(b) the use of footpedals;
(c) the need for bimanualness;
(d) eye–hand coordination;
(e) the handling requirements;
(f) the weight of objects handled.

Tables of adjustment factors are available for various categories of each of these six factors.

The Westinghouse Company devised a system in about 1927 in which four characteristics were considered: the skill used, the effort required, the conditions prevailing and the consistency required. A numerical scale is attached to each of these characteristics (Table 8.2). Unlike the two systems mentioned above, the Westinghouse system is used to rate a job rather than the separate elements of the job. For this reason it is sometimes referred to as a *levelling system* rather than a rating system. A separate rating for each element is made for each area and the sum of the four figures represents the final rating factor for each element, e.g.

$$\text{Observed (actual) element time} = 0.45 \text{ minutes}$$

$$\begin{aligned}
\text{Element rating} \quad &= +0.06 \text{ (skill)} \\
&\phantom{=} +0.12 \text{ (effort)} \\
&\phantom{=} +0.00 \text{ (conditions)} \\
&\phantom{=} +0.01 \text{ (consistency)} \\
\hline
&\phantom{=} +0.19
\end{aligned}$$

$$\begin{aligned}
\text{Basic time for element} \quad &= 0.45 \times (1.00+0.19) \\
&= 0.54 \text{ minutes}
\end{aligned}$$

Whichever one of these or other methods of rating or levelling is used the basic time corresponds to the observed time after rating, i.e.

$$\text{basic time for element or job} = \text{observed time} \times \frac{\text{observed rating}}{\text{standard rating of 100}}$$

*Allowances*

The basic time does not contain any allowances and is merely the time required by the worker to perform the task at a standard rate without any interruptions or delays. Allowances are normally given as a percentage of the basic element times and usually include:

1. Relaxation allowances: = WICONT.
   (a) fatigue allowances to give the workers time to recover from the effort (physiological and psychological) required by the job;
   (b) personal needs—to visit toilets, washrooms, etc.

**Table 8.2**  *Factors and point values in the Westinghouse system of performance rating or levelling.*

| Skill | Effort | Conditions | Consistency |
|---|---|---|---|
| +0.15 A1 Superskill | +0.13 A1 Excessive | +0.06 A  Ideal | +0.04 A  Perfect |
| +0.13 A2 | +0.12 A2 | +0.04 B  Excellent | +0.03 B  Excellent |
| +0.11 B1 Excellent | +0.10 B1 Excellent | +0.02 C  Good | +0.01 C  Good |
| +0.08 B2 | +0.08 B2 | 0.00 D  Average | 0.00 D  Average |
| +0.06 C1 Good | +0.05 C1 Good | −0.03 E  Fair | −0.02 E  Fair |
| +0.03 C2 | +0.02 C2 | −0.07 F  Poor | −0.04 F  Poor |
| 0.00 D  Average | 0.00 D  Average | | |
| −0.05 E1 Fair | −0.04 E1 Fair | | |
| −0.10 E2 | −0.08 E2 | | |
| −0.16 F1 Poor | −0.12 F1 Poor | | |
| −0.22 F2 | −0.17 F2 | | |

2. Contingency allowances given to compensate for the time required by the workers to perform all necessary additional and periodic activities which were not included in the basic time because of infrequent or irregular occurrence and the difficulty of establishing the times, e.g. reading drawings, cleaning machinery. *EXTRA WORK*
3. Tool and machinery allowance to compensate the worker for the time necessary for adjusting and sharpening tools, setting up equipment, and so on. *DELAY*
4. Reject allowance, necessary where a proportion of defective items must necessarily be produced.
5. Interference allowance to compensate for time unavoidably lost because of the stoppage of two or more machines, attended by one worker, at the same time.
6. Excess work allowance to compensate for the extra work necessary because of unforeseen or temporary changes in the standard conditions.

Total allowances are often of the order of 15 to 20 per cent, so inaccuracies are of some consequence.

*Calculate standard time*

The standard time for an element or a job is calculated as follows:

$$\text{Standard time} = \left( \text{observed time} \times \frac{\text{rating}}{100} \right) + \text{total allowance}$$

For example, where the worker is observed to be working at greater than the standard rate the three element times may bear a relationship to one another, as shown in Figure 8.2.

The *standard minute* is the unit of measurement of work, consisting partly of work and partly of relaxation. It represents the output in one minute if the work is performed at the standard rate. By means of work measurement we can express the work content of jobs in terms of single units—standard minutes (SMs)—irrespective of the differences between the jobs themselves.

Note that an SM is a measure of *work* and not a measure of time. It is connected with time only in that one SM of work will take one minute of time at 100 performance. SMs can therefore be used in calculating wages and performance. For example, performance can be measured by:

$$\frac{\text{Output of work in SMs}}{\text{Total labour time in minutes}}$$

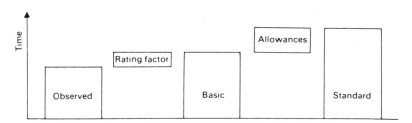

**Figure 8.2**  *Breakdown of the standard minute.*

## Activity sampling

The work measurement techniques we have described so far are appropriate where we are concerned with short-cycle repetitive work. If, however, it is necessary to establish work standards in situations where long, irregular-cycle work is conducted, or where many different jobs are performed, these techniques may be quite inappropriate.

It may be necessary to study the activities of several workers on several machines in order to establish the proportion of time each worker spends on various activities, or to determine the utilization of resources, space, etc., and in such cases some form of sampling procedure is invaluable.

Memomotion photography, discussed in the previous chapter, was a sampling technique by which, in particular circumstances, we are able to obtain enough information about jobs or activities without conducting a continuous study. In memomotion study the sampling interval was constant, but in certain cases we may wish to sample at irregular intervals in order to avoid any chance of our observations regularly coinciding with some particular feature of the activity being studied.

The accuracy of our sample as a measure of the actual activity is clearly dependent on the number of observations we take. If we are willing to take many observations, our confidence in the result can be high, but this will have been obtained only at higher cost.

Again, we must decide what confidence level and accuracy we require before we can decide how many observations to take. Furthermore, a pilot study must be conducted to establish the frequency of occurrence of the activity being studied; then for a confidence level of 95 per cent the formula to determine the number of observations required is:

$$N^1 = \frac{4p\,(100 - p)}{L^2}$$

Where $N^1$ = number of observations needed

$\quad\quad\quad p$ = percentage of total time occupied by the activity with which we are concerned, as obtained from a pilot study.

$\quad\quad\quad L$ = required limits of accuracy (expressed as a percentage)

Activity sampling is normally used to determine the percentage of the total time that a person or machine spends on certain activities. In the simplest case, the requisite number of random observations is taken to determine the percentage of total time spent by either a worker or a machine in working or not working.

## Rated activity sampling

Occasionally it is practical to sample activities at regular rather than random intervals because of the random nature of the activities concerned. In such circumstances it is possible to use an extension of activity sampling known as *rated activity sampling* or *rated systematic sampling*.

---

### EXAMPLE: A PACKING JOB

A woman is performing a packing job which has an irregular cycle and consists of a maximum of three elements of work. Observations are made at regular intervals of 0.1 minute; the number of items produced during the period of the study is determined and the operator is rated at each observation. Determine the *basic minutes* for each element and for each item produced.

The table shows the results of the sampling. The figures in the columns indicate not only which element was being performed on each observation, but also the performance rating for that element at that time.

The output during this two-minute study was ten items.

| Observation number (0.1 minute intervals) | Rating (%) for element 1 | Rating (%) for element 2 | Rating (%) for element 3 | Rating (%) for idle |
|:---:|:---:|:---:|:---:|:---:|
| 1 | 100 | | | |
| 2 | | 100 | | |
| 3 | 95 | | | |
| 4 | | | 110 | |
| 5 | 95 | | | |
| 6 | | | | 100 |
| 7 | | 100 | | |
| 8 | 95 | | | |
| 9 | 100 | | | |
| 10 | | | 105 | |
| 11 | | 100 | | |
| 12 | | | | 100 |
| 13 | | 100 | | |
| 14 | 95 | | | |
| 15 | | 100 | | |
| 16 | 110 | | | |
| 17 | | 110 | | |
| 18 | | | 95 | |
| 19 | | | | 100 |
| 20 | 100 | | | |
| Total ('00) | 7.9 | 6.1 | 3.1 | 3.0 |

The basic minutes for each element per product can be calculated using the following formula:

$$\text{BM/element} = \frac{\text{sum of all ratings}}{100} \times \frac{\text{observation interval}}{\text{output}}$$

i.e. For element 1:
BM = 7.9×0.1/10
= 0.079

For element 2:
BM = 6.1×0.1/10
= 0.061

For element 3:
BM = 3.1×0.1/10
= 0.031

The total basic minutes for each item is of course the sum of the above figures, i.e. 0.171.

**Indirect work measurement**

### Synthetic timing (elemental, standard or basic data)

Work measurement data are often classified and stored with this possible use in mind, and the process of reconstruction is usually referred to as synthesizing. As time studies are completed the 'elemental' data are coded and stored. Periodically these data are examined to determine whether there is any consistency between times for similar elements. When enough consistent data have been gathered the information can be condensed as tables, graphs or equations for easy future application. If elemental times are being collected for this purpose the definitions of work elements should be more precise than would normally be required. Furthermore, because of the slow accumulation of data suitable for synthesizing, it is often preferable to plan the entire work measurement activity with the object of obtaining accurate data.

The generation of data for machine elements normally involves comparatively little trouble, since such times are often either constant or the functions of known variables. Similarly, constant 'worker' elements provide little difficulty, since an equal time will be required whenever the job or element is performed.

It is more difficult to deal with variable elements. First, we must examine the variations in time which occur in our accumulated data to establish whether the variation is a result of a difference in the nature of the element itself, or whether it results from the action of one or more variables. If the variations are particularly large there may be fundamental differences in the nature of the elements, in which case the data cannot be assembled together. The remaining variation can usually be attributed to variables such as distance, size and weight, and graphs or tables can then be constructed.

Synthetic data are reliable and consistent, since normally they have resulted from many studies over a period of time. They can be used to establish time standards for short-run work on which there would be insufficient time to conduct a direct time study, and to construct time standards for jobs not yet begun.

A practical advantage is that there is no need for the use of a stopwatch, but it can be expensive and time consuming to develop synthetic data. It is normal to synthesize basic times to which allowances must be added. The need to rate the job under consideration is avoided and, since the synthetic data will probably have been derived from numerous studies, the consequence of inaccuracies in the original studies is reduced.

### Predetermined motion time systems (PMTS)

In BS 3138 PMTS is defined as 'a work measurement technique whereby times established for basic human motions (classified according to the nature of the motion and the conditions under which it is made) are used to build up the time for a job at a defined level of performance'. A PMT system therefore consists of a list of all motions that a worker can use in doing a task, together with time values for these motions at a specified level of performance and in specified circumstances.

#### MTM–1 (methods time measurement)

The first MTM system (MTM–1) provided times for basic motions, the argument being that, because such motions approximated to the 'lowest common denominators' of all work, it was possible to construct time standards for all jobs from a set of tabular data.

MTM–1 classifies all hand motions into basic units as follows:

| | |
|---|---|
| *Reach* (R) | the basic element employed when the predominant purpose is to move the hand to a destination or general location |
| *Move* (M) | the basic element employed when the predominant purpose is to transport an object to a destination |
| *Turn* (T) | a movement which rotates the hand, wrist and forearm |
| *Apply pressure* (AP) | the element employed whenever pressure is applied |
| *Grasp* (G) | a hand or fingers element employed when an object is required for further operation |
| *Position* (P) | the basic element employed to align, orient or engage one object with another, when motions used are minor and do not justify classification as other basic elements |
| *Release* (RL) | the basic element employed to relinquish control of an object by the fingers or hand |
| *Disengage* (D) | the basic element employed to break contact between objects |
| *Eye travel and eye focus (ET, EF)* | |
| *Body, leg and foot motions* | |

The times for various sub-groups of each of these units, and under various conditions, are shown in Figure 8.3. Table 8.3 shows how the MTM–1 notation is constructed.

The time units used in MTM are 'time measurement units' where:

$$1 \text{ TMU} = 0.0006 \text{ min.}$$

It should be noted that because MTM–1 was developed in America, TMU values do not necessarily correspond to 100 on the BS rating scale. There has been a good deal of controversy over the relationship of the ratings included in the TMU values and the BS scale, but recently it has been suggested that for all practical purposes job times derived using MTM values should be accepted as equivalent to a BSI rating of 83.

## MTM–2

The main disadvantage of the use of MTM–1 is the considerable amount of time normally needed to construct element and job times from such detailed information. For this reason certain 'second generation' systems were developed which relied on the use of elements rather than basic motions.

MTM–2 was synthesized for MTM–1 data and consists of nine motions—Get; Put; Apply pressure; Regrasp; Eye action; Crank; Step; Foot motion; Bend and arise. Only Get and Put have variable categories, so the MTM–2 data card has only 39 time standards. As with MTM–1, the motions and their various sub-categories are closely defined and precise rules govern their use.

**TABLE I—REACH—R**

| Distance Moved Inches | Time TMU | | | | Hand In Motion | | CASE AND DESCRIPTION |
|---|---|---|---|---|---|---|---|
| | A | B | C or D | E | A | B | |
| ¾ or less | 2.0 | 2.0 | 2.0 | 2.0 | 1.5 | 1.6 | A Reach to object in fixed location, or to object in other hand or on which other hand rests. |
| 1 | 2.5 | 2.5 | 3.6 | 2.4 | 2.3 | 2.3 | |
| 2 | 4.0 | 4.0 | 6.9 | 3.8 | 3.5 | 2.7 | |
| 3 | 5.3 | 6.3 | 7.3 | 5.3 | 4.5 | 3.6 | B Reach to single object in location which may vary slightly from cycle to cycle. |
| 4 | 6.1 | 6.4 | 8.4 | 6.8 | 4.9 | 4.3 | |
| 5 | 6.5 | 7.8 | 9.4 | 7.4 | 6.3 | 5.0 | |
| 6 | 7.0 | 8.6 | 10.1 | 8.0 | 5.7 | 5.7 | |
| 7 | 7.4 | 9.3 | 10.8 | 8.7 | 6.1 | 6.5 | C Reach to object jumbled with other objects in a group so that search and select occur. |
| 8 | 7.9 | 10.1 | 11.5 | 9.3 | 6.5 | 7.2 | |
| 9 | 8.3 | 10.8 | 12.2 | 9.9 | 6.9 | 7.9 | |
| 10 | 8.7 | 11.5 | 12.9 | 10.5 | 7.3 | 8.6 | |
| 12 | 9.6 | 12.9 | 14.2 | 11.8 | 8.1 | 10.1 | |
| 14 | 10.5 | 14.4 | 15.6 | 13.0 | 8.9 | 11.5 | D Reach to a very small object or where accurate grasp is required. |
| 16 | 11.4 | 15.8 | 17.0 | 14.2 | 9.7 | 12.9 | |
| 18 | 12.3 | 17.2 | 18.4 | 15.5 | 10.5 | 14.4 | |
| 20 | 13.1 | 18.6 | 19.8 | 16.7 | 11.3 | 15.8 | |
| 22 | 14.0 | 20.1 | 21.2 | 18.0 | 12.1 | 17.3 | |
| 24 | 14.9 | 21.5 | 22.5 | 19.2 | 12.9 | 18.8 | E Reach to indefinite location to get hand in position for body balance or next motion or out of way. |
| 26 | 15.8 | 22.9 | 23.9 | 20.4 | 13.7 | 20.2 | |
| 28 | 16.7 | 24.4 | 25.3 | 21.7 | 14.5 | 21.7 | |
| 30 | 17.5 | 25.8 | 26.7 | 22.9 | 15.3 | 23.2 | |

**TABLE II—MOVE—M**

| Distance Moved Inches | Time TMU | | | | Wt Allowanc | | | CASE AND DESCRIPTION |
|---|---|---|---|---|---|---|---|---|
| | A | B | C | Hand In Motion B | Wt (lb.) Up to | Factor | Constant TMU | |
| ¾ or less | 2.0 | 2.0 | 2.0 | 1.7 | 2.5 | 1.00 | 0 | |
| 1 | 2.6 | 2.9 | 3.4 | 2.3 | | | | |
| 2 | 3.6 | 4.6 | 5.2 | 2.9 | 7.5 | 1.06 | 2.2 | A Move object to other hand or against stop. |
| 3 | 4.9 | 5.7 | 6.7 | 3.6 | | | | |
| 4 | 6.1 | 6.9 | 8.0 | 4.3 | 12.5 | 1.11 | 3.9 | |
| 5 | 7.3 | 8.0 | 9.2 | 5.0 | | | | |
| 6 | 8.1 | 8.9 | 10.3 | 6.7 | 17.5 | 1.17 | 5.6 | |
| 7 | 8.9 | 9.7 | 11.1 | 6.5 | | | | |
| 8 | 9.7 | 10.6 | 11.8 | 7.2 | 22.5 | 1.22 | 7.4 | |
| 9 | 10.5 | 11.5 | 12.7 | 7.9 | | | | |
| 10 | 11.3 | 12.2 | 13.5 | 8.6 | 27.5 | 1.28 | 9.1 | B Move object to approximate or indefinite location. |
| 12 | 12.9 | 13.4 | 15.2 | 10.0 | | | | |
| 14 | 14.4 | 14.6 | 16.9 | 11.4 | | | | |
| 16 | 16.0 | 15.8 | 18.7 | 12.8 | 32.5 | 1.33 | 10.8 | |
| 18 | 17.6 | 17.0 | 20.4 | 14.2 | | | | |
| 20 | 19.2 | 18.2 | 22.1 | 15.6 | 37.5 | 1.39 | 12.5 | |
| 22 | 20.8 | 19.4 | 23.8 | 17.0 | | | | |
| 24 | 22.4 | 20.6 | 25.5 | 18.4 | 42.5 | 1.44 | 14.3 | C Move object to exact location. |
| 26 | 24.0 | 21.8 | 27.3 | 19.8 | | | | |
| 28 | 25.5 | 23.1 | 29.0 | 21.2 | 47.5 | 1.50 | 16.0 | |
| 30 | 27.1 | 24.3 | 30.7 | 22.7 | | | | |

**TABLE III—TURN AND APPLY PRESSURE  T AND AP**

| Weight | Time TMU for Degrees Turned | | | | | | | | | | |
|---|---|---|---|---|---|---|---|---|---|---|---|
| | 30° | 45° | 60° | 75° | 90° | 105° | 120° | 135° | 150° | 165° | 180° |
| Small 0 to 2 Pounds | 2.8 | 3.5 | 4.1 | 4.8 | 5.4 | 6.1 | 6.8 | 7.4 | 8.1 | 8.7 | 9.4 |
| Medium 2.1 to 10 Pounds | 4.4 | 5.5 | 6.5 | 7.5 | 8.5 | 9.6 | 10.6 | 11.6 | 12.7 | 13.7 | 14.8 |
| Large 10.1 to 35 Pounds | 8.4 | 10.5 | 12.3 | 14.4 | 16.2 | 18.3 | 20.4 | 22.2 | 24.3 | 26.1 | 28.2 |

APPLY PRESSURE CASE 1  16.2 TMU    APPLY PRESSURE CASE 2  10.6 TMU

**TABLE IV—GRASP—G**

| Case | Time TMU | DESCRIPTION |
|---|---|---|
| 1A | 2.0 | Pick Up Grasp—Small, medium or large object by itself, easily grasped. |
| 1B | 3.8 | Very small object or object lying close against a flat surface. |
| 1C1 | 7.3 | Interference with grasp on bottom and one side of nearly cylindrical object. Diamer larger than ½. |
| 1C2 | 8.7 | Interference with grasp on bottom and one side of nearly cylindrical object. Diameter ¼ to ½. |
| 1C3 | 10.8 | Interference with grasp on bottom and one side of nearly cylindrical object. Diameter less than ¼. |
| 2 | 5.6 | Regrasp. |
| 3 | 5.6 | Transfer Grasp. |
| 4A | 7.3 | Object jumbled with other objects so search and select occur. Larger than 1" × 1" × 1". |
| 4B | 9.1 | Object jumbled with other objects so search and select occur. ¼" × ¼" × ⅛" to 1" × 1" × 1". |
| 4C | 12.9 | Object jumbled with other objects so search and select occur. Smaller than ¼" × ¼" × ⅛". |
| 6 | 0 | Contact, sliding or hook grasp. |

**TABLE V—POSITION—P**

| CLASS OF FIT | | Symmetry | Easy To Handle | Difficult To Handle |
|---|---|---|---|---|
| 1—Loose | No pressure required | S | 5.6 | 11.2 |
| | | SS | 9.1 | 14.7 |
| | | NS | 10.4 | 16.0 |
| 2—Close | Light pressure required | S | 16.2 | 21.6 |
| | | SS | 19.7 | 25.3 |
| | | NS | 21.0 | 26.6 |
| 3—Exact | Heavy pressure required | S | 43.0 | 48.6 |
| | | SS | 46.5 | 52.1 |
| | | NS | 47.8 | 53.4 |

* Distance moved to engage—1" or less.

**TABLE VI—RELEASE—RL**

| Case | Time TMU | DESCRIPTION |
|---|---|---|
| 1 | 2.0 | Normal release performed by opening fingers as independent motion. |
| 2 | 0 | Contact Release. |

**TABLE VII—DISENGAGE—D**

| CLASS OF FIT | Easy to Handle | Difficult to Handle |
|---|---|---|
| 1 Loose Very slight effort, blends with subsequent move. | 4.0 | 5.7 |
| 2 Close Normal effort, slight recoil. | 7.5 | 11.8 |
| 3 Tight Considerable effort, hand recoils markedly. | 22.9 | 34.7 |

**TABLE VIII—EYE TRAVEL TIME AND EYE FOCUS—ET AND EF**

Eye Travel Time = $15.2 \times \frac{T}{D}$ TMU, with a maximum value of 20 TMU.

where T = the distance between points from and to which the eye travels.
D = the perpendicular distance from the eye to the line of travel T.

Eye Focus Time = 7.3 TMU.

**TABLE IX  BODY, LEG AND FOOT MOTIONS**

| DESCRIPTION | SYMBOL | DISTANCE | TIME TMU |
|---|---|---|---|
| Foot Motion  Hinged at Ankle | FM | Up to 4" | 8.6 |
| With heavy pressure | FMP | | 19.1 |
| Leg or Foreleg Motion | LM— | Up to 6" | 7.1 |
| | | Each add'l inch | 1.2 |
| Sidestep  Case 1  Complete when leading leg contacts floor | SS-C1 | Less than 12" | Use REACH or MOVE Time |
| | | 12" | 17.0 |
| | | Each add'l inch | 6 |
| Case 2  Lagging leg must contact floor before next motion can be made | SS-C2 | 12" | 34.1 |
| | | Each add'l inch | 1.1 |
| Bend, Stoop, or Kneel on One Knee | B, S, KOK | | 29.0 |
| Arise | AB, AS, AKOK | | 31.9 |
| Kneel on Floor  Both Knees | KBK | | 60.4 |
| Arise | AKBK | | 76.7 |
| Sit | SIT | | 34.7 |
| Stand from Sitting Position | STD | | 43.4 |
| Turn Body 45 to 90 degrees— | | | |
| Case 1  Complete when leading leg contacts floor | TBC1 | | 18.6 |
| Case 2  Lagging leg must contact floor before next motion can be made | TBC2 | | 37.2 |
| Walk | W-FT | Per Foot | 5.3 |
| Walk | W-P | Per Pace | 15.0 |
| Walk | W-PO | Per Pace | 17.0 |

**Figure 8.3**  *MTM–1 application data in TMU.*

**Table 8.3** *Examples of MTM–1 notation.*

| Motion | Code | Meaning and TMU value |
|--------|------|----------------------|
| Reach | R7A | Reach, path of movement 17.5 cm, class A. Hand not in motion at beginning or end<br>(7.4 TMU) |
| Move | M6A | Move, 15 cm, class A, object weighs less than 1.1 kg<br>(8.9 TMU) |
| Turn | T90M | Turn, 90° object weighing 0.95 to 4.5 kg<br>(8.5 TMU) |
| Grasp | G1C1 | Grasp, case 1C1<br>(7.3 TMU) |
| Position | P2NSE | Position, close fit, non-symmetrical part. Easy to handle.<br>(21.0 TMU) |
| Release | RL1 | Release, case 1<br>(2.0 TMU) |
| Disengage | D1D | Disengage, loose fit, difficult to handle<br>(5.7 TMU) |
| Eye travel | ET10/12 | Eye travel, between points 25 cm apart, line of travel 30 cm from eye<br>(12.7 TMU) |

| | |
|---|---|
| *Get* (G) | a motion with the predominant purpose of reaching with the hand or fingers to an object, grasping the object, and subsequently releasing it<br>Class A—no grasping motion required<br>Class B—grasping involving closing of the hand or fingers with one motion<br>Class C—complex grasping motion<br>Class W—*get weight*, the action required for the muscles of the hand or arm to take up the weight of an object |
| *Put* (P) | a motion with the predominant purpose of moving an object to a destination with the hand or fingers<br>Class A—continuous smooth motion<br>Class B—discontinuous motion, but without obvious correcting motion (i.e. unintentional stop, hesitation or change in direction)<br>Class C—discontinuous motion with obvious correcting motions<br>Class W—*put weight,* is an addition to a put action depending on the weight of the object moved |
| *Apply pressure* (A) | an action with the purpose of exerting muscular force on an object |
| *Regrasp* (R) | the hand action performed with the purpose of changing the grasp of an object |
| *Eye action* (E) | the action with the purpose of either (a) recognizing a readily distinguishable characteristic of an object, or (b) shifting vision to a new viewing area |
| *Crank* (C) | a motion with the purpose of moving an object in a circular path more than 180° with hand or fingers |

| | |
|---|---|
| *Step (S)* | either (a) a leg motion with the purpose of moving the body or (b) a leg motion longer than 30 centimetres |
| *Foot motion (F)* | a short foot or leg motion the purpose of which is *not* to move the body |
| *Bend and arise (B)* | bend, stoop or kneel on one knee and subsequently arise |

The time standard, in TM units, for each of the motions is easily obtained from the MTM–2 data card (Figure 8.4). The values for the seven motions without variable categories are given at the bottom of the card, while the remaining figures on the card relate to Get and Put. The time standard for both of these is determined by the category of the motion and the distance involved. The left-hand column gives distance in centimetres. The time standards for GW and PW are shown on the card; in the case of the former, a time value of 1 TMU per kilogram applies, and in the case of the latter 1 TMU per 5 kilograms, i.e the TMU associated with 'Getting' an object of effective net weight 10 kg (GW 10) is 10 TMU, whereas the time standard for PW 10 is 2 TMU.

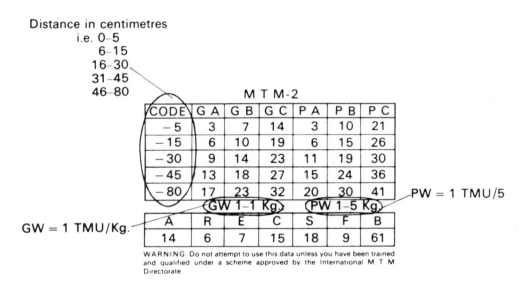

Distance in centimetres
  i.e. 0–5
    6–15
    16–30
    31–45
    46–80

M T M-2

| CODE | G A | G B | G C | P A | P B | P C |
|---|---|---|---|---|---|---|
| – 5 | 3 | 7 | 14 | 3 | 10 | 21 |
| – 15 | 6 | 10 | 19 | 6 | 15 | 26 |
| – 30 | 9 | 14 | 23 | 11 | 19 | 30 |
| – 45 | 13 | 18 | 27 | 15 | 24 | 36 |
| – 80 | 17 | 23 | 32 | 20 | 30 | 41 |

GW 1–1 Kg        PW 1–5 Kg

PW = 1 TMU/5

GW = 1 TMU/Kg.

| A | R | E | C | S | F | B |
|---|---|---|---|---|---|---|
| 14 | 6 | 7 | 15 | 18 | 9 | 61 |

WARNING Do not attempt to use this data unless you have been trained and qualified under a scheme approved by the International M T M Directorate

**Figure 8.4** *The MTM–2 data card. Reproduced with the permission of the MTM Association of UK.*

*Other MTM-derived PMTS*

MTM–3

MTM–3 is a development of MTM–2. Introduced in 1970, it is more quickly applied and intended primarily for small-batch work where there is considerable variation in work method from cycle to cycle.

## 4M DATA

There are many other MTM-based PMTS. The 4M DATA system (O'Neil and Moore (1980)), developed specifically for use in a computerized PMTS, combines the basic MTM–1 motions into only two categories: GET and PLACE.

## MOST

The MOST (Maynard Operations Sequence Technique) (Zandin (1980)) was derived from MTM–1 with the objective of simplifying and accelerating application without loss of accuracy. MOST identifies eight key activities which occur in three fixed sequences. Index numbers ascribed to the variables for each activity reflect the relative simplicity or complexity of the sequence or move. Thus the 'compression' of a single activity into a short formula is achieved, enabling MOST to be used (it is claimed) up to 40 times faster than MTM–1 and up to 15 times faster than MTM–2.

## Clerical PMTS

Most of the techniques described above are of value in the study of most types of manual work. However, a MTM-derived PMTS has been developed specifically for use in work study for clerical jobs. MTM–C is a two-level standard data system. Synthesized from MTM–1 motion data, MTM–C covers a wide range of filing, typing, key entry, and general clerical tasks. The activities covered include:

1. Get/place
2. Open/close
3. Fasten/unfasten
4. Organize/file
5. Read/write
6. Typing
7. Handling
8. Walking/body motions
9. Office machines

Level 1 of MTM–C, the more detailed, provides three distance ranges for elements involving reach and move. Level 2 provides these elements in the intermediate distance range.

### *Analytical estimating*

Analytical estimating is described as 'a work mesurement technique, whereby the time required to carry out elements of a job at a defined level of performance is established from knowledge and practical experience of the elements concerned' (BS 3138).

Analytical estimating is intended to replace a procedure known as *rate fixing*, which was occasionally used to establish time standards for non-repetitive work such as maintenance. In such circumstances there are often insufficient synthetic data available to allow time standards to be established and consequently standards must be constructed using whatever data are available, plus estimates of the basic times for the remaining elements. Clearly a requirement in analytical estimating is that the estimator is completely familiar with, and preferably skilled and experienced in, the work concerned.

The procedure used is much the same as before, in that jobs are first divided into appropriate elements, synthetic data being used for as many of those elements as possible while basic times are estimated for the remainder. Rather than applying allowances to individual elements, relaxation and contingency allowances are applied as overall or blanket figures for the whole job.

## COMPUTERS IN WORK STUDY

Computer programs and computer systems might be of value to the work study practitioner in the following areas:

(a)   preparation of detailed work methods description;
(b)   methods development and analysis (and workplace layout);
(c)   storage and retrieval of data on work methods and times;
(d)   development of workplace layout;
(e)   analysis of direct time study data;
(f)   determination of time standards;
(g)   computerized PMTS.

Of the above, (a), (b) and (c) relate specifically to method study and were discussed in Chapter 7, while (e) (f) and (g) relate specifically to work measurement and are discussed below.

In the remainder of this chapter we shall look first at computer applications in work measurement before concluding with a review of the impact of computers in the broad field of work study.

## COMPUTERS IN WORK MEASUREMENT

At the simplest level, computer programs have been written to analyse direct time study data. For example, such a program might take observed times for elements with ratings, and information on the frequency of the elements per cycle, etc., and provide a listing with observed data, cumulative element times, average times and average ratings for elements. Such applications are simple 'number-crunching' uses of a computer to take over some of the more tedious aspects of work measurement. At a slightly more sophisticated level, programs are available to 'attach' element times to elements by reference to PMTS tables. Thus if the elements are identified by appropriate code reference can be made to the table of element times and these can then be attached to the elements and standard times for the job, etc., can be calculated. This application is in fact one step removed from that of a fully computerized PMTS system. In such a system element and job times will be calculated, for a given job description, by reference to PMTS tables. In addition, by reference to filed data, the computer is able to print out a fully detailed statement of the job method using full element description, PMTS code, etc., and also perhaps by checking against certain rules or heuristics is able to ensure that the method does not violate any of the rules and procedures for effective work methods, e.g. by checking that sequences of elements do not incorporate any difficult motion sequences. In addition such a program might determine various indices as measures of the effectiveness of the method, e.g. the number of difficult motions used.

Using computers in work measurement, indeed in the whole field of work study, it will often be appropriate to employ some form of 'data capture'. In its simplest form data-capture equipment simply replaces the traditional stopwatch and time study record sheets. At a more sophisticated level, data-capture equipment is available to enable observers to time elements automatically (for example using a built-in clock or cassette recorder running at a known speed), to store element descriptions and times for a particular job and then input that data either directly or remotely to a computer for subsequent editing and analysis, or to perform some local analysis on the data, e.g. checking for missing times, determining job times, etc. Most such equipment is now able to interface with a computer and in effect therefore operates as a remote terminal for that computer, but provides for storage of data on the terminal during the period in which the observer is measuring or describing the job.

Increasingly, in using computer systems, data-capture terminals, etc., the objective is to deploy the facilities for the benefit of both method study and work measurement. Although at present computer systems perhaps provide greater benefits in work measurement than in method study, there is now a trend towards the development of more comprehensive applications.

## Comprehensive work study

A comprehensive computerized work study system will provide facilities in the seven categories listed earlier and will therefore be of relevance and value to the work study practitioner in all aspects of his or her work. Such comprehensive systems will involve not only the use of computers (with printers, disc files, etc.) but also electronic equipment for gathering and inputting data. None of the systems provides a fully comprehensive computer-based work study system but their further development will rapidly lead to such a system becoming available. Consideration of a hypothetical system will give some indication of the scope for the use of computers in work study. The scope of a hypothetical 'comprehensive' computer-based work study system is illustrated by Figure 8.5 (which in turn is derived from Figure 7.1, which was used to outline the structure of work study). The facilities provided by a comprehensive computer-based work study system are described in this diagram. The configuration required to support such a system might resemble that shown in Figure 8.6.

## FURTHER READING

Anderson, J. and Hosni, Y. A. (1981) Time standards by microcomputers, *Industrial Engineering*, September, pp. 18–21.

Brisley, C. L. and Dossett, R. J. (1980) Computer use and non-direct labour measurement will transform profession in the next decade, *Industrial Engineering*, August, pp. 34–42.

Duncanson, G. (1981) Electronic time study really arrives, *Management Services*, February, pp. 6–8.

Karger, D. W. and Bayha, F. H. (1955) *Engineered Work Measurement*, 2nd edition, New York: Industrial Press. Deals with MTM.

O'Neal, M. H. and Moore, C. (1980) Multi-plant computer systems for standards provides tools for overall manufacturing control, *Industrial Engineering*, August, pp. 54–80.

Seabourne, R. G. (1971) *Introduction to Work Study and Statistics*. Harlow: Longman.

Zandin, K. B. (1980) MOST Work Measurement Systems. New York: Dekker.

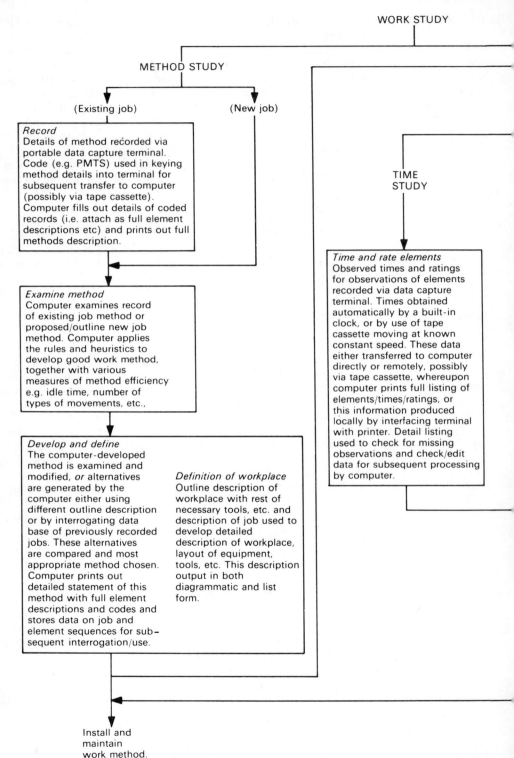

WORK STUDY

METHOD STUDY

(Existing job)                    (New job)

**Record**
Details of method recorded via
portable data capture terminal.
Code (e.g. PMTS) used in keying
method details into terminal for
subsequent transfer to computer
(possibly via tape cassette).
Computer fills out details of coded
records (i.e. attach as full element
descriptions etc) and prints out full
methods description.

TIME
STUDY

**Examine method**
Computer examines record
of existing job method or
proposed/outline new job
method. Computer applies
the rules and heuristics to
develop good work method,
together with various
measures of method efficiency
e.g. idle time, number of
types of movements, etc.,

**Time and rate elements**
Observed times and ratings
for observations of elements
recorded via data capture
terminal. Times obtained
automatically by a built-in
clock, or by use of tape
cassette moving at known
constant speed. These data
either transferred to computer
directly or remotely, possibly
via tape cassette, whereupon
computer prints full listing of
elements/times/ratings, or
this information produced
locally by interfacing terminal
with printer. Detail listing
used to check for missing
observations and check/edit
data for subsequent processing
by computer.

**Develop and define**
The computer-developed
method is examined and
modified, *or* alternatives
are generated by the
computer either using
different outline description
or by interrogating data
base of previously recorded
jobs. These alternatives
are compared and most
appropriate method chosen.
Computer prints out
detailed statement of this
method with full element
descriptions and codes and
stores data on job and
element sequences for subsequent interrogation/use.

**Definition of workplace**
Outline description of
workplace with rest of
necessary tools, etc. and
description of job used to
develop detailed
description of workplace,
layout of equipment,
tools, etc. This description
output in both
diagrammatic and list
form.

Install and
maintain
work method.

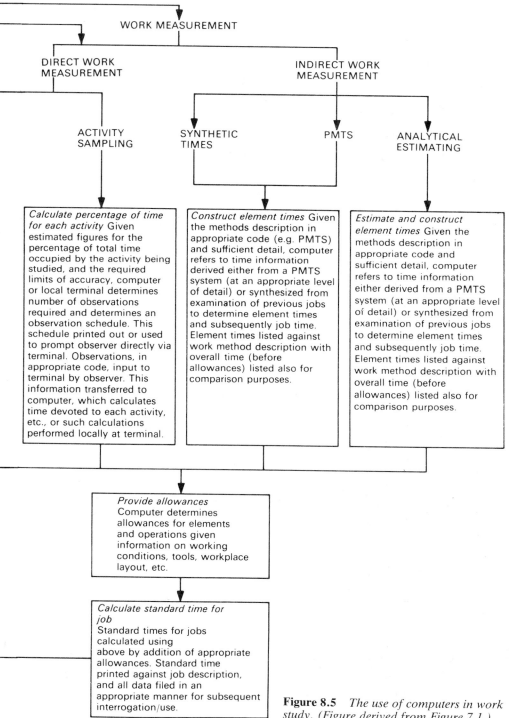

**Figure 8.5** *The use of computers in work study. (Figure derived from Figure 7.1.)*

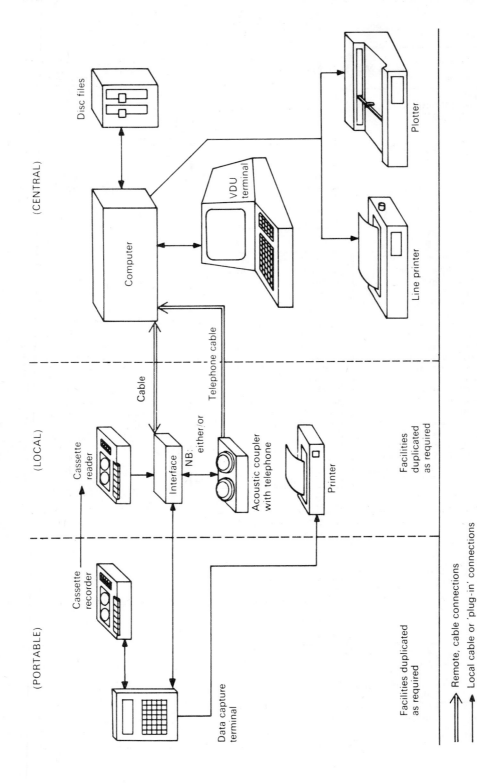

**Figure 8.6** *Possible configuration of a computer system's hardware for work study applications.*

## QUESTIONS

**8.1** The figures below are the observed times obtained by stopwatch during 25 observations of a single element of a manual task. Have sufficient observations of this element been made to provide an accuracy of ± 5 per cent with a confidence interval of 95 per cent?

| Observation number (N) | Time for element (in 1/100 min) |
|:---:|:---:|
| 1 | 40 |
| 2 | 45 |
| 3 | 43 |
| 4 | 42 |
| 5 | 45 |
| 6 | 47 |
| 7 | 40 |
| 8 | 48 |
| 9 | 47 |
| 10 | 42 |
| 11 | 40 |
| 12 | 39 |
| 13 | 42 |
| 14 | 41 |
| 15 | 43 |
| 16 | 44 |
| 17 | 46 |
| 18 | 43 |
| 19 | 42 |
| 20 | 42 |
| 21 | 44 |
| 22 | 43 |
| 23 | 40 |
| 24 | 42 |
| 25 | 45 |

**8.2** The Westinghouse method of rating (see Table 8.2) was used to rate the performance of the element for which the observed times given in the previous question were also obtained. The rating is to be made on a basis of the following:

| | |
|---|---|
| Skill | C1 |
| Effort | B2 |
| Conditions | E |
| Consistency | D |

Calculate the standard time for the element if a personal allowance of 5 per cent is given.

**8.3** Using the data given on the sheet shown below and the following information, calculate the output of an operator at standard performance for an eight-hour shift.

| Study | Operator | Times | Date | Sheet |
|---|---|---|---|---|
| | Male | 1/10 min | | 1 |

| Element number | Rating | Observed time | Ineffective time | Basic time | Element number | Rating | Observed time | Ineffective time | Basic time |
|---|---|---|---|---|---|---|---|---|---|
| 1 | 110 | 0.45 | | | 1 | 105 | 0.45 | | |
| 2 | 100 | 0.70 | | | 2 | 110 | 0.70 | | |
| 3 | 110 | 0.35 | | | 3 | 115 | 0.40 | | |
| 1 | 105 | 0.50 | | | 1 | 100 | 0.45 | | |
| 2 | 110 | 0.65 | | | 2 | 100 | 0.80 | | |
| 3 | 105 | 0.40 | | | 3 | 90 | 0.50 | | |
| 1 | 100 | 0.45 | | | 1 | 95 | 0.52 | | |
| 2 | 100 | 0.72 | | | 2 | 100 | 0.75 | | |
| 3 | 100 | 0.42 | | | 3 | 110 | 0.45 | | |
| — | | | 3.80 | | 1 | 100 | 0.45 | | |
| | | | | | 2 | 100 | 0.75 | | |
| | | | | | 3 | 100 | 0.40 | | |
| 1 | 100 | 0.47 | | | 1 | 110 | 0.52 | | |
| 2 | 90 | 0.85 | | | 2 | 100 | 0.75 | | |
| 3 | 110 | 0.50 | | | 3 | 100 | 0.38 | | |
| 1 | 100 | 0.45 | | | | | | | |
| 2 | 100 | 0.75 | | | — | | | | |
| 3 | 110 | 0.48 | | | Adjust jig every 25 cycles | | | | |

Allowances: Fatigue   5 per cent
Personal   10 per cent
Delay   2 per cent

**8.4** Assume that after the application of appropriate work simplification techniques you have taken a direct time study and, after subtraction, you get the following results (time in minutes):

| Cycle number | Element number | | | | |
|---|---|---|---|---|---|
| | 1 | 2 | 3 | 4 | 5 |
| 1 | 0.15 | 0.62 | 0.33 | 0.51 | 0.23 |
| 2 | 0.14 | 0.58 | 0.20 | 0.50 | 0.26 |
| 3 | 0.13 | 0.59 | 0.36 | 0.55 | .0.24 |
| 4 | 0.18 | 0.61 | 0.37 | 0.49 | 0.25 |
| 5 | 0.22 | 0.60 | 0.34 | 0.45 | 0.27 |

(a) Elements 2 and 4 are machine paced.
(b) You have a decision rule which states that any reading which varies by more than 25 per cent from the average of all readings for an element will be considered 'abnormal'.

(c) The operator is rated at 120 per cent.
(d) Allowances have been set at (for an eight-hour shift):

| | |
|---|---|
| personal time | 30 minutes |
| unavoidable delay | 36 minutes |
| fatigue | 5 per cent |

(e) The operator, who is paid on a straight time rate, receives 50p per hour.
(f) Material costs are 3p per piece.
(g) Overhead costs are calculated at 80 per cent of the sum of direct labour and material costs.

How many pieces per shift should each operator produce and what is the production cost per piece? Discuss the appropriateness of these estimates for planning purposes.

**8.5** 'The principal benefit in using predetermined motion time systems to develop work standards is the avoidance of performance rating, and hence the avoidance of undue dispute over the resultant standards.' Discuss.

**8.6** Discuss the function of performance rating in the determination of work standards. Compare stopwatch study and work sampling in the determination of work standards.
You have obtained the following work sample from a study during a 40-hour work week:

| | |
|---|---|
| idle time | 20 per cent |
| performance rating | 135 per cent |
| total parts produced | 280 |

The allowance for this particular type of work is 10 per cent. Determine the standard time per part.

**8.7** The technique of rated activity sampling is used to study the activities of three workers employed on an assembly line. The first two workers on the line have two elements to perform on each item, whereas the third worker has one element of work for each item.
At the beginning of the study the line is empty. Sufficient parts to enable the assembly of ten items are then provided, and observations are taken at 0.1-minute intervals as follows:

| Time | Observed worker |
|---|---|
| 0.1 | A |
| 0.2 | B |
| 0.3 | C |
| 0.1 | A |
| 0.2 | B |
| 0.3 | C |
| etc. | etc. |

These observations result in the ratings shown in the table below.

What are the basic times for each of the five work elements and for each of the three workers?

| Observation number | | | Worker A | | | Worker B | | | Worker C | |
|---|---|---|---|---|---|---|---|---|---|---|
| A | B | C | E11 | E12 | Idle | E13 | E14 | Idle | E15 | Idle |
| 1 | 2 | 3 | 80 | | | | | 100 | | 100 |
| 4 | 5 | 6 | | 110 | | 90 | | | | 100 |
| 7 | 8 | 9 | | 100 | | | | 100 | 75 | |
| 10 | 11 | 12 | | 90 | | | 80 | | 85 | |
| 13 | 14 | 15 | | | 100 | | | 100 | 90 | |
| 16 | 17 | 18 | 110 | | | | | 100 | | 100 |
| 19 | 20 | 21 | | 100 | | 100 | | | | 100 |
| 22 | 23 | 24 | | | 100 | 100 | | | 100 | |
| 25 | 26 | 27 | | 75 | | | 85 | | 110 | |
| 28 | 29 | 30 | 120 | | | 110 | | | 100 | |
| 31 | 32 | 33 | | | 100 | 85 | | | 120 | |
| 34 | 35 | 36 | | | 100 | | | 100 | | 100 |

# CHAPTER 9

# Human Factors in Work System Design

In this chapter we shall concentrate on working conditions and the worker. The topics covered here are complementary to those covered in Chapters 7 and 8. To a large extent this chapter introduces the 'behavioural' dimension into our consideration of the design of work and work systems.

This chapter is divided into two parts as follows:

1. *Working conditions*. In this part we shall look at the design of the workplace and ergonomics. We shall also consider health and safety considerations.
2. *The worker*. Here we shall look at the design of jobs in the work organization from the worker's viewpoint and also consider aspects of worker variability and learning.

## THE WORKING CONDITIONS

### Ergonomics

In this section we shall be concerned with people at work, and particularly with the design of workplaces and equipment with people in mind.

Despite increasing automation of work in industry and business, people are still associated with, and are essential to, most operating systems. Certainly the worker's role is changing, the worker being relieved of many routine and/or hazardous tasks. This trend will continue, but there will always be a need for some people, and the emphasis will therefore move to the design and management of worker–machine systems.

The efficiency with which the worker functions depends on environmental factors, on his or her own characteristics, such as age, motivation, training and experience, and on the efficiency with which the machine provides the information feedback and accepts control measures.

**147**

If we accept, for our present purposes, that workers and their characteristics are largely fixed, this leaves us with only three aspects of the worker–machine system to discuss:

(a)  design of information displays;
(b)  design of controls;
(c)  environmental factors.


### Design of information displays


The most common means of displaying or communicating information is visual. We can identify two categories of visual display: analogue and digital. Analogue methods, such as the circular graduated scale, are in common use, but this is mainly due to expediency rather than functional merit. The use of digital displays is a more recent phenomenon.

We can further classify visual display as follows:

1.  Displays used without controls:

    (a)  for quantitative measurement, e.g. clocks, voltmeters; the purpose of these is to determine whether the correct value exists, or whether corrective action is necessary;
    (b)  for check reading, i.e. to determine the proximity of a characteristic to a desired value, and not for obtaining a precise measurement;
    (c)  for comparison, e.g. to compare the readings on two dials;
    (d)  for warning; although warning systems often include audible devices, lights are also frequently used.

2.  Displays used with controls:

    (a)  for controlling, i.e. to extract information and measure the effect of corrective action;
    (b)  for setting, i.e. to use a control and display to ensure that a correct value is obtained, for example setting the running speed of an engine after starting up;
    (c)  for tracking, i.e. to use a control continuously to correct movement or to compensate for external factors, for example keeping two indicators synchronized, or on target, by means of a control.

Many of the handbooks on ergonomics and human engineering present standards and design data for visual displays. They are not identical in their recommendations, but the following list contains most of the important points relating to the design of dials, etc.

1.  Instruments should enable the worker to read information as accurately as necessary, but not more so.
2.  The scale used should be both simple and logical, using the minimum number of suitable divisions.
3.  The scale should provide information in an immediately usable form, and no mental conversions should be necessary.
4.  Scales that must be read quantitatively should be designed so that workers need not interpolate between marks.
5.  Vertical figures should be used on stationary dials and radial figures used on rotating dials.
6.  Scales should not be obscured by the pointer.

Also in the visual category are written or printed information, radar, and VDUs. Visual methods of communication involving permanent copies, such as line output from computers, are particularly valuable where the message must be retained for future reference, where there is no urgency in the transmission of the information, and where long or complex messages are involved.

Instruments such as gauges and dials are of value where many sets of information are to be transmitted, and where the worker's job permits him or her to receive such information when it arrives.

Aural information 'displays', such as telephones, buzzers, bells and speech, are more appropriate where speed of transmission is important, where messages are short and uncomplicated, and where a record of the message need not be retained. Often aural communication is essential in industry, where visual channels are overloaded or where the environment does not permit visual communication. However, within the context of the worker–machine, aural communication is infrequent, except where workers are able to determine the state of equipment from the sound of operation.

## Design of controls

The types of controls commonly used and their suitability for various tasks are shown in Table 9.1. The first and most important step is to select the type of control best suited to the requirements. This will involve answering the following questions:

1. What is the control for?
2. What is required, e.g. in terms of precision, force, speed, number of settings?
3. What information must be displayed by the control, i.e. must the control be identified from the others, must it be picked out in the dark, and should the worker be able to tell how the control is set?

**Table 9.1** *Suitability of various controls for different purposes.* (Reproduced from 'Ergonomics for Industry No. 7', Ministry of Technology, 1965, by permission of the Controller, HMSO.)

| Type of control | Speed | Accuracy | Force | Range | Loads |
|---|---|---|---|---|---|
| Cranks | | | | | |
| small | Good | Poor | Unsuitable | Good | Up to 40 in/lb |
| large | Poor | Unsuitable | Good | Good | Over 40 in/lb |
| Handwheels | Poor | Good | Fair/Poor | Fair | Up to 150 in/lb |
| Knobs | Unsuitable | Fair | Unsuitable | Fair | Up to 15 in/lb |
| Levers | | | | | |
| horizontal | Good | Poor | Poor | Poor | Up to 25 lb[a] |
| vertical (to-from body) | Good | Fair | { *Short* Poor <br> { *Long* Good | Poor | Up to 30 lb[a] |
| vertical (across body) | Fair | Fair | Fair | Unsuitable | { One hand up to 20 lb[a] <br> { Two hands up to 30 lb[a] |
| joysticks | Good | Fair | Poor | Poor | 5–20 lb |
| Pedals | Good | Poor | Good | Unsuitable | 30–200 lb; depends on leg flexion and body support (Ankle only up to 20 lb) |
| Push buttons | Good | Unsuitable | Unsuitable | Unsuitable | 2 lb |
| Rotary selector switch | Good | Good | Unsuitable | Unsuitable | Up to 10 in/lb |
| Joystick selector switch | Good | Good | Poor | Unsuitable | Up to 30 lb |

[a] When operated by a standing operator depends on body weight.

4.  How do environmental conditions affect or limit the use of the control?

Finally, having selected the most appropriate types of controls to use, they should be logically arranged, clearly marked and easily accessible. They should suit the capabilities of the operator and should be positioned to distribute the loads evenly among them. Functionally similar controls may be combined, as for example in the combined sidelights, headlights and flasher switch on many cars; also as far as possible, controls should 'match' the changes they produce in the machine or the system (e.g. clockwise rotation to 'increase' something, etc.). There should be consistency in the direction of movement of controls and they should be close to, and identifiable with, their associated displays.

### Environmental factors

The provision of good workplace lighting, heating, ventilation, etc., is often a statutory requirement, and is necessary, though insufficient, to motivate workers and provide job satisfaction.

### Lighting

Good lighting is not achieved merely by adding extra lights, since the type of lighting system adopted will depend on the type of work being performed, the size of objects, the accuracy, speed and duration of the work, etc. An adequate lighting system should provide:

(a) sufficient brightness;
(b) uniform illumination;
(c) a contrast between brightness of job and of background;
(d) no direct or reflected glare.

Although a considerable amount of research has been conducted to establish optimum levels of illumination for various jobs, there is little agreement on the subject, and American recommendations in particular differ from British in suggesting higher levels of illumination.

Lighting should be arranged to avoid 'flicker' and to provide an acceptable amount of shadow. Notice that freedom from shadow is not always desirable, since in certain circumstances, e.g. inspection, shadows can be used to improve the visibility of details by accentuating or 'modelling' surface details.

### Noise

We can make the obvious distinction between continuous and intermittent noise, both of which are to some extent inevitable in industry; both can have detrimental effects on behaviour and may even cause physical damage to the worker.

Noise levels and the effect on workers can be reduced by controlling noise at its source, by putting barriers between the worker and the source of noise, by providing protective devices for the workers, or by modifying work processes to reduce workers' exposure to noise. Prolonged exposure to continuous noise levels in excess of 90 dB (decibels) is likely to result in hearing loss; 40 dB is an acceptable maximum level for comfort.

Sudden noises greatly in excess of the background noise level can and do produce a reaction, shock, or startling effect which could have disastrous consequences for workers employed on or close to machinery. Regular intermittent noise is a common feature in industry where, for example, automatic machines such as presses are involved, but there is a danger of underestimating its effect by assuming an eventual adjustment by the worker to the situation.

## Temperature and ventilation

Figure 9.1 shows that the type of work and its duration determines the individual's tolerance to heat, and Table 9.2 indicates the relationship between space requirements and ventilation.

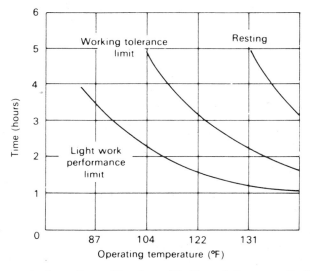

**Figure 9.1**   *Tolerance to heat. From Woodson, W. E. and Conover, D. W. (1964)* Human Engineering Guide for Equipment Designers. *Berkeley: University of California Press.*

**Table 9.2**   *Relationship between space requirements and ventilation.* (From Fogel, L. J. 1963 *Biotechnology: Concepts and Applications.* New Jersey: Prentice-Hall. Reproduced with permission.)

| Net volume of space (cubic feet) / Fresh air supply (cubic feet per minute) | Volume of space required per person (cubic feet) |
|---|---|
| 1000 | 500 |
| 600 | 450 |
| 400 | 400 |
| 200 | 300 |
| 100 | 200 |
| 60 | 150 |
| 35 | 100 |
| 22 | 65 |

## Workplace design

The design of workplaces and equipment was mentioned in Chapter 7, and all the comments made there are relevant here.

In many jobs the worker has to remain sitting or standing for long periods of time while performing a given series of tasks. Rarely is the detailed design of the product or its components influenced by the ergonomic requirements of the workers responsible for making it, except of course in such cases as the need for access during assembly. Commonly, however, other aspects of workplace design are influenced by ergonomic considerations. Inadequate design of workplaces will inhibit the ability of the worker to perform his or her tasks and may result in injuries, strain or fatigue, or a reduction in quality or output.

Determination of workplace requirements will involve an examination of the work elements which constitute the work cycle and an examination of the body measurements, reach and movement capacities of the worker.

### *Anthropometric data*

Using anthropometric data, i.e. body dimensions, information of the type given in Figures 9.2, 9.3, 9.4, 9.5 and 9.6 can be determined. Figures 9.2 and 9.3 give the normal and maximum working areas in the horizontal and vertical planes. The optimum horizontal working area is given in Figure 9.4. Figures 9.5 and 9.6 present dimensions for working space and work area height for seated and standing workers.

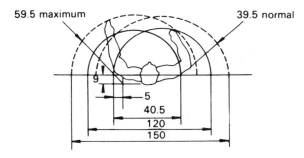

**Figure 9.2**   *Normal and maximum working areas in horizontal plane (cm).*

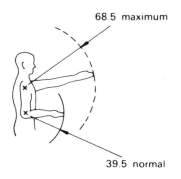

**Figure 9.3**   *Normal and maximum working areas in vertical plane (cm).*

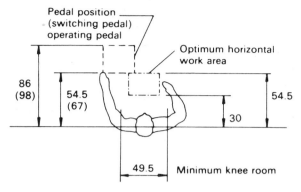

**Figure 9.4**   *Optimum working area, pedal positions and knee room (cm).*

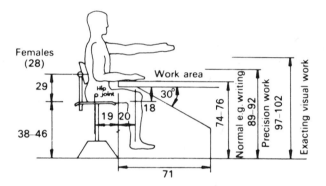

**Figure 9.5**   *Space for seated work (cm).*

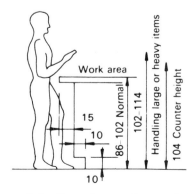

**Figure 9.6**   *Space for standing work (cm).*

The data given in these figures are offered *for guidance purposes only*. They have been extracted from several specialist books (see Further Reading), each of which provides more detailed information should this be required.

## VDU (visual display unit) work

A substantial proportion of workers in offices and factories work with VDUs. In the typical situation the worker works with a VDU and keyboard connected to a computer. Such working situations are commonplace in all types of office work, in retailing, banking and insurance, and in many aspects of factory work, as well as in computer installations. Similar situations exist in connection with the use of microfilm readers, VDU readout terminals (without input keyboards), etc. The VDU, with or without input keyboard, as a self-contained unit or linked to a remote computer, is increasingly becoming a dominant feature in people's working environments.

The impact of VDUs on work will continue to increase, and already we see the evolution of 'Homo termino-videns' (terminal-viewing man) at work. Such is the importance of the VDU that the design of VDU-dominated working environments merits special reference in this chapter.

Trade unions and workers' representatives, employers and legislators have come to be particularly concerned about the effects of VDUs on workers. There is evidence of VDU work giving rise to physical discomforts, especially relating to visual fatigue, headaches, back and shoulder ache, etc. Clearly adequate ergonomic design of a VDU-dominated workplace is essential. Much of the previous discussion is also relevant in this context, but here there are additional factors which in some countries have given rise to legislation or publication of guidelines governing VDU work.

The sections below outline some of the major considerations in the design of VDU-dominated work environments. These factors are increasingly likely to be the subject of legislation or collective agreement.

### Visual conditions

A major problem in designing VDU workplaces is the distribution of luminescences (light emissions) at the workplace. A compromise must be found between the low luminescence required of the display screen and the high luminescence required for reading the keyboard and printed documents.

Symbols on the VDU are produced by an electron beam which excites an emission of light in the phosphor coating of the screen. There is a choice of different phosphors, and this influences not only luminous intensity but also colour, flicker, and the life of the screen. The legibility of symbols on the screen depends on the contrast, and it has been suggested that a contrast of 10:1 is near optimum, while the maximum and minimum values are 15:1 and 2.5:1 respectively. Depending on the level of illumination in the room the symbol luminescence of 90 cd/m$^2$ is near optimum, with maximum and minimum values of 160 and 20 respectively. Symbol colour is not considered to be of critical importance; however, 'flicker' is a major factor. A 'critical flicker frequency' is that at which the individual can just detect a flicker in a light source. This varies from person to person but is normally in the range 20 to 60 Hz. It is dependent also on the flicker area, the shape of the light source, its illumination, location in the visual field, etc. The closer the worker to the screen and the higher the luminescence, the higher the critical flicker frequency. The surface of VDUs, being convex and glossy, can reflect surrounding features, and this can reduce symbol contrast and increase strain. Such reflections can be muted by surface treatment or the use of filters.

The cabinet surrounding the VDU tube should have a higher reflection factor than the screen itself to provide a smooth transition to the normally brighter surroundings. The luminescence of keyboards should not differ substantially from that of screens, which in most situations will necessitate the use of a dark-coloured keyboard. Concave keys can result in reflections.

Normally the level of illumination required for reading a manuscript will be higher than that required for other aspects of VDU work. However, substantial contrast with the level of illumination at the workplace is undesirable, so in most cases 'manuscript illumination' will be lower than provided for normal office work; hence legibility must be good. Printed character size, character colour and paper colour will affect legibility.

Ambient lighting conditions in working environments where VDUs exist will often be influenced by the needs of other workers on different types of work. In such cases VDUs must be positioned and oriented to prevent glare and to minimize the contrast between screen, keyboard and manuscript illumination, and levels of background illumination. It has been suggested that the area surrounding the VDU workplace should have a horizontal illumination of 300 lx and a background luminescence of 20 to 40 cd/m$^2$.

### Heat and noise

The power delivered to the VDU and associated equipment is partly converted to heat and can result in a higher temperature than is desirable unless adequate local ventilation is provided. The largest contributor to local heat production will be the control unit for the VDU; the heat output of such units, typically in the range 75 to 100 W, must be considered in determining the thermal balance for working environments. Convection effects which might produce draughts and humidity requirements must also be considered.

Several sources of noise are associated with the operation of a VDU: mechanical ventilation of a VDU can add considerably to the local noise level, and keyboard noise and the noise caused by printers can be substantial. A recommended noise level below 55 dB(A) has been recommended, while VDU tasks requiring high levels of mental concentration might be adversely affected by background noise levels greater than 45 dB(A).

### Ergonomic considerations

The checklists below deal specifically with a VDU working environment comprising VDU screen, keyboard, manuscript or printed material (being read) and operator.

### Terminal desk

1. Adjustable desk height is desirable. A height indicator to facilitate adjustment by different workers is beneficial.
2. The desk top should be large enough to allow for all items used by the operator and for readjustment/repositioning of those items.
3. The desk top should consist of one piece with no gaps, joints, etc.
4. The desk top should have a non-reflecting surface and a pleasant (not a cold) feel.

Keyboard

1. The thickness/height of the keyboard should not exceed 20 mm including the second row of keys and it should be as narrow as possible.
2. Keyboards with a height greater than 30 mm should be sunk into the desk (although this reduces the possibility of relocation, etc.).
3. It should be easy to push or turn the keyboard.
4. The keyboard should stand firmly.
5. The keyboard should not be attached to the screen unit.
6. The slope of the keyboard should be as small as possible.
7. The keyboard should not have more keys than are needed for the work in question.
8. It will often be better to change from one keyboard to another to accommodate different types of work rather than have a comprehensive, over-large keyboard to accommodate all requirements.

Keys

1. The force required to press a key should be 0.25 to 1.5 N.
2. The distance of travel in key depression should be 3 to 4.8 mm.
3. The length of a square key should be 12 to 15 mm.
4. The distance from centre to centre of adjacent keys should be 18 to 20 mm.
5. The function keys should be larger than, and perhaps a different colour from, other keys.
6. The symbols should be engraved in the key surface or printed below a non-reflecting transparent cap.
7. The keys should be concave but only enough to match the convexity of fingers and not so much as to cause undue reflection.
8. Guide keys should be marked with a small raised dot for easier location in touch typing.

Screen unit

1. It should be possible to adjust the height of the screen unit and to tilt or turn it without tools.
2. It should be possible to push the screen unit backwards and forwards on the desk. Distance markers will facilitate adjustment.
3. The screen unit should stand firmly and not be too heavy to move.

Manuscript

1. A manuscript stand should be stable and adjustable in height and sideways. It should also tilt.
2. The best position for the manuscript is at the same distance from the eyes as the screen, and as close to the screen as possible. Abrupt changes in luminescence and reflection must be avoided.

Work schedules

Views on the definition of fair rest periods for VDU workers are numerous and varied. An early report published in Austria recommended that a break of at least one hour should follow not more than one hour's work at a VDU, but more recently collective agreements in industry have envisaged rather shorter breaks after rather longer periods, e.g. 15 minutes minimum after two hours' work at a VDU. Clearly the 'relaxation' allowance provided (see Chapter 8) in VDU work will be significant in most situations. This is an area in which legislation and collective agreements will undoubtedly have considerable impact.

## Health and safety

Our discussion of working conditions and job design leads us to consider issues relating to health and safety at work—important aspects for operations managers who in many cases are legally responsible for the health and safety of their subordinates. For example in the UK, with the enforcement of Health and Safety at Work Act 1974, much of the legal responsibility for the health and safety of workers is placed on management. Employees are of course required to carry responsibility for the safety of themselves and their colleagues through both the observance of safety practices and the adoption of those working methods in which they have been instructed. The employer or manager is required to provide an overall working environment, including adequate training of the operator, so that it is safe and healthy for employers to undertake their jobs. In effect, therefore, the safety of workers becomes the individual responsibility of managers responsible for departments as well as the responsibility of the employing organization as a whole. In such circumstances individual managers become legally responsible and therefore liable to criminal prosecution for failure to observe the requirements of the Act.

In considering health and safety we are concerned in effect with the prevention of accidents or ill health. Such subjects should of course be considered in a preventive rather than a remedial sense, since it is in the interests of all parties to prevent the occurrence of illness or accidents, but in order to indicate the magnitude of the problem it will be appropriate to remind ourselves of the effects of accidents and the extent to which accidents have occurred in industry and commerce in the past.

### *Industrial accidents*

Currently in the UK and in most other industrialized countries the number of work days lost through industrial injury exceeds those lost through industrial disputes, strikes and grievance activity. In the UK at the present time the relationship is of the order of two to one. Approximately 300 000 accidents are reported in factories annually in the UK, approximately 1 per cent of which are fatal. It should be noted, however, that in general a large proportion of the accidents which occur in industry and business are never reported and therefore do not feature in local or national statistics. Statistics concerning accidents are therefore a poor indicator of the magnitude of the problem, since for such purposes an accident is considered to be something which 'causes disablement for more than three days' and is therefore legally notifiable. Thus a large number of accidents are not reported and, furthermore, a large number of the accidents which do cause disablement for more than three days are reported under other headings, e.g. sickness, absence, etc.

In general, at least in factories, the major source of accidents is concerned with the handling of goods, e.g. lifting, placing, movement, etc., at the workplace and between workplaces. Falls, and accidents caused by machinery, are the next most important source of accidents. Most severe accidents occur as a result of individuals becoming 'involved' with machinery, while accidents occurring during the handling of goods comprise a major proportion of those accidents causing lesser or shorter periods of disablement. Fires and explosions are also a major source of accidents.

Among the economic implications to the employer deriving from the occurrence of an accident are the following:

(a) working time lost by the employee;
(b) time lost by other employees who choose to or must of necessity stop work at the time of or following the accident;
(c) time lost by supervision, management and technical staff following the accident;
(d) proportion of the cost of employing first aid, medical staff, etc.;
(e) cost of disruption to the operation;
(f) cost of any damage to the equipment or any cost associated with the subsequent modification of the equipment;
(g) cost of any compensation payments or fines resulting from legal action;
(h) costs associated with increased insurance premiums;
(i) reduced output from the injured employee on return to work;
(j) cost of reduced morale, increased absenteeism, increased labour turnover among employees.

This is, of course, only one side of the equation, since the injured person, his or her dependants, colleagues, etc. must also 'pay' some cost as a result of the occurrence of an accident. Certainly it would be socially, morally and probably legally unacceptable to consider accidents only in terms of direct and indirect cost to the employers.

### Preventive action

The prevention of illness and accidents requires efforts on the part of employees and management, the latter including those responsible for the design of the operating system and its staffing. Some of the steps which might be taken to reduce the frequency and severity of accidents are as follows:

(a) developing a safety consciousness among staff and workers and encouraging departmental pride in a good safety record;
(b) developing effective consultative participation between management, workers and unions so that safety and health rules can be accepted and followed;
(c) giving adequate instruction in safety rules and measures as part of the training of new and transferred workers, or where working methods or speeds of operation are changed;
(d) materials handling, a major cause of accidents, to be minimized and designed as far as possible for safe working and operation;
(e) ensuring a satisfactory standard from the safety angle for both basic plant and auxiliary fittings such as guards and other devices;
(f) good maintenance—apart from making sound job repairs, temporary expedients to keep production going should not prejudice safety.

Fire prevention and control represent a further area for preventive action. The main causes of fire in industry and commerce tend to be associated with electrical appliances and installations. Smoking is a major source of fires in business premises. The Fire Protection Association (of the UK) suggest the following guidelines for fire prevention and control:

1. Management should accept that fire prevention policies and practices must be established and reviewed regularly.
2. Management should be aware of the possible effects and consequences of fires in terms of loss of buildings, plant and output, damage to records, effects on customers and workers, etc.
3. Fire risks should be identified, particularly as regards sources of ignition, presence of combustible materials, and the means by which fires can spread.
4. The responsibility for fire prevention should be established.
5. A fire officer should be appointed.
6. A fire prevention drill should be established and practised.

As for other sources of illness and accidents, there are detailed guidelines for fire prevention and checklists for use in assessing the adequacy of existing procedures and in designing new procedures.

## THE WORKER

### Job design and work organization

No longer is the design of work and jobs simply the application of method study and work measurement. There is a need to give considerable thought to the behavioural aspects of work and job design, and this is the focus of this section.

### *The job enlargement and enrichment philosophy (job redesign)*

Throughout the period up to the 1970s there was a continuing trend towards the increasing rationalization of work. The principles of work study developed and first applied by Taylor and Gilbreth were adopted widely and largely unquestioningly, but then it was argued that rationalized work was incapable of fulfilling the basic work needs, i.e. the needs for achievement, recognition and so on, and that as a consequence job satisfaction was minimal. During the 1970s, therefore, a philosophy evolved which advocated the design or redesign of jobs so that workers might use their skills and abilities more, determine their own work pace, make decisions about work methods, quality, etc. The emphasis was on worker self-motivation and job satisfaction *alongside* operational efficiency and productivity.

### *Job redesign and work organization*

The job redesign 'experiments' which were undertaken in effect involved one or both of two basic approaches, i.e. the *enlargement* of work content through the addition of one or more related tasks, and job *enrichment,* involving the increase in the motivational content of jobs through, for example, the addition of different types of tasks or the provision of increased worker involvement and participation. Both approaches are concerned with the content of jobs. A quite different approach involves changing the way in which jobs are organized. The provision of job rotation, i.e. workers moving between jobs in either a self-organized or a scheduled manner, and the provision of some opportunities for workers to organize their own jobs are examples of this approach. We shall describe this approach as work organization. This two-part categorization is summarized in Figure 9.7. It is argued that the opportunity for the satisfaction of higher-order needs is provided through job enrichment but not through the simple enlargement or extension of the existing content of jobs. The difference between job redesign and work organizational changes helps highlight the fact that, although the objective of many changes is the modification of the tasks undertaken by workers, such changes are often dependent on, or perhaps brought about only by, appropriate organizational change. Thus job rotation, an organizational change, may provide for job enlargement, and some degree of worker self-organization may give rise to, or be a necessary prerequisite for, certain types of job enrichment.

Our objective here is to develop a checklist which can be used in the redesign of jobs and in work organizations. For this we must look in more detail at the 'mechanics' of redesign and organizational changes (i.e. the means) and at the objectives (i.e. the ends) of such change.

Table 9.3 identifies most of the desirable job characteristics which have been advocated by authors, i.e. those characteristics which are considered to give rise to job satisfaction and worker motivation. These are further considered below.

Examination of the items listed in Table 9.3 suggests that some characteristics are in

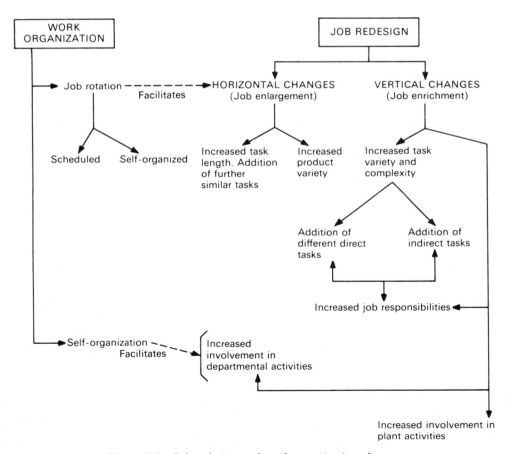

**Figure 9.7**   *Job redesign and work organization changes.*

**Table 9.3** *Desirable characteristics of jobs (for job satisfaction and motivation).*

*Job/Work*
1. Work content
    A  'Closure', i.e. complete module of work
    B  Obvious relationship between tasks
    C  New and more difficult tasks added
    D  Increased variety of tasks
    E  Make use of workers' valued skills and abilities
    F  Include some auxiliary and preparatory tasks
    G  Individual inspects own work
    H  Assembler repairs defective items
    I  Operator sets up machines
    J  Operator responsible for cleanliness of work area
    K  Operator responsible for maintenance
    L  Perceived contribution to product's utility
    M  Work content such that job is meaningful and worthwhile
2. Work method
    A  No machine pacing

*Organization*
3. Work organization
    A  Give worker some choice of method
    B  Worker discretion
    C  Operator plans own work
    D  Operator organizes own work
    E  Self-regulation
    F  Worker responsible for controlling own work
    G  Operator sets own performance goals
    H  Subgoals to measure accomplishment
    I  Individual accountable for own work
    J  Job responsibilities (generally)
    K  Worker autonomy
    L  Operator involved in solving problems
    M  Workers participate in design and improvement of own job
    N  Workers involved in decision-making concerning work
    O  Workers receive performance feedback at regular intervals
4. Job opportunity
    A  More than minimum required training provided
    B  Worker able to learn new things about process
    C  Promotion prospects for worker
    D  Specific or specialized tasks enable worker to develop expertise
    E  Increased challenge for worker
5. Social conditions/relations
    A  Conversation either easy or impossible
    B  Facilitates workers' movement about factory

fact prerequisites for the existence of others, i.e. some must be provided in order that others might exist. In fact by re-organizing these characteristics we can develop a type of 'means' and 'ends' model. The model is summarized in Figure 9.8. This model does not necessarily provide a complete checklist; nor does the information reviewed above yield only to this interpretation. However, the structure is of value in that it helps to distinguish between those aspects of jobs which might be manipulated and those job features which result.

The model suggests that certain types of task and work methods should exist in order that particular task relationships might exist, and so that certain work organization changes can be made. These task relationships, methods of work organization and other opportunities can give rise to work and jobs which have the attributions necessary for the provision of job satisfaction and worker motivation.

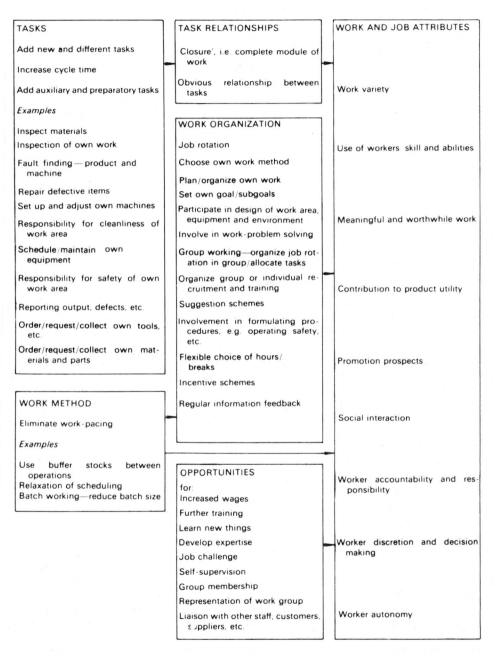

**Figure 9.8**   *Model relating the characteristics and attitudes of work and jobs. (From Wild, R. (1975)*
Work Organization. *New York: Wiley.)*

## EXAMPLE: WORK REORGANIZATION IN CONTRACT CLEANING

| | |
|---|---|
| Organization: | Texas Instruments, USA |
| Jobs: | Factory and office cleaners |
| Original arrangement: | Contract workers do all cleaning |
| Problem: | Poor standard of work of contract cleaners |
| New arrangement | Groups of cleaners established (employed by company) |
| | Groups given specific areas of responsibility |
| | Groups responsible for organizing their own work in each area |
| | Groups plan and control own work schedules |
| | Groups given training in work simplification |
| Results: | Cleanliness improved |
| | 71 personnel used in place of 120 |
| | Turnover of staff substantially reduced |
| | Saving $103 000 p.a. |

## WORKER VARIABILITY AND LEARNING EFFECTS

An implicit assumption in work measurement is that of worker consistency. Certainly, in establishing work times through direct measurement it is normal to average several readings or observations. To some extent this overcomes the problems of worker variability, and of course minimizes the effects of inaccuracies of measurement. However, the objective nevertheless is to obtain a single time estimate or measure. This single figure is then frequently used without recognition of the fact that, in practice, work times will vary around it, and that at best it represents only the mean work time. In virtually all circumstances human manual work times will vary and some account must be taken of this characteristic. For example, where work is undertaken in a series of sequential operations, unless some allowance is made for work time variability at each stage, substantial idle time and/or work congestion will result. Such worker variability will be considered in more detail in Chapter 15 in the discussion of flow system design.

### Learning curves

The concept of learning is complex, so much so that there is as yet little agreement about the true nature of the processes involved. We cannot examine this complex subject here and it will be sufficient for our present purposes to consider learning as the process by which an individual acquires skill and proficiency at a task which, in turn, has the effect of permitting increased productivity in performance of that task. Here we are concerned primarily with the speed at which a task can be executed and thus the duration of that task, the extent to which this speed increases or duration reduces, and the influence of various factors on the learning phenomenon. We are in fact concerned with the phenomenon of the *learning curve* (sometimes called the *improvement curve* or the *progress function*). The learning curve of the type shown in Figure 9.9 reflects three factors:

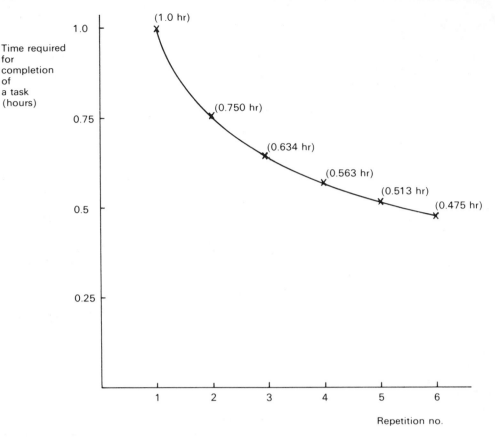

**Figure 9.9**   *75 per cent learning curve.*

1. The time required to complete a task or unit of work will reduce with repeated performance of that task.
2. The rate of reduction will decrease over time.
3. This reduction in time will follow a general pattern.

The learning curve shown in Figure 9.9 represents a 75 per cent rate of improvement. The curve shows a performance improvement resulting from learning equivalent to a constant rate of improvement of 75 per cent, i.e. the first performance of the task requires one hour and thereafter every doubling of the number of performances or number of repetitions shows a 75 per cent improvement. Thus the second performance requires $1 \times 0.75$, i.e. 0.75 hours, the fourth performance requires 0.75 $\times$ 0.75, i.e. 0.56 hours, etc. This performance improvement, shown on arithmetic scales as in Figure 9.9, shows a characteristic asymptotic pattern and is covered by the following formula:

$$\bar{y} = ax^b$$

where $\bar{y}$ = accumulative work hours for any quantity, $x$, of units produced by $x$ repetitions of the task.

$a$ = work hours for first unit, i.e. for first performance of the task
$x$ = number of completed units, i.e. number of repetitions of the task

$b$ = exponent representing the rate of improvement (i.e. the percentage learning rate divided by 100)

Thus the work hours required for a total of ten repetitions of a task where the first performance takes one hour and where a 75 per cent learning effect exists = $1 \times 10^{0.75}$ = 5.59 hours.

---

## EXAMPLES OF LEARNING CURVE CALCULATIONS

1. A worker is to repeat a job 20 times. It is estimated that the first time the job is done it will take 1.5 hours. It is estimated that an 80 per cent learning effect will exist. How long will it take to finish all 20 jobs?
   *Answer.* For 20 units at 80 per cent learning, total time = 1.5 (10.484) = 15.73 hours
2. It is known that the average time for a job over a 'run' of 15 identical jobs is three hours. What is the time required for the first and the last jobs if the learning rate is 75 per cent?
   *Answer.* Total time for 15 units (for an initial time of 1 hour = 7.319

   Average time for 15 units (for an initial time of 1 hour) = $\dfrac{7.319}{15}$ = 0.4879 hours

   Hence:

   Time for first unit $\dfrac{3}{0.4879}$ = 6.149 hours

   Time for last unit  0.325 (6.149) = 1.998 hours

---

### *Factors influencing learning*

Task learning is doubtless influenced by numerous factors. The most important for our purposes are as follows:

1. Task length, i.e. the longer the task, in general the slower the learning, not only in terms of the total time required to reach a particular level of performance, but also in terms of the number of repetitions required to reach that level of performance.
2. Task complexity.
3. The capability or skill of the worker and his or her familiarity with the type of work to be learned.
4. Task similarity, i.e. the extent to which the task being learned is similar to that undertaken previously by the worker.
5. Worker motivation and personal characteristics.
6. External influences, e.g. physical conditions, etc.

In certain circumstances, particularly where work has begun on a particular task, it will be possible to estimate the learning percentage and thus to predict, using the formula above, the time required to complete a task or the performance level at some future date. Thus it will be possible to predict the relatively steady state performance, i.e. the work standard for a particular task. In other circumstances, especially where work has not begun on a particular task, it will be necessary to estimate the learning percentage in order to predict the 'relatively steady state' work standard. Prediction might be undertaken either by comparing the task to be completed with similar work undertaken in similar circumstances or by analysing the nature of the task by comparison with other tasks.

Because of this learning phenomenon it will be unrealistic to assume that a constant time is required for the completion of particular tasks, i.e. that a particular work standard will always apply. Thus in direct time study it will be necessary to take some account of the level of learning accomplishment of the worker in order to 'correct' the work standard based on the observed time. Thus if the worker being observed during direct time study is inexperienced, it must be assumed that a more experienced worker will be able to perform the task in a shorter time. However, if a work standard is being determined for a new job, the learning effect must be allowed. Similarly, in establishing work standards for jobs some account must be taken of the 'life' of such jobs. If a worker is to perform a job for some considerable length of time then it is reasonable to assume that he or she will achieve a level of performance equivalent to the relatively steady state level. If, however, the task is to be performed for a relatively short time it might be assumed that learning will still be taking place when the last cycle is completed. In applying indirect work measurement, e.g. PMTS, an allowance must also be made for the learning effect. In general, PMTS times will provide work standards for fully trained, skilled and accomplished workers, i.e. steady state learned performances. Some allowances must be made in such times to provide for the learning effect during the start-up period.

## Learning effects

It follows from the above that consideration of learning effects, as shown by learning curves, will be of relevance wherever it is necessary to establish a time for a worker to perform a task, and wherever such times are to be used. For example, learning curves, as a means of determining the amount of time required for tasks and/or the amount of capacity available for undertaking work, are of relevance in applications such as the following:

1. In capacity planning. It is suggested in Chapter 11 that capacity will increase over time as increasing familiarity with the task increases labour efficiency.
2. Pricing products and services. If the labour cost component for a product or service is to be costed in terms of the labour hours required to execute the task then the cost will decrease over time. Thus a long 'run' involving greater repetition should result in reduced cost, therefore perhaps reducing price.
3. Scheduling. If the time required for a task is reduced because of the effects of learning, this fact should be taken into account in scheduling repetitive operations. It is possible that, initially at least, increasing repetition of a task will lead to greater efficiency not only in terms of the time required to complete the task but also in the achievement of quality standards, i.e. greater standards of accuracy, etc. This form of learning effect may need to be taken into account in the planning and implementation of quality control procedures. (Notice, however, that equally it might be argued that excessive repetition might lead to a form of 'over-familiarity' and lack of attention, which might result in reduced quality.)

## FURTHER READING

Corlett, E. N. and Richardson, J. (1981) *Stress, Work Design and Productivity*. Chichester: Wiley. Ergonomics and human factors engineering with case examples, etc.
Davis, L. E. and Taylor, J. C. (ed.) (1972) *Design of Jobs*. Harmondsworth: Penguin. A book of readings.
European Foundation for the Improvement of Living and Working Conditions (1981) *The Working Environment and VDUs*. Shankill: Euro Foundation.
Hirschmann, W. B. (1964) Profit from the learning curve, *Harvard Business Review*, February, p. 118.
Mackay, C. (1983) People and VDUs, *Archimedes*, February, pp. 28–30. A good review of the topic.
Osborne, D. (1982) *Ergonomics at work*, Chichester: Wiley. Practical ergonomics.

## QUESTIONS

**9.1** Propose, discuss and compare the principal requirements of displays used for the following purposes:
(a) indicating road speed of car to driver;
(b) indicating domestic oven temperature required (i.e. set) and actual temperatures;
(c) indicating time of day in an airport departure lounge.

**9.2** Propose, discuss and compare the principal requirement of controls used for the following purposes:
(a) setting temperature required for a domestic oven;
(b) emergency 'off' control for metal-cutting lathe;
(c) controls for a hi-fi stereo radio receiver.

**9.3** Outline and justify the ambient conditions required for the following working environments:
(a) an engineering drawing office;
(b) an electronic instrument assembly workshop;
(c) a hospital operating room.

**9.4** How might anthropometric data be used in the design of the following items:
(a) an adult's cycle;
(b) a typist's chair;
(c) the driver's seat and controls of a car?

**9.5** Discuss and compare the nature of the manual jobs likely to be associated with a moving-belt, fixed-item assembly line for small products (see Chapter 15) and a toolroom grinding machine.

**9.6** How might the following jobs be enriched:
(a) copy typist;
(b) bank teller;
(c) a domestic appliance service/repair worker?
Indicate any assumptions about the jobs and their circumstances.

**9.7** What factors might be expected to influence the learning, i.e. the rate of performance improvement, of a worker operating a new piece of office machinery? How might the standard performance for such a task be determined and what factors would influence the procedure employed?

**9.8** (a) An 80 per cent learning effect is known to exist in a situation in which the first performance of a manual task takes 100 hours. What is the average performance time for the task after 32 task repetitions?
(b) how many hours are required for the eighth task performance?
(c) how many repetitions of the task are required before a target performance level of 41 hours is achieved?

# CHAPTER 10

# Organizational Factors in Work System Design

Our focus in this chapter is an 'organizational' one. We shall consider the process of change, in particular technological change within the organization, and the design and operation of the reward or incentive system for work undertaken within the organization. These topics complement those discussed in Chapters 7, 8 and 9, and should be considered alongside them.

## TECHNOLOGICAL CHANGE AND WORK

We have noted in Chapter 9 that because of continuing mechanization and automation of operations, workers' roles are changing. It is appropriate now, having also discussed organization design and technology, to look more closely at the nature and effects of mechanization and automation.

### The nature of mechanization and automation

Automation in one industry may contrast both in level of development and in characteristics with automation elsewhere, but in general the elimination of direct manual involvement in *control activities* is the principal feature of automation. Mechanization may be viewed as an aspect of automation, the latter also being seen as a function of the integration of operations and the use of control systems which are largely independent of manual involvement. It is reasonable, therefore, to view both mechanization and automation as trends rather than states, both being associated with the replacement of human activities by the activities of inanimate objects. The two terms will be used in this manner throughout the remainder of this chapter, i.e. automation will be taken to subsume mechanization.

We can identify four basic components of operations in order to aid examination of the nature and effects of automation:

(a) power technology—sources of energy used;
(b) processing technology—tools and techniques used in operations performed on materials;
(c) materials handling technology—transfer of materials and items between processes;
(d) control—regulation of quality and quantity of output and throughput.

It has been suggested that the substitution of inanimate for human work, i.e. the process of automation, usually occurs in the order: first, processes; second, handling; and third, control. Thus a hierarchy of levels of automation such as that shown in Table 10.1 might be envisaged. In each case level 1 is fully manual work, while levels 2, 3 and 4 are the intermediate steps to the achievement of level 5, where fully automatic work is obtained.

**Table 10.1** *Dimensions of automation.*

*Automation of process* (i.e. assembly, measurement, etc.)

Level 1.  Use of hand and handtool
2.  Use of powered handtool
3.  Use of machine—hand controlled
4.  Use of machine—automatic cycle—hand activated
5.  Use of machine—automatic

*Automation of handling* (i.e. transport, load/unload, location, storage)

Level 1.  Use of hand and handtool
2.  Use of powered handtool
3.  Use of machine—hand controlled
4.  Use of machine—automatic cycle—hand activated
5.  Use of machine—automatic

*Automation of control* (i.e. (a) activation, (b) monitoring, (c) regulation and (d) rectification and maintenance of processes and handling)

Level 1.  Manual (a), (b), (c) and (d)
2.  Product activated or timed with manual (b), (c) and (d)
3.  Automatic (a), (b); manual (c), (d)
4.  Automatic (a), (b), (c); manual (d)
5.  Fully automatic

## The effects of automation

Studies of the effect of automation have typically involved examination of work in process industries. Here, with increasing automation, jobs tend to become more demanding, varied, interesting and challenging for many workers, although in some cases such changes may be of a temporary nature—a result of a 'start-up' situation. Technical know-how tends to become more important and workers may expect increased job content resulting from automation, together with increased demands on skills, knowledge and training. In general, greater job complexity and responsibility, and therefore greater intrinsic rewards, are associated with work in automated systems, but often at the expense of increased worker inactivity.

Often the greater distance between workers in automated systems results in reduced social interaction. However, as full automation is approached, the central grouping of controls gives rise to grouping of workers. Up to a certain level, therefore, automation increases the ratio of working space to people and therefore inhibits social relationships. The relationship of operators and their supervisors is also considered to be affected by automation, the general view being one of increased contact and improved worker/supervisor relations. An increased separation of workers from both operations and their outputs is often found. Increased training needs are often associated with the wider responsibilities of automated jobs, while emphasis on vigilance and monitoring duties, the importance of minimizing process disruption, the consequences of breakdowns, and the comparative inactivity of workers are considered to lead occasionally to increased stress.

The above comments relate mainly to situations approaching full automation, i.e. those in which there is automation of control. The effects of lower levels of automation have received less attention; however, we can conclude tentatively that such developments tend to give rise to:

(a) the increasing isolation of workers and hence a reduction in social interaction;
(b) a reduction in the amount of physical effort required, largely due to reduced handling requirements;
(c) a loss of worker control of work pace and worker independence from the machine cycle;
(d) improved working conditions and increased safety;
(e) increased use of shift working.

The degree to which workers' jobs are affected is one area in which many authors have been at pains to distinguish between the effects of mechanization and automation. For example, it has been suggested that the principal effect of mechanization is to restrict workers' actions, while automation takes over these actions: workers who are 'in-line' with the operating system may have work tasks which have the repetitiveness and tensions of similar, non-mechanized work. It would seem that in many cases mechanization affects jobs adversely by increasing the division of labour, rendering certain skills obsolete, removing control of the work pace and increasing the 'distance' between worker and product. It is generally accepted that both in mechanization beyond a certain stage and in automation, the emphasis on inspection, monitoring and control tasks increases while the amount of direct work activity decreases. High levels of mechanization appear to necessitate the use of greater skills, wider knowledge and the performance of supervisory duties, and thus the effects may differ little from those of automation. However, to achieve this situation the various stages of partial mechanization, characterized by the retention of some manual work in either processing or handling, appear to necessitate a somewhat different role for the worker.

## PAYMENT AND INCENTIVES

### Nature of remuneration

Here we are concerned with the remuneration of work undertaken in an employment context. All such work will be associated with some form of remuneration, the major element of which will be financial. We shall focus on financial rewards, particularly wages. In fact we might identify four classes of financial remuneration as follows:

(a) wages, i.e. payment received by employees on a periodic basis, e.g. weekly or monthly;

(b) bonuses, e.g. lump sum awards, often provided on an annual basis;
(c) benefits, e.g. insurance benefits, pensions, allowances and non-monetary rewards such as the use of company cars;
(d) long-term rewards, i.e. lump sum rewards over a long period of time, typically five years, and/or on termination of contract or on completion of contract employment period.

## The significance of wages

We must distinguish between those factors which encourage an individual to work and those factors influencing satisfaction at work. Financial reward is undoubtedly a major factor in the former, although beyond a certain level and in certain circumstances job satisfaction may be influenced largely by factors other than wage levels and the wage system. Adequate wage levels and an acceptable wage payment system may therefore be seen as a foundation or 'platform' upon which other aspects or remuneration might be built and without which other aspects might not exist.

Needless to say, payment of wages represents a major cost source in many organizations. Not only do companies compete with one another as regards wage levels, but also their competition in the marketplace, being affected by price, is indirectly affected by wages as one factor affecting price and margins. The value added during operations, e.g. the value added to materials, is influenced by wage levels, while the ability to recruit and retain labour and the attitudes and therefore to some extent the behaviour of labour are also influenced by wage levels and the nature of payment systems. In these respects, therefore, the design and administration of wage payment systems are of relevance to the operations manager.

## Wage payment systems and structures

The objectives of any payment system are numerous and might include the following (see Bowey in Further Reading):

(a) to enable the employee to earn a good and reasonable salary or wage;
(b) to pay equitable sums to different individuals, avoiding anomalies;
(c) to be understandable and acceptable to the employees and their seniors;
(d) to reward and encourage high-quality work;
(e) to encourage employees to accept transfers between jobs;
(f) to encourage employees to accept changes in methods of working;
(g) to discourage waste of materials and equipment;
(h) to encourage employees to use their initiative and discretion;
(i) to encourage employees to develop better methods of working;
(j) to reward and encourage high levels of output;
(k) to discourage and lead to a decrease in overtime working.

In general, the design of a wage payment system to meet some or all of the above objectives will require some consideration of (a) pay structure and (b) pay systems.

The development of an adequate pay structure will require some consideration of the pay to be provided and the differentials between various jobs, i.e. the establishment of the 'relative worth' of different jobs in different circumstances. It will, in most cases, be necessary to establish some scale or gradation of jobs based on some objective assessment and to relate jobs measured on this scale to pay rates or

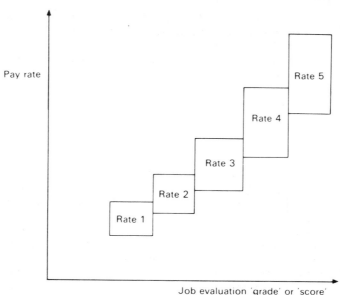

Pay rate

Rate 5

Rate 4

Rate 3

Rate 2

Rate 1

Job evaluation 'grade' or 'score'

**Figure 10.1**   *A pay/job structure.*

levels in the manner shown in Figure 10.1. The establishment of such a scale will often provide some form of career or job structure for employees.

Various schemes are available under the general heading 'job evaluation' for the establishment of such structures; however, it should be remembered that in many cases the establishment of pay levels or pay bands for particular jobs will be a matter of negotiation between employees (often represented by trade unions) and employers. In many cases, of course, there will be national agreements between employers or employers' associations and trade unions. Such agreements will often stipulate pay bands or minimum pay levels for particular jobs and conditions of service, etc.; in supplementing such national agreements there may be certain local negotiating and bargaining machinery to establish pay and wage structures at local or company level.

The design of the wage payment system will require the consideration of questions such as: 'To what extent will the wage be paid through some form of incentive payment system? How might such an incentive payment system operate? How will standards of performance be established and what control system will be introduced to monitor payment levels, earnings, etc.?' In many cases some form of incentive payment system will be employed, although, as we have noted, in recent years there has been a move towards the introduction of non-financial incentives.

The following sections consider in outline both job evaluation and incentive systems.

## Job evaluation

'Job evaluation' is a term used to cover a number of separate and distinct methods of systematically measuring the relative worth of jobs, using yardsticks which are derived from the content of the jobs. A job evaluation scheme will enable new jobs to be placed in a proper relationship with existing jobs by the use of easily explained and acceptable facts and principles. Thus the principal purpose of job evaluation is to rank jobs as a basis for a pay structure. It aims, therefore, to compare all jobs under review using common criteria, to define the relationship of one job to another. It is essentially concerned with establishing relationships and not with absolutes. In comparing jobs it is the job content which is considered, and job evaluation is used primarily for establishing basic pay levels or wage bands.

There are four main methods of job evaluation.

(a) job ranking;
(b) job classification;
(c) points evaluation;
(d) factor comparison.

Points evaluation is by far the most popular system, followed by job classification, job ranking and finally factor comparison. All systems may be applied to jobs at different levels, although the factor comparison system perhaps has more limitations in this respect.

Other techniques have been developed and are in use. For example, the job profile method,[1] the guide chart profile method (the well-known Hay job evaluation method),[2] the time span of discretion method[3] and the decision band method[4] are among those in fairly general use. Brief descriptions of the four schemes listed above are given below. Further detail can be obtained through the sources listed in 'Further Reading'.

## Job ranking

This is perhaps the simplest job evaluation method. Job descriptions are prepared for each job to identify the duties, responsibilities and qualifications necessary for the job. Such descriptions may be developed jointly by management and unions, and should certainly be agreed by both parties. In some cases 'key' jobs are chosen which adequately cover the whole range of jobs and these are compared with one another in order to produce a ranking of jobs. Where few jobs exist it will be possible to develop a ranking for the entire list at the outset. Given this ranking of jobs on the basis of difficulty, importance to the firm, etc., job grades are established through an examination of the relative importance or merit of adjacent jobs on the scale. Thus grade boundaries may be established between jobs in the ranking which are agreed to have substantially different importance or difficulty ratings. Pay levels or ranges are then attached to each job grade. A somewhat more sophisticated approach involves the use of paired comparisons. Again, where many jobs exist, key jobs will be chosen and each pair of jobs compared with one another by a panel of judges. This process will enable a ranking to be established and thereafter the above procedure is followed.

The job ranking method is simple and straightforward. It is relatively cheap to install and is flexible. It does, however, suffer the disadvantage of relying heavily on judgement and having a relatively minor objective or quantitative content. In the use of this job ranking system there is a tendency to rank jobs to reflect current pay levels. Furthermore, the resultant ranking of jobs reflects only their rank order

---

[1] Butterworth, J. 'The job profile method', Chapter 5 in Bowey (1975) (see Further Reading at the end of this chapter).
[2] Younger, W. F. 'The guide chart profile method', Chapter 15 in Bowey (1975) (see Further Reading at the end of this chapter).
[3] Jaques, E. (1961) Time span of discretion method, *Equitable Payment*. London: Heinemann.
[4] Patterson, T. I. (1966) Decision band method, *Management Theory*. London: Business Publications.

importance and does not provide for the quantitative assessment of differences between jobs.

## Job classification

Using this procedure a number of job grades are first determined and then the existing jobs are allocated to these predetermined grades. Each grade will normally have recognizable characteristics, taking account of such features as the skill required in jobs, and their responsibilities. Each grade may be represented by a 'benchmark' job, which, taking account of the majority of factors, is most representative of the job grade. The job descriptions are then prepared for each of the existing jobs or each of the jobs to be allocated to the job structure. These jobs are then allocated to the existing grades through a process of comparison with the job grade descriptions or with the predetermined 'benchmark' jobs. Thus the procedure is much the same as in job ranking except that jobs are allocated against an existing or required job structure. In both cases whole jobs may be treated and in both systems jobs may be evaluated on a variety of factors as agreed or as considered important within the particular circumstances. Skill and responsibilities are usually considered, and job difficulty and job-holder qualifications are also usually of some importance.

## Points evaluation

This, one of the most popular job evaluation schemes, was developed in 1924 in the USA by M.R. Lott. Unlike the above systems, it relies on the identification and comparison of job factors rather than the whole job. Factors are selected, e.g. skill, effort, responsibility and working conditions, which are common to all or most of the jobs within the organization. These *compensatable* factors are defined and a weighting

**Table 10.2**  *Job evaluation by points rating.*

| Elements and factors | Possible points rating |
|---|---|
| *Skill* | *(50)* |
| 1. Education | 10 |
| 2. Experience | 30 |
| 3. Initiative/ingenuity | 10 |
| *Effort* | *(50)* |
| 4. Physical | 30 |
| 5. Mental/visual | 20 |
| *Responsibility* | *(60)* |
| 6. Equipment or process | 15 |
| 7. Material or product | 15 |
| 8. Safety of others | 15 |
| 9. Work of others | 15 |
| *Job conditions* | *(40)* |
| 10. Working conditions | 25 |
| 11. Unavoidable hazards | 15 |
| *(200)* | 200 |

is allocated to each to indicate its relative importance to the organization. Thus for a total points weighting of 200, skill may be allocated 50 points, effort 50 points, responsibility 60 points and job conditions 40 points. Each of these factors is then broken down into sub-factors which are again defined and weighted, the sum of the weightings for each sub-factor being equal to the points weighting given to the main factor. Table 10.2 lists eleven sub-factors as identified in the NEMA (National Electrical Manufacturers Association of the USA) version of the points evaluation scheme. In some cases sub-factors are further broken down and again points allocated to each. Job descriptions are then prepared for each job to be evaluated and jobs are evaluated against the sub-factors, points being allocated to each job for each sub-factor. The total points score for each job then represents the total evaluation or 'merit' of the job. Jobs are then ranked according to the total points score, job grades are established and pay scales or ranges agreed for each job grade as in the above scheme.

Unlike the above systems the points evaluation system provides a semi-objective means of job evaluation. Because of the detail which might be introduced through the identification and definition of sub-factors, the scheme might be employed consistently and agreement may be achieved relatively easily. The use of this scheme provides not only a means of establishing job rankings and a job structure but also a means of quantitatively identifying differentials between jobs and grades.

### *Factor comparison*

This method is an extension of points evaluation and uses five factors:

(a) mental effort required in the job;
(b) skills required for the job;
(c) physical effort required for the job;
(d) responsibility of the job;
(e) job conditions.

A number of key jobs are selected and then a panel of 'experts' determines the proportion of the total wage paid for each constituent factor. Each factor is given a monetary value for the key jobs. This allows a scale to be established for each factor and other jobs can then be compared with them, factor by factor, to yield a ranking of all jobs. Since the initial exercise is carried out in terms of monetary values, interpolation will yield wage rates for all jobs. This method is more complex and difficult to both describe and implement because it uses, in one process, job evaluation and the allocation of monetary values.

### Incentive wage systems

Although the use of incentive payment systems is not a necessary corollary of a work measurement exercise, it is a fact that the installation or use of an incentive payment scheme is one of the usual reasons for work measurement.

It is also a fact that there is a great deal of confused thinking about the merits, design and use of methods of incentive payment. Consequently, while we do not wish to comment directly on the merits of such schemes, it is perhaps worth while to describe some of the more popular schemes.

## 100 per cent participation or one for one schemes

This is one of the simplest and most widely used incentive payment systems. Under this system, increases in production efficiency above a certain level lead to directly proportional increases in wages. In its simplest form, incentive payment is provided for outputs above 100 performance, there being a guaranteed payment of a base rate for performances at 100 or less. In other words, earnings are calculated on a time basis as follows:

$$E = RH + R (S-H)$$

where $E$ = earnings for a given period
$R$ = base pay rate
$H$ = hours worked
$S$ = standard hours allowed for job
= standard hours for each piece $(s) \times$ number of pieces $(N)$

---

EXAMPLE

Base pay rate = 250 pence/hour
Hours worked = 8
Standard minutes (SM)/piece = 20
Output = 30 pieces

$$E = 250(8) + 250 \left[ \left( \frac{20}{60} \times 30 \right) - 8 \right]$$

$$= 2000 + 250(10 - 8)$$
$$= \quad 2000 \quad + \quad 500$$
$$\text{(base pay)} \quad \text{(incentive pay)}$$
$$= 2500 \text{ p (total pay)}$$

---

Normally 100 per cent participation or one for one schemes begin at a level less than 100 performance, i.e. incentive payment is offered to workers who exceed a performance of perhaps 75 or 80. As with the previous scheme, it is usual to guarantee minimum base rate earnings. In this case earnings are calculated as follows:

$$E = RH + R \left( \frac{100S}{X} - H \right)$$

where $X$ = the performance at which participation begins, e.g. 75 or 80.

## Less than 100 per cent participation or geared schemes

A large number of schemes have been developed which differ from those described previously in that they do not offer 100 per cent increases in payment for 100 per cent increases in performance. Such schemes differ mainly in the extent to which workers participate as a result of increased performance. For example, in a 50/50 scheme earnings increase by ½ per cent for every 1 per cent increase in performance beyond 100. The main benefit of such incentive payment schemes is that they provide some measure of safeguard for management in circumstances where allowed times may have been estimated inaccurately. An additional safeguard can, of course, be provided by applying an upper limit to incentive earnings.

The formula for calculating earnings for geared schemes without an upper earnings limit, and starting at a performance level of 100, is as follows:

$$E = RH + YR(S - H)$$

where $Y$ = the extent of the gearing, e.g. 0.5 for a 50/50 plan.

---

## EXAMPLE

Base pay rate $= 250$ pence/hour
Hours worked $= 8$
SM/piece $\quad = 20$
Output $\qquad = 30$ pieces
Gearing $\qquad = 50/50$

$$E = 250(8) + 0.5(250) \left| \frac{20 \times 30}{60} - 8 \right|$$

$$= 2000 + 125(10 - 8)$$

$$= \quad\quad 2000 \quad + \quad\quad 250$$
$$\text{(base pay)} \quad \text{(incentive pay)}$$
$$= 2250 \text{ p (total pay)}$$

---

As before, participation may begin at a level below 100, in which case earnings are calculated by the following formula:

$$E = RH + YR \left( \frac{100S}{X} - H \right)$$

## Piece-work

This is one of the oldest methods of incentive payment, under which workers are paid a fixed amount for each piece produced. In fact the piece-work system is very similar to the 100 per cent participation or one for one system previously described, the principal difference being that in piece-work the standard is described in terms of money and not time. As with the previous systems, it is usual to operate the incentive payment system in conjunction with a guaranteed minimum payment level.

The piece-rate $(P)$ is defined as follows:

$$P = Rs$$

Consequently earnings $(E)$ over a period of time are calculated by means of the following simple equations:

$\quad\quad\quad E = RsN \quad$ (where performance is above 100)
$\quad\quad\quad E = RH \quad\quad$ (where performance is below 100)

EXAMPLE

Base pay rate = 250 pence/hour
Hours worked = 8
SM/piece = 20
Output = 30

Piece-rate = $Rs$

$$= 250 \times \frac{20}{60}$$

$$\text{Performance} = \frac{\text{standard hours produced}}{\text{hours worked}} \times 100$$

$$= \frac{\frac{20}{60} \times 30}{8} \times 100$$

$$= 125$$

$\therefore$ Earnings $(E) = RsN$

$$= 250 \times \frac{20}{60} \times 30$$

$$= 2500 \text{ p}$$

Finally, it should be noted that certain practical complexities must be accommodated during the operation of any incentive payment method. For example, a certain amount of waiting time will be incurred throughout most working periods and, in addition, unmeasured work may be undertaken. It is usual to pay both of these at base rate or at day-work rate and, consequently, care must be taken to include these in the wage calculations.

EXAMPLE

Base pay rate = 250 pence/hour
Total hours worked = 9½
Hours worked on unmeasured work = ½
Waiting hours = 1
SM/piece for measured work = 20
Output of measured work = 30 pieces

Using a 100 per cent participation system above a 100 performance.

$$E = 250(9\tfrac{1}{2}) + 250\left[\left(\frac{20}{60} \times 30\right) - (9\tfrac{1}{2} - 1\tfrac{1}{2})\right]$$

$$= 2375 + 500 \text{ (incentive pay)}$$
$$= 2875 \text{ p (total pay)}$$

## Measured day work

The use of the measured day/work system avoids some of the problems normally encountered in the design and administration of incentive wage systems. It avoids the need for continual measurement of performance and adjustment of wage levels based on such performance, yet it provides a form of incentive wage system. Measured day work offers a fixed rate of pay for a defined standard of performance. Work measurement is used to establish standard times for various jobs and to negotiate the pay rate for such jobs at different levels of performance. Workers are then guaranteed a regular weekly wage if they are able consistently to achieve a given level of performance. Having demonstrated the ability to maintain a level of performance over a minimum period, they are paid an appropriate wage. Subsequent failure to achieve this level of performance results first in some form of discipline or review by management, and subsequently in a reduction to a lower wage level. Measured day work therefore incorporates elements of normal incentive pay with some other benefits of a straight time rate system, in that wage levels do not fluctuate as much as in incentive pay, yet an incentive element remains.

## Premium payment scheme

The approach here is similar to that of measured day work, but the time scale is often extended so that performance reviews take place at long intervals; hence stability is high.

## Multi-factor incentives

Increasingly, incentive payment schemes are based on multiple performance or achievement criteria. In particular such schemes take into account factors other than the output-related or throughput-related criteria used in the schemes described above. At the simplest level, multi-factor schemes will also provide for the reward of quality, attendance and timekeeping achievements. At this level they can readily be applied to individuals, but in general multi-factor schemes are more appropriate for group incentive payment (see below). In these cases, factors such as output (or throughput) quality, resource utilization and customer service criteria can be accommodated. With this approach a high base rate is supplemented by an 'incentive' earning usually calculated on a 'points' basis, points being awarded for a level of achievement on each factor. Factors may carry different weightings to reflect their relative importance in the particular situation, and the total incentive earning may be obtained by adding the weighted points achievements for each factor and converting the total to a money equivalent, to be added to the base pay.

Such schemes offer the following benefits:

1. The incentive has a broad base and can be designed more readily to reflect the organization's needs.
2. Overall performance/achievement is rewarded, and the risk of high achievement on one factor being achieved at the expense of another is reduced.
3. The setting and weighting of factors offer opportunities for the participation of all groups involved.

4. Flexibility can be built into the scheme by allowing for changes in factors weighting.

### Group incentive schemes

The schemes described above are *primarily* applied to individuals. Derivatives of these schemes, in particular measured day work, premium payments and multi-factor schemes, may be applied to small groups of people employed in related tasks in a particular area, but in general other types of schemes, with a distinctive philosophy, are used to provide incentive pay to groups of workers. Many such schemes exist, ranging from the schemes developed for a particular application, e.g. the Scanlon plan, to those based on general principles, which are relevant in a variety of organizations. Such group incentive schemes might be applied to small groups of workers engaged together on a task and working interdependently, to departments, and in some cases to entire organizations. In general the larger the group involved in such incentive pay the greater the problem of designing a scheme which has perceived *relevance* and *immediacy*. In other words, the larger the group and the more 'remote' the criteria for determining the amount of incentive pay, the greater the likelihood that individuals will see the factors which influence their incentive pay as being beyond their direct influence, and the greater the risk that the time lag in providing the incentive pay will limit the development of individuals' motivation. These, therefore, are the principal motivational obstacles of such schemes, but on the other hand such schemes do emphasize the sharing of achievements and productivity gains, and with that the need for team working, and perhaps the development of some greater identification with organizational goals, etc.

Group incentive payment schemes will, in general, emphasize participation in productivity improvement. Such schemes may be based on productivity improvements as measured by reduced labour costs, or increased value added, or other criteria, including many of those outlined in our discussion of performance measurement in Chapter 21. An alternative approach allows the beneficiaries of such schemes to participate in their design through the establishment of some form of representative committee whose task will be to identify objectives associated with productivity/ performance improvement and thus specify the criteria for group incentive reward. Such approaches require considerable employee/management discussion and 'negotiation' during the design process, but have been common replacements for individual, and in particular piece-work, systems in the manufacturing industries, and are especially appropriate in industries where output cannot be measured easily. Thus such schemes are popular in retailing, transport, etc.

Some approaches to group incentive payment are outlined below.

#### Profit-sharing schemes

An index or formula can be negotiated to relate incentive payments to profits (usually pre-tax), normally above a base level. Generally profits are shared between the company and its employees, e.g. a 60:40 share.

Employees' bonus for period = 0.4 (profit earned less base line profit)

The major disadvantage of such schemes, apart from problems of 'immediacy' (see above), is that profits can be affected by factors which are beyond employees' control.

*Sales value schemes*

Such schemes are similar to the above except that increases of sales value over a base line are distributed between employees and the organization. Again there can be the problem of 'immediacy', and of course sales revenue will be influenced by pricing policy decisions, as well as by factors influenced by employees. Such schemes, however, are a popular means of incentive payment in supply organizations, where sales targets are often established and used as a base from which to calculate PBR for sales personnel, etc.

*Added value (AV) schemes*

The use of the AV concept permits changes in performance, particularly labour productivity, to be expressed in terms of value.

AV can be defined as 'the value added to input materials', i.e. the difference between the value of output (e.g. sales) and the costs of the materials used in creating those sales. From this added value must be paid all the other costs incurred in the operation, e.g. wages, administrative costs, capital charges. Hence (see Figure 21.1):

$$AV = \text{Sales revenue } \textit{less} \text{ Total external purchases}$$

$$AV \text{ productivity} = \frac{\text{Added value}}{\text{Labour costs} + \text{Capital charges}}$$

$$= \frac{\text{Added value}}{\text{Internal expense}}$$

The major benefits of using the AV productivity measure as an indication of the overall performance of a unit and a basis for incentive payment include:

1. It clearly demonstrates that increases in wages must be met from increases in the value of outputs, not simply from sales or turnover (which might result from non-profitable activity).
2. Value can be increased in numerous ways, e.g. rationalization of activities (eliminating low-value work), increased capital expenditure, improved resource utilization, modified pricing; thus the AV productivity criterion emphasizes overall effort, not simply output and worker-controlled factors.
3. The comparison of the performance of different units or organizations is easier, since AV (unlike profit measure) is not influenced by depreciation, etc.
4. The measurement of AV productivity requires consideration of the whole organization's activities and therefore demands meaningful participation and negotiation within the organization.

## FURTHER READING

Bowey, A. (ed.) (1975) *Handbook of Salary and Wage Systems*. Epping: Gower. Thirty-two chapters covering most aspects of pay, pay systems and their context.

Husband, T. M. (1976) *Work Analysis and Pay Structure*. New York: McGraw-Hill. The structure and organization of rewards, jobs analysis, job evaluation and pay systems.

*Industrial Engineering*, **14**(11) (1982) Incentive systems—another look. Four articles on pp. 52–80.

# QUESTIONS

**10.1** Refer to Question 8.3. The operator on that job produces 2600 pieces during an eight-hour working shift. He is working on a 10 per cent participation incentive scheme, in which the basic rate is £3 per hour, and in which incentive payment is given for outputs in excess of 75. What are the operator's total gross earnings for the shift?

**10.2** Show how any two of the job evaluation schemes described in this chapter would be used to evaluate:
(a) the job of a supermarket check-out desk operator;
(b) the job of a draughtsman or draughtswoman;
(c) your job.

**10.3** A worker is capable of giving a regular 125 performance over a working week of 40 hours. If she is employed on testing work and if the standard hour (SH) per item tested is 0.75, what would be the gross total pay per week on a base rate of 270 pence per hour under the following systems of payment:
(a) 100 per cent participation with incentive payment for performances over 100;
(b) 100 per cent participation with incentive payment for performances over 75;
(c) 50/50 scheme with incentive payment for performances over 100;
(d) 50/50 scheme with incentive payment for performances over 75?
What piece-rate must be paid to the worker if her gross total weekly earnings under a piece-work system are to equal the largest gross total weekly earnings provided by one of the above incentive schemes?

# PART 5

# THE MANAGEMENT OF CAPACITY

# INTRODUCTION TO PART 5

*In this chapter we deal in some detail with what is perhaps the most difficult, and certainly the most important, problem and decision area for operations management. Unless the capacity of the operating system is managed effectively, the operations manager is unlikely to achieve his or her twin objectives. Good decision-making and effectiveness in other areas are unlikely to compensate for or conceal poor capacity management.*

*This is one of the 'principal' problem areas of operations management as defined in Chapter 1. The nature of the capacity management problem is influenced by the operating system structure, but equally capacity decisions can change the operating system structure. Further, the choice of a strategy for the management of capacity will be influenced by the objectives which the operations manager is to achieve, in particular the relative importance of achieving high resource utilization and high customer service. However, given some freedom of choice, the operations manager may prefer a strategy which protects the operating system from external uncertainties, e.g. in demand or supply.*

# CHAPTER 11

# Capacity Management

In this chapter we shall consider only capacity management, one of the three interrelated 'principal' problem areas of operations management. Activity scheduling will be dealt with in the next chapter, while inventory management will be dealt with in Chapter 17. Both activity scheduling and inventory management decisions may be considered to be subsidiary to capacity management. A particular approach to, or strategy for, the management of capacity will often be implemented largely through scheduling and inventory decisions.

The effective management of capacity is perhaps the most important responsibility of operations management. It is the principal planning responsibility of operations managers. All other operations planning takes place within the framework set by capacity decisions. Initially we shall look at the nature of capacity management, the various strategies for the management of capacity, and their relevance to different situations. Then we shall outline the procedures and methods available for decision-making in this area and relate these to the approaches which might be appropriate in different types of operating system.

## THE CAPACITY MANAGEMENT PROBLEM

The objective of capacity management, i.e. the planning and control of system capacity, is to match the level of operations to the level of demand. It is the uncertainty of demand level which gives rise to this problem, i.e. the expectation of changing demand levels without the possibility of accurate prediction. This uncertainty of demand level may be caused by:

(a) uncertainty about the number of orders to be received; and/or
(b) uncertainty about the amount of resources required for the satisfaction of particular customer orders.

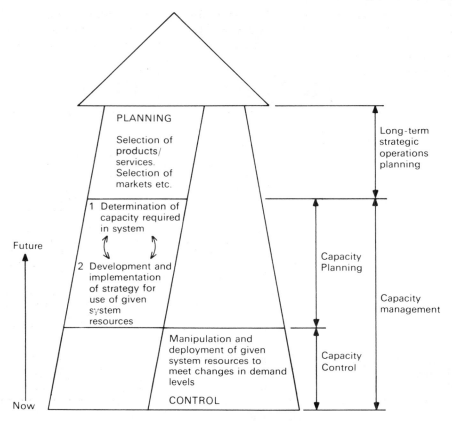

**Figure 11.1**   *The timescale of capacity management.*

Capacity management is a medium- to long-term problem area. Figure 11.1 locates the two elements along such a timescale. Here we are concerned largely with planning decisions. In discussing activity scheduling and inventory management in Chapters 12 and 17 we shall, in effect, be dealing with control decisions.

## CAPACITY PLANNING

The capacity of a system is a reflection of the amount of resources available for the performance of the function. A system has zero capacity unless it has at least some of each type of resource necessary for the performance of its function. If resources are available to satisfy average demand, and if fluctuations about this level can be accommodated, a satisfactory capacity situation exists. In some cases, periods during which demand exceeds average may be offset against periods below average. In others, demand above expectations may be lost unless we maintain capacity in excess of expected requirements as a safeguard. In most cases demand levels lower than expected will give rise to either an under-utilization of capacity and/or a build-up of resources beyond expectations.

While it is convenient to consider capacity planning as occurring in two stages, i.e.

determination of average level and planning for meeting variations about this level, these two aspects are clearly interdependent. The capacity provided may be influenced by the manner in which adjustments may be made. Constraints on adjustment may necessitate provision of 'excess' capacity.

Examples of capacity planning are given in Table 11.1.

**Table 11.1** *Examples of capacity planning problems.*

| Examples of operating systems | Type of capacity planning problem |
|---|---|
| *Manufacture* Builder (of 'one-off' houses to customer order) | Houses are built as, when, how and where required by particular customers. Resources must be obtained for each job but, since each house is different, it will not be possible to predict exactly how many resources are needed. The builder must complete the houses on time and therefore must provide excess resources or be able to subcontract. |
| *Supply* Wholesaler | The wholesale business supplies retailers in an area with goods. They need to provide a good service, but don't want to hold too much stock. They will try to forecast demand, in particular to identify seasonal variations. They will then have to decide how much of each item to stock, and what to do if stocks are insufficient at any time. |
| *Transport* Furniture removal | The furniture remover will want to give a good service, and in particular will not want customers to wait too long. However, it is known that demand will fluctuate. The business doesn't want to have too many spare, unused vans, drivers, etc., so will hope to have enough resources to deal with most demand most of the time. |
| *Service* Fire service | A fire service cannot keep its customers waiting; nor can demand be forecast accurately. It will probably be necessary to have enough capacity (e.g. vehicles, staff, etc.) to deal with most situations, but also to arrange for other facilities to be 'on call', e.g. from other towns. |

## STRATEGIES FOR CAPACITY MANAGEMENT

Faced with fluctuating and uncertain demand levels there are two basic strategies.

### Strategy 1: Provide for efficient adjustment or variation of system capacity

Usually system capacity can be changed within certain limits. Temporarily, more useful capacity might be created by providing more resources and/or providing for their more efficient or intense utilization. Temporary reductions in capacity might be achieved through the transfer of resources to other functions or, of course, the temporary reduction in the resources on hand or the input rate of resources consumed.

Table 11.2 lists some of the means available for the adjustment of system capacity. They are discussed in more detail later in the chapter.

### Strategy 2: Eliminate or reduce the need for adjustments in system capacity

In some cases it may be impossible, undesirable or time-consuming to provide for temporary adjustment in system capacity. In general it will be difficult to provide for

**Table 11.2**   *Means available for capacity adjustment.*

| Resources | Capacity increases | Capacity reductions |
|---|---|---|
| *All* | Subcontract some work | Retrieve some previously subcontracted work |
| | Buy rather than make (manufacture only) | Make rather than buy (manufacture only) |
| *Consumed* *Material* | Reduce material content Substitute more readily available materials | |
| | Increase supply schedules | Reduce supply schedules |
| | Transfer from other jobs | Transfer to other jobs |
| *Fixed* | Scheduling of activities, i.e. speed and load increases | |
| Machines | Scheduling of maintenance, i.e. defer, hire or transfer from other functions | Scheduling of maintenance, i.e. advance Subcontract or transfer to other functions |
| Labour | Hours worked, i.e. overtime, rearrangement of hours, shifts, holidays. | Hours worked i.e. short time, rearrangement of hours, shifts, holidays |
| | Workforce size, i.e. staffing levels, temporary labour transfer from other areas | Workforce size, i.e. layoffs, transfer to other areas |

temporary capacity adjustments in systems which employ large quantities of a large variety of resources without incurring considerable expense and/or delay. Complex process plants which normally work around the clock present little scope for capacity adjustments to meet temporary demand increases, while reductions in demand will often give rise to under-utilization of major resources. Similarly, in systems which use highly specialized resources, such as skilled labour, it may be desirable to avoid the need for temporary capacity adjustments.

In such situations a strategy of minimizing the need for system capacity adjustments will be more appealing. The adoption of such a strategy might involve the provision of excess capacity and therefore the acceptance of perhaps considerable under-utilization of resources, in order to increase the probability of being able to meet high or even maximum demand. Such an approach might be desirable where there is little possibility of providing temporary increases in capacity, and where customer service is of paramount importance. The provision of some excess capacity, yet insufficient to meet maximum demand, necessitates the acceptance that during periods of peak demand either customers will be lost or they must wait or queue until demand levels fall. In practice such an approach is frequently adopted, for in many cases very considerable excess resources must be provided to ensure that peak demand can be satisfied.

In systems where output stock can exist, the provision of inventories of goods is a conventional strategy for the smoothing of demand. Such inventories not only insulate the function from fluctuations in demand levels and thus facilitate the use of relatively stable resource levels and high utilization, but also enable customers to be provided with goods with little delay.

A similar situation exists where customer waiting or queuing is feasible. In such cases, despite a fluctuating demand rate, the rate at which customers are dealt with, i.e. the system capacity, might remain fairly stable.

This strategy for capacity management involves the following approaches, which might be adopted individually or in combination, i.e.

(a)  Maintain 'excess' capacity.

(b) (i) Accept loss of customers; and/or require customer queuing or waiting.
    (ii) Provide output stocks.

Notice that only some approaches permit the accommodation of temporary demand reduction without the risk of reductions in capacity utilization. Notice also that the provision of excess capacity alone is rarely a sufficient basis for accommodating demand fluctuations. In most cases it will be necessary to take some action aimed at reducing or smoothing the effect of fluctuations on the function. The relevance of these means for implementing capacity strategy 2 are outlined in Table 11.3.

**Table 11.3** *Approaches for eliminating or reducing the need for adjustments in system capacity (capacity planning strategy 2).*

| | Relevance | |
|---|---|---|
| Approach | Accommodation of temporary demand increases | Accommodation of temporary demand reductions |
| (a) Maintain 'excess' capacity | Yes | Not directly relevant |
| (b) Accept loss of customers | Yes—in effect some demand ignored | Not directly relevant |
|     Customer queuing or waiting | Yes—queue increases | Yes—queue reduces |
|     Output stocks | Yes—stocks reduce | Yes—stocks increase |

## CAPACITY STRATEGY AND TYPE OF OPERATING SYSTEM

In many cases organizations would prefer to have demand level fluctuations eliminated or reduced. To some extent they may be able to smooth demand by offering inducements or by requiring customers to wait. Failing or following these efforts to reduce the effects of demand level fluctuations, operations managers will seek to accommodate fluctuations by adjusting capacity. However, the opportunities (or indeed the need) to adopt these strategies for capacity planning will be influenced or limited by the structure of the system. We shall consider only those structures in which resource stocks are maintained, since capacity planning as outlined above is needed only where resources are acquired in anticipation of requirements. In these cases capacity planning will aim to deal with uncertainty about the number of orders to be received and perhaps also uncertainty about the resources needed to satisfy the orders received. The feasibility of each strategy for each of the four structures is outlined in Figure 11.2 and discussed below.

Operating systems which provide for output stocks permit accommodation of fluctuations in demand level through the use of physical stocks, which not only protect the function against unexpected changes in demand level, but also permit a relatively stable level of function activity and thus high capacity utilization. The stock levels employed will often reflect the variability of demand and the 'service level' to be provided, i.e. the acceptable level of probability of stock-out situations with the consequent risk of loss of trade or customer waiting. Systems which are unable to operate with output stocks will in most cases have relatively fixed capacity, hence during temporary high-demand periods they will either require customer waiting or suffer loss of trade. Since some excess capacity will normally be provided, capacity utilization will often be low, especially when demand is highly variable.

Transport and service systems do not permit function in anticipation of demand,

| STRATEGY / STRUCTURE | 1. PROVIDE FOR EFFICIENT ADJUSTMENT OF SYSTEM CAPACITY | 2. ELIMINATE OR REDUCE NEED FOR ADJUSTMENT OF SYSTEM CAPACITY | | | |
|---|---|---|---|---|---|
| | | a. Maintain excess capacity | b. Reduce or smooth effect of demand level fluctuations | | |
| | | | (i) Fix upper capacity limit with effect of | | (ii) Use stock to absorb demand fluctuations |
| | | | Loss of trade | Customer queuing/waiting •• | |
| 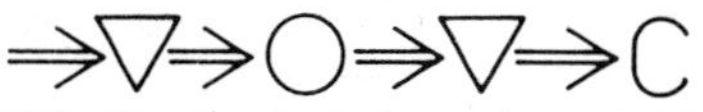 | Feasible and often desirable to supplement strategy 2b(i) | Feasible, but not necessary | Feasible, but not normally necessary | Waiting feasible but not normally necessary | Feasible, and normally adopted |
|  | Feasible and often desirable to supplement strategy 2b(ii) | Feasible, and may be necessary in conjunction with or instead of 2b1 | Feasible and normally adopted | Waiting feasible and normally adopted | Not feasible |
| 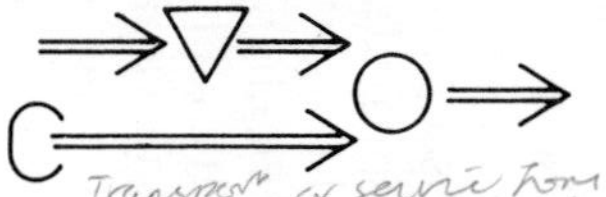 | Feasible and desirable in conjunction with 2a | Feasible and normally adopted | Might be feasible depending on nature of function | Not feasible | Not feasible |
| 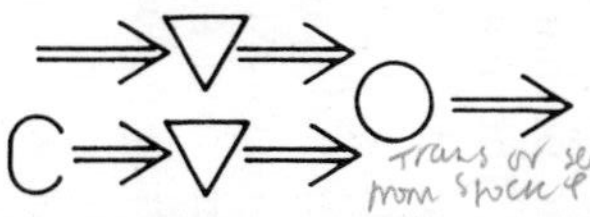 | Feasible and often desirable to supplement strategy 2b(i) | Feasible, but not necessary | Feasible and might be adopted | Queuing feasible and normally adopted | Not feasible |

• Customer push
•• Customer pull

**Figure 11.2** *Capacity planning strategies for systems with resource stocks. From Wild, R. (1977) Concepts for Operations Management. New York: Wiley. Reproduced with permission.*

hence either a relatively fixed capacity will be under-utilized despite efforts to maximize the ability of the system to adjust, or customer queuing will be required. The queue size will depend on relative levels and variabilities of demand and function capacity, and in some cases, through the use of scheduling (e.g. appointment) systems, customer queuing can be planned.

The relative values of strategy 1 (provide for efficient adjustment of system capacity) and strategy 2 (eliminate or reduce the need for adjustment in system capacity) are influenced by operating system structure feasibility. Other factors, however, will influence the choice of strategy. If, for example, there is a limit to the size of output stocks, then although strategy 2b (ii) (see Figure 11.2) is feasible it may not be possible to rely on this means for meeting demand level changes. In most situations it will be desirable to consider providing effective capacity adjustment to meet demand level change, but in most cases effective capacity management will also depend on a preventive strategy, either through the absorption of fluctuation through stock or through customer queuing and waiting. Systems which permit function in anticipation of demand will normally use output stock to protect against demand level fluctuations. Hence the management of the finished goods inventory is of crucial importance. Other systems will normally rely on customer queuing and will, where possible, seek to schedule customer arrivals.

The types of approach which might be employed in managing capacity in these cases are outlined in Table 11.4.

## CAPACITY PLANNING PROCEDURES

Capacity planning has been shown to involve:

(a) the determination of the capacity required in the system;
(b) the development and implementation of the strategy for the use of given system resources to meet demand fluctuations.

This section deals with these two tasks: first, the determination of the capacity required and the factors affecting the choice of capacity, and second, meeting demand level fluctuations.

### Determining the capacity required

The objective in this aspect of capacity planning will be the determination of required capacity through either measurement or estimation of the demand to be placed on the system. Estimation or forecasting of future demand will normally be necessary where resources and/or output are stocked. In other situations, since no output or resources are provided prior to receipt of customer order, demand can be measured, hence estimation is unnecessary and the capacity planning problem is considerably simplified.

When forecasting future demand for capacity planning purposes, fluctuations will be expected but to some extent ignored. For example, where there is no trend in expected demand, a capacity equal to average expected demand might be provided. If, however, a strategy of providing excess capacity is to be adopted a higher capacity may be provided. Where demand is expected to increase or fall, correspondingly increasing or reducing capacity may be provided.

**Table 11.4**  *The nature of capacity: examples.*

| Example | Operating system structure | Capacity planning | | Principal objectives |
|---|---|---|---|---|
| | | Determination of capacity required | Capacity planning strategy (see Tables 11.2 and 11.3) | |
| Builder (of 'one-off' houses) | →O→C | Demand is measured. Capacity is provided to meet each demand. | 1 and/or 2(b)(i) i.e. Provide for capacity adjustment and/or some excess capacity | Maximum customer service (in particular through minimizing completion time) + Maximum utilization of (consumed) resource |
| Fire service | ▷→O↑ ; C→ | Expected demand is forecast. Capacity is provided to meet maximum or near maximum demand. | 2(a) with some possibility of 1. i.e. Eliminate or reduce need for adjustment in system by providing excess capacity with further possibility of providing some capacity adjustment | No customer queuing + High resource productivity |
| Furniture removal | ▷→▷→O↑ ; C→ | Expected demand is forecast. Capacity is provided to meet average or 'sufficient' demand. | 2(b)(i) (with customer queuing and possibly loss of trade), with possibility of 1. i.e. Eliminate or reduce need for adjustment in system capacity by smoothing effect of demand level fluctuations through fixing upper capacity limit and accepting loss of trade with the further possibility of providing some capacity adjustment. | Minimum customer queuing and/or loss of trade + High resource productivity |

*[Handwritten marginal annotations: "manufacture & supply = pull", "pull", "Push. Service", "Transport or service from stock", "pull", "Transport", "Manufacture or supply to customer", "Transport or service from stock or from customer", "Transport from stock and from customer queue"]*

## Demand forecasting

The length of the forecast period will depend largely on the nature of system resources and the nature of the market. Capacity plans may involve periods in excess of five years where there is sufficient stability or predictability of the nature of demand. A long-term view may be essential where there is a long lead time on the provision or replacement of resources. In contrast, a shorter-term view would be appropriate where the nature of demand is less stable or less predictable, and where resources are more readily provided or replaced, or where the manner in which the function is accomplished may change, through for example technological change.

Where the nature of future demand is unknown, future demand cannot be estimated. Here capacity planning is simpler and the future time period is zero. In fact capacity planning as described above does not occur since demand can be measured and appropriate capacity provided. However, in most cases there will remain some uncertainty in determining required capacity, since every customer request will be different. It will therefore be necessary to provide for some capacity level adjustment.

In forecasting demand for goods or services it is appropriate to recognize that in many cases demand is a function of time. The classic life-cycle curve shown in Figure 11.3 illustrates one such relationship. This curve will normally apply in the case of goods or services consumed directly by the public (e.g. domestic appliances, sport and leisure facilities). The time scale will depend on the nature of the product or service. Various mathematical formulae exist for the description of such curves. Exponential functions are often employed to describe the incubation and growth periods. Various policies might be employed for the provision of capacity to satisfy such demand. At one extreme, sufficient capacity to meet all expected demand might be provided from the outset, with attendant benefits of economies of scale in ordering, acquisition, training, etc. Alternatively, capacity might be matched to demand by incremental change over time, with benefits in utilization, etc.

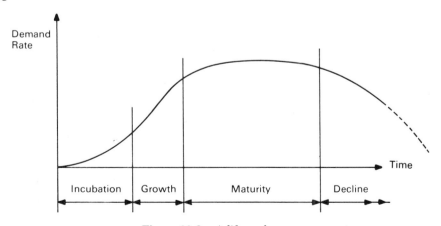

**Figure 11.3** *A life-cycle curve.*

## Aggregation

The term 'aggregate planning' is often employed in the capacity context. The implication is that such planning is concerned with total demand, i.e. all demands collected together. This is of relevance only in multi-channel systems where different goods or services are provided, and in such cases aggregate or capacity planning will seek to estimate or measure all demands and express the total in such a way as to enable sufficient of all resources (or total capacity) to be provided. Demand for all outputs must therefore be expressed in common capacity-related units such as the number of resources or resource hours required. An operating system may, for example, provide three types of service, or service three types of customer. The estimated demand for each source expressed in, for example, hours per unit time (e.g. week) required for each type of resource must be identified and totalled. Given this aggregate demand, a sufficient quantity of each resource can be provided.

### Resource improvement and deterioration

In determining the quantity of resources required to meet either forecast or measured demand, it should be noted that the capability, or capacity, of a given set of resources might also change with time. The reliability of machinery might change and the efficiency of labour might improve, due to the learning effect. It is sufficient for our purposes to consider learning to be the process by means of which an individual or an organization acquires skill and proficiency at a task which in turn permits a higher task performance (e.g. shorter time required for completion). Figure 9.9 shows a typical learning or improvement curve. Clearly the effect of such learning is to increase the capacity of a given quantity of labour resource. Such capacity change effects may be of considerable importance in capacity planning.

### Economic operating levels

Figure 11.4 shows the relationship between the unit cost of processing and the throughput rate for a hypothetical situation. It will be evident from the figure that the economic throughput rate is $p^1$ since this is the rate at which the unit cost is least. The

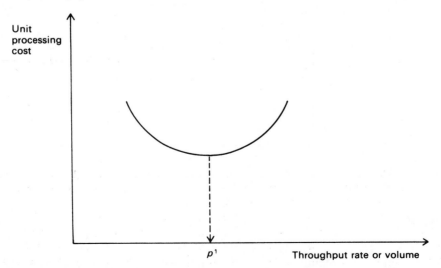

**Figure 11.4** *Unit cost/volume relationship.*

use of a higher throughput rate involves higher unit costs, as does a lower throughput rate. Such a situation will often exist, especially where an operating system has been designed specifically to process items or customers at a particular rate.

If, in an operating system comprising a set of resources which provide the relationship shown in Figure 11.4, it is now considered appropriate to increase the level of resources in order to provide for a greater throughput rate, then it may be possible to shift the entire curve as shown in Figure 11.5. This implies that the facilities have been rearranged or set up in a different manner so that the intended rate is now $p^2$. Again, departures from this throughput rate $p^2$ can incur increased unit costs.

This concept of an 'economic operating level' is relevant in many situations and is of value in capacity planning since, where curves such as those shown in Figures 11.4 and 11.5 are available or can be approximated, the cost of changing capacity through the adoption of capacity planning strategy 1 can be established for different magnitudes of change.

Notice that in some situations the cost/throughput rate relationship is not a 'smooth' one. For example, in some situations a throughput rate can be increased only incrementally. However, whatever the nature of the relationship, providing it is known or can be approximated, the economic level of operations can be found and the cost of capacity changes above or below a particular level can be obtained.

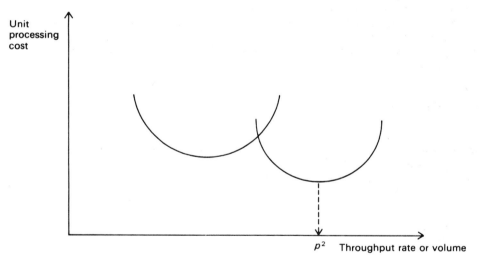

**Figure 11.5** *Unit cost/volume relationships.*

## Cumulation

The capacity provided to satisfy estimated or measured demand will, as mentioned above, be influenced by the strategy employed for meeting demand fluctuations. The use of *cumulative curves* is a method of examining alternatives.

Table 11.5 gives the estimated monthly demand for a one-year period. The figures are plotted cumulatively in Figure 11.6, which also shows two possible cumulative capacity curves. Curve 1 corresponds to a capacity of 37.5 resource hours per day—the minimum required to ensure that capacity is always equal to or in excess of expected demand for this period. The adoption of a strategy of providing sufficient

**Table 11.5** *Estimated monthly demand.*

| Month | Working days | Cumulative days | Estimated demand (in resource hours) | Cumulative estimated demand |
|---|---|---|---|---|
| Jan. | 20 | 20 | 500 | 500 |
| Feb. | 18 | 38 | 650 | 1150 |
| Mar. | 22 | 60 | 750 | 1900 |
| Apr. | 18 | 78 | 900 | 2800 |
| May | 21 | 99 | 700 | 3500 |
| June | 20 | 119 | 500 | 4000 |
| July | 20 | 139 | 300 | 4300 |
| Aug. | 10 | 149 | 300 | 4600 |
| Sept. | 20 | 169 | 450 | 5050 |
| Oct. | 21 | 190 | 500 | 5550 |
| Nov. | 20 | 210 | 550 | 6100 |
| Dec. | 18 | 228 | 300 | 6300 |

excess capacity to eliminate the need for capacity adjustment (strategy 2(a), Figure 11.2) would lead to the provision of such capacity. The provision of approximately 30 resource hours per day—curve 2—might result from the adoption of a different strategy for the use of resources (strategy 2(b), Figure 11.2). Such an arrangement would give rise to either increasing output stock or reducing customer waiting time during the period up to day 50 and after day 160, when capacity exceeds demand. Day 50 to day 160 would see:

(a)  stock diminishing or depleted, and/or
(b)  increased customer waiting time, and/or
(c)  loss of trade,

since capacity would be lower than expected demand.
    Both curves 1 and 2 require no capacity adjustment during this period. The

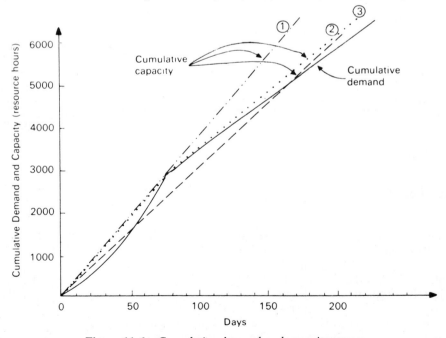

**Figure 11.6** *Cumulative demand and capacity curves.*

adoption of an approach relying wholly upon or involving the strategy of providing for efficient adjustment in capacity (strategy 1, Figure 11.2) might give rise to the provision of capacity in the manner of curve 3, in which one capacity adjustment is made (at day 75) and which provides for the satisfaction of all forecast demand without the use of output stocks, customer queuing or loss of trade, yet with better capacity utilization than curve 1.

In practice the use of cumulative graphs in planning must take into account the lead time normally required between the use of capacity or resources and the satisfaction of customers. For example, the expected customer demand in April equivalent to 900 resource hours (Table 11.5) would necessitate the provision of appropriate capacity at an earlier period. Hence the capacity curves in Figure 11.6 should in fact be displaced forward by the amount of this lead time.

## Meeting demand-level fluctuations

In this section we shall examine the means by which capacity management strategies might be implemented and the factors which will influence their relative merit and cost.

### *Adjustment of capacity*

Some aspects and implications of the strategy of adjusting system capacity are considered below.

#### *Make or buy/subcontract*

An organization may find another willing to take some of the excess demand. This will often involve a higher cost per unit processed because of subcontractor overheads and profit and increased cost of inspection, administration, transport, etc. Such an approach is least reliable, most expensive and least flexible when it is needed most, since a need for greater capacity is often associated with a general increase in total 'industry' demand. At such time, potential subcontractors will also be busy.

#### *Workforce and hours changes*

Not all system outputs will necessarily be subject to high demand simultaneously. If labour can move from one function/system to another and machinery is also flexible, high demand for one output may be offset by low demand elsewhere. Again this approach may be least reliable when most needed, for the reasons given above. The additional costs incurred derive from the time and effort invested in multi-job training and lower performance during learning periods.

Changes in labour force and working hours are the normal means of adjusting system capacity. The most used method for increasing labour capacity is overtime working. Overtime and shift premiums are added costs, and productivity may be lower, supervision and service costs higher, etc. Long hours may also lead to more accidents, illness and greater absenteeism. Where layoffs are undesirable, overtime working is preferable to adding temporary workers. Adding workers to the payroll increases the costs of recruitment and training. Employment often can be reduced without formal layoffs. Normal labour turnover may help reduce labour capacity. Again this approach may be unavailable when most required. An alternative to layoffs is shorter work weeks or idle time. The latter requires the company to carry the cost of underutilized capacity.

### Deferred maintenance

In periods of temporary high demand it is possible to keep resources operating longer by not closing down as scheduled. Demand reductions will permit shutdowns earlier than originally scheduled. The costs involved in such an approach may derive from the difficulties of scheduling the use of maintenance facilities, earlier breakdowns, etc.

### Activity scheduling

The selection of the appropriate activity schedules, including if possible the scheduling of customer arrivals, can contribute considerably to the ability of the system to meet demand fluctuations. Such changes, which will not affect capacity substantially, are relevant only for capacity increase. Costs incurred derive from the increased complexity of scheduling and control, perhaps to some extent offset by higher capacity utilization.

## Avoidance or reduction of need for capacity adjustment

Some aspects and implications of this strategy are examined below.

### Refusing business, reducing service and adjusting backlogs

An organization may decline an order when its capacity is fully utilized. If capacity is short throughout an industry the organization may be able to lengthen its deliveries, and therefore its customer queues, without loss of trade. In such cases the customer's order may simply be added to the backlog of work. In the opposite situation reduction of the backlog is desirable. Given customer queuing during periods of high demand, greater flexibility may exist in selecting orders to fill in the gaps in activity schedules. This may give better capacity utilization but poorer customer service, which may be tolerated if competitors offer similar delivery at a comparable price.

### Adjustments in inventory levels

An output stock permits the utilization of capacity during low demand periods and relieves the congestion, helps avoid queuing, etc., during peak loads. In some cases partly completed output may be stocked, and finished on receipt of order. Customer service might be improved and this may bring an increased share of the demand, greater workloads and further capacity problems. The costs of inventory are related primarily to the opportunity costs of the capital invested and the risks of obsolescence.

*Changing price levels*

To maintain operations, prices can be manipulated, especially on goods and services where individual price quotations are offered subject to negotiation. When demand is high, prices can be increased to increase total contribution; and in low demand periods, prices can be lowered towards variable costs to help reduce the fall in demand placed on the system.

## FURTHER READING

Wild, R. (1977) *Concepts for Operations Management.* New York: Wiley. Chapter 7 discusses the nature of capacity management, while Chapter 10 outlines procedures and techniques in the manner covered in this chapter.
Eilon, S. (1973) The production smoothing problem. *Production Engineer*, **52**, pp. 123–129.

## QUESTIONS

**11.1** What are the two basic capacity management strategies? Describe, with examples, the use of each, and their use together.

**11.2** Identify and discuss the relevance of the various approaches available for the adjustment of capacity. Indicate what factors or considerations might encourage or prevent the use of each.

**11.3** What is aggregate planning? Show, using your own figures, how the cumulative graph method might be used to compare alternative capacity plans for a future one-year period given the forecast demand for the three products produced by a company.

**11.4** How might the learning effect, i.e. the improvement of human performance with the repeated performance of a task, be taken into account in planning future capacity requirements? In what situations might such a procedure be necessary?

# OPERATIONS SCHEDULING

# INTRODUCTION TO PART 6

*Here we deal with the scheduling of the conversion activities of the operating system. We try first to identify types of scheduling problems which can be encountered in different types of operating systems, and then consider some techniques for their solution. The techniques and the types of problems which are of particular importance are dealt with in depth in Chapters 13, 14 and 15.*

*The scheduling of the activities within the operating system is another principal problem area of operations management, as defined in Chapter 1. The nature of the activity scheduling problem will be influenced by the operating system structure, but equally, activity scheduling decisions can change the operating system structure. Further, the objectives being pursued by the operations manager, in particular the relative importance of resource utilization and customer service, will influence the selection of an activity scheduling strategy but, given some freedom of choice, the operations manager may prefer to employ an approach which insulates the operating system from external uncertainties, e.g. demand changes.*

# CHAPTER 12

# Activity Scheduling

Activity scheduling is concerned with the activities which take place *within* the operating system. An activity schedule will show the times (or dates) at which all of these activities are to be undertaken. The fixing of such times determines the manner in which items will flow through the operating system. The activity scheduling problem (sometimes called activity planning) is concerned with the fixing of these times in advance. The manner in which the problem is tackled will depend largely on the situation in which activity scheduling is undertaken. For example, if an operating system is working in anticipation of demand, the scheduling problems will differ from those in an operating system which is working specifically to satisfy individual customers' 'due date' requirements. Other factors will influence the nature of the activity scheduling problem and therefore the techniques which might be appropriate for the solution of that problem. In order better to understand the nature of the activity scheduling problem we shall first consider two factors:

(a) whether scheduling is to be 'internally' or 'externally' oriented;
(b) whether demand is 'dependent' or 'independent'.


## FACTORS INFLUENCING THE ACTIVITY SCHEDULING PROBLEM

### Internally or externally oriented scheduling

Consider as an example a situation in which products are manufactured against a specific customer order. Each customer order specifies exactly what is to be produced and when it is required—the 'due date'. Here the internal activities which create end products (e.g. the manufacture of components and sub-assemblies) must all be scheduled so that each end product is available on the required 'due' or delivery date.

A similar situation can exist in non-manufacturing organizations. Here those activities which are necessary to satisfy a particular service or transport requirement must be performed in time to satisfy a particular customer's request. In all such cases the customer has a *direct* influence on the timing of activities within the operating system, so activity scheduling can be seen to be *externally* oriented in that the timing of all activities are fixed to satisfy *particular* external customer timing requirements.

In contrast, consider a situation in which items are manufactured for stock in anticipation of future customer orders. Here there need be no *direct* influence from a particular customer on the internal activity schedule. Customers are satisfied from stock and the need to replenish this stock gives rise to the need to schedule activities within the operating system. A similar situation can exist in service and transport systems, where a system is 'buffered' from its customers by an input queue. In these circumstances the activity scheduling can be mainly *internally oriented*, and in such cases there can be more freedom in activity scheduling, so schedules can be fixed more easily to maximize resource utilization, etc.

Thus the nature of the activity scheduling problem can in part be defined by the *orientation* of scheduling.

---

### EXAMPLE: ACTIVITY SCHEDULING FOR A 'BESPOKE' TAILOR

In this case an externally oriented activity scheduling strategy will be employed. The customers will influence the entire system directly, excluding input resource stocks. Customer orders, together with their required, quoted and/or agreed delivery dates, will be fed directly into the activity scheduling function along with necessary information on the work content, method of manufacture and resource requirements. A reverse scheduling procedure will normally be applied, all separate operations being scheduled to commence so that, given available capacity limits, the garment will be completed on or before the required due date. For simple garments this reverse scheduling procedure might involve one operation only (i.e. 'manufacture garment'), the normal throughput time for manufacture of such a garment being known with some accuracy. For more complicated garments, especially those requiring several different operations using different resources, the reverse scheduling procedure may recognize several separate operations, each with known or estimated throughput time and each scheduled to be performed sequentially or, in some cases, concurrently (e.g. concurrent manufacture of the pieces of a suit).

Materials will be withdrawn from input inventories according to the specified manufacturing schedule. Inventories of consumable items will therefore be depleted; this in turn will lead to the placing of replenishment orders.

The principal objective of activity scheduling in this case will be the provision of high due date performance, that is, the provision of a high proportion of goods on or before due date or the minimization of lateness, for example average lateness of jobs or the percentage of late jobs. A simultaneous objective will be the achievement of adequate resource utilization.

---

### Dependent or independent demand

Another way of describing the activity scheduling situation is to consider the relationship between demand for the outputs of the operating system (i.e. the products or services) and the need to perform the various activities which take place within the operating system. Consider as an example the manufacture of a complex product consisting of several components, parts, sub-assemblies, etc.

If in this case we know the parts and components which are required to produce a particular end product, and if we know the demand for that product, then we can, for a particular period of time, calculate exactly what activities must be performed within the system to satisfy that demand. Thus there is a completely *dependent* relationship between demand, which is known, and the activities required within the operating system. A similar situation can exist in the non-manufacturing organization where the satisfaction of a particular customer requirement, e.g. a service or transport, requires the performance of particular activities within the system and where demand for that service is known and hence the particular activities which must be performed can be calculated and known with certainty.

Thus we can describe a *dependent activity demand situation* as one in which a knowledge of customer demand in terms of both *what* is required and *when* it is required permits us to calculate what activities must be performed within the operating system in a particular period of time. Notice that in most cases we shall be concerned with a particular scheduling period, i.e. the need to schedule particular activities to be performed within a particular period, e.g. a month. This will often correspond to the planning period, or the period for which demand is forecast.

It will be appreciated that, in many respects, the scheduling of activities in a dependent activity demand situation is relatively straightforward, since there are few uncertainties. All that is required is that a known amount of work is scheduled to take place so that known customer requirements are satisfied by particular times or dates. In addition to this objective it will, of course, be appropriate to try to schedule these activities to take place, within these constraints, in such a manner that resource utilization is maximized.

In contrast, an *independent activity demand situation* can be said to exist where it is impossible to calculate exactly what activities are required within the operating system in a particular period of time. Such a situation can exist *either* where there is not enough knowledge about demand, i.e. customers' orders are not known in advance or there is a good deal of uncertainty about future customer orders, *or* where there is no clear relationship between the nature of the product, service, transport, etc., required by the customer and the nature of the activities which must be performed by the operating system to satisfy that customer requirement. In an independent activity demand situation, therefore, the activity scheduling problem is more complex since there are more uncertainties. In this type of situation it will often be necessary to estimate or forecast in some way the amount of activities required to satisfy some future, as yet unknown, demand, and then to schedule those activities to take place so that the end products are available at what is expected to be the right time, or so that the service or transport is available when customers arrive.

## TYPES OF ACTIVITY SCHEDULING PROBLEM

The distinction between the internal and external orientation of scheduling, and that between dependent and independent activity demand, are relevant in identifying different types of activity scheduling situations. These two factors are *interrelated* and normally those responsible for the scheduling of activities will find themselves dealing with a situation in which there is either dependent activity demand and externally oriented scheduling or, in total contrast, independent activity demand and internally oriented activity scheduling. These are the two normal and distinctive activity scheduling situations but a third situation is possible, as outlined in Table 12.1. The two normal situations are described in more detail below.

### Externally oriented activity scheduling with dependent activity demand

The nature of the customers' demand on the system is known, whether for products, services or transport. The customers have been identified and their requirements determined in terms of both the nature of the things required and the time when those things are required. There is a known relationship between the nature of products or

**Table 12.1** *Activity scheduling situations.*

|  | Externally oriented activity scheduling | Internally oriented activity scheduling |
|---|---|---|
| Dependent activity demand | 1<br>*Situation*<br>Customer demand known in terms of what is required, quantities and due dates. Hence the activities required to satisfy this demand can be calculated.<br><br>*Activity scheduling problems*<br>Determine when known activities must be done to satisfy given customer due dates while also satisfying internal requirements.<br>*Appropriate techniques*<br>MRP (Chapter 12). 'Reverse' network analysis (i.e. with scheduled project completion dates) (Chapter 13). Line of balance (Chapter 14). Reverse scheduling (Chapter 12) for production and supply. Forward scheduling (Chapter 12) for service and transport. | 3<br>*Situation*<br>Customer demand known in terms of what is required, quantities and due dates, but due dates not taken into account *or* demand stated only in terms of what is required and the quantities (i.e. no due date requirement). The activities which are needed can be calculated.<br><br>*Activity scheduling problems*<br>Determine when known activities must be done to satisfy internal requirements.<br><br><br>*Appropriate techniques*<br>Forward network analysis (i.e. without scheduled project completion dates) (Chapter 12). Sequencing (Chapter 12). Batch scheduling (Chapter 14). Dispatching (Chapter 12). Assignment (Chapter 12). Forward scheduling for production and supply (Chapter 12). Flow scheduling (Chapter 15). Timetabling (Chapter 12). |
| Independent activity demand | 4<br><br><br><br>Does not normally exist | 2<br>*Situation*<br>Activities to be completed in a given time period must be *estimated*.<br>*Activity scheduling problems*<br>Determine when activities must be done to satisfy the estimated overall requirements for the period while satisfying internal requirements.<br>*Appropriate techniques*<br>Forward network analysis (i.e. without scheduled project completion dates) (Chapter 12). Sequencing (Chapter 12). Dispatching (Chapter 12). Assignment (Chapter 12). Forward scheduling for production and supply (Chapter 12). Batch scheduling (Chapter 14). Flow scheduling (Chapter 15). Timetabling (Chapter 12). |

services provided by the organization and the types of activities which must be performed within the organization so that these outputs are available. Thus given the knowledge of demand and given this relationship, the activities required by the operating system and the dates by which these activities must be completed can be calculated. Here the activity scheduling problem is that of determining when to do given activities such as to satisfy given customer due date requirements, while also satisfying certain internal requirements, e.g. capacity requirements.

Appropriate scheduling techniques for this type of activity scheduling situation will include:

1. Materials requirements planning (see this chapter).
2. Network analysis using scheduled project completion dates (see Chapter 13).
3. Line of balance (see Chapter 14).
4. Reverse or forward scheduling (see this chapter).

## Internally oriented activity scheduling with independent activity demand

Here we have little information about customer demand. It is not possible to calculate actual activity requirements, so the nature and quantity of the activities which must be performed within the operating system will be obtained by direct forecasting of activity requirements. The activity scheduling problem in this situation therefore involves the timing of an estimated activity requirement in order to satisfy a period's estimated needs while also satisfying internal, e.g. capacity, requirements. In this situation there are no known customers and no definite due dates.

Appropriate techniques for use in this type of situation might include:

1. Network analysis without the use of schedule end dates (see Chapter 13).
2. Sequencing (see this chapter).
3. Dispatching (see this chapter).
4. Assignment (see this chapter).
5. Forward scheduling (see this chapter).
6. Batch scheduling (see Chapter 14).
7. Flow scheduling (see Chapter 15).
8. Timetabling (see this chapter).

## NATURE OF OPERATIONS, AND ACTIVITY SCHEDULING TECHNIQUES

The discussion above has identified which types of scheduling techniques might be appropriate in different activity scheduling situations. A third factor will influence which type of technique is employed in a particular situation: this factor is concerned with the nature of the process involved within the operating system. Let us take as an example a system in which the operating system provides services to satisfy different customer requirements. No two customers ever come to the system with precisely the same requirements, so the operating system must respond to quite different customer needs. This is a form of 'one-off' situation. A similar situation can exist in the manufacturing industry where items are to be manufactured against specific customer orders and where such orders are never repeated. In the manufacturing context this will be referred to as project production.

In contrast, there are manufacturing systems which produce one type of item only to satisfy the needs of a particular set of customers; this might be a form of repetitive production. A similar situation can exist in service or transport industries where an operating system exists solely to provide one particular service or transport for customers who require or are prepared to accept that service or transport. There are also intermediate situations in which jobbing or batch processes are employed.

The type of scheduling technique used in a particular situation will depend on the factors outlined in Figure 12.1, and in addition on whether the activities are to be scheduled in a project, jobbing, batch or repetitive manner. This distinction is rather simplistic, since there are areas of overlap between the four categories; however, it is sufficient for our present purposes. Table 12.2 lists the activity scheduling techniques previously introduced in Table 12.1. Each technique is described briefly and some indication is given of where the technique will be appropriate for project and/or jobbing and/or batch and/or repetitive processes.

Reference to Tables 12.1 and 12.2 will indicate which scheduling technique might be appropriate for a given situation.

## MATERIALS REQUIREMENTS PLANNING (MRP)
### *(see also Chapter 16)*

The principal applications of MRP are in manufacture, particularly batch manufacture. In this context it has some similarities with the line of balance technique (see Chapter 14). There are also similarities with group technology (see Chapter 14) and the reverse scheduling methods (see this chapter). MRP is, however, in principle, of relevance in other situations, both in manufacture and in service operations. Where an MRP approach is appropriate it will often provide the framework within which all scheduling and also inventory decisions are made.

### The principles of MRP

Materials requirements planning is concerned primarily with the scheduling of activities and the management of inventories. It is particularly useful where there is a need to produce components, items or sub-assemblies which themselves are later used in the production of a final product or, in non-manufacturing organizations, where the provision of a transport or service for a customer necessitates the use or provision of certain sub-systems. For example it may be used when a customer orders a motor vehicle from a manufacturing organization, which must first manufacture or obtain various components which are then used in the final assembly of that vehicle for that customer. Similarly, in treating a patient in a hospital, e.g. for a major operation, the hospital must, in order to satisfy this service requirement, provide accommodation for the patient, diagnostic tests, anaesthetics and post-care facilities as well as surgical facilities so that the patient's total requirements are satisfied. In these two cases the product or service requested by the customer can be seen to be the 'final' output of the system, which derives from certain lower-level provisions. These lower-level provisions are considered to be *dependent* on the customer's final requirement. Given a measure or forecast of the total number of customers requiring the final provision of the system, the demand at lower levels can be obtained. The materials requirement planning technique is used for precisely this purpose, i.e. to break down or explode the final customer requirements into their component parts and then, taking into

**Table 12.2**  *Activity scheduling techniques for project, jobbing, batch and flow systems.*

| Scheduling technique | Brief description | Project | Jobbing | Batch | Flow | See Chapter: |
|---|---|---|---|---|---|---|
| A  Material requirements planning (MRP) | A technique by which known customer demand requirements are 'exploded' to produce 'gross' parts, components or activity requirements. These 'gross' requirements are compared with available inventories to produce 'net' requirements which are then scheduled within available capacity limitations. MRP is for scheduling and also for inventory management and capacity management. | ? | ? | √ | | 12 |
| B  Reverse scheduling (Gantt charts) | A technique by which the durations of particular activities are subtracted from a required completion date, i.e. the schedules for all the activities required for the satisfaction of some particular customer requirement are determined by scheduling in reverse from the required due date. | √ | √ | √ | | 12 |
| C  Forward scheduling (Gantt charts) | The opposite of reverse scheduling, where the scheduled times for a particular set of activities are determined by forward scheduling from a given date in order ultimately to obtain a date for completion of a particular set of activities or project. | √ | √ | √ | | 12 |
| D  Sequencing | The determination of the best order for processing a known set of jobs through a given set of facilities in order to, for example, minimize total throughput time, minimize queuing, minimize facility idle time, etc. | | √ | ? | | 12 |
| E  Dispatching | A technique by which it is possible to identify which of an available set of jobs to process next on an available facility in order to minimize, over a period of time, throughput times, lateness, etc. | | √ | ? | | 12 |
| F  Assignment | A technique by which it is possible to assign or allocate an available set of jobs against an available set of resources (where each job may be undertaken on more than one resource), in order to minimize throughput time, maximize resource utilization, etc. | ? | √ | ? | | 12 |

**Table 12.2**   *(cont)*

| Scheduling technique | Brief description | Project | Jobbing | Batch | Flow | See Chapter: |
|---|---|---|---|---|---|---|
| G   Timetabling | Techniques resulting in the development of a schedule, timetable or rota indicating when certain facilities or resources will be available to those wishing to use them. | | | | ✓ | 12 |
| H   Network analysis (or critical path analysis) | A technique by which the various interrelated and interdependent activities required in the completion of a complex project can be scheduled, with any slack or free time being identified. The technique can be used in scheduling activities from a start date (forward NA) or by working backwards from a required completion date (backward NA). | ✓ | ? | ? | | 13 |
| I   Batch scheduling | A technique involving the determination of optimum batch sizes and a schedule for the completion of such batches on a set of facilities. The batch sizes are determined by comparing set-up (or change) costs with holding or inventory costs. The schedule is determined by reference to these batch sizes. The technique is concerned with both scheduling and inventory management. | | | ✓ | ? | 14 |
| J   Line of balance (LOB) | A technique which permits the calculation of the quantities of the particular activities or parts and components which must have been completed by a particular intermediate date, in order that some final delivery schedule might be satisfied. It is therefore a scheduling and a control technique. | | | ✓ | | 14 |
| K   Flow scheduling | A technique for establishing appropriate facilities for the processing of items and customers where each item or customer passes through the same facilities in the same order. The technique is concerned primarily with meeting certain output requirements in terms of cycle time and balancing the use of the resources within the system. | | | ? | ✓ | 15 |

account available capacity, existing inventories, etc., to schedule the provision of these component parts so that the customer's final requirement is satisfied on time. The materials requirement planning procedure therefore takes as one of its inputs the measured or forecast demand for the system's outputs. It breaks down this demand into its component parts, compares this requirement against existing inventories, and seeks to schedule the parts required against available capacity. The MRP procedure produces a schedule for all component parts, if necessary through to purchasing requirements, and where appropriate shows expected shortages due to capacity limitations. The basic procedure is illustrated in Figure 12.1. The procedure will be undertaken on a repetitive basis, the 'explosion' and scheduling procedure being repeated at regular intervals perhaps corresponding to the intervals at which demand forecasting is undertaken or as and when required as a result of changes in known demand. The use of this procedure involves considerable data processing, even for relatively simple outputs. The popularity of the MRP technique and its extensive use have resulted largely from the availability of cheap computing power within organizations.

## The use of MRP

The manner in which MRP operates will be described by reference to a manufacturing situation. The principal *inputs* to the MRP process are as follows:

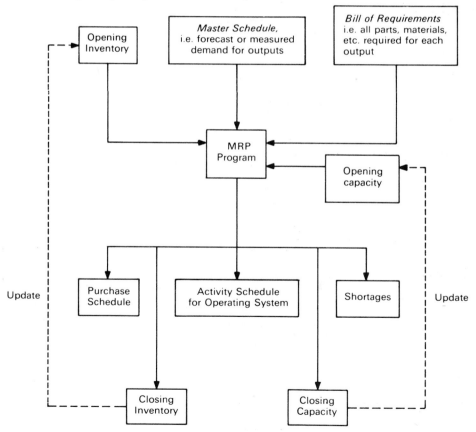

**Figure 12.1** *Basic MRP procedure.*

1. The *bill of requirements*. This, in effect, identifies the component parts of a final output product. (The terms 'bill of materials' or 'product structure record' might be employed.) At each 'level' the different components, materials or sub-assemblies are shown, thus the bill of requirements shows not only the total number of sub-parts but also the manner in which these parts eventually come together to constitute the final product. The lead time between levels is also shown. The arrangement is shown diagrammatically in Figure 12.2. There are several different methods of structuring the bill of requirements data. The most appropriate structure will depend on the nature of the application and on computing requirements, e.g. file structures. In general, however, the final product level will be referred to as level zero. Below this, at level 1, are the principal sub-assemblies, etc., which together make up the final product. At level 2 are the components, etc., of the principal sub-assemblies, and so on through as many levels as appropriate to reach the level of raw materials or bought-in items. Each item is assigned to one level only, and each item at each level has a unique coding. The different levels and/or branches may correspond to different design or manufacturing responsibilities. For example, in organizing the components of a motor vehicle in this format, level 1 may comprise major sub-assemblies such as engines, bodies,

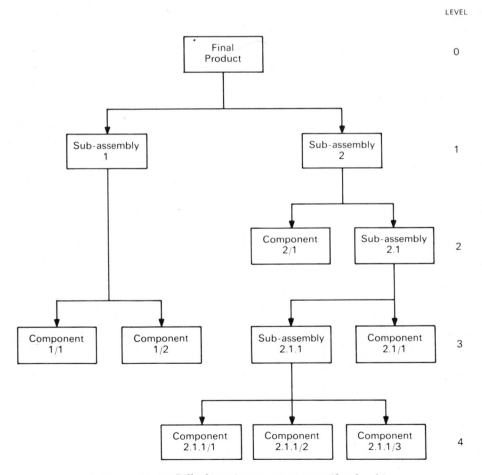

**Figure 12.2**   *Bill of requirements structure (five levels).*

frames, etc., such that below that level the various component parts in effect correspond to particular areas of manufacturing responsibility. Where complex end products may be made in several different possible configurations from a large number of parts or sub-assemblies which may be assembled in different ways, it is common to use a 'modular' bill of requirements structure. Using this approach, even though there may be a very large range of end products differing in detail from one another, it will not be necessary to have a large number of different, unique bill of requirements structures, but will be enough to specify those modules from a composite bill of requirements structure which together constitute the required end product.

2. The *master production schedule* is based on known or forecast demand for a specified future period, e.g. the forecasting period. The schedule shows how much of each end item is wanted and when the items are wanted. It is in effect the delivery or the 'due date' schedule for each product expressed in terms of both quantity and timing. The period over which this demand is expressed will depend on the type of product concerned and the capacity planning procedures used by the organization. In general, however, the time period should allow enough time for the acquisition of all materials, the manufacture of all components, parts and sub-assemblies, and the assembly of the final product.

3. *Opening inventory*. This record will show the available inventories of all materials, components, sub-assemblies, etc., required for the manufacture of the end product. In general the file will show both total and free (i.e. unallocated) inventory. The latter is more important in the context of MRP, since the objective is to compare component or parts requirements against available stock (i.e. excluding those items already committed to the manufacture of other products), in order to determine purchase and manufacture requirements for items for a particular delivery schedule.

4. *Opening capacity*. If the MRP procedure is to be used to provide a production schedule it will be necessary to have available information on free capacity. The MRP programme will allocate component manufacturing requirements against this capacity so that the appropriate components at each level in the bill of requirements are available at an appropriate time, in order to ensure that the final product is available to the customer at the required time. In this respect the procedure is very similar to that used in the line of balance technique (Chapter 14).

The basic procedure involves the 'explosion' of the final product requirements into constituent component and materials requirements. This procedure (sometimes referred to as 'netting') is performed level by level through the bill of requirements. The gross requirements for each item at each level are compared with available inventory so that the outstanding parts, components or materials requirements can be determined. This procedure determines how many units of each item are required to meet a given production schedule and also when those units are required, in order that manufacturing lead times might be satisfied. The result of this procedure will be the production of a schedule of purchase requirements, a schedule of manufacturing requirements (i.e. manufacturing activity schedule) and, if appropriate, a schedule showing the shortages that will occur as a result of there being insufficient capacity available to meet component/item manufacturing requirements.

Thus the principal *outputs* from the MRP procedure are as follows:

1. Purchase requirements: including which items are to be ordered, at what time, and in what quantities.
2. Manufacturing activity schedules indicating which items are to be manufactured, in what quantities and by what date.
3. Expected shortages (and/or items which must be expedited).

4. Resultant free inventory following satisfaction of the master schedule.
5. Available free capacity.

The above procedure will be undertaken in a reiterative manner. Basically there are two types of approach available. Using the *regenerative* approach the entire MRP procedure as described above, is repeated periodically. The time period between repetitions will normally conform to the time period between demand forecasts, the two usually being undertaken on a regular basis, e.g. once a month. The approach using the regenerative system is in effect to undertake an entirely new MRP calculation on each occasion, i.e. to undertake each set of calculations as if there had been no previous MRP study. In each cases the inventory inputs to the system will assume that all current stocks are free and that none of the available capacity is committed. Thus each MRP repetition takes into account all known demand for the schedule period, and from the demand, bill of requirements, inventory and capacity data, calculates a new schedule. Such an approach may be appropriate where the output schedule changes to a relatively small extent. In such circumstances the amount of computation may not be too great and the differences between the schedules produced for successive calculations may not be substantial. An additional advantage of the regenerative approach is that data errors are not repeated or compounded.

Where there is considerable change in the output schedule, or where forecasts are subject to large margins of error, or where the bill of requirements details change, e.g. as a result of design changes, it may be more appropriate to adopt a *net change* approach to materials requirements planning. Using this procedure only the alterations to the master schedule and/or the other input data are taken into account as and when necessary. These changes are considered and their effects on purchase and manufacturing schedules, inventories, capacity factors, etc., are considered. While the regenerative approach might be useful in a relatively stable situation, in a volatile situation the net change approach might be more appropriate. The net change system requires more processing and will not normally be used when the volumes are high.

## REVERSE SCHEDULING

External due date considerations will directly influence activity scheduling in certain structures. The approach adopted in scheduling activities in such cases will often involve a form of reverse scheduling with the use of bar or Gantt charts.

A major problem with such reverse or 'due date' scheduling is in estimating the total time to be allowed for each operation, in particular the time to be allowed for waiting or queuing at facilities.

Some queuing of jobs (whether items or customers) before facilities is often desirable since, where processing times on facilities are uncertain, high utilization is achieved only by the provision of such queues.

Operation times are often available, but queuing times are rarely known initially. The only realistic way in which queuing allowances can be obtained is by experience. Experienced planners will schedule operations, making allowances which they know from past performances to be correct. Such allowances may vary from 50 per cent to 2000 per cent of operation times and can be obtained empirically or by analysis of the progress of previous jobs. It is normally sufficient to obtain and use allowances for groups of similar facilities or for particular departments, since delays depend not so much on the nature of the job, as on the amount of work passing through the departments and the nature of the facilities.

Operations schedules of this type are usually depicted on Gantt or bar charts. The advantage of this type of presentation is that the load on any facility or any department is clear at a glance, and available or spare capacity is easily identified. The major disadvantage is that the dependencies between operations are not shown and, consequently, any readjustment of such schedules necessitates reference back to operation planning documents. Notice that, in scheduling the processing of items, total throughput time can be minimized by the batching of similar items to save set-up time, inspection time, etc.

## FORWARD SCHEDULING

For a manufacturing or supply organization a forward scheduling procedure will in fact be the opposite of that described above. This approach will be particularly relevant where scheduling is undertaken on an internally oriented basis and the objective is to determine the date or times for subsequent activities, given the times for an earlier activity, e.g. a starting time.

In the case of supply or transport organizations, the objective will be to schedule forward from a given start date, where that start date will often be the customer due date, e.g. the date at which the customer arrives into the system. In these circumstances, therefore, forward scheduling will be an appropriate method for dealing with externally oriented scheduling activities.

## SEQUENCING

Sequencing procedures seek to determine the best order for processing a set of jobs through a set of facilities.

Two types of problems can be identified. First, the static case, in which all jobs to be processed are known and are available, and in which no additional jobs arrive in the queue during the exercise. Second, the dynamic case, which allows for the continuous arrival of jobs in the queue. Associated with these two cases are certain objectives. In the static case the problem is merely to order a given queue of jobs through a given numbers of facilities, each job passing through the facilities in the required order and spending the necessary amount of time at each. The objective in such a case is usually to minimize the total time required to process all jobs: the throughput time. In the dynamic case the objective might be to minimize facility idle time, to minimize work in progress or to achieve the required completion or delivery dates for each job. Sequencing procedures are relevant primarily for static cases.

Several simple techniques have been developed for solving simple sequencing problems, for example the sequencing of jobs through two facilities, where each job must visit each facility in the same order. Fairly complex mathematical procedures are available to deal with more realistic problems, but in all cases either a static case is assumed or some other simplifying assumptions are made.

## DISPATCHING

A more useful approach for dealing with realistic sequencing problems is provided by dispatching procedures.

The principal method of job dispatching is by means of priority rules. The use of priority rule dispatching is an attempt to formalize the decisions of the experienced 'human' dispatcher. Most of the simple priority rules that have been suggested are listed below.

1. *Job slack (S).* This is the amount of contingency or free time, over and above the expected processing time, available before the job is completed at a predetermined date ($t_0$), i.e.

$$S = t_0 - t_1 - \Sigma a_i$$

   where   $t_1$ = present date (e.g. day or week number, where $t_1 < t_0$)
   $\Sigma a_i$ = sum of remaining processing times

   Where delays are associated with each operation, e.g. delays caused by interfacility transport, this rule is less suitable, hence the following rule may be used.
2. *Job slack per operation,* i.e. $S/N$, where $N$ = number of remaining operations. Therefore where $S$ is the same for two or more jobs, the job having the most remaining operations is processed first.
3. *Job slack ratio,* or the ratio of the remaining slack time to the total remaining time, i.e.

$$\frac{S}{t_0 - t_1}$$

   In all the above cases, where the priority index is negative the job cannot be completed by the requisite date. The rule will therefore be to process first those jobs having negative indices.

4. *Shortest imminent operation* (SIO). i.e. process first the job with the shortest processing times.
5. *Longest imminent operation* (LIO). This is the converse of (4).
6. *Scheduled start date.* This is perhaps the most frequently used rule. The date at which operations must be started in order that a job will meet a required completion date is calculated, usually by employing reverse scheduling from the completion date, e.g.

$$x_i = t_0 - \Sigma a_i$$
$$\text{or} \quad x_i = t_0 - \Sigma (a_i + f_i)$$

   where $x_i$ = scheduled start date for an operation
   $f_i$ = delay or contingency allowance

   Usually some other rule is also used, e.g. first come, first served, to decide priorities between jobs having equal $x_i$ values.
7. *Earliest due date,* i.e. process first the job required first.
8. *Subsequent processing times.* Process first the job that has the longest remaining process times, i.e. $\Sigma a_i$ or, in modified form, $\Sigma (a_i + f_i)$.
9. *Value.* To reduce work in progress inventory cost, process first the job which has the highest value.
10. *Minimum total float.* This rule is the one usually adopted when scheduling by network techniques.

11. *Subsequent operation.* Look ahead to see where the job will go after this operation has been completed and process first the job which goes to a 'critical' queue, that is a facility having a small queue of available work, thus minimizing the possibility of facility idle time.
12. *First come, first served* (FCFS).
13. *Random* (e.g. in order of job number, etc.).

Rules 12 and 13 are random since, unlike the others, neither one depends directly on job characteristics such as length of operation or value.
   Priority rules can be classified further, as follows:

1. *Local rules* depend solely on data relating to jobs in the queue at any particular facility.
2. *General rules* depend on data relating to jobs in the queue at any particular facility and/or data for jobs in queues at *other* facilities.

Local rules, because of the smaller amount of information used, are easier and cheaper to calculate than general (sometimes called *global*) rules. All of the above rules with the exception of rule 11 are local rules.
   One further classification of rules is as follows:

1. *Static rules* are those in which the priority index for a job does not change with the passage of time, during waiting in any one queue.
2. *Dynamic rules* are those in which the priority index is a function of the present time.

Rules 4,5,6,7,8,9,10,11,12 and 13 are all static, whereas the remainder are dynamic.
   Perhaps the most effective rule according to present research is the SIO rule, and, more particularly, the various extensions of this rule. Massive simulation studies have shown that, of all 'local' rules, those based on the SIO rule are perhaps the most effective, certainly when considered against criteria such as minimizing the number of jobs in the system, the mean of the 'completion distribution' and the throughput time. The SIO rule appears to be particularly effective in reducing throughput time, the 'truncated SIO' and the 'two-class SIO' rules being perhaps the most effective derivatives, having the additional advantage of reducing throughput time variance and lateness.
   The 'first come, first served' priority rule has been shown to be particularly beneficial in reducing average lateness, whereas the 'scheduled start date and total float' rule has been proved effective where jobs are of the network type.

## ASSIGNMENT

Frequently, when attempting to decide how orders are to be scheduled onto available facilities, one is faced with various alternative solutions. For example, many different facilities may be capable of performing the operations required on one customer or item. Operations management must then decide which jobs are to be scheduled onto which facilities in order to achieve some objective, such as minimum cost or minimum throughput time.
   One simple, rapid, but approximate method of facility/job assignment is best described by means of an example.

## EXAMPLE

A company must complete five orders during a particular period. Each order consists of several identical products and each can be made on one of several facilities. Table 12.3 gives the operation time for each product on each of the available facilities.

**Table 12.3**  *Operation time per item on each facility.*

| Order no. (i) | No. of items in order ($Q_1$) | Operation time per item on facility j (hours) | | |
|:---:|:---:|:---:|:---:|:---:|
| | | A | B | C |
| 1 | 30 | 5.0 | 4.0 | 2.5 |
| 2 | 25 | 1.5 | 2.5 | 4.0 |
| 3 | 45 | 2.0 | 4.0 | 4.5 |
| 4 | 15 | 3.0 | 2.5 | 3.5 |
| 5 | 10 | 4.0 | 3.5 | 2.0 |

The available capacity for these facilities for the period in question is:

$$A = 100 \text{ hours}$$
$$B = 80 \text{ hours}$$
$$C = 150 \text{ hours}$$

The index number for a facility is a measure of the cost disadvantage of using that facility for processing, and is obtained by using this formula:

$$I_j = \frac{X_{ij} - x_i \text{ min.}}{x_i \text{ min.}}$$

where
$I_j$ = index number for facility
$X_{ij}$ = operation time for item $i$ on facility $j$
$x_i$ min. = minimum operation time for item $i$

*For order 1:*

$$I_A = \frac{5.0 - 2.5}{2.5} = 1.0$$

$$I_B = \frac{4.0 - 2.5}{2.5} = 0.6$$

$$I_C = \frac{2.5 - 2.5}{2.5} = 0$$

Table 12.4 shows the index numbers for all facilities and orders. Using Table 12.4 and remembering that the index number is a measure of the cost disadvantage of using that facility, we can now allocate orders to facilities. The best facility for order 1 is C ($I_C = 0$); the processing time for that order (75 hours) is less than the available capacity. We can therefore schedule the processing of this order on this facility. Facility A is the best facility for order 2, but also the best for order 3. Both cannot be accommodated because of limitations on available capacity, so we must consider the possibility of allocating one of the orders to another facility. The next best facility for order 2 is facility B ($I_B = 0.67$) and for order 3 the next best facility is also facility B ($I_B = 1$). Because the cost disadvantage on B is less for order 2, allocate order 2 to B and 3 to A as shown in the table. The best facility for order 4 is B but there is now insufficient capacity available on this facility. The alternatives now are to reallocate order 2 to another facility or to allocate order 4 elsewhere. In the circumstances it is better to allocate order 4 to facility C. Finally order 5 can be allocated to its best facility, namely, facility C.

**Table 12.4**

| Order no. | No. of items in order | Facility A | | Facility B | | Facility C | |
|---|---|---|---|---|---|---|---|
| | | Index no. | Processing time for order (h) | Index no. | Processing time for order | Index no. | Processing time for order |
| 1 | 30 | 1.0 | 150 | 0.6 | 120 | 0 | 75 |
| 2 | 25 | 0 | 37.5 | 0.67 | 62.5 | 1.67 | 100 |
| 3 | 45 | 0 | 90 | 1.0 | 180 | 1.25 | 202.5 |
| 4 | 15 | 0.2 | 45 | 0 | 37.5 | 0.4 | 52.5 |
| 5 | 10 | 1.0 | 40 | 0.75 | 35 | 0 | 20 |
| Capacity (% utilization) | | | 100 (90) | | 80 (78) | | 150 (98) |

The disadvantages of this method are readily apparent. First, with problems involving more orders and facilities than the one used here, the allocation and reallocation of orders might be very tedious. Second, we have not considered the possibility of splitting an order. For example, rather than reallocate all of order 2 to facility B, it might have been economically better to allocate 10 hours of work (6 products) to A (the remaining available capacity) and reallocate only the remaining 19 products to facility B. Assuming that it is possible to split batches in this way, the benefits of doing so depend on the costs of setting up the machines. These costs, being fixed and not varying with order quantity, are not considered in the index method.

The problem of assigning jobs to available facilities, discussed above, can also be solved by linear programming. The objectives and the constraints can be formulated as a set of linear inequalities, which might then be solved using, say, the Simplex method.

When more than one facility is assigned to a single operator a phenomenon known as *machine interference* may occur. For example, if one operator attends three weaving machines, when one stops—either at the end of its production cycle or for any other reason (e.g. breakdown)—then the operator will attend to it. If, however, while it is being attended to, one of the other machines stops, then, since the operator is unable to attend to both, a certain amount of machine idle time must result. This is known as machine interference.

The assignment of two or more facilities to one operator is a common feature in many industries, and, of course, the nature of the work being done on such facilities will determine the amount of attention required from the operator. This will, in turn, determine the optimum number of facilities to assign to the operator. This worker–facility assignment, since it determines the system capacity, is of considerable importance during operations planning.

The mathematical treatment of multi-facility assignments has been attempted by many authors, but the problem is a particularly complex one, especially when the operators have their duties other than simply attending to the facility, and when the characteristics of the facilities differ.

## TIMETABLING

The timetabling of activities is of particular relevance in respect of repetitive functions. Bus, train and air services usually operate to a timetable. Similarly, the activities of certain service systems, e.g. cinemas, are timetabled. These are customer push systems, so customers are required to take advantage of the function at predetermined times. The function is not performed at other times, so customers arriving at the wrong time must wait, and, of course, an absence of customers at the time selected for the performance of the function, or the availability of insufficient customers to utilize fully the facilities provided, will necessarily give rise to under-utilization of capacity. In many situations timetables are necessary, since common resources are deployed to provide a variety or series of functions. In many transport systems, for example, vehicles travel a set route providing movement for individuals between points along that route. In certain service systems, for example hospitals, common resources such as specialists provide a service in a variety of departments, or for a variety of types of customer, in a given period of time. Certain out-patients clinics operate in this fashion. In all such cases a timetable will normally be developed and made available to customers. Much the same situations may apply in 'customer pull' systems, where functions occur at given times. It follows that in all such cases the nature of demand must be predictable since, in effect, function is undertaken in anticipation of demand. In fact, in such cases, the absence of (sufficient) customers at the time selected for the performance of the function may give rise to the creation of output stock. Alternatively, output may be lost or wasted. The timetabling of such activities is an exercise in internally oriented scheduling, since no direct account is taken of individual customers' demands. The development of timetables will take into account the time required for, or the duration of, activities, and in many cases (e.g. transport systems) the required or preferred order or sequence.

Few quantitative techniques are relevant in the development of such timetables. 'Routeing', flow planning and vehicle scheduling procedures are of relevance in timetabling transport systems. In some cases the problem will resemble that of sequencing outlined above, while in others it may be convenient to use Gantt charts and simulation procedures in both the development and the evaluation of timetables.

## CRITERIA IN SCHEDULING

In most situations it will not usually be feasible, and in some cases not desirable, to attempt to develop optimum activity schedules. Because of the dynamics of situations and the unpredictability of demand, a degree of control is essential. The relative importance attached to scheduling or control will depend to some extent on the type of situation and particularly the type of structure existing. In general, scheduling will be more complex in 'function to order' situations where scheduling decisions will be required to absorb external (i.e. demand) fluctuations directly. Furthermore, in such situations the degree of function repetition may be less, therefore the need for control may be greater. In contrast, in 'function to stock' situations, scheduling will be somewhat easier, therefore the need for control somewhat less. In 'demand push' situations, where stocks exist between function and customer, scheduling will tend to be easier and the need for control less. Demand levels may also influence the relative complexity and importance of scheduling and control activities. In general, high-demand levels will be associated with function repetition and the provision of special-purpose resources together with product or service specialization. In contrast, relatively low demand levels may be associated with relatively low function repetition, high product or service variety and the use of general-purpose resources, hence scheduling may be complex and there will be a relatively greater dependence on control. In situations where demand predictability, i.e the nature of demand, permits the provision, i.e. stocking, of resources and where demand levels are high, the provision of special-purpose equipment may give rise to an emphasis on the provision of balance, the avoidance of interference and consideration of learning or improvement effects. In such situations much of the internally oriented scheduling will be 'built in' to the system. In contrast, in situations where demand predictability is low and where demand levels are also low, accurate scheduling will be impossible, hence low equipment utilization, high work in progress, and /or customer queuing will be evident. In these situations the use of local dispatching rules, resource smoothing, allocation of jobs, etc., together with an emphasis on control, will be evident.

Criteria or measures of effective activity scheduling and control might include the following:

(a) the level of finished goods or work in progress (for systems with output stocks);
(b) percentage resource utilization (all systems);
(c) percentage of orders delivered on or before due date (for function to order systems only);
(d) percentage stock-outs/shortages (for systems with output stocks only);
(e) number of customers (all systems);
(f) down time/set-ups, etc. (all systems);
(g) customer queuing times (for systems in which customers wait or queue).

In virtually all cases there will be a need to avoid sub-optimization, that is, it will be easy in most cases to satisfy each of the above criteria individually. However, as we pointed out earlier, the objective of operations management, and therefore an objective of activity scheduling, is to obtain a satisfactory balance between customer service criteria and resource utilization criteria.

## FURTHER READING

Eilon, S. (1979) Production scheduling, in Haley, K.B. (ed.) *OR 78*. pp. 237–264. North Holland Publishing Co. A review of production scheduling problems and methods for their solution.
New, C. (1978) *Requirements Planning*. Aldershot: Carver.
Niland, P. *Production Planning, Scheduling and Inventory Control*. London: Macmillan. Deals largely with scheduling decisions in manufacture, including forecasting and inventory control.
Wild, R. (1977) *Concepts for Operations Management,* Chapters 8 and 11. Chichester and New York: Wiley.

# QUESTIONS

**12.1** Distinguish between the sequencing and the dispatching problems. How important is the sequencing problem in activity scheduling and how useful in practice are the various algorithms which can be used to provide optimal solutions to such problems?

**12.2** Ten jobs are waiting to be processed on a machine.
(a) Given the information below, arrange these jobs in priority order (the one with highest processing or dispatching priority first) according to the following priority rules:
  1. job slack;
  2. job slack per operation;
  3. job slack ratio;
  4. shortest imminent operation;
  5. longest imminent operation;
  6. scheduled start date;
  7. earliest due date;
  8. subsequent processing time;
  9. first come, first served.

| Job | Scheduled completion date (week no.) | Sum of remaining processing times (weeks) | Number of remaining operations | Duration of operations on this machine | Arrival order at this machine |
|-----|-----|-----|-----|-----|-----|
| 1 | 17 | 4 | 2 | 1 | 1 |
| 2 | 15 | 6 | 3 | 2 | 10 |
| 3 | 17 | 3 | 4 | 1 | 2 |
| 4 | 16 | 5 | 1 | 3 | 4 |
| 5 | 19 | 7 | 2 | 0.5 | 9 |
| 6 | 21 | 4 | 5 | 2 | 3 |
| 7 | 17 | 2 | 4 | 0.5 | 5 |
| 8 | 22 | 8 | 3 | 3.5 | 8 |
| 9 | 20 | 6 | 2 | 2 | 6 |
| 10 | 25 | 10 | 1 | 2 | 7 |

NB: The present date is week no. 12.

(b) Use the 'first come, first served' (FCFS) priority rule to resolve 'ties' given by the above rules.

**12.3** Describe some of the activity scheduling problems which may occur and the techniques available for their solution, in the following situations:
(a) an emergency ward in a hospital;
(b) a furniture removal company;
(c) a take-away food shop (e.g. a hamburger shop).

**12.4** Holdtight Company Ltd have just received orders from four customers for quantities of different 'expanderbolts'. Each order is to be manufactured over the same very short period of time, during which three machines are available for the manufacture of the bolts.

The table below shows the manufacturing time in hours/bolt for each of the three machines and the total available hours capacity on each for the period in question.

Assuming that each order is to be manufactured on one machine only, how should orders be allocated to machines?

| Order no. | Number of expanderbolts | Manufacturing time (hours/bolt) | | |
|---|---|---|---|---|
| | | M/cA | M/cB | M/cC |
| 1 | 50 | 4 | 5 | 3 |
| 1 | 75 | 3 | 2 | 4 |
| 3 | 25 | 5 | 4 | 3 |
| 4 | 80 | 2 | 5 | 4 |
| Total capacity (hours) | | 175 | 275 | 175 |

# CHAPTER 13

# Network Scheduling

This chapter will deal exclusively and in detail with the use of network techniques in activity scheduling and planning. The topic was introduced briefly in Chapter 12, where it was noted that this approach provides a means of establishing schedules for sequentially interdependent activities taking account of precedence and sometimes resource constraints. The technique is of wide relevance, is used extensively in the scheduling of complex projects, and merits consideration in detail. Our description throughout will refer to projects, the planning of projects, etc. We should note that such projects might relate to manufacture, supply, service or transport.

The rudimentary steps in operations planning by network analysis are as follows:

1. Construct an arrow or network diagram to represent the project to be undertaken, indicating the sequence and interdependence of all necessary jobs in the project.
2. Determine how long each of the jobs will last and insert those times on the network.
3. Perform network calculations to determine the overall duration of the project and the criticality of the various jobs.
4. If the project completion date is later than required, consider modifying either the network and/or the individual job durations so that the project may be completed within the required time.

This is the extent of the planning phase of simple network analysis; there are, however, subsequent steps concerned with the control of operation and these will be dealt with in Chapter 18. Furthermore, this simple description of the procedure has omitted all considerations of costs and resources, and these will be dealt with later in this chapter.

## THE CONSTRUCTION OF NETWORKS

Any project may be represented by means of an arrow diagram in which the arrangement of arrows indicate the sequence of individual jobs and their dependence on other jobs. Arrow diagrams consist of two basic elements: *activities* and *events*.

An activity is a time-consuming task and is represented by an arrow or line. An event is considered as instantaneous, i.e. a point in time. An event may represent the completion or the commencement of an activity and is represented by a circle. A sequence of events is referred to as a path.

Unlike bar charts, the scale to which activities are drawn has no significance. The length of an activity arrow on a network diagram is unrelated to the duration of that activity. It is normal to number events as in Figure 13.1 so that paths within the network can be easily described, but, other than for identification, event numbers have no significance.

**Figure 13.1**

The network diagram is constructed by assembling all activities in a logical order. For example, the networks shown in Figures 13.2 and 13.3 relate to a decorating job.

No activity may begin until all the activities leading to it are completed. In Figure 13.2 only after the walls have been cleaned can they be painted. In Figure 13.3 starting

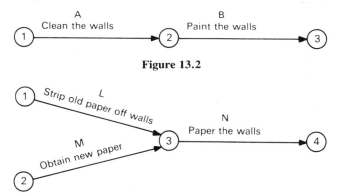

**Figure 13.2**

**Figure 13.3**

to paper the walls is dependent not only on the old paper having been removed but also on the new paper being available.

Activities occurring on the same path are *sequential* and are directly dependent on each other. *Parallel* activities on different paths are independent of one another (Figure 13.4).

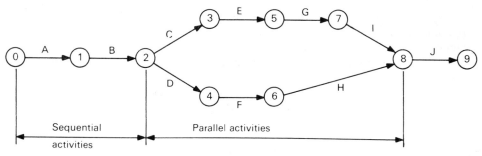

**Figure 13.4**

The convention in drawing networks is to allow time to flow from left to right, and to number events in this direction so that events on the left of the diagram have smaller numbers than, and occur before, events on the right of the diagram.

It is not usually possible to use network diagrams in which 'loops' or 'dangles' occur; a loop such as that in Figure 13.5 may be a perfectly legitimate sequence of operations

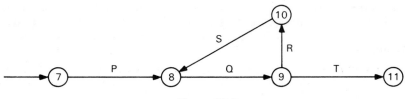

**Figure 13.5**

where, for example, a certain amount of reprocessing of materials or rectification takes place but, because of the calculations which must later be performed on the diagram, it cannot be accepted in network analysis.

Although there are certain computer programs which will accept multiple-finish and multiple-start events on networks, it is not normally possible to leave events 'dangling' as in Figure 13.6.

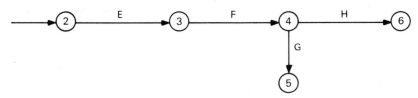

**Figure 13.6**

## Dummy activities

The activities discussed above represent some time-consuming operation or job to be performed during the project. Dummy activities consume no time; they are of zero duration and are used solely for convenience in network construction. Dummy activities, represented by dotted lines, may be necessary on the following occasions:

1. To provide the correct logic in the diagram. In Figure 13.7 the completion of activities C and D is necessary before either E or F may begin. If in practice only activity E depends on the completion of both activities C and D, and activity F depends on D alone, then to represent this logic a dummy activity is required (Figure 13.8).

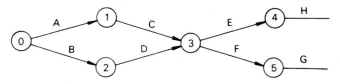

**Figure 13.7**

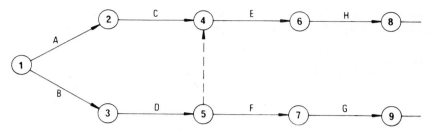

**Figure 13.8**

2. To avoid having more than one activity with the same beginning and end event (Figure 13.9). It is not usually possible to represent activities in this manner since activities B and C would be described from their event numbers as 3–4, so a dummy activity is necessary (Figure 13.10).
3. For convenience in drawing. The two networks in Figure 13.11 are equivalent, but the use of dummy activities facilitates representation. This is often necessary in complex networks.

**Figure 13.9**

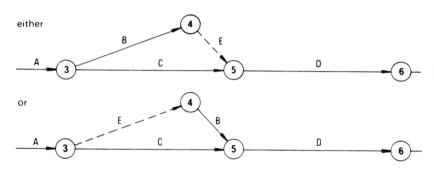

**Figure 13.10**

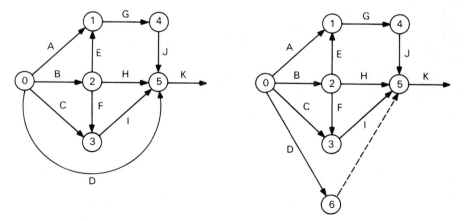

**Figure 13.11**

It may be necessary to use dummy activities when initially constructing networks to avoid complicated and untidy diagrams. Nevertheless, since the amount of subsequent analysis is dependent on the number of activities in a diagram, redundant dummies should be eliminated in order to save calculation time.

In drawing large networks for projects with many activities we have often found it to be easier to begin from the end of the project and work backwards. It is often helpful to consider large projects in separate parts, i.e. certain sections of the project or, if more appropriate, certain periods during the project, and then to piece together several smaller networks rather than try to construct the complete network from scratch. For example, the manufacture of a large water turbine could be divided into rotating parts (impeller, shafts, etc.) and stationary parts (housing, ducting, etc.). Alternatively it may be considered in terms of two time periods, the first covering the cutting, forming and welding of the parts, and the second the machining and assembling.

Except in the case of simple projects it is usually beneficial to construct the network around the important activities. Identify the important or major parts, locate the important activities on the diagram, then attach all the other, secondary activities to construct the complete network.

## NETWORK CALCULATIONS

### Dates

The objective of initial network calculations is to determine the overall duration of the project either so that a delivery date can be given to the customer or so that we can consider what alterations are necessary for the project to be completed on or before a date to which we are already committed.

To perform the network calculations two things are required: first an *activity network* representing the project, and second the durations of all the activities in that network. Network analysis is only a tool; its value depends entirely on the way in which it is used and the information on which it is based. Consequently, the collection of activity durations from records, or the estimation of durations, is an important part of the exercise.

If the activities have been performed previously then, assuming the use of the same resources and procedures, the durations may be obtained from records. On the many occasions where the activities have no direct precedent some form of estimation is necessary. For the time being we shall ignore the possibility of using multiple estimates of activity durations and consider only the case in which each activity is given one duration.

### *Earliest start date for activities (ES)*

The earliest start date for each activity is calculated from the *beginning* of the network by totalling all preceding activity durations ($d$).

Where two (or more) activities lead into one event the following activity cannot begin until both of the preceding activities are completed. Consequently, the last of these activities to finish determines the start date for the subsequent activity.

In Figure 13.12 the earliest start date for activity I is day 17 (assuming the project starts at day 0), since the start date of activity I will depend on the completion of the later of the two activities G and H, which is H.

Therefore, when calculating *ES* dates, work from the *beginning* of the network and use the *largest* numbers at junctions.

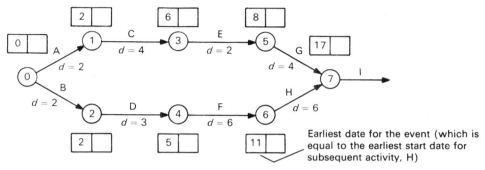

**Figure 13.12**

### Latest finish dates for activities (LF)

This is calculated from the *end* of the project by successively subtracting activity durations (*d*) from the project finish date.

Where two (or more) activities stem from one event the earliest of the dates will determine the latest finish date for previous activities.

In Figure 13.13 the latest finish date for activity A is day 3, since activity B must start at day 3 if the project is not to be delayed.

Therefore, when calculating *LF* dates begin from the *end* of the network and use the *smallest* numbers at junctions.

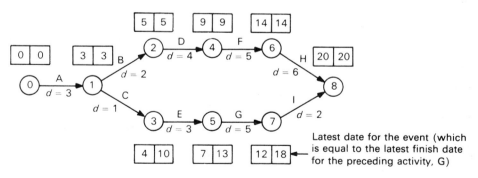

**Figure 13.13**

### Earliest finish date for activities (EF)

The earliest finish date for any activity is determined by that activity's earliest start date and its duration, i.e. for any activity: $EF = ES + d$.

### Latest start date for activities (LS)

The latest start date for any activity is determined by that activity's latest finish date and its duration, i.e. for any activity: $LS = LF - d$.

### Float

In the previous example the earliest completion date for the project, i.e. the date of event 8, is determined by the $EF$ dates for activities H and I. Activity I could finish at day 14 (the $EF$ date for activity I is $ES + d = 12 + 2$), but activity H cannot finish until day 20 and it is the activity which determines the finish date for the project. In fact, it is the path consisting of activities ABDFH which determines the project's earliest finish date rather than path ACEGI.

The earliest finish date for any project is determined by the longest path through the network; consequently, it follows that the shorter paths will have more time available than they require. The difference between the time available for any activity and the time required is called the *total float (TF)*.

In Figure 13.13 the time required for activity I is 2 but the time available is 8 and hence the $TF$ on activity I is 6.

$$\text{Time available} = LF - ES$$
$$\text{Time required} = d$$
$$\text{Total float} = LF - ES - d$$

i.e. for any activity (say G), using our notation the $TF$ can be expressed as in Figure 13.14.

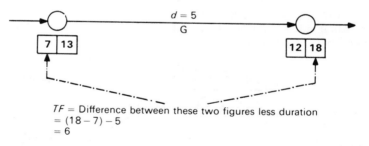

$TF$ = Difference between these two figures less duration
$= (18 - 7) - 5$
$= 6$

**Figure 13.14**

Total float is a characteristic of a path and not a characteristic of a single activity. For example, in Figure 13.13 the total float on activities A,C,E,G, and I is 6. If the total float is used up at any time by delays or lateness in one of the activities then it is no longer available to any of the other activities on that path.

### The critical path

The critical path is the longest path through the network and is, therefore, the path with minimum total float (zero $TF$ in the above example). Any delay in the activities on the critical path will delay the completion of the project, whereas delay in activities not on the critical path will initially use up some of the total float on that path and not affect the project completion date.

## EXAMPLE 13.1

The table below lists all the activities which together constitute a small engineering project. The table also shows the necessary immediate predecessors for each activity and the activity durations.

1. Construct an activity network to represent the project.
2. Determine the earliest finish date for the entire project, assuming the project begins at day 0.

| Activity | Immediate predecessors | Activity duration (days) |
|---|---|---|
| A | — | 2 |
| B | A | 3 |
| C | A | 4 |
| D | A | 5 |
| E | B | 6 |
| F | CD | 3 |
| G | D | 4 |
| H | B | 7 |
| I | EFG | 2 |
| J | G | 3 |

Answer:

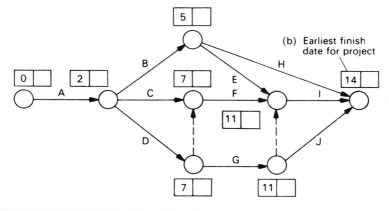

## EXAMPLE 13.2

For the project described in Example 13.1 determine:
(a) the total float on each activity;

(b)  the critical path;
(c)  the latest start date for activity B;
(d)  the earliest finish date for activity F;
(e)  the effect on the project duration if activity I were to take three days;
(f)  the effect on the project duration if activity F were to take six days.

Answer:

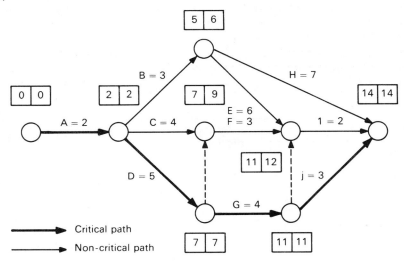

(a) *Activity*    A B C D E F G H I J
         *TF*   0 1 3 0 1 2 0 2 1 0
(b) Critical path = ADGJ
(c) Latest start date for B = *LF* − duration
                  = 6 − 3
                  = day 3
(d) Earliest finish date for F = *ES* + duration
                  = 7 + 3
                  = day 10
(e) No effect, but since increase in duration is equal to total float on activity, this activity would become critical.
(f) Project would be delayed by one day since only two days *TF* are available on activity.

## Schedule dates

At the beginning of this section we indicated that one objective of network calculations is to calculate the earliest completion date for the project and to compare this with the desired completion date. We may be committed to complete a project by a certain date and, if the calculated earliest finish date for the project occurs after this scheduled finish date, it will be desirable to try to reduce the project duration. If we had used the schedule completion date in the calculations then we would have obtained negative total float values, the greatest negative values occurring on the critical path and indicating the minimum amount by which the project would be late unless some alterations were made. Schedule dates may also be placed on intermediate events. If it is necessary to complete one of the intermediate activities by a given date, e.g. so that the customer or the main contractor may inspect or test the partly completed product, then an *intermediate schedule date/late* may be used. If this date is earlier than the *LF* date for that activity it would be used in the network calculations instead of the calculated *LF* date. If one of the intermediate activities cannot be started until a given date for some reason, e.g. because of the delivery of materials, then an *intermediate schedule date/early* may be used. If this date is later than the *ES* date for that activity it would be used instead of the calculated *ES* figure.

In the example in Figure 13.15 the final schedule date, day 20, is earlier than the calculated finish date for the project and therefore replaces the calculated *LF* date. The same applies to the intermediate schedule date/late for the completion of activity C. The intermediate schedule date/early for the start of activity J has no effect since this date is earlier than the calculated *ES* date for that activity.

Using schedule dates it is possible to obtain not only negative values of total float but also different values along the critical path. In the example in Figure 13.15 the *TF* on activities A and C is $-2$, and on E and I it is $-1$, but all four activities form a critical path.

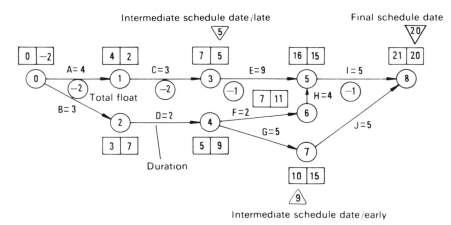

**Figure 13.15**

## MULTIPLE TIME ESTIMATES

We have previously assumed that a single time can be given for the duration of every activity. There are many occasions, however, when the duration of activities is not certain or when some amount of variation from the average duration is expected. For example, in maintenance work unexpected snags may occur to increase the activity duration, or failures may be found to be less serious than had been expected and the activity duration reduced. In construction work jobs may be delayed because of unfavourable weather, etc.

In such cases it is desirable to be able to use a time distribution rather than a single time for activity durations to represent the uncertainty that exists.

In network analysis uncertainty in durations can be accommodated and the following notation is usually used:

$m$ = the most likely duration of the activity
$a$ = the optimistic estimate of the activity duration
$b$ = the pessimistic estimate of the activity duration

These three estimates can be used to describe the distribution for the activity duration. It is assumed that the times are distributed as a 'beta' distribution (Figure 13.16).

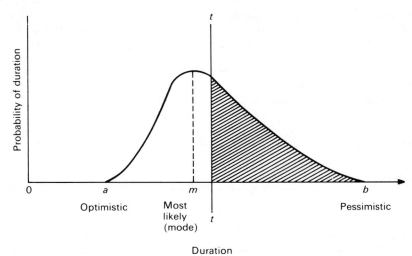

**Figure 13.16**

where  $t$ = the expected time − the mean of the distribution
$\sigma$ = the standard deviation (which is a measure of the spread of the distribution)
$\triangleq$ the range between the extreme values divided by 6

$$\equiv \frac{b - a}{6}$$

If certain assumptions are made about the distribution, the mean ($t$) and the variance ($\sigma^2$) can be expressed as follows:

$$\text{Mean (the expected time) } t = \frac{a + b + 4m}{6}$$

$$\text{Variance} \qquad \sigma^2 = \frac{(b - a)^2}{36}$$

## Probability of achieving scheduled dates

Suppose we have two sequential activities, A and B, for which the durations are:

$$a_A = 0.5 \text{ days} \qquad a_B = 4 \text{ days}$$
$$b_A = 3.5 \text{ days} \qquad b_B = 12 \text{ days}$$
$$m_A = 2 \text{ days} \qquad m_B = 8 \text{ days}$$

Using these formulae, for activity A the expected duration $t_A$ is 2 days and the variance $\sigma^2$ is 0.25 days, and for activity B the expected duration $t_B$ is 8 days and variance $\sigma_B^2$ is 1.75 days. Assuming activity durations to be independent, the expected duration for the pair of activities is 10 days and, since the variances may be added together, the variance for the pair is 2 days. It is usually assumed that the distribution for the duration of a series of activities corresponds to the 'normal' probability curve; consequently, in this case, the probability that the two activities will be completed in a minimum of 10 days is 50 per cent, since the normal distribution is symmetrical about the mean (Figure 13.17) and consequently the probability is given by the proportion of the area to the left of the mean of 10 days (50 per cent).

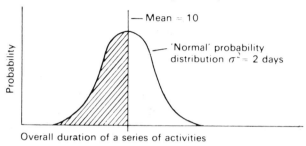

**Figure 13.17**

Suppose we have three activities which represent the critical path in a network, as in Figure 13.18. If we assume that these durations are independent, i.e. that the duration of activity A does not affect that of B, and so on, and that the normal distribution applies for the project duration, then we can calculate the probability that the project will be completed on or before the required schedule date.

$$\text{Expected project duration } (t) = 2 + 8 + 5 = 15$$
$$\sigma^2 = 3$$

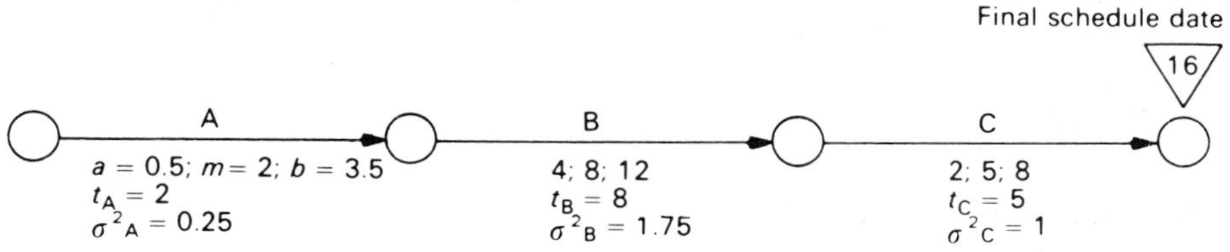

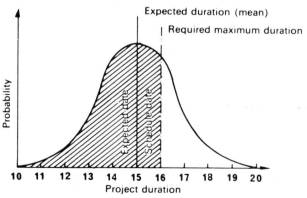

**Figure 13.18**

**Figure 13.19**

In the distribution shown in Figure 13.19 the probability of meeting the schedule date is represented by that portion of the area under the curve to the left of the 16-day ordinate. This area can be obtained from normal distribution tables if the diagram is first converted to a standardized scale.[1] In this case the probability of completing the project by day 16 is 0.72, since the area to the left of the 16-day ordinate is 72 per cent of the total area.

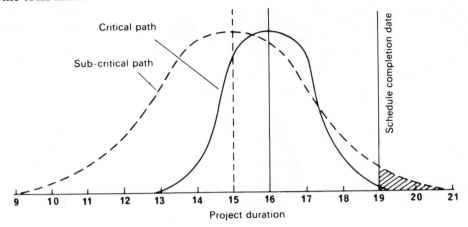

**Figure 13.21**

The assumptions underlying the use of probabilities in this way in network analysis are, to say the least, of doubtful validity. The assumptions that the distribution for each activity duration corresponds to a 'beta' distribution and that the distribution of the duration of a sequence of activities can be regarded as 'normal' are not based on thorough research and should be regarded only as empirical rules which, over a period of time, have been found to work. Furthermore, in calculating the probability on project end dates only the critical path is used, but where the duration of each activity in the network is uncertain any path through the network has a certain probability of being critical and we should perhaps examine more than one path.

---

[1]  The standardized scale is used solely for convenience. The standardized normal distribution has a total area of 1.00, a mean value of 0, and variance $\sigma^2$ of 1 (Figure 13.20).

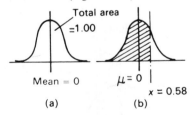

**Figure 13.20**

where $s$ = schedule date
$t$ = expected date
$\sigma$ = standard deviation
$x$ = standardized value for the ordinate required, i.e. the schedule date

$$x = \frac{s-t}{\sigma} = \frac{16-15}{\sqrt{3}} = 0.58$$

This value can then be located in normal distribution tables and the area to the left of the value found.

Suppose that in a network in which most of the activities' durations are uncertain the critical path has an expected duration of 16 days and a standard deviation of 1 day. In the same network there is a path of expected duration 15 days with a standard deviation of 3 days. According to the usual practice we ought to consider only the critical path in calculating our probabilities, but to do so in this case would mislead us, since there is a possibility that it will be the second path which will determine the project duration (Figure 13.21).

Had our scheduled completion date been day 19 then, considering the critical path only, we would be almost certain of meeting it, but the probability would be less if we considered the sub-critical path since, although the expected duration of this path is shorter, it is subject to greater variance.

---

## EXAMPLE 13.3

The three time estimates (optimistic, likely, pessimistic) for the duration of the individual activities which form a small project are shown on the network diagram below.

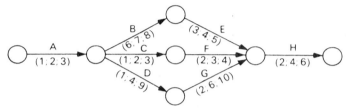

(a) Calculate the expected project duration.
(b) Determine the probability of finishing the project by day 18 or earlier.

Answer: (a)

| Activity | t days | $\sigma^2$ |
|----------|--------|------------|
| A | 2 | 4/36 |
| B | 7 | 4/36 |
| C | 2 | 4/36 |
| D | 4.33 | 64/36 |
| E | 4 | 4/36 |
| F | 3 | 4/36 |
| G | 6 | 64/36 |
| H | 4 | 16/36 |

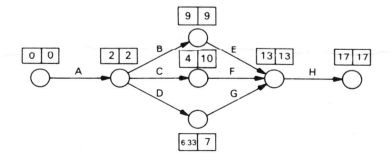

Expected project duration = 17 days
(b) Considering critical path ABEH:

$$t = 17$$
$$\sigma^2 = 4/36 + 4/36 + 4/36 + 16/36$$
$$= 0.776$$

$$x = \frac{s - t}{\sigma} = \frac{18 - 17}{\sqrt{0.776}}$$

$$x = 1.14$$

From normal probability tables $x \equiv 87.3\%$
Considering sub-critical path ADGH:

$$t = 2 + 4.33 + 6 + 4$$
$$= 16.33$$
$$\sigma^2 = 4/36 + 64/36 + 64/36 + 16/36$$
$$= 4.1$$

$$x = \frac{s - t}{\sigma} = \frac{18 - 16.33}{\sqrt{4.1}}$$

$$x = 0.825$$

From normal probability tables $x = 79.6\%$

---

In using three activity duration estimates to calculate the probabilities of completing projects or parts of projects on or before given scheduled completion dates, it is important to consider sub-critical paths. This is particularly important when the length of such paths approaches the length of the critical path, and also where the duration of the activities on such paths is subject to comparatively large variance.

Unless jobs have been done before, it is often difficult to obtain accurate estimates of activity durations. One advantage of using multiple estimates is that it encourages people to commit themselves to estimates when they might be reluctant to give a single estimate. But if this method is used principally for this reason, then there is little to be said for using these figures and subsequently calculating project durations and probabilities to several places of decimals. In such cases it may be sufficient merely to take the average of the three estimates; in fact many computer programs provide this facility.

## RESOURCES

Our treatment of network analysis so far has assumed that only time is important in executing tasks. There are certainly many situations where time is indeed the only or the most important factor, but in the majority of cases other factors affect our ability to do the job. We have assumed, for example, that the correct facilities have been available and in the correct quantities. The availability of such facilities as labour, plant, etc., determines not only our ability to do the job but also the time required to do it. Estimates of activity duration will rely implicitly on our capability to undertake those activities, so it is a little unrealistic to speak of activity durations in the abstract.

An estimate of the duration of an activity may differ substantially depending on the time at which the activity is undertaken. When very little other work is being undertaken an activity duration is likely to be shorter than when facilities are already heavily loaded or committed.

Each estimate of durations is based on the assumed use of a certain amount of resources, and consequently, when the project duration is initially calculated, we may also calculate the forward resource utilization, e.g. Figure 13.22.

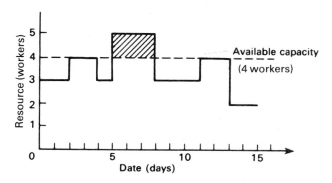

**Figure 13.22**

In this example an overload occurs from day 5 to day 8; consequently, unless we arrange to either subcontract this work or obtain additional resources, we cannot expect to meet our project completion date. The only remaining alternative is to reschedule some of the jobs which constitute this overload. We can, for example, delay three work-days of work from this period until days 8–11 and avoid overloading the resources.

Consider the part of a network shown in Figure 13.23. To be completed in four days, activity C requires six workers and four machines; activity D requires eight

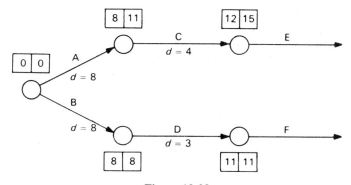

**Figure 13.23**

workers and five machines for three days. The total resources available are eight workers and six machines, therefore activities C and D cannot occur together. The solution is to:

1. Subcontract one of the activities.
2. Obtain additional resources.
3. Reschedule one or both of the activities.

Solutions (1) and (2) are particularly suitable where large overloads would occur and where this occurrence can be predicted well in advance. Often rescheduling is undertaken, and certainly where the overload is small and has occurred unexpectedly this is perhaps the only solution. The question is how we can reschedule the project to avoid overloading the resources and yet incur a minimum delay in completion. Activity D is on the critical path (it has a total float of 0) and the total float of activity C is three days, so activity D should be undertaken before C and this results in no additional project delay (Figure 13.24).

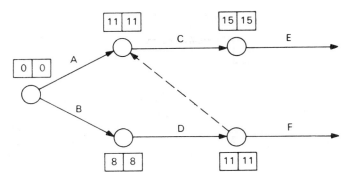

**Figure 13.24**

Resource aggregation, i.e. calculating the total resources necessary in any period to complete the project as in Figure 13.22, is a straightforward job, but resource allocation, as in Figure 13.24, can involve extensive computation for a large project. Networks involving more than a few hundred activities are normally processed on a computer, but the use of one of the numerous computer/network analysis programs is still economic for networks of fewer activities if resource allocation is to be undertaken. Although methods of resource allocation suitable for manual processing are available, in practice almost all resource allocation in network analysis occurs during computer processing.


## COSTS


The duration of an activity depends on the quantity of resources allocated to it. At additional cost more resources can usually be acquired and the activity duration decreased. In many cases this additional expenditure can be justified by the earlier completion of the activity and of the project. If a heavy penalty clause applies for late completion of the project, or if the project must be completed by a given date so that it can begin earning revenue (e.g. a hotel or holiday camp ready for the beginning of the holiday season), then additional expenditure during manufacture may be economically justifiable. In network analysis it is assumed that cost is linearly related to activity duration, and that as duration decreases the cost increases (Figure 13.25).

When it is possible to reduce an activity duration by engaging extra resources at additional cost, two extreme cases are assumed to exist:

1. *Normal* activity duration at normal cost, utilizing the normal quantity of resources.
2. A shorter *crash* activity duration at crash cost, utilizing additional resources.

Where the difference between normal and crash durations results from the use of a

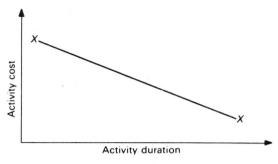

**Figure 13.25**

different method or process, no intermediate duration may be possible. For example, an estate of houses built by conventional techniques may require 50 days and cost £200 000 but an estate of 'industrialized' buildings may require 25 days and cost £330 000. Since two entirely different resources are used no compromise state exists on the same cost/duration function, whereas where the difference between normal and crash duration results from the use of additional similar resources, the two extremes may be interpolated, as in Figure 13.25.

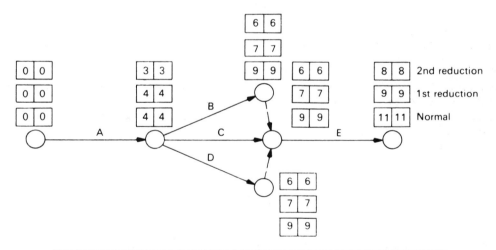

| Activity | Normal | | Crash | |
|---|---|---|---|---|
| | Duration (days) | Cost (£) | Duration (days) | Cost (£) |
| A | 4 | 30 | 3 | 40 |
| B | 5 | 12 | 2 | 18 |
| C | 3 | 10 | 2 | 20 |
| D | 5 | 10 | 3 | 12 |
| E | 2 | 15 | 1 | 30 |
| | Total 77 | | | |

N.B. Indirect fixed cost—£5/day

**Figure 13.26** *(a) Network diagram and comparison between cost of normal and crash activities.*

The total cost of a project is determined not only by variable costs such as production resources, but also by fixed or overhead costs such as rent for buildings, insurance, power, and administration. Consequently the project duration involving minimum total cost is not necessarily the duration with minimum cost of resources.

The network diagram for a small construction project, activity cost data and network dates are shown in Figure 13.26(a). Only the activities on the critical path affect the project duration, therefore reduction in project duration must be sought on the critical path and from those activities offering time savings at least cost. Initially there are two critical paths—ABE and ADE—and the least cost time saving is two days from both activities B and D. After activities B and D have been reduced from five to three days all three paths are critical and, since no further reduction is possible on activity D, savings must be obtained from activities A and E. Activity A can be reduced by one day at a cost of £10, then activity E by one day at a cost of £15. This procedure for reducing the project duration is given in the table in Figure 13.26(b),

Normal duration = 11 days
Normal cost = £77

| Job | Cost day saved | Reduction (days) | Total reduction (days) | Additional cost (£) | Duration (days) |
|---|---|---|---|---|---|
| Initial critical paths = $\begin{cases} A\,B\,E \\ A\,D\,E \end{cases}$ | | | | | |
| Least cost saving occurs on B and D | | | | | |
| $\left. \begin{array}{c} B \\ D \end{array} \right\}$ | 2 + 1 | 2 | 2 | 6 | 9 |
| Now three critical paths = $\begin{cases} A\,B\,E \\ A\,C\,E \\ A\,D\,E \end{cases}$ | | | | | |
| Least cost saving on A | | | | | |
| A | 10 | 1 | 3 | 16 | 8 |
| Least cost saving on E | | | | | |
| E | 15 | 1 | 4 | 31 | 7 |

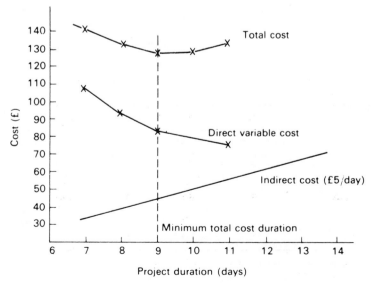

**Figure 13.26**  *(b) Activity variable cost/duration relationships for Figure 13.26 (a).*

which also shows the construction of the total cost/project duration curve. The least cost project duration is nine days.

Before terminating our discussion of costs we must draw attention to a rather interesting 'twist' or variation of the procedure followed in the preceding example. Again we shall consider a simple example in order to explain the variation. Consider the simple project represented by Figure 13.27. Let us calculate the total cost associated with the completion of this project in firstly one and then two days less than the normal duration.

The normal duration of the project is 32 days at a normal cost of £1620. Under those conditions the critical path is 0 1 4 3 5 6 (see Figure 13.27 and Table 13.1). To reduce this duration by one day, one of the jobs on the critical path must be reduced by one day. The cheapest reduction is available on job 1–4 (£15), consequently a project duration of 31 days is achieved at a cost of £1635.

There are now three critical paths (0 1 4 3 5 6, 0 2 4 3 5 6 and 0 1 3 5 6), consequently a reduction of the project duration by a further day is achieved by reducing each of

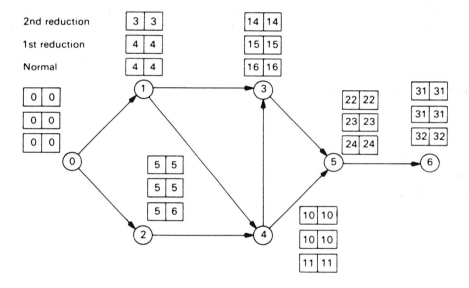

| Activity | Normal | | Crash | |
|---|---|---|---|---|
| | Duration (days) | Cost (£) | Duration (days) | Cost (£) |
| 0–1 | 4 | 200 | 3 | 230 |
| 0–2 | 5 | 180 | 4 | 200 |
| 1–3 | 11 | 200 | 9 | 240 |
| 1–4 | 7 | 150 | 6 | 165 |
| 2–4 | 5 | 150 | 4 | 170 |
| 4–3 | 5 | 170 | 4 | 190 |
| 3–5 | 8 | 170 | 7 | 265 |
| 4–5 | 8 | 200 | 8 | 200 |
| 5–6 | 8 | 200 | 8 | 200 |
| | Total 1620 | | | |

N.B. Indirect fixed cost considered to be zero.

**Figure 13.27**

these paths by one day. Job 1–4 cannot be reduced any further, hence the cheapest direct method of reducing the project duration from 31 to 30 days is reducing by one day the duration of job 1–3 (thereby reducing critical path 0 1 3 5 6) and the duration of job 4–3 (thereby reducing the duration of *both* paths 0 1 4 3 5 6 and 0 2 4 3 5 6). Thus the additional cost incurred is £40 and the total cost for a project duration of 30 days is £1675. Notice that although three critical paths were involved, job 4–3 was common to two of those and it was necessary only to alter the duration of two jobs.

Job 0–1 is also common on two critical paths and we could therefore have reduced the duration of this job and that of either job 0–2 or 2–4 to reduce the duration of the project, but such a solution would have been more expensive than that outlined previously. One further means of reducing the duration of the project would have been to reduce the duration of jobs 0–1 and 4–3. This again would have been a more expensive solution than the original. Notice, however, that both jobs 0–1 and 4–3 are common to two paths. Reduction of job 0–1 would reduce both path 0 1 3 5 6 and path 0 1 4 3 5 6, while reduction of job 4–3 would reduce path 0 1 4 3 5 6 and path 0 2 4 3 5 6. The reduction of both of these jobs by one day would reduce path 0 1 4 3 5 6 by two days, hence an alternative method of obtaining a project duration is to reduce by one day jobs 0–4 and 4–3, and to *increase* by one day job 1–4. In fact this alternative is cheaper than the previous one, the cost of the reduction being 30 + 20 − 15, i.e. £35 compared with the £40 cost of the previous method.

**Table 13.1**

| Job or activity | Cost/day saved | Reduction | Total reduction | Additional cost | Duration |
|---|---|---|---|---|---|
|  |  |  |  |  | 32 |
| Critical path 0 1 4 3 5 6 |  |  |  |  |  |
| Least cost reduction occurs on path 1–4 | 15 | 1 | 1 | 15 | 31 |
| Critical paths $\begin{cases} 0\ 1\ 4\ 3\ 5\ 6 \\ 0\ 2\ 4\ 3\ 5\ 6 \\ 0\ 1\ 3\ 5\ 6 \end{cases}$ |  |  |  |  |  |
| *Method 1* $\left.\begin{array}{l} 1\text{–}3 \\ 4\text{–}3 \end{array}\right\}$ | 20 + 20 | 1 | 2 | 55 | 30 |
| *Alternative method* $\left.\begin{array}{l} 0\text{–}1 \\ 4\text{–}5 \end{array}\right\}$ | 30 + 20 | 1 | 2 | 50 | 30 |
| 1–4 | − 15 (increase duration) |  |  |  |  |

This interesting twist occurs only infrequently; nevertheless it is worth while keeping a lookout for this type of solution when the analysis involves more than one critical path—when two or more reducible activities are common to these paths which themselves contain previously reduced activities.

## FURTHER READING

Battersby, A. (1978) *Network Analysis for Planning and Scheduling Studies in Management,* 3rd edition. London: Macmillan. Possibly the best British book on network methods.

## QUESTIONS

**13.1** Construct a network diagram for the following activities:

| Activity | A | B | C | D | E | F | G | H | J | K | L | M | N | O |
|---|---|---|---|---|---|---|---|---|---|---|---|---|---|---|
| Necessary preceding activities | – | – | A | AB | C | C | D | D | E | EF | GH | H | JK | LM |

**13.2** Draw an activity network for the following activities. Assuming that the project starts at day 0, calculate the earliest start and latest finish dates for all activities, and the project earliest completion date. Calculate also the total float on all activities and identify the critical path.

| Activity | A | B | C | D | E | F | G | H | I |
|---|---|---|---|---|---|---|---|---|---|
| Immediate predecessors | – | – | A | AB | BC | CD | CD | EF | EGF |
| Activity duration (days) | 3 | 5 | 6 | 2 | 4 | 7 | 3 | 4 | 5 |

**13.3** The following table describes the various activities of a small project. What is the probability that the project will be completed in 22½ days or less?

| Activity | Immediate predecessor(s) | Estimates of activity duration (days) | | |
|---|---|---|---|---|
| | | Optimistic | Likely | Pessimistic |
| A | – | 2 | 4 | 6 |
| B | A | 1 | 5 | 9 |
| C | A | – | 9 | – |
| D | C | 5 | 6 | 7 |
| E | B | 5 | 7 | 9 |
| F | B | 4 | 10 | 16 |
| G | DE | – | 7 | – |
| H | F | 6 | 9 | 12 |

**13.4** A small civil engineering project consists of 15 activities and can be represented by the network diagram below:

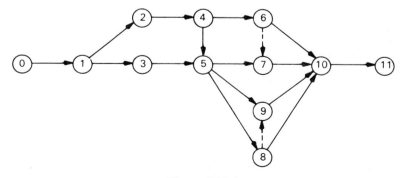

**Figure Q13.4**

The duration of each of the activities is given in the following table.

| Activity | | Duration (days) |
|---|---|---|
| Begin event | End event | |
| 0 | 1 | 10 |
| 1 | 2 | 5 |
| 1 | 3 | 6 |
| 2 | 4 | 3 |
| 3 | 5 | 4 |
| 4 | 5 | 3 |
| 4 | 6 | 8 |
| 5 | 7 | 4 |
| 5 | 8 | 5 |
| 5 | 9 | 9 |
| 6 | 7 | Dummy |
| 6 | 10 | 7 |
| 7 | 10 | 2 |
| 8 | 10 | 3 |
| 9 | 8 | Dummy |
| 9 | 10 | 6 |
| 10 | 11 | 9 |

(a) If the project is to start at, say, day 0 and is to end as soon as possible, calculate the total float (TF) on each activity and identify the critical path.

(b) Activity 3–5 is 'lay 150 mm pipe'.
Activity 6–10 is 'lay 250 mm pipe'.

The project is begun on day 0 but the supplier of the pipes informs the company that the 150 mm pipe will be delivered on day 18 and the 250 mm pipe on day 34.
(i) What effect do these deliveries have on the earliest completion date of the project?
(ii) What is the new critical path?

**13.5** If certain multiple time estimates are used for the duration of individual jobs in a project, probabilities may be calculated for the completion of the project or part of the project by certain schedule dates.

What are the basic assumptions necessary for such calculations, and how justified are such assumptions in practice?

Under what circumstances is this procedure likely to be beneficial, and in what circumstances are the results likely to be either inaccurate or unrealistic?

Wherever possible, construct numerical examples to illustrate your answer.

**13.6** The following network diagram has been drawn up by a project planner. The diagram represents the sequence of jobs which will be undertaken during the service of a large component which must be completed by day 35. Using the estimates of the job durations given by the managers of the various departments, the project planner has calculated event dates which indicate that the project will be completed one day before the scheduled completion date.

The information given on the diagram has been submitted to you, the project executive, for approval prior to being distributed to the various departments. What are your reactions and why?

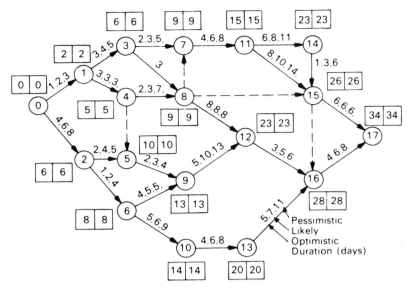

**Figure Q13.6**

**13.7** From the information given below construct a network diagram.
  (a) Neglecting resource considerations, what is the earliest finish date for the project?
  (b) Assuming that each activity begins as early as possible, construct a graph showing the amount of resources used during each period.
  (c) The maximum number of resources available is 19 workers. Again, assuming that activities are begun as soon as possible, redraw the network so that the resources used at any time do not exceed 19 workers, and so that a minimum project delay is incurred.
  (d) What project delay is incurred through this adherence to the resource limit?

| Activity | Immediate predecessor | Duration (days) | Number of workers used |
|----------|-----------------------|-----------------|------------------------|
| A | – | 8 | 4 |
| B | – | 7 | 8 |
| C | A | 6 | 5 |
| D | B | 8 | 4 |
| E | B | 4 | 8 |
| F | B | 8 | 6 |
| G | CD | 5 | 5 |
| H | E | 6 | 4 |
| I | F | 6 | 5 |
| J | CHI | 10 | 6 |

NB: Because of the nature of the work, jobs cannot be interrupted and must be finished once begun.

# CHAPTER 14

# Scheduling for Batch Processing

Although batch systems tend to be associated with batch manufacture, and our discussion in this chapter will to some extent focus on such applications, it should be remembered that batch flow processing might be evident in a variety of other situations. A batch flow system might exist in supply, in that the function might seek to transfer items from input stock to customers in batches rather than in unit quantities. For example, where the cost of supply, i.e. transfer from input stock to customer, is high there may be some benefit in dealing with several customers at one time, given the possibility of accumulating 'customers' for particular types of item. Equally, in supply systems which operate without input stocks, i.e. in which items are acquired for particular customers, there may be benefits in operating on a batch processing system. The acquisition and sale of shares, some commodities, etc., is undertaken in this way. In service systems customers may be processed in batches. For example, certain entertainment services operate in this way in that the service is provided when a given number or minimum number of customers are available. Such a situation might exist in systems in which resources are stocked, as in certain entertainment facilities or in situations which must acquire resources to satisfy customer needs. Likewise certain transport systems might operate on a batch processing arrangement. Transport, for example, might be available only when a certain number of customers have presented themselves. Thus a function might be triggered by the growth of the queue of customers to or beyond a certain minimum limit.

Thus batch processing systems may exist in all four functions and for most system structures. A common characteristic is the need to identify appropriate batch sizes at which the function is triggered. Equally there is usually a need to utilize the resources within the system for the processing of the different types of item or customer; indeed, it is because the available resources normally provide capacity in excess of that required for a particular type of item or customer that batch working is employed; thus, between the times at which particular items are processed, facilities may be used for processing different items or customers. In manufacture, batch processing might be employed in systems which have output stocks, i.e. batches of items are produced in anticipation of demand. Also the batch processing method might be employed in the manufacture of items to order, providing of course, orders are received for sufficiently similar items. (See 'Group Technology in Manufacture' later in this chapter.)

For transport and service systems it is likely that batch processing can be employed only where customer input queues exist, since it is unlikely that batches of customers will present themselves to the organization but rather that they will be allowed to accumulate over time. In all cases, of course, the use of batch processing at the expense of customer waiting or queuing time is feasible only in certain market situations, while the use of batch processing to provide a stock of items in anticipation of demand will be appropriate in circumstances where customer waiting or queuing is to be minimized.

In general the planning of batch processing requires the solution of three problems:

(a) batch sequencing, i.e. the determination of the order in which batches of different items or customers will be processed;
(b) the determination of batch sizes, i.e. the quantity of items or customers to be processed at one time;
(c) batch scheduling, i.e. the timing of the processing of batches of items for customers.

## BATCH SEQUENCING

It is possible that the cost of setting up, i.e. preparing, a set of facilities for the processing of a particular batch of items or customers will depend not only on the type of items or customers to be processed in that batch, but also on the type which was previously processed on the same facilities. Thus, for example, if, among other items, two very similar types of items (A and B) are to be processed in batches on a set of facilities, the cost of changing the set-up of facilities from that which is appropriate for processing item A to that which is appropriate for processing item B may be relatively low compared with the cost of changing the set-up from that appropriate for processing either of these types of items to that appropriate for processing quite a different type of item. Here the set-up cost is a function of the sequence of items, and it is appropriate to try to determine the appropriate sequence in order to minimize total set-up costs. Thus if four types of items, A, B, C and D, are to be processed in batches on a common set of facilities, and the set-up cost for each batch is influenced by the type of item which was previously processed on the facilities, and where that cost is known, an optimum sequence for these four items can be determined to minimize total set-up cost for the processing of a batch of each of the four types of items. The assumption here, of course, is that each batch must be processed the same number of times, i.e. that a repetitive sequence involving one batch of each item can be established. This is the normal situation, and a solution can often be found using the assignment method of linear programming. (The problem is identical to that of determining the optimum sequence for batches of items to be processed on a mixed-model repetitive/flow processing system. This is described in Chapter 15.)

### Processing 'families' of items

A situation might exist in which several different types of item each require a similar, but not identical, set-up, while other items which must be processed on the facility require a different type of set-up. In this situation those items which require the same type of set-up may be seen as a 'family' of similar items. It will be sensible when setting up the facilities to process a batch of any one of the items in the family to take advantage of that set-up and process a batch of all the other items within the family, especially where the cost of the set-up is relatively high.

For example, in the situation shown in Table 14.1, the set-up costs incurred between the processing of items B, C and D are small whereas the cost of setting up the process between either A or E and any of the family B, C and D is relatively high. In this case, therefore, there will be some merit in processing the 'family' of items B, C and D in succession, possibly in the order C, B, D, with the other two items produced at another time, possibly in the order A, E. In fact the sequencing problem shown in Table 14.1 is an example of the type of situation which *cannot* be solved using the assignment method referred to above; this is because of the configuration of the cost within the matrix. In such cases, particularly where a 'family' of items exist, an alternative approach will be required.

One approach to the solution of the 'family' sequencing problem is as follows:

1. Identify the items within a 'family'.
2. Determine the 'processing cycle' for these items (i.e. the time interval between the successive processings of the family) together with the batch quantity for each item.
3. Determine the optimum sequence for the remaining items and process these items as required between families.

**Table 14.1**   *Set-up costs.*

| Preceding item | Succeeding item | | | | |
|---|---|---|---|---|---|
| | A | B | C | D | E |
| A | 0 | 100 | 90 | 110 | 60 |
| B | 105 | 0 | 10 | 5 | 60 |
| C | 95 | 20 | 0 | 25 | 70 |
| D | 100 | 15 | 10 | 0 | 80 |
| E | 70 | 75 | 80 | 75 | 0 |

The procedure for determining the optimum processing cycle for a set of items is given later in this chapter.

(Notice that the 'family' processing problem has some similarities with the approach discussed in the section on group technology later in this chapter.)

## DETERMINATION OF BATCH SIZES

Batch quantities which are too large will result in high stock levels and cause a large amount of capital to be tied up in stock which might otherwise be invested elsewhere. Additionally, unduly high stock levels will incur other costs, such as the cost of stock-keeping, insurance, depreciation, etc. On the other hand, batch quantities which are too small will result in both low stock levels, which may be insufficient to meet large fluctuations in demand, and the frequent processing of small batches, each time incurring costs associated with set-up, ordering, etc.

The problem, then, is to determine the batch size which minimizes total costs; consequently we must consider the following:

(a)  stock holding;
(b)  processing;
(c)  set-up and preparation of machines and equipment.

## Minimum cost batch size

The minimum cost batch size can easily be determined providing, of course, that the assumptions made in deriving the formula are justified in practice, and providing also that the various costs can be determined accurately.

We shall consider first a simple *static* and *deterministic* situation, i.e. one in which both processing and consumption rates are *known* and *constant*. Let us assume that items are delivered into stock as a complete batch at the end of the processing period. In other words we are considering the type of batch processing system shown in Figure 14.1.

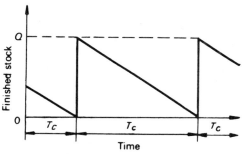

**Figure 14.1**   *Batch processing in a 'pure' inventory system.*

Our notation is as follows:

$Q$  = Process batch quantity
$C_s$ = Set-up or preparation cost/batch
$C_1$ = Stock-holding cost/item/unit of time
$r$  = Consumption rate/unit of time
$q$  = Process rate/unit of time

Then:

$$\text{Average stock level} = Q/2$$

$$\text{Minimum cost batch size} = Q^* = \sqrt{\frac{2C_s r}{C_1}}$$

$$\text{Total cost/unit of time} = C$$

$$\therefore C^* = \sqrt{2rC_sC_1}$$

$$\text{Processing cycle time}, t = \frac{Q}{r}$$

$$\therefore t^* = \frac{Q^*}{r}$$

These formulae are very simple to use, but often, to simplify matters even further, nomographs, tables or charts are used.

## EXAMPLE 14.1

Watertight Ltd are the manufacturers of a range of plastic overshoes. The complete range consists of 14 different types (i.e. sizes and styles). Type BB (Big and Black) is sold in the largest quantities, demand being reasonably stable at 4500 pairs per month.

All overshoes are manufactured in batches, the production process being such that the entire batch is completed at the same time.

(a) Given the following information, use the formulae above to determine the economic batch production quantity:

    Machine set-up cost per production batch = £150
    Stock-holding cost per pair     = £3.75 per annum

(b) The present production policy is to manufacture BB overshoes in batch sizes of 3000 pairs at regular intervals. How does the actual production cycle time compare with the optimum production cycle time?

(a)        $r = 4500$ per month
         $C_s = £150$

$$C_1 = 3.75 \times \frac{1}{12} = £0.313 \text{ per month}$$

$$\therefore Q^* = \sqrt{\frac{2C_s r}{C_1}} = \sqrt{\frac{2 \times 150 \times 4500}{0.313}}$$

$$= 2070 \text{ pairs}$$

(b)        $t^* = \dfrac{Q^*}{r}$

$$= \frac{2070}{4500}$$

$$= 0.46 \text{ months}$$

  Actual $Q = 3000$ pairs

$$\therefore \text{ Actual } t = \frac{Q}{r} = \frac{3000}{4500}$$

$$= 0.67 \text{ months (45\% longer interval than optimum policy)}$$

One might extend this simple model to include the possibility of stock shortages or 'stock-outs'. This introduces an additional cost factor, the cost of shortages, $C_2$. The model, which still assumes known and constant demand, is depicted in Figure 14.2. The areas below the horizontal axis, i.e. periods $t_2$, represent demand which would have been satisfied had adequate stock been available. The cost of such shortage, in terms of loss of profit, etc., must be introduced into the formula, since it will influence the choice of batch size.

Using the previous notation, plus $C_2$ = shortage cost/item/unit of time:

$$Q^* = \sqrt{\frac{2rC_s}{C_1}} \sqrt{\frac{C_1 + C_2}{C_2}}$$

$$C^* = \sqrt{2rC_1 C_s} \sqrt{\frac{C_2}{C_1 + C_2}}$$

$$t^* = \frac{Q^*}{r}$$

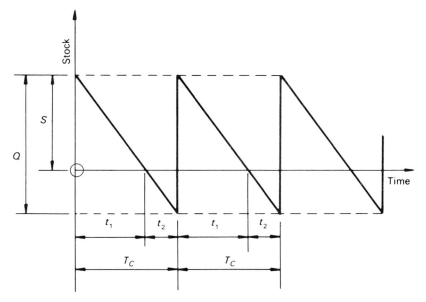

**Figure 14.2** *A stock/batch processing model allowing shortages.*

---

## EXAMPLE 14.2

$$r = 9500 \text{ per month}$$
$$C_1 = £5 \text{ per item per annum}$$
$$C_s = £1250$$
$$C_2 = £2 \text{ per item per month}$$

Compare the optimum processing quantities for:

(a) a policy in which stock-outs are permitted;
(b) a policy in which stock-outs are not to occur.

(a)

$$Q^* = \sqrt{\frac{2rC_s r}{C_1}} \sqrt{\frac{C_1 + C_2}{C_2}}$$

$$= \sqrt{\frac{2 \times 1250 \times 9500}{5/12}} \sqrt{\frac{5/12 + 2}{2}}$$

$$= 7520 \times 1.1$$
$$= 8250$$

(b)

$$Q^* = \sqrt{\frac{2C_s r}{C_1}}$$

$$= 7520$$

---

Now instead of considering the total processing batch to be delivered into stock at the same time, we shall consider a situation in which the items which constitute the batch are delivered into stock continuously throughout the process period. Such a situation is depicted in Figure 14.3.

We can again calculate optimum batch quantities, etc., as follows (adopting the notation used above):

Average inventory $= B + \dfrac{Q}{2}(1 - r/q)$

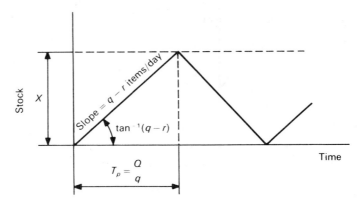

**Figure 14.3**

$$Q^* = \sqrt{\frac{2C_s r}{C_1 (1 - r/q)}}$$

$$C^* = \sqrt{2rC_s C_1} \sqrt{1 - (r/q)}$$
$$t^* = \frac{Q^*}{r}$$

---

## EXAMPLE 14.3

A product is sold at a constant rate of 600 per day, the processing rate for the item being 2000 per day. It is known that set-up costs are £10 per batch and that stock-holding costs, including notional loss of interest on capital, are £0.5 per item per year. If a buffer stock of 500 items is maintained, what is the minimum cost processing batch quantity?

$$C_s = £10$$
$$B = 500$$
$$q = 2000$$
$$r = 600$$

Assuming that there are 250 working days per year:

$$C_1 = \frac{0.5}{250} = £0.002 \text{ per item per day}$$

$$Q^* = \sqrt{\frac{2 \times 10 \times 600}{0.002(1 - 6/20)}}$$

$$Q^* = 2925$$

---

## The 'production' range (or processing range)

Because of the frequent difficulty of accurately establishing costs such as $C_1$ and $C_s$ it is fortunate that the total cost curve is fairly flat at the point of minimum cost, since this means that the total variable cost is not very sensitive to deviations from optimal batch size. It is possible, therefore, to adopt a batch size which differs slightly from the optimal without incurring substantially increased costs. This feature of the total cost curve gives rise to the 'production range' concept (see Figure 14.4). Batch quantities within this range are considered as acceptable.

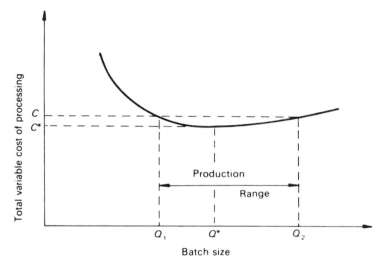

**Figure 14.4** *Economic batch size.*

Eilon[1] has developed a procedure for the determination of an acceptable processing range which is dependent on knowing the allowable increase in the total variable costs of production, i.e. let:

$$c = \frac{\text{Actual variable costs per unit}}{\text{Minimum variable costs per unit}}$$

$$q = \frac{\text{Actual batch size}}{\text{Minimum cost batch size}}$$

then:

$$q = c \pm \sqrt{c^2 - 1}$$

and the two limits of 'production' range are:

$$Q_1 = Q^*(c - \sqrt{c^2 - 1}) = Q^*q_1$$
$$Q_2 = Q^*(c + \sqrt{c^2 - 1}) = Q^*q_2$$

The values of $q_1$ and $q_2$ can be found from the curve given in Figure 14.5 and consequently the production range can be calculated.

---

[1] Eilon, S. (1969) *Elements of Production Planning and Control*. London: Collier-Macmillan.

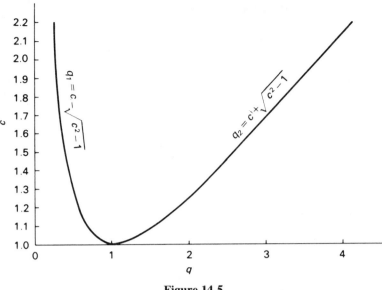

**Figure 14.5**

---

## EXAMPLE 14.4

In our previous example the optimal batch size was 2925 units. A policy of an allowable increase in cost per unit of 10 per cent has been adopted, i.e. $c = 1.1$. From Figure 14.5:

$$q_1 = 0.65$$
$$q_2 = 1.55$$
$$Q_1 = Q^*q_1 = 2925(0.65) = 1901$$
$$Q_2 = Q^*q_2 = 2925(1.55) = 4533$$

---

## SCHEDULING FOR BATCH PRODUCTION

Having now decided the optimal size of the batch for each item which is to be processed, we must consider when these batches are to be processed. Here we shall focus on one particular aspect of the scheduling problem which is peculiar to batch processing and then on one further technique which is of relevance in this area. Previously we have considered each item in isolation, whereas we must now consider how these batches are to be processed on the available equipment and how they affect one another.

As an illustration of the batch scheduling problem, consider a situation in which only two items (A and B) are to be processed successively on the same equipment. The economic (minimum cost) batch quantity for each item has been calculated by use of one of the previous formulae and the processing schedule is shown in Figure 14.6. In this case there is no idle time on the equipment and the optimum and individually calculated processing policies for the two batches do not clash, so we must think ourselves particularly lucky. Quite easily we could have found ourselves in a far from

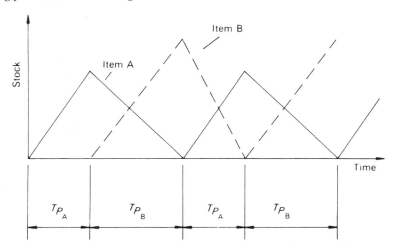

**Figure 14.6** *Successive processing of batches of A and B on the same equipment: ideal situation.*

ideal situation in which, for example, the sum of the processing times for the batches of items was either greater or less than the time available. Alternatively a situation might have resulted in which processing of successive batches of one item was constrained to take place at greater than the desired interval and consequently stocks of that item would fall to a level below the desirable safety or buffer stock level. Any of these situations is quite likely to arise if, in a multi-item situation, we attempt to calculate batch sizes and processing cycles for items individually and without reference to their effect on one another.

Very often the order or sequence in which the different items are to be processed will be determined either by the process itself or by the setting-up or preparation requirements for each item. For example, in a paint-manufacturing process it is desirable to manufacture lighter colours first and darkers colours later. In the manufacture of engineering components, the order in which batches of items are manufactured is often determined by the change-over costs of jigs and tools. In such cases the only problems to be solved are the desirable length of the complete manufacturing cycle (i.e. the time required to manufacture one batch of all the products) and the frequency of the cycles.

The problem is to find the most economical cycle, i.e. that which minimizes set-up and holding or inventory costs. As before, the set-up costs increase and the holding costs decrease as the number of cycles increases, but to obtain a satisfactory solution the cycle time for all items must be set simultaneously.

## THE LINE OF BALANCE TECHNIQUE

Our previous discussion has taken for granted the fact that batch processing proceeds in a series of steps. For example, we have assumed that in a process consisting of several operations, 1, 2, 3, etc., the entire batch is completed on operation 1 before being passed to operation 2 and so on. This type of situation is desirable to some extent, since it provides easier operations control. On the other hand there are disadvantages in this iterative type of procedure. For example, the throughput time for any batch will be high, the work in progress will be high and, consequently, a large amount of storage space will be required. Ideally, therefore, we must look for a procedure in which batches of items might be divided, i.e. processing begun on subsequent operations before the complete batch has been processed on previous operations, and yet a procedure which enables adequate control of operations to be exercised. Such a situation might be desirable in manufacture, supply or service systems in certain conditions.

When batches are kept complete during processing and when an activity schedule for each batch on each operation is available, it is an easy matter to determine whether processing is proceeding according to plan. If the dividing of batches is allowed then the situation is more complex and it is often quite difficult both to establish an activity schedule and to determine whether progress is satisfactory or not. It is difficult, for example, to determine whether, at a given time, sufficient items have completed sufficient operations.

For example, consider the completion schedule shown in Table 14.2. Twelve finished items must be completed at the end of week 1, another fourteen at the end of week 2, and so on. It is clear from this that, at the end of the fifth week, forty items should have completed the final operation. What is not clear, however, is how many items should have passed through the previous operations at this date so as to ensure completion of the requisite quantity of items in later weeks.

**Table 14.2**  *Job completion requirements.*

| Week no. | Delivery of finished items required | Cumulative completions |
|:---:|:---:|:---:|
| 0 | 0 | 0 |
| 1 | 12 | 12 |
| 2 | 14 | 26 |
| 3 | 8 | 34 |
| 4 | 6 | 40 |
| 5 | 10 | 50 |
| 6 | 12 | 62 |
| 7 | 14 | 76 |
| 8 | 16 | 92 |
| 9 | 18 | 110 |
| 10 | 22 | 132 |

The 'line of balance' technique was developed to deal with precisely this type of situation. It originated at the US Goodyear Company in the early 1940s, was developed during the 1950s at the request of the US Department of Defence, and has been used largely by the US Army and Navy.

The line of balance technique is an example of 'management by exception' since it deals only with the important or crucial (exceptional) operations in a job, establishes a schedule or plan for them and attracts attention to those which do not conform to this schedule (those about which something must be done if the progress of the entire job is not to be jeopardized). It is particularly useful where large batches of fairly complex items requiring many operations are to be delivered or completed over a period of time.

The technique can be regarded as a slightly more sophisticated form of the Gantt chart, the objective being to study the progress of jobs at regular intervals, to compare progress on each operation with the progress necessary to satisfy the eventual delivery requirements, and to identify those operations in which progress is unsatisfactory.

We can best describe the technique by means of a simple example. Two pieces of information are required: first the completion requirements and second an operation programme, i.e. the sequence and duration of the various operations. Four stages are involved in the use of the technique:

(a) the completion schedule;
(b) the operation programme;
(c) the programme progress chart;
(d) analysis of progress.

## The completion schedule

Construction of the completion schedule is the first step. The cumulative complete requirements must be calculated and presented as either a table (Table 14.2) or, and this is more useful later, a graph (Figure 14.7), which may also be used to record deliveries in the manner shown.

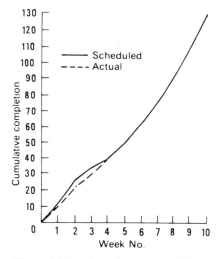

**Figure 14.7** *Cumulative completions.*

## The operation programme

The operation programme depicts the 'lead time' of the various operations, i.e. the length of time prior to the completion of the final operation by which intermediate operations must be completed.

In a simple job it is possible to show such information for *all* operations in the job, but in more complex jobs we concern ourselves only with those operations which are important or critical to the progress of the job and the satisfaction of the schedule.

The operation programme is best depicted as a chart, with the final delivery date as zero. Figure 14.8 is such an operation programme. The final completion date (completion of operation 15) is zero and the time scale runs from right to left. This programme shows that items B and C must be combined (operation 14) two days before completion. Item C, prior to this combination, undergoes two conversion operations; the second must be finished five days before final completion, and the first two days before that. Purchase of the material for item C must be completed by ten days before final combination. The item with longest lead time, 17 days, is B.

These two pieces of information—completion schedule and operation

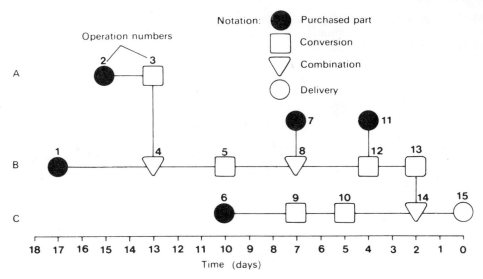

**Figure 14.8**   *Operation programme.*

programme—are prerequisites for use of the line of balance technique. They need to be constructed only once for any job, unlike the following documents, which must be constructed each time the schedule and progress are examined.

## The programme progress chart

This chart shows the number of items which have been finished at each of the critical or important operations at a given date. Suppose, for example, the review date is week 4, by which, according to the completion schedule, 40 items should have been completed, i.e. 40 items should have passed operation 15 of the operation programme. The number of items that have completed this and each of the other operations can be obtained simply by checking inventory levels. The results can then be depicted by means of a histogram. Figure 14.9 shows the programme performance at week 4.

Since the object of the exercise is to compare actual progress with scheduled or planned progress, the information given in Figure 14.9 must be compared with required progress. This is done by constructing a line on the programme progress chart which shows the number of items which should have been finished at each operation at the time of review. This line—the line of balance—can be constructed analytically or graphically, the latter method being perhaps the more convenient for our purposes. The line of balance shows the total number of items which should have been finished at each operation. Clearly, since a cumulative completion of 40 items is required for week 4, a total of 40 items must have completed operation 15 by this date. Operation 14 has a lead time of two days, consequently at week 4 sufficient items must have completed operation 15 to ensure that completion requirements two days later are satisfied. From the completion schedule the delivery for week 4 plus two days is 44 units (assuming five working days a week). The longest lead time, operation 1, is 17 days, so at week 4 enough items to satisfy the delivery requirements for week 4 plus 17 days, i.e. 82 units, should have been finished. The graphical procedure shown in Figure 14.10 is a convenient way of performing these calculations.

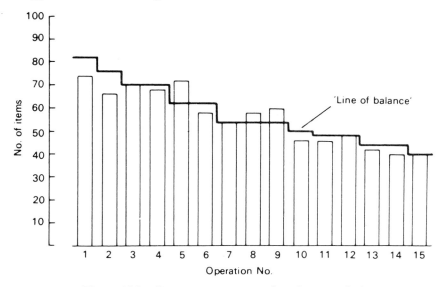

**Figure 14.9** *Programme progress chart (as at week 4).*

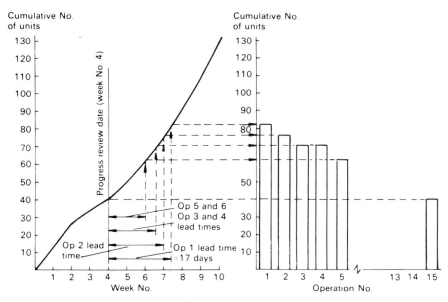

**Figure 14.10** *Construction of a line of balance.*

## Analysis of progress

In comparing required with actual progress it is again convenient to work backwards, beginning with the last operation (15). From Figure 14.9 it is clear that the required number of completed items have been delivered to the customer (operation 15 = 40), a fact which is reflected by the actual performance line on the completion schedule.

Clearly there is a shortage on both operations 13 and 14 and, unless processing can be expedited in some way, completion during the next week may fall short of requirements. When shortages occur, obviously we must attempt to ascertain the reasons. If operations other than those considered as critical are the cause of shortages then those operations must be included in subsequent versions of the progress and line of balance chart. As an aid to control, colour codes might be used for the 'bars' on the progress chart to depict responsibility; alternatively, additional charts might be constructed containing progress information on operations in various processing areas. Figure 14.11 shows three additional programme progress charts, each containing one type of operation. From these it is clear that performance on the purchasing operations may well jeopardize future deliveries. We must therefore attempt to ensure that items, particularly on operations 1 and 2, are purchased more quickly, or failing this we should alter the lead time on these operations. Charts such as these might be issued to and used by departmental managers or production controllers.

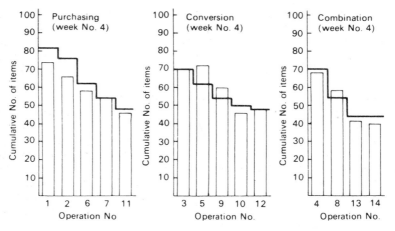

**Figure 14.11**   *Additional programme progress charts.*

The line of balance is a simple and useful planning and control technique, its main advantage being, like network analysis, that it formalizes and enforces a planning discipline which in itself is useful. It is a simple but powerful procedure which relies on several assumptions. For example, we have assumed that the lead times shown in Figure 14.8 are constant, and that the type and sequence of operations are independent of production quantities. Such assumptions are very often justified in practice and consequently the technique as it has been presented here is of direct value.

## GROUP TECHNOLOGY IN MANUFACTURE

The principal precondition for large-scale (large batch and mass) processing is a stable and high demand for items. The principal benefits of this type of processing are high machine utilization, few machine set-ups and low work in progress. Group technology is an attempt to obtain these benefits in situations where the necessary precondition does not exist and it attempts to do this by concentrating on components rather than products.

In conventional batch processing work, batch sizes and operations sequences are determined from the information available to the appropriate manager. Such information normally derives directly from the sales order or works order documents; consequently batch sizes are usually related directly to customer order sizes. The net result of this type of situation is that similar parts are often passed through widely differing sequences of operations and usually constitute different processing batches. This situation leads directly to low efficiency because of frequent machine set-ups and high work in progress.

Traditionally, in batch production, each time a particular item is manufactured a batch is produced so that an output stock might be built up in order to satisfy demand until that item is manufactured again. The appropriate, i.e. most economic, batch size is a function of the cost of setting up facilities for the manufacture of an item and the cost of holding completed items in stock. As the setting-up cost increases, for a given stock-holding cost the economic batch size will increase. As the setting-up cost reduces, then for a given stock-holding cost the economic batch size will fall. In general, the more similar the items to be made, the smaller the facilities set-up cost. Further, the more flexible the facilities to be used, i.e. the more easily adaptable they are to the manufacture of different items, the smaller the facilities set-up cost. Thus, if items can be grouped in families, and if inherently flexible manufacturing facilities can be used, a particularly efficient method of 'batch' production can be employed, in which batch sizes are small, throughput time is reduced, and output stock levels are minimized.

The concept of family or group production has been employed for some time. However, the recent availability of inherently flexible manufacturing facilities has begun to transform traditional batch production. In the engineering industry, for example, the use of computer-controlled machine tools with automatic tool-changing facilities, together with the automatic transport of items between machines and automatic loading using robotic devices, all under computer control, have resulted in the development of flexible manufacturing systems (FMS). The use of an FMS in the manufacture of 'family grouped', i.e. similar, items gives rise to a particularly efficient form of manufacture in comparison with the traditional batch working method through a function or process-type layout.

Efficient computer-controlled flexible manufacture is increasingly important in other manufacturing industries, e.g. foodstuffs, pharmaceuticals and clothing, where there is a need for the manufacture of a range of possibly similar products, where, for economic reasons, work in progress and throughput times must be reduced, delivery times must be reduced, and output stocks must be kept to a minimum.

Adopting a group technology method, the following stages are achieved:

1. The parts of each of the items processed are examined and placed into logical classes or families and the operations sequence for each class of parts is determined and specified.
2. Groups of facilities suitable for the processing of these classes of parts are specified using the operations planning details and forecasted demand for the items and hence the components.
3. The sequencing of each class of parts for each group of facilities.

For purposes of implementing group technology, two types of family or group and three methods of processing can be identified. The two types of family are:

1. *Type A,* consisting of parts which are similar in shape and which have all or the majority of processing operations in common.
2. *Type B,* consisting of apparently dissimilar parts which are related by having one or more processing operations in common.

The three methods of processing using group technology are therefore as follows:

1. *Method 1*—processing of a type-A family on a group of different conventional machines.
2. *Method 2*—processing of a type-A and/or type-B family on one or more similar and conventional machines.
3. *Method 3*—processing of a type-B family on a group of different machines.

In conventional terms the processing of a large quantity of type-A parts by method 1 corresponds to flow processing, which is, of course, an efficient method since it maximizes machine utilization. It is the object of group technology, by identifying common features in parts, to extend this type of application and to obtain increased efficiency in processing by adopting one of the three methods described above.

## Formation of parts families

On occasions the selection of the parts for inclusion in a family may be relatively simple; hence the use of one of the more rigorous techniques will be unnecessary. Such a situation may occur when the item range is fairly static, when there are large numbers of parts with similar shapes, and when several obviously exclusive categories of parts exist.

*Classification* in this context refers to the assignment of parts into predefined groups or classes, while *coding* is the allocation of identities to these groups. The type and amount of information contained in the code depend on the potential uses of the system. A designer may wish to retrieve designs to obtain relevant information and to use existing parts in new items, while retrieval is also necessary in connection with costing, planning, variety reduction, etc. For this reason the design of a classification and coding system is normally a compromise that attempts to satisfy as many potential demands as possible.

The demands made on the system require not only that it should establish what types of parts are being processed, but that it should also facilitate the arrangement of parts into groups suitable for manufacture by the group method. The size of some groups formed will be such that their process is not economically feasible, but by merging such groups together their group processes may become economic.

A different type of approach relies on the classification of operation or process routes for parts to identify families which use the same group of facilities, or which can be readily re-routed to do so. In production flow analysis a progressive form of analysis is used, consisting of three basic steps as follows:

1. *Factory-flow analysis.* The objective of this is to identify the best division of facilities into departments. The operations routeings for all parts (obtained from route cards) are coded to indicate the department visited by each item and then sorted by this code to create groups of parts with the same interdepartmental routeings.
2. *Group analysis.* The route cards for all parts processed in each department are analysed to identify the best division into groups. This is achieved by sorting cards into packs containing items with the same operation routeing, these packs then being combined to form viable facility/operation groupings.
3. *Line analysis.* The objective here is to obtain the best sequence of facilities in groups through study of the flow patterns within these groups. This is the layout problem in group technology, which will be discussed more fully in the next section.

## Facilities grouping

The facilities necessary to perform all operations on the parts family, and the expected load on each piece of equipment, can be listed for each family identified. It may be necessary at this stage to eliminate certain parts from families, or to add others to avoid low or uneven machine utilization. Rarely, however, will it prove possible to achieve full utilization of all machines in a group, and some flexibility of labour is probably required—a characteristic which distinguishes group technology from classic flow processing.

Several techniques suitable for assisting in the determination of the arrangement of facilities in a group-technology system have been developed.

Singleton[2] outlined a simple method for determining a layout sequence for a number of operations or machines through which a variety of parts is processed, each part having a particular route through the operations. This method involves converting the process or operation sequence for each part to a common length scale of 100 units, the spacing of operations on this scale being equal to $100/N$, where $N$ is the number of operations for that part. Histograms are plotted for each operation, showing its placing on the percentile scale for each part, the occurrences being weighted by the processing quantity for each part. These distributions are then ranked in order of their means to give a suitable sequence of operations, i.e. the operation with the lowest mean is placed first on the line and the one with highest mean is placed last. Backtracking or by-passing of operations by parts is indicated by the overlapping of the distributions, while distributions with a large spread or range might suggest that alternative operations routeings for parts be examined to improve part flow.

*Travel or cross charts* are of some value in developing layouts (see Chapter 6). Such a chart can show the nature of inter-operation movements for all parts for a given period of time. The row totals on the chart show the extent of movement from an operation, and the column totals show movement to an operation. Each cell of the chart shows the relative frequency of movement between two operations; an ideal movement pattern suitable for use on a flow line is indicated when all the entries in the matrix appear in the cells immediately above the diagonal. Such travel charts can be used to help develop a sequence of operations. For example, operations with a low 'to/from' ratio (i.e. row-total/column-total ratio) receive parts from relatively few sources but distribute work to a large number of destinations. Hence, if in-sequence movement is to be maximized and backtracking is to be minimized, such operations should be placed at the beginning of the sequence of operations. Conversely, operations with a high 'to/from' ratio should be placed towards the end of the sequence, since they receive work from a large number of sources but distribute to comparatively few destinations. This heuristic approach is simple and attractive, and clearly has considerable practical merit.

## Sequencing

The determination of the sequence in which batches of parts are loaded onto a group-technology cell or 'line' will be influenced by the desire to reduce setting cost and minimize throughput time. The problem is entirely congruent with the multi-model line batch sequencing problem and can be approached in the same way (see Chapter 15). If component batching is not adopted, individual components will

[2] Singleton, W. T. (1962) Optimum sequencing of operations for batch production, *Work Study and Industrial Engineering*, **3**, pp. 100–110.

be launched into the cell in much the same manner as in mixed-model line production. However, in this case, launch discipline and model sequence are unlikely to be important, because of the far greater throughput time and component idle time.

## FURTHER READING

For readings on techniques, particularly analytical techniques related to batch sizes, schedules, etc., see books on inventory management (Chapter 17).

Burbidge, J. L. (1975) *The Introduction of Group Technology*. London: Heinemann. The techniques of group technology.

Gallagher, C. C. and Knight, W. A. (1973) *Group Technology*. London: Butterworth. Classification and organization of group or family processing systems.

Lumsden, N. P. (1972) *Line of Balance Method*. Oxford: Pergamon. A clear and concise treatment of the subject. Possibly the best book on line of balance.

Ránky, P. (1983) *The Design and Operation of Flexible Manufacturing Systems*. Bedford: IFS (Publications).

## QUESTIONS

**14.1** What circumstances necessitate the use of batch processing in manufacture, supply, transport and service systems? What are the principal characteristics of this method of processing and what are the principal managerial problems involved?

**14.2** (a) Calculate:
   (i) the optimum processing batch quantity;
   (ii) the processing cycle time, given the following information:

| | |
|---|---|
| Set-up cost per batch | = £17 |
| Stock-holding cost per item per month | = £0.05 |
| Buffer stock required | = 25 items |
| Demand rate per year | = 12 000 (stable) |
| Process rate per month | = 1500 |
| Processing cost per item | = £25 |

The process is such that all items in a batch are completed at the same time.
   (b) Because of deterioration in the processing facilities, the processing rate per month drops from 1500 to 900. How does this change affect the economic batch quantity?

**14.3** Experimental Brewers Ltd are the sole manufacturers of 'Instant Beer'. Because of the market potential for this new style of beverage, an entirely new manufacturing facility has been established, the capacity of which is 5000 litres (equivalent) per day. At the moment demand for 'Instant Beer' is stable at 3000 litres (equivalent) per day. The product is manufactured intermittently, set-up costs for the facility being £250, and storage costs per day per 10 000 litres (equivalent) being £100.

The company is prepared to tolerate the occasional stock-out, which it estimates to cost £500 per 10 000 litres (equivalent) per day.

In what batch quantities should 'Instant Beer' be manufactured?

**14.4** The assembly section of a factory uses a certain component at a rate of 200 units per day. The associated set-up cost is £100, the manufacturing cost is £5 per unit, and the inventory holding is £0.1 per unit per day.

If the management is prepared to tolerate an increase of up to 1 per cent in the minimum total cost per unit, what flexibility does this give in the choice of batch quantities and what is the total cost per unit of the cheapest solution if, for technical reasons, production batches are restricted to multiples of 50 units?

**14.5** Discuss the advantages, disadvantages and limitations of the line of balance planning and control technique. Compare and contrast it with any other planning and control technique, such as network analysis, with which you are familiar.

**14.6** The delivery schedule of items and the operation programme for the manufacture of these items are given below.

| Week no. | Delivery required | Cumulative delivery |
|---|---|---|
| 0 | 0 | 0 |
| 1 | 12 | 12 |
| 2 | 15 | 27 |
| 3 | 12 | 39 |
| 4 | 20 | 59 |
| 5 | 5 | 64 |
| 6 | 10 | 74 |
| 7 | 15 | 89 |
| 8 | 10 | 99 |
| 9 | 27 | 126 |
| 10 | 15 | 141 |
| 11 | 20 | 161 |
| 12 | 17 | 178 |

Cumulative delivery requirements:

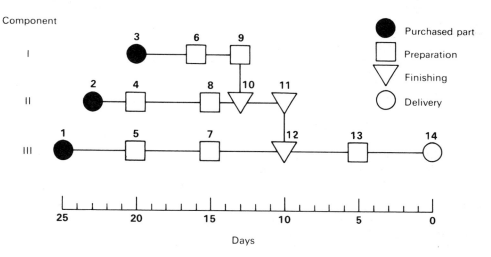

**Figure Q14.6** *Operations programme for each item.*

Construct the line of balance for weeks 3, 6 and 10. Indicate how you would use the line of balance to analyse production progress in the several different departments involved in the production of the items.

**14.7** What is group technology, and what benefits are likely to be obtained by introducing group technology, if appropriate, into a manufacturing company?

What steps would be followed during an investigation to determine whether group technology is appropriate in a given manufacturing situation?

Describe briefly the principal methods of component classification, designed for use in group technology.

# CHAPTER 15

# The Design and Scheduling of Flow Processing Systems

Here we shall focus on the characteristics, design and scheduling of the flow processing type of system, which, because of its importance, merits individual attention.We shall take as our principal focus the manufacturing flow or assembly line. Certainly flow line manufacturing systems are of considerable importance; however, we should not overlook the fact that similar types of system are to be found in other situations. For example, the passage of paperwork through offices in a company, or patients through various departments in a hospital, can be seen as flow processing systems.

Flow lines are a principal feature of mass production systems. While the details may differ somewhat, the concept remains the same: the items are manufactured or assembled as they pass through a series of work stations. Raw materials or components are fed in at the beginning of, and at certain points along, the line, and goods are delivered from the end of the line. In the assembly of motor vehicles the body unit is delivered to the first work station on the line and the workers at subsequent stations add the engine, transmission, suspension, body, trim and so on, until the vehicle is completed.

The mass production of complex discrete items such as cars using the flow principle is one of the most important achievements in manufacturing technology and one of the most important aspects of mass production. However, the general term 'mass production' embraces two technologies (Figure 15.1), the development of the simpler *quantity production* having preceded the development of *flow production*. We use the term 'quantity production' here to describe the manufacture, in large quantities, of relatively simple items using single facilities. In such cases there is no flow through facilities. Mass production and flow production are therefore not necessarily the same, since mass production gives rise to flow production only when necessitated by the nature of the product, i.e. where it is complex enough to require the use of several facilities or production 'stages'.

Flow production consists of basically two subsections: flow processes, designed for the manufacture of large quantities of bulk, fluid or semi-fluid products, and flow lines, which use the same principle of efficient material and product flow in the

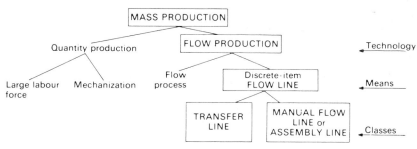

**Figure 15.1** *Mass production systems. From Wild, R. (1972)* Mass Production Management. *New York: Wiley. Reproduced with permission.*

manufacture of large quantities of complex, discrete items.

Flow lines which are engaged, essentially, in product assembly are often referred to as manual flow lines or assembly lines, while those which use automatic material transfer between the automatic machining 'stations' are normally referred to as transfer lines.

We have identified two classes of production flow line, and can now identify various subdivisions of these classes (Table 15.1). Both classes of flow line can be used for the manufacture of either one or more products. The production of one product or model on either class of line can be accomplished without the need to alter the 'set-up' of the line, i.e. without the need to change tools or work allocations, etc. The production of more than one product, however, gives rise to more complex situations. In such cases two alternative strategies are available:

1. The production of the two or more products in separate batches. This we shall refer to as the multi-model situation, and it necessitates the rearrangement of the flow line between batches.
2. The production of the two or more products simultaneously on the line. This we shall call the mixed-model situation, which gives rise to rather complex design problems, and will be discussed in some detail later.

**Table 15.1** *Classes and varieties of flow line (From Wild, R. (1972)* Mass Production Management. *New York: Wiley. Reproduced with permission.)*

| Flow line description | | Number of products | Product changes | Flow of items | Setting of equipment and allocation of work |
|---|---|---|---|---|---|
| Class | Variety | | | | |
| Transfer line | Single model | 1 | None | Regular | No changes required |
| | Multi-model | >1 | Batch changes | Regular batches | Changes of equipment setting and/or work allocation required on change of batch |
| Manual flow line | Single model | 1 | None | Irregular[a] | No changes required |
| or assembly line | Multi-model | >1 | Batch changes | Irregular[a] | Changes of equipment setting and/or work allocation required on batch change |
| | Mixed model | >1 | Continual[c] | Irregular | Changes of equipment setting and/or work allocation normally required[b] |

[a] Because of variable work-station times—characteristic of manual flow lines.
[b] Alternatively, as in 'group technology', tools and equipment might be permanently allocated a specific group of components.
[c] At any time the line contains a mixture of product types.

Whichever strategy is adopted, if more than one model or product is to be manufactured on the line, these products must have similar work contents. The greater the similarity the easier it will be to provide either multi-model or mixed-model production. More flexibility is normally available on assembly lines; consequently in certain circumstances it may be possible to design such lines for either multi-model or mixed-model operation. For example, many car assembly lines work on the mixed-model principle, different 'builds' of the same vehicle, and occasionally different types of vehicle, being produced simultaneously on the line. In contrast, transfer lines are far less flexible. They are normally confined to single-model, or occasionally large-batch multi-model, operation.

There is only one fundamental prerequisite for mass production, and that is mass demand. Since flow-line production is one means of mass production, its use also depends on mass demand. The term 'mass demand' must be qualified; in particular, we must consider not only the level of demand, but also the continuity. In practice, flow-line production will be justified for certain products when demand is both high and reasonably continuous. Nevertheless, in certain circumstances it may be justifiable to establish a flow line to produce items to satisfy one very large order (i.e. to accommodate high-level, but not continuous, demand). In practice such situations are likely to be rare, and some degree of demand continuity will normally be a prerequisite for flow-line production.

## THE DESIGN OF 'SIMPLE' FLOW LINES

We must begin by considering the nature and design of 'simple' flow lines. The reason for the use of the term 'simple' will become apparent later in the chapter, and here it is sufficient to recognize that certain simplifying assumptions will be made.

A production flow line consists, essentially, of a series of work stations, these stations consisting either of (in a transfer line) one or more machines or of (in a manual flow line) one or more workers, probably equipped with some tools.

The total work content of the product or item, i.e. the total time required to complete the item, is divided among these stations so that, as the item travels down the line, it becomes incrementally more complete at each station.

One objective in designing flow lines is to attempt to allocate equal amounts of work to each station, i.e. to divide the total work content of the job as evenly as possible between the stations. This is known as *line balancing.* Without such balance a certain amount of inefficiency or loss must inevitably occur, since some stations will have more work to perform than others. All stations will normally be required to process the same number of items within a given period of time.

The time required to complete the work allocated to each station is known as the *service time.* The time available at each station for the performance of the work is known as the *cycle time,* the cycle time normally being larger than the service time. The cycle time at a station is the time interval between the completion or the starting of work on successive items, and therefore includes both productive and non-productive work as well as any idle time. Non-productive work in both manual flow lines and transfer lines will include the transfer of the product between stations, and in the former will also include a certain amount of handling, movement, etc.

$$\text{Cycle time} = (\text{service time}) + (\text{idle time or loss})$$
$$= \frac{\text{productive}}{\text{work time}} + \frac{\text{non-productive}}{\text{work time}} + (\text{idle time or loss})$$

The total work content of the job consists of the total productive work plus the total non-productive work.

Total work content = (total productive work) + (total non-productive work)

The manner in which work can be allocated to stations on the line is influenced by certain constraints. Each job will consist of certain work elements, and normally the order in which some of these elements of work can be performed will be influenced by technological or *precedence* constraints. For example, it is necessary to drill a hole before it can be tapped. Such precedence constraints will limit the flow-line designer's ability to achieve balance in allocating work (i.e. work elements) to stations.

The allocation of elements to stations will also be limited by *zoning* constraints. Such constraints will necessitate or preclude the grouping of certain work elements at certain stations. For example, it may be essential that two work elements are not allocated to the same station if they might in some way interfere with one another, e.g. the grouping at one station of a delicate assembly and a heavy forging operation. Such a constraint is known as a negative zoning constraint, in contrast to a positive zoning constraint, which necessitates the grouping of two or more work elements at one station, as might be the case when the maximum utilization of a single expensive piece of equipment is to be achieved. Because of such constraints, perfect line balance is rarely achieved in practice, and a certain amount of *balancing delay* and *balancing loss* is normally inevitable. Balance delay is the difference between the total time available for completion of the job and the total time required. For example, at any one station the balance delay is the difference between the cycle time and the service time. The percentage balancing loss for any station is given by the difference between the cycle time and the service time, expressed as a percentage of the cycle time. Similarly, the balancing loss for a complete line is given by the difference of the total time available (e.g. the sum of the cycle times) and the total time required (i.e. the sum of the service times), expressed as a percentage of the total time available.

## Simple flow-line balancing

### The line balancing problem

The cycle time can be calculated, at least theoretically, from the required output. For example, if $N$ items are to be produced in $T$ minutes, then the cycle time ($C$) should be:

$$C = \frac{T}{N}$$

Furthermore, given these two figures and knowing either the total work content or each of the element times ($t$), the minimum number of work stations ($n_{min.}$) can be calculated.

$$n_{min.} = \frac{N\Sigma t}{T}$$

In fact, since we must have a whole number of work stations, $n_{min.}$ will be the integer equal to or greater than $N\Sigma_t/T$.

The average work station time ($\bar{c}$) is simply the total work content ($\Sigma t$) divided by the actual number of stations, $n$.

$$\bar{c} = \frac{\Sigma t}{n}$$

Almost invariably, this figure is less than the cycle time ($C$). Hence:

$$\text{Balancing loss} (\%) = \frac{C - \bar{c}}{C} \times 100$$

$$\text{or} = \frac{n(C) - \Sigma t}{n(C)} \times 100$$

Although we have spoken of idle time resulting from imperfect line balance, in practice, periods of idleness caused by the difference between cycle times and work station times rarely exist because a worker will normally be inclined to perform his or her work operations in the time available. In fact, a Parkinson's law type of situation will exist in which the work will expand to fill the available time. Nevertheless, the consequences are precisely the same because an under-utilization of labour will result.

It has been estimated that the balancing loss occurring in industry today is between 5 and 20 per cent.

The objective of assembly line balancing is that, given a desired cycle time or output rate, the minimum rational work elements and their standard times, and other constraints, one should attempt to assign work elements to work stations in order to:

(a)  minimize idle time or balancing loss;
(b)  minimize the number of work stations;
(c)  distribute balancing loss evenly between stations;
(d)  avoid violating any constraints.

### Methods of simple assembly line balancing

*The Kilbridge and Wester method[1]*

This simple heuristic method of assembly line balancing is best described by means of an example.

Assembly of a simple component requires the performance of 21 work elements which are governed by certain precedence constraints, as shown in Figure 15.2. This

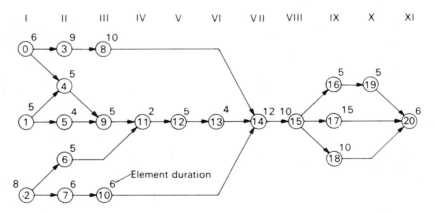

**Figure 15.2**  *Precedence diagram of work elements.*

[1] Kilbridge, K. and Wester, L. (1961) A heuristic method of assembly line balancing, *Journal of Industrial Engineering*, **VXII**(4), p. 292.

**Table 15.2**   *Tabular presentation of data in Figure 15.2.*

| Column no. in precedence diagram (a) | Element no. (b) | Transferability of element (c) | Element duration (d) | Duration for column (e) | Cumulative duration (f) |
|---|---|---|---|---|---|
| I | 0<br>1<br>2 | II (with 4, 7, 10) | 6<br>5<br>8 | 19 | 19 |
| II | 3<br>4<br>5<br>6<br>7 | III–V (with 8)<br><br><br>III<br>III–V (with 10) | 9<br>5<br>4<br>5<br>6 | 29 | 48 |
| III | 8<br>9<br>10 | IV–VI<br><br>IV–VI | 10<br>5<br>6 | 21 | 69 |
| IV | 11 | | 2 | 2 | 71 |
| V | 12 | | 5 | 5 | 76 |
| VI | 13 | | 4 | 4 | 80 |
| VII | 14 | | 12 | 12 | 92 |
| VIII | 15 | | 10 | 10 | 102 |
| IX | 16<br>17<br>18 | <br>X<br>X | 5<br>15<br>10 | 30 | 132 |
| X | 19 | | 5 | 5 | 137 |
| XI | 20 | | 6 | 6 | 143 |

precedence diagram shows circles representing work elements placed as far to the left as possible, with all of the arrows joining circles sloping or pointing to the right. The figures above the diagram are column numbers. Elements appearing in column I can be started immediately, those in column II can be begun only after one or more in column I have been completed, and so on.

The data shown on this diagram can now be represented in tabular form as shown in Table 15.2. Column (c) of this table describes the lateral transferability of elements among columns; for example, element 6 can be performed in column III as well as in column II without violating precedence constraints. Element 8 can also be performed in any of the columns IV to VI, as can element 10. Element 3 can also be performed in any of the columns III to V provided element 8 is also transferred, as can element 7.

Suppose it is our objective to balance the assembly line for a cycle time of 36, then in this case we would proceed as follows:

1. Is there a duration in column (f) of the table equal to the cycle time of 36? *No.*
2. Select the largest duration in column (f) less than 36, i.e. 19 *for column I.*
3. Subtract 19 from 36 = 17.
4. Does one or more of the elements in the next column (II) equal 17? *No, the nearest is 16 for elements 4, 6 and 7, which will give a work station time of 35.*
5. Select the smallest duration from column (f) which is larger than 36, i.e. *48 for columns I and II.*
6. Can one or more of the elements in columns I and II be transferred beyond column II so as to reduce the duration to 36? *No, but element 3 (with 8) plus 6 can be transferred to give a work station time of 34.*

7. Select the next largest duration from column (f), i.e. *69 for columns I, II and III.*
8. Can one or more of the elements in columns I, II and III be transferred beyond column III so as to reduce the duration to 36? *No, the nearest are elements 3, 8, 7 and 10, which would give a duration of 38, which is too large.*
9. Will an improved allocation of elements for station 1 be obtained by considering a large duration from column (f)? *No.*
10. Adopt the best allocation found previously, *i.e. step 4, which gave a work station time of 35.*
11. Rewrite the table to show this allocation, and calculate new cumulative figures for column (f) (Table 15.3).

**Table 15.3**

| Column no. in precedence diagram (a) | Element no. (b) | Transferability of element (c) | Element duration (d) | Duration of column (e) | Cumulative duration (f) | |
|---|---|---|---|---|---|---|
| I | 0 | | 6 | | | |
| | 1 | | 5 | | | |
| | 2 | | 8 | | | |
| II | 4 | | 5 | | | |
| | 6 | | 5 | | | |
| | 7 | | 6 | | (35) | Station 1 |
| III | 3 | III–V (with 8) | 9 | | | |
| | 9 | | 5 | | | |
| | 5 | | 4 | | | |
| | 10 | IV–VI | 6 | 24 | 24 | |
| IV | 8 | V–VI | 10 | | | |
| | 11 | | 2 | 12 | 36 | |
| V | 12 | | 5 | 5 | 41 | |
| VI | 13 | | 4 | 4 | 45 | |
| VII | 14 | | 12 | 12 | 57 | |
| VIII | 15 | | 10 | 10 | 67 | |
| IX | 16 | | 5 | | | |
| | 17 | X | 15 | | | |
| | 18 | X | 10 | 30 | 97 | |
| X | 19 | | 5 | 5 | 102 | |
| XI | 20 | | 6 | 6 | 108 | |

12. Is there a duration in column (f) of the new table equal to 36? *Yes, for columns III and IV.*
13. Allocate the elements in these columns to the second work station and redraw the table showing new figures for column (f) (Table 15.4).
14. Is there a duration in column (f) of the new table equal to the cycle time of 36? *No.*
15. Select the largest duration in column (f) which is less than 36, *i.e. 31 for columns V, VI, VII and VIII.*
16. Subtract 31 from 36 = 5.
17. Does one or more of the elements in the next column (IX) equal 5? *Yes, element 16.*

**Table 15.4**

| Column no. in precedence diagram (a) | Element no. (b) | Transferability of element (c) | Element duration (d) | Duration of column (e) | Cumulative duration (f) | |
|---|---|---|---|---|---|---|
| | 0 | | | | | Station 1 |
| | 1 | | | | | |
| | 2 | | | | | |
| | 4 | | | | | |
| | 6 | | | | | |
| | 7 | | | 35 | (35) | |
| III | 3 | | 9 | | | Station 2 |
| | 9 | | 5 | | | |
| | 5 | | 4 | | | |
| | 10 | | 6 | | | |
| | 8 | | 10 | | | |
| IV | 11 | | 2 | 36 | (36) | |
| V | 12 | | 5 | 5 | 5 | |
| VI | 13 | | 4 | 4 | 9 | |
| VII | 14 | | 12 | 12 | 21 | |
| VIII | 15 | | 10 | 10 | 31 | |
| IX | 16 | | 5 | | | |
| | 17 | X | 15 | | | |
| | 18 | X | 10 | 30 | 61 | |
| X | 19 | | 5 | 5 | 66 | |
| XI | 20 | | 6 | 6 | 72 | |

**Table 15.5**

| Column no. in precedence diagram (a) | Element no. (b) | Transferability of element (c) | Element duration (d) | Duration of column (e) | Cumulative duration (f) | |
|---|---|---|---|---|---|---|
| | 0 | | | | | Station 1 |
| | 1 | | | | | |
| | 2 | | | | | |
| | 4 | | | | | |
| | 6 | | | | | |
| | 7 | | | 35 | (35) | |
| | 3 | | | | | Station 2 |
| | 9 | | | | | |
| | 5 | | | | | |
| | 10 | | | | | |
| | 8 | | | | | |
| | 11 | | | 36 | (36) | |
| V | 12 | | 5 | | | Station 3 |
| VI | 13 | | 4 | | | |
| VII | 14 | | 12 | | | |
| VIII | 15 | | 10 | | | |
| IX | 16 | | 5 | 36 | (36) | |
| IX | 17 | | 15 | | | |
| | 18 | | 10 | 25 | 25 | |
| X | 19 | | 5 | 5 | 30 | |
| XI | 20 | | 6 | 6 | 36 | |

18. Allocate the columns concerned and that element to the work station and redraw the table (Table 15.5).
19. Is there a duration in column (f) of the new table equal to 36? *Yes, for columns IX, X and XI.*
20. Allocate the element in these columns to the work station.

All 21 elements have now been assigned to four work stations, the balancing loss involved being:

$$\frac{n(C) - \Sigma t}{n(C)} \times 100$$

$$= \frac{4(36) - 143}{4(36)} \times 100$$

$$= 0.7\%$$

As can readily be seen from the example, this heuristic method is rapid, easy and often quite efficient. The allocation of elements is basically determined by precedence relationships, lateral transferability of elements being used to aid allocation when necessary.

### Ranked positional weights[2]

The *ranked positional weight* procedure (developed by Helgerson and Birnie) is a rapid, but approximate, method which has been shown to provide acceptably good solutions quicker than many of the alternative methods. It is capable of dealing with both precedence and zoning constraints. The procedure is best illustrated by considering a simple example.

Assembly of a very simple component involves 11 minimum rational work elements. There are constraints on the order in which these elements are to be undertaken, but there are no zoning constraints. Figure 15.3 is a precedence diagram

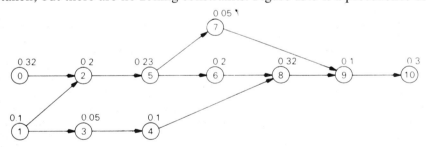

**Figure 15.3** *Element precedence diagram.*

in which the circles depict work elements. Element 2 must follow elements 0 and 1 and must precede element 5, etc. The standard element times (hours) are also shown in Figure 15.3. In Figure 15.4 this same information is listed: in the first column the element number is given, and in the second its standard time. The middle of the table shows the element precedences; for example, element 0 is immediately followed by element 2, which in turn is followed by 5, which is followed by 6 and 7, and so on. A single mark indicates the element which follows immediately, and crosses indicate elements which follow because of their relationship with other elements. The final

[2] Helgerson, N. B. and Birnie, D. P. (1961) Assembly line balancing using the ranked positional weight technique, *Journal of Industrial Engineering*, **XII**(6), p. 394.

| Element number | Element time (hours) | 0 | 1 | 2 | 3 | 4 | 5 | 6 | 7 | 8 | 9 | 10 | Positional weight |
|---|---|---|---|---|---|---|---|---|---|---|---|---|---|
| 0 | 0.32 | | | I | | | + | + | + | + | + | + | 1.72 |
| 1 | 0.1 | | | I | I | + | + | + | + | + | + | + | 1.65 |
| 2 | 0.2 | | | | | | I | + | + | + | + | + | 1.40 |
| 3 | 0.05 | | | | | I | | | | + | + | + | 0.87 |
| 4 | 0.1 | | | | | | | | | I | + | + | 0.82 |
| 5 | 0.23 | | | | | | | I | I | + | + | + | 1.20 |
| 6 | 0.2 | | | | | | | | | I | + | + | 0.92 |
| 7 | 0.05 | | | | | | | | | | I | + | 0.45 |
| 8 | 0.32 | | | | | | | | | | I | + | 0.72 |
| 9 | 0.1 | | | | | | | | | | | I | 0.40 |
| 10 | 0.3 | | | | | | | | | | | | 0.30 |

**Figure 15.4**  *Precedence and positional weights table.*

column of the table gives the *positional weight (PW)* for each element. This is calculated by summing the element's own standard time and the standard time for all following elements. Thus, in the case of element 0:

$$
\begin{aligned}
PW = \text{element}\ \ 0 &= 0.32 \\
+ \text{element}\ \ 2 &= 0.20 \\
+ \text{element}\ \ 5 &= 0.23 \\
+ \text{element}\ \ 6 &= 0.20 \\
+ \text{element}\ \ 7 &= 0.05 \\
+ \text{element}\ \ 8 &= 0.32 \\
+ \text{element}\ \ 9 &= 0.10 \\
+ \text{element}\ 10 &= 0.30 = 1.72
\end{aligned}
$$

The positional weight is therefore a measure of the size of an element and its position in the sequence of elements.

In Table 15.6 the elements, their times and the immediate predecessors are given in order of decreasing positional weights.

We are required to design an assembly line with the minimum number of stations to provide a cycle time of 0.55 hours (i.e. an output of 1.82 per hour). Using Table 15.6, elements are allocated to work stations in order of decreasing positional weights and without violating precedence constraints. Element 0, with the highest PW, 1.72, is allocated first to station 1. This allocation is acceptable because element 0 has no immediate predecessors, and furthermore its element time is less than the spare time available in station 1 (see Table 15.7).

Element 1 is the next to be allocated since it has the next highest PW. It is acceptable in station 1 since no precedence constraints are violated and there is sufficient unassigned cycle time left to accommodate it.

**Table 15.6**  *Elements in order of positional weights.*

| Element no. | 0 | 1 | 2 | 5 | 6 | 3 | 4 | 8 | 7 | 9 | 10 | Total |
|---|---|---|---|---|---|---|---|---|---|---|---|---|
| Element time | 0.32 | 0.1 | 0.2 | 0.23 | 0.2 | 0.05 | 0.1 | 0.32 | 0.05 | 0.1 | 0.3 | 1.97 |
| PW | 1.72 | 1.65 | 1.4 | 1.2 | 0.92 | 0.87 | 0.82 | 0.72 | 0.45 | 0.40 | 0.30 | |
| Predecessors (immediate) | – | – | 0.1 | 2 | 5 | 1 | 3 | 4.6 | 5 | 7.8 | 9 | |

**Table 15.7** *Element allocation for cycle time of 0.55 hours.*

| Work station | Element | PW | Immediate predecessor | Element time | Cumulative station time ($X$) | Unassigned station time ($C - X$) |
|---|---|---|---|---|---|---|
|   | 0 | 1.72 | – | 0.32 | 0.32 | 0.23 |
| 1 | 1 | 1.65 | – | 0.1 | 0.42 | 0.13 |
|   | 3 | 0.87 | 1 | 0.05 | 0.47 | 0.08 |
|   | 2 | 1.4 | 0,1 | 0.2 | 0.2 | 0.35 |
| 2 | 5 | 1.2 | 2 | 0.23 | 0.43 | 0.12 |
|   | 4 | 0.82 | 3 | 0.1 | 0.53 | 0.02 |
| 3 | 6 | 0.92 | 5 | 0.2 | 0.2 | 0.35 |
|   | 8 | 0.72 | 4,6 | 0.32 | 0.52 | 0.03 |
|   | 7 | 0.45 | 5 | 0.05 | 0.05 | 0.50 |
| 4 | 9 | 0.4 | 7,8 | 0.1 | 0.15 | 0.40 |
|   | 10 | 0.3 | 9 | 0.3 | 0.45 | 0.10 |

$C = 0.55$

$$\text{Balancing loss} = \frac{4(0.55) - 1.97}{4(0.55)} \times 100 = 10.4\%$$

The next highest PW belongs to element 2, but this cannot be assigned to station 1, even though its immediate predecessors have been assigned, because the unassigned station time remaining (0.13) is less than the element time (0.2).

Element 5 cannot be allocated because it must follow element 2; nor is there sufficient time available.

Element 6 cannot be allocated to station 1 for the same reasons.

Element 3 can be allocated to station 1 since its immediate predecessor is already allocated and there is enough time available.

Of the remaining elements only 7 is short enough for accommodation in station 1, but it cannot be allocated here because it must follow element 5.

The same procedure is now repeated for the remaining stations.

Four work stations are required for this assembly line, and the initial allocation gives a balancing loss of 10.4 per cent. Notice that there is unassigned time at each station, the largest work station time of 0.53 hours occurring at station 2.

For the specified output required (1.82 per hour) there is no better solution than the one given above, but, if other considerations permit, the cycle time could be reduced to 0.53 hours with a corresponding increase in output to 1.89 per hour and a reduction of balancing loss to 7 per cent. A reduction of the cycle time to less than 0.53 hours would necessitate the use of five work stations.

There is really little point in retaining a cycle time of 0.55 hours in this case, since to do so is merely to introduce inefficiency into the system for the sake of obtaining a given output. Here, as in many cases of assembly line balancing, it is desirable to modify output in order to minimize balancing loss. In this case, therefore, the assembly line balancing procedure would be first to seek a balance for a given cycle time, $C$, and then to minimize the cycle time for the same number of work stations.

## Multi-model and mixed-model line design

The use of flow techniques certainly leads to highly efficient production when product variety is small or non-existent, but any increase in the variety of the product not only leads to more complex design and management problems but also results inevitably in reduced operating efficiency. The increasing affluence and discretion of consumers and increasing competition from other manufacturers restrict a company's ability to rationalize production, and consequently, for example, few if any motor-vehicle assembly lines are now devoted to the continuous production of single uniform products, and a similar situation exists in many other industries. Multi-model or mixed-model lines must therefore be used and hence designed.

1. *Multi-model line*
   Again assuming a simple line design problem, this approach requires the following major decisions to be made:

   (a) How will the line be 'balanced'?
   (b) What will be the production batch sizes of the models?
   (c) In what order will the batches be manufactured? (The batch sequencing problem.)

2. *Mixed-model line*
   Here the major decisions are:

   (a) How will the line be balanced?
   (b) In what order will the models be launched into the line? (The model sequencing problem.)

### *Multi-model lines*

The multiple models may be either different products or different versions of the same product, but in either case the different models or products will have similar, though not identical, manufacturing requirements, since otherwise there would be little justification in manufacturing them on the same basic assembly line. In practice the line is set up for one model, then adjustments are made to the line prior to the manufacture of a batch of the second model, and so on. We can therefore consider the problem as a succession of separate assembly line design problems, hence decisions (a) and (b) above may be treated in the manner outlined previously. Decision (b), batch sizes, was dealt with in detail in Chapter 14.

The optimum manufacturing sequence for the batches of different models is clearly influenced by the cost of setting up the assembly line. The total cost of setting up the line comprises the cost of tool and machine changeovers, tool and machine resetting, machine and labour idle time, etc., and is clearly influenced by the nature of the preceding and succeeding models. The problem, therefore, is to determine the sequence order of the model batches to minimize the total setting-up cost over a given period of time. It is highly unlikely that line set-up costs will be constant, but, of course, if this were the case the sequence order of model batches would be immaterial. A solution to this problem can often be obtained using the assignment method of linear programming.

*Mixed-model lines*

The advantage of this type of production is that, unlike multi-model lines, a steady flow of models is produced in order to meet customer requirements, theoretically without the need for large stocks of finished goods. The major disadvantages arise from the differing work contents of the models, resulting in the uneven flow of work and consequent station idle time and/or congestion of semi-finished products.

Line balancing for mixed-model assembly lines might be considered merely as several single-model balancing problems, i.e. each model could be considered separately and the total work content divided as equally as possible between the work stations. Consider a case where a line is built for the assembly of two similar models of a product, A and B. The work elements of model A are allocated to the work stations so that during the periods in which A is being assembled, balancing loss is minimized. Similarly, the work elements of B are allocated to work stations in order to minimize balancing loss during the assembly of model B. Such a procedure is often adopted and is fairly satisfactory when the models to be produced are of a similar nature, i.e. when the production of each model involves similar work elements to be undertaken in a similar order or when the production of all models merely involves the repetition of similar work elements. When such circumstances apply, the workers at each station will be required to do the same type of work irrespective of which model is being produced. If, on the other hand, basically dissimilar models are to be produced, then independent line balancing for each will often result in dissimilar work elements, e.g. work involving different skills, necessitating different training, etc., being allocated to each station. In circumstances such as these, balancing should be undertaken in such a way as to ensure that similar work elements are allocated to the same work stations or groups of stations, irrespective of which model is being produced. A method by which this might be achieved (not described here) is to assign elements to stations on a total time rather than a cycle time basis.

The efficient design and operation of mixed-model assembly lines depends also on the solution of the model sequencing problem. The problem (not dealt with here) is concerned both with the time interval between the 'launching' or starting of models onto the line and also with the *order* in which models are launched onto and flow along the line. The objective of such sequencing is to provide for the best utilization of the assembly line, high utilization being associated with minimum station idle time and minimum congestion of work along the line (item waiting).

## THE DESIGN OF 'COMPLEX' FLOW LINES

### Human aspects of assembly line design

This phenomenon of work element or service time variability is the fundamental difference between assembly lines involving human operators and those depending exclusively on machines, i.e. transfer lines. It is not invalid to assume that machines at stations on transfer lines require a constant time for elements of work, but it certainly is quite unrealistic to make the same assumption about human beings. The procedures described above are adequate by themselves for the design of transfer lines, but insufficient for the design of assembly lines involving human workers.

Clearly, if we were to design assembly lines in which workers were allowed a fixed standard time, neither more nor less, in which to complete an operation, we might find that on some occasions the worker would easily complete the task within this time, while on other occasions he or she would be prevented from doing so. This type of situation is referred to as *rigid pacing*. There is no 'freedom' for workers, since they are confined to perform each and every operation in a given time. This rigid pacing causes both worker idle time and incompleted work.

These losses or inefficiencies, often referred to as *system loss,* can be reduced only by reducing or eliminating the pacing effect. There are two ways in which we can attempt to do this; both involve making the items available to the worker for a longer period of time. Take, for example, an assembly line consisting of workers sitting at a bench above which jobs travel by means of a conveyor belt with suspended baskets. The workers must take the job off the belt, perform the operation and replace it on the belt, which carries it to the next station. Jobs spaced at 5 m intervals on a belt moving at 5 m/min will produce an output of 60 products/hour. The same output will result from a spacing of 10 m and a belt speed of 10 m/min, or a spacing of 2.5 m and a belt speed of 2.5 m/min. But each of these different arrangements has different consequences for the seated workers, who can reach only a certain distance either side of their work stations. If they can reach 2.5 m either way, then in the first case each job will be within their reach and available to them for one minute only, in the second case for half a minute, and in the last case for two minutes. Clearly the greater the time the job is available to the worker the lower the pacing effect, and system loss is reduced.

On assembly lines where jobs pass directly from one worker to the next, every worker, except the one at the first station on the line, is dependent on the previous worker. Under such conditions the work must be strictly paced in order to avoid excessive labour idle time. If, for example, because of faulty material or a mistake in assembly, a worker at one station takes longer than the cycle time to complete the operation, then the worker at the next station on the line will have to wait for work (unless coincidentally he or she has also exceeded the cycle time). This coupling or interdependence of stations necessitates pacing, but if the stations could be decoupled in some way the pacing effect, and also system loss, could be reduced.

The way in which this is done is to introduce buffer stocks of several jobs between stations, so that temporary hold-ups or delays at stations do not immediately result in idle time at subsequent stations. There are certain disadvantages of using buffer stocks on assembly lines. Work-in-progress stock and hence tied-up capital will be increased, and additional space will be required. In fact, in many cases, because of the size of the items, it may be quite unrealistic to consider using buffer stocks. (Introducing inter-station buffer stocks onto a motor-vehicle final-assembly line would not be a suggestion that the company accountant or the works manager would receive too enthusiastically.) However, in many situations buffer stocks are an important feature of assembly line operation.

## FURTHER READING

Sawyer, J. H. F. (1970) *Line Balancing.* Machinery Publishing Company, Brighton, Sussex, 1970. Dealing solely, but comprehensively, with the flow system balancing problem.

Wild, R. (1972) *Mass Production Management.* New York: Wiley. A comprehensive treatment of discrete-item mass-production flow systems. The only book currently available on the subject.

## QUESTIONS

**15.1** A multi-station assembly line is to produce a minimum of 6000 completed items per 40-hour working shift. The assembly of one item consists of 25 elements of work together constituting a total work content of 11 minutes.

What is the minimum number of work stations for this assembly line and what will the cycle time ($C$) ideally be?

**15.2** What will be the balancing loss of the assembly line, the requirements of which are given above?

**15.3** The diagram shown below indicates the necessary precedence requirements of 12 work elements which together constitute the total work content of a simple assembly task.

Using the assembly line balancing technique devised by Kilbridge and Wester, design an assembly line (i.e. assign work elements to the required number of work stations) to produce as near as possible to, and no less than, three items per hour.

What is the balancing loss for the line that you have designed?

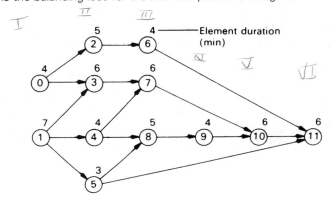

**Figure Q15.3**

**15.4** The work involved in assembling a small component can be described in terms of 11 minimum rational work elements whose element times are as follows:

| Element | Time (min.) |
|---------|-------------|
| 0 | 4 |
| 1 | 3 |
| 2 | 3 |
| 3 | 3 |
| 4 | 7 |
| 5 | 5 |
| 6 | 4.5 |
| 7 | 9.5 |
| 8 | 5 |
| 9 | 7 |
| 10 | 7 |

Certain precedence constraints apply to the work; these are shown diagrammatically in Figure Q15.4.

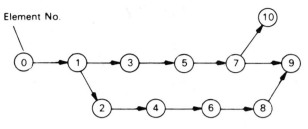

**Figure Q15.4**

Furthermore, because of the nature of the work it is necessary to ensure that elements 0 and 3 *do not* occur at the same work station, elements 3 and 5 *do not* occur at the same work station, and the elements 8 and 10 *do* occur at the same work station. Two assembly lines are to be designed (without buffer stocks), one producing components at a rate of 4.61 per hour and the other components at a rate of 5.0 per hour.

Use the ranked positional weight method to assign work elements to work stations in order to minimize the number of work stations and the balancing loss on each line. Calculate the balancing loss in both cases.

Describe the heuristic device you are using to solve this problem and justify its use as a method of assembly line balancing.

**15.5** What is 'system loss', how is it caused, and how can it be reduced?

**15.6** Analytical line balancing procedures are sufficient for the successful design of 'transfer lines' but are they adequate themselves for the design of mass production systems in which human operators are involved in executing the work?

What are the 'human' problems associated with the design and operation of mass production systems such as flow lines?

# INVENTORY MANAGEMENT AND THE SUPPLY OF RESOURCES

# INTRODUCTION TO PART 7

*Here we deal with the management of items, products and customers throughout the operating system, from inputs to outputs. We first identify different approaches to this task of materials management, and then consider those topics which are of particular and direct relevance to the operations manager.*

*Again, especially when dealing with inventory management in Chapter 17, we shall consider 'principal' or 'characteristic' operations management problem areas, i.e. problems which are influenced by the operating system structure and where the approaches employed are influenced by the operations objectives.*

# CHAPTER 16

# Materials Administration, Purchasing and Distribution

*Materials administration* has been defined as the methods and principles by which we endeavour to plan, organize, co-ordinate, control and review the flow of materials throughout an organization. It involves, therefore, some form of overall control of materials throughout an organization, and offers a distinctive and increasingly popular approach to materials management. In the absence of a materials administration approach within an organization the management (i.e. the planning, organizing, co-ordinating, controlling and reviewing) of materials, materials stocks, materials flows, parts stocks, materials in progress and, where appropriate, the flow of customers will be the responsibility of several departments or individuals. This is the more decentralized approach and has been the traditional approach in most businesses to date.

## CENTRALIZED v. DECENTRALIZED MATERIALS MANAGEMENT

The benefits of a centralized or overall approach to materials management, e.g. through the use of the materials administration concept, might be seen to include:

1. Avoidance of problems of divided responsibility.
2. Avoidance of possible conflicting objectives and priorities.
3. Avoidance of duplication of effort.
4. Ease of communications throughout the organization.
5. Ease of, and better representation of, the materials management function at board/policy level.
6. Better career/developmental opportunities.
7. Economies of scale.

The benefits of a decentralized approach to materials management, i.e. through the use of different departments or functions operating essentially individually but with appropriate communication and perhaps overall control from board level, might be seen to include:

1. Greater opportunity for functional specialization.
2. Greater flexibility.
3. Greater opportunity for materials managers to act as integral parts of geographically dispersed organizations (rather than being seen as separate head office/personnel staff).

The type of approach employed for materials management within an organization will depend largely on the relevance of the above advantages and the circumstances in which the organization is to work. For example it might be argued from organizational theory that a centralized (materials administration) approach might be more appropriate in 'static' situations subject to few uncertainties. In such situations the organization will face fewer changes in markets, demand, customer behaviour, supplier behaviour, technology, etc., and thus it may be possible to implement and stick to relevant rules, procedures, etc., for materials management throughout the organization. Where there is a greater degree of uncertainty, for example because of demand changes, product changes, changes in the nature of the service and technological changes, particularly where these affect different parts of the organization in different ways, then there may be some merit in a decentralized approach which facilitates rapid response to their changing circumstances from different parts of the organization. In this book our description of materials management is a decentralized one. The remainder of this chapter deals with purchasing and distribution, while in Chapter 17 we concentrate on inventory management, i.e. the management of input and output, and process inventories. Together these two chapters will cover most of the materials management tasks for most types of organization.

## PURCHASING AND SUPPLY

Although rarely their sole responsibility, the purchasing or procurement function clearly concerns operations managers. Operations managers are responsible for providing goods or services of the right specification and quality, at the right time, in the right quantity and at the right price, and purchasing or procurement managers are, in the same terms, responsible for purchasing materials and items of the right specification and quality, at the right time, in the right quantity, from the right source and at the right price. Theirs, in other words, is the responsibility of obtaining those items required by the operating system. They are concerned with the input to the operating system, i.e. the flow of physical resources to the operating system.

### The objectives of purchasing

The objectives of purchasing have been identified as follows:

1. (a) To supply the organization with a steady flow of materials and services to meet its needs.
   (b) To ensure continuity of supply by maintaining effective relationships with existing sources and by developing other sources of supply either as alternatives or to meet emerging or planned needs.

2. To obtain efficiently, by any ethical means, the best value for every unit of expenditure.
3. To manage inventory so as to give the best possible service at lowest cost.
4. To maintain sound co-operative relationships with other departments, providing information and advice as necessary to ensure the effective operation of the organization as a whole.
5. To develop staff, policies, procedures and organization to ensure the achievement of the foregoing objectives.

Reference to the management of inventories above raises the question of the relationship of purchasing as a process to inventory management as discussed in Chapter 17. Purchasing will, in some cases, become concerned with the provision of goods to input inventories, i.e. in those system structures in which inventories exist, the purchasing function, whether a part of the operations management area of responsibility or not, will be concerned with the link between customers and input inventories. In some cases this responsibility for supplying items and materials to input inventory will be matched with some responsibility for the maintenance of such inventories. In other situations inventory replenishment needs will be identified, thus giving rise to purchase requirements executed by the purchasing function. Again it is unimportant to argue about the responsibility for such input inventories. We shall deal with inventory management in Chapter 17. The topics covered there are of relevance in purchasing, as indeed the topics covered here are relevant to inventory management.

Deriving from the above objectives, we might identify the following as being the principal benefits to be gained from the effective management of the purchasing process:

(a) lower prices for materials and items used;
(b) faster inventory turnover;
(c) continuity of supply;
(d) reduced replenishment lead times;
(e) reduced transport cost;
(f) reduced materials obsolescence;
(g) improved vendor relationships;
(h) better control of quality;
(i) effective administration and minimization of organizational effort;
(j) maintenance of adequate records and provision of information for the operations managers.

Clearly the purchase of items and materials has relevance in all types of operating system, since in all such systems there will be some dependence on the use of physical items. While the principles and objectives of purchasing might also be applied in the acquisition of labour, capital, etc., the purchasing process is concerned primarily with obtaining physical items for use in, and conversion through, the operating system. Most operating systems need such items. Hospitals, for example, need a regular reliable supply of consumable items such as medicines and sterile equipment and transport operations are dependent on an adequate supply of consumable materials such as fuel and tyres. Supply organizations naturally are dependent on an adequate, reliable and efficient supply of those items which are to be passed to customers, while manufacturing organizations are entirely dependent on the supply of consumable and non-consumable materials and items.

## The organization of purchasing

A major issue in this context is the degree to which purchasing as a function should be centralized. In recent years there has been a trend towards the establishment of centralized purchasing functions. This trend has been particularly noticeable in health services and in local and central government supply, as well as in manufacturing. The principal benefits thought to be associated with central purchasing are summarized below:

(a) the possibility of standardizing specifications and establishing common needs, as regards quantity, quality, specification, etc.;
(b) the possibility of more economic purchase through, for example, larger batch quantities;
(c) the reduction in administrative cost through the purchase of larger quantities on few occasions, possibly from fewer sources;
(d) the possibility of purchase staff specialization and thus increased knowledge of sources and supplies;
(e) the possibility of the use of more effective, detailed and accurate purchase information and records;
(f) the possibility of more detailed accurate and rapid budgetary and financial control procedures;

The principal advantages derive from the possibility of increased purchase volumes, from standardization, and from specialization. Disadvantages of centralized purchasing, however, might include:

(a) difficulties of communication within the organization, deriving perhaps from geographical separation;
(b) slow response to new or unusual supply needs from the organization;
(c) possible increased dependence on a smaller number of suppliers resulting from increased volume and from standardization.

Thus the merits of centralized purchasing will depend on the possible financial savings through volume and variety considerations as against the possibility of reduced response times and flexibility.

## Sourcing and suppliers

An important function of purchasing is the identification of suitable sources of supply. The systematic investigation and comparison of sources, the evaluation and monitoring of performance of supply sources and the development of appropriate procedures with suppliers are therefore of importance. Vendor rating is discussed briefly below and in more detail in Chapter 19. Although market research will not be discussed in detail here, it will be appreciated that supplier market research is of importance in obtaining adequate supply sources for the organization.

Figure 16.1 outlines the procedure normally involved in selecting suppliers. The model suggests that the buyer, on receipt of a request to purchase, first checks whether the organization is currently committed to the particular supplier for the supply of such items and, if not, whether an existing source might satisfy the requirement. Repeat ordering with an existing source would be normal unless for some reasons necessitating a review of such an arrangement. Such reasons might include recent price increases, recent extensions in supplier supply lead time, failing to

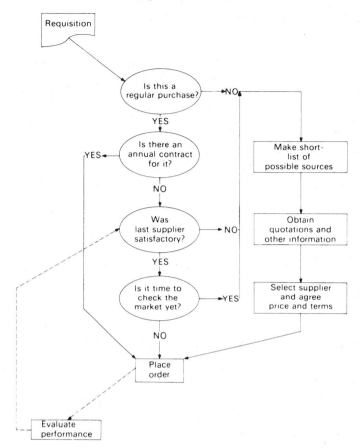

**Figure 16.1** *Outline of procedures for selecting suppliers. The broken line indicates steps taken after the order has been placed. From Baily, P. J. H. (1970)* Design of Purchasing Systems and Records. *Epping: Gower Press. Reproduced with permission.*

meet specifications, decline in vendor rate performance, etc. Buyer source loyalty is a well-documented phenomenon, and clearly offers benefits in terms of reduced administrative difficulty, improved vendor/buyer understanding and relationship. In fact, benefits accrue both to supplier and to vendor. Vendors tend also to give preference to existing customers.

Often an investigation of possible sources for the supply of new items and materials will reveal several alternatives, hence the question of single or multiple sourcing often arises. Factors to be considered in this respect include the following:

1. Effect on price, i.e. single sourcing of increased quantities may reduce purchase price. Alternatively, in certain circumstances, multiple sourcing may in fact reduce price as a result of supplier competition for orders.
2. Effect on supply security, i.e. while organization of supply will be simpler with a single source, the organization will be dependent and thus a great risk as a result of any disruptions through, for example, strikes, etc.
3. Effect on supplier motivation. Although the security resulting from regularly supplying large quantities to an organization might increase supplier motivation, and thus increase willingness to improve specifications, etc., undoubtedly in some circumstances increased motivation might also result from a competitive situation.

4. Effect on market structure of single sourcing may in the long term result in the development of a monopolistic situation with the eventual elimination of alternative sources of supply.

The process of identifying and determining supply sources will often involve obtaining competitive bids and analysing such bids and proposals. The latter will often involve price and delivery comparisons, but in most cases more detailed analysis will be necessary. The following factors may be among those considered:

(a) price and cost factors, i.e. cost, delivery costs, insurance costs, price breaks etc.;
(b) delivery factors, including delivery lead times, delivery quantities and delivery frequencies;
(c) specifications factors and quality control/assurance practices;
(d) legal factors, e.g. warranty, in terms of condition etc.

## Considerations in purchasing policy and procedures

Special considerations will apply in the purchasing of commodities in which speculation, the purchase of 'futures' and price forecasting are of considerable importance.

This specialist area will not be dealt with here. Further details can be obtained from the 'Further Reading' at the end of the chapter.

Value analysis and value engineering have been dealt with in Chapter 3 and, while the make or buy decision has already been introduced, it is relevant to refer again to the issue in this context. Table 16.1 provides a checklist for the make or buy decision. Such decisions can be complex and therefore past, present and future market conditions will normally be analysed.

Documentation procedures for purchasing will not be considered here; however, it should be noted that, because of the often considerable amount of money involved in

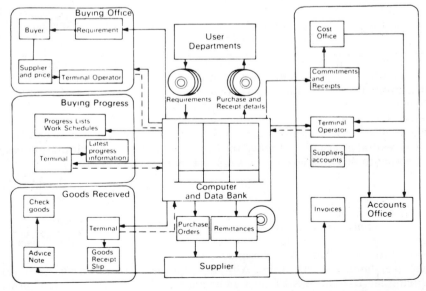

**Figure 16.2** *A computer-based purchase record system. From Baily, P. and Farmer, D. F. (1977)* Purchasing Principles and Techniques. *London: Pitman. Reproduced with permission.*

**Table 16.1** *A make or buy checklist* (From Baily, P. and Farmer, D. H. (1977) *Purchasing Principles and Techniques*. London: Pitman. Reproduced with permission.)

| If currently purchased from an outside source | If currently being manufactured within the company |
|---|---|
| (1) Does capacity exist within own company? | (1) Is there a matter of secrecy to be considered? |
| (2) If so, is such capacity likely to be available for the planning period involved? | (2) If the item is withdrawn from production, would redundancies result? |
| (3) Is the necessary raw material available now at economic rates? | (3) If 'yes', what action would need to be taken by management regarding these redundancies? |
| (4) Will that material continue to be available at economic rates for the planning period? | (4) If tooling is involved, what is its condition? Can it be used by the prospective source? |
| (5) If tooling is involved: (a) what is the cost? (b) what is the expected life? (c) what is the delivery? | (5) Will the machinery involved on current manufacture be fully utilized for alternative work if the part is withdrawn? |
| (6) Are we satisfied that the current suppliers are the most economic source? | (6) Is there a possibility of development work being done on the part? If so, can this be done satisfactorily in conjunction with an outside supplier? |
| (7) Is there a patent involved and thus the possibility of royalties to be paid? | (7) Will the quantities involved interest an outside supplier? |
| (8) Is VAT chargeable (e.g. printing)? | (8) Do we know the true cost of alternative supply against manufacture (e.g. transport and handling costs)—present and forward? |
| (9) Are the current suppliers doing development work towards an improved version of the item? | (9) Is the item part of an integral production route involving several stages of manufacture? If so, can outside manufacture be satisfactorily coordinated with production schedules and machine loading in our shops? |
| (10) Have the current suppliers had difficulty with quality, quantity or time factors, and have their costs escalated as a result, thus affecting their selling price? | (10) What is the forward market position for the item concerned for the relevant planning period? |
| (11) If their quality has been affected: (a) has the suppliers' quality system been vetted? (b) what has been the extent of quality failures? (c) is our production department confident that the specified quality can be economically maintained in internal production? (d) are we over-specifying? | (11) Are all drawings current? |
| | (12) Is there any advantage in our supplying raw materials/components if a decision to buy is made? |
| (12) If their other costs are escalating: (a) what are the reasons? (b) are we confident that we will not be affected in the same way? | (13) Can we indicate to the potential supplier the remaining life of the product? |
| (13) If the item is currently being imported, what is the cost breakdown? If duty is payable, what rates are applied? What duty, if any, will be payable on the relevant raw materials/components if they are imported? | (14) Can the potential supplier suggest ideas for taking cost out of the product? |

purchase and purchase decisions, adequate records must be maintained, and because of the often complex situations which exist, computer-based records and control procedures are often desirable. Figure 16.2 shows in outline a computer-based system used by one aircraft-manufacturing organization. The system was designed to provide a bank of reliable and readily available information for interrogation using terminals. It aims to increase the amount of time the buyer is able to spend in negotiating with suppliers and to reduce the amount of time spent in maintaining information of supply. The system also provides benefits in offering interface with company production and financial systems.

It covers all purchases including bought-out equipment, standard parts, raw materials, subcontract work, repairs, services, commercial equipment and stationery. It assist in the following functions:

(a) accumulation of the requirement to buy;
(b) printing of purchase orders;
(c) recording the progression of the purchase order;
(d) receipts;

(e) inspection;
(f) accumulation of the purchase history;
(g) supply analysis.

## Material requirements planning *(see also Chapter 12)*

Although developed primarily for use in batch manufacturing situations, materials requirements planning has potential in other manufacturing and non-manufacturing situations. The procedure is discussed in detail in Chapter 12 and will only be summarized here.

The principles involved in MRP differ little from those employed for the purchase of materials and parts in many organizations in recent years. Justification for the discussion of these procedures as a separate topic derives largely from the fact that the recent application of computers in this area made possible the use of a purchasing procedure of a scale not hitherto generally feasible.

In batch manufacture, particularly in situations where items are assembled in batches, certain components may be required in large quantities at infrequent intervals, i.e. to suit the batch assembly schedule. In many such situations, therefore, there will be little benefit in maintaining stocks of all parts and items at all times, since at most times these stocks will not be drawn upon. Thus if a procedure can be developed by which those items required for assembly are available at the times required and stocks of these items are not maintained, or are maintained at a far lower level, at other times, an efficient purchasing/stock-holding policy may result. Given this situation the high cost of maintaining unnecessary stock is avoided while items will still be available when required. Materials requirements planning provides such a procedure. It is based on the use of a 'bill of materials' file and a production or assembly schedule. The bill of materials file provides information on all parts and materials required for all finished products and the production schedule provides information on the production or assembly schedule for all finished products.

Co-ordination of this information together with a knowledge of supply lead times permits the procurement of parts as and when required by the production/assembly schedule. MRP, which has some similarities with reverse or due date scheduling and network analysis (see Chapter 13), aims to keep inventories low in order to facilitate purchasing, to ensure a supply of parts and materials when needed and to highlight exceptions and priorities. It is an effective means to an adequate link between the purchasing or procurement and the manufacturing function.

In non-manufacturing situations the material requirements planning procedure may be of relevance, particularly when the system requires the acquisition of inputs specific to particular operations, jobs or outputs, i.e. when a batch processing procedure is employed. In, for example, certain supply operations where items are acquired against particular customer orders, a materials requirements procedure may be of value in that it might provide an effective means of planning, controlling and monitoring the purchase of large quantities of a large range of items in order to satisfy the requirements of a large number of customers each of whom has particular delivery or due date requirements.

## PHYSICAL DISTRIBUTION AND CUSTOMER CHANNELS

In goods output systems (i.e. manufacturing and supply) the responsibility of distribution is that of getting goods *to* the customer. A similar responsibility exists in 'customer input' type systems (i.e. service and transport), where the responsibility is to get customers, whether they be people or things, into the system. In the simplest situation these responsibilities involve the organization in direct relationships with the ultimate or end customers, possibly through inventories, and the input of customers, possibly through customer queues. In more complex cases there will be intermediate stages.

In this section we shall deal with the management of both types of 'channel'. The term 'customer channels' will be used to remind us that we are concerned with flows from or to customers. We shall consider the terms 'distribution' or 'physical distribution' to apply to the management of physical flows through both types of customer channels.

## Physical distribution management (PDM)

PDM, concerned with the dynamics of distribution and with customer channel behaviour, may be defined in our context as the process by which appropriate quantities of items or customers are passed through the distribution channel to or from customers. This definition suggests that, given certain channels, the task of PDM is to make them work. However, it begs the question of 'influence' or 'control'. An enterprise may have a one-stage customer channel, i.e. dealing directly with its own ultimate customers, perhaps through a stock or customer queue over which it has some direct control. The manner in which it operates, i.e. its stock-holding, the service level provided to customers and its coverage of the market, can therefore be determined entirely by itself. If, however, more stages exist, e.g. there are intermediaries between the organization and its end customer, then each party may have some influence over such decisions.

Ideally an enterprise would like to influence all stages in the distribution channel between itself and the final customer, and this is easily achieved for organizations with one-stage customer channels. The extent of the influence or the 'reach' of the enterprise along the customer channel will affect its PDM decision. An enterprise which controls its entire distribution channel to or from the final customer will make decisions affecting all stages in that channel, whereas an enterprise with less influence may make decisions affecting only a part of the channel.

## PDM decisions

The principal interrelated decision areas in PDM are as follows:

(a)  the choice, design and implementation of a channel of distribution;
(b)  the 'level of service' to be provided to customers;
(c)  inventory decisions.

These are outlined in the following section, which can provide only an introduction to this subject. Notice that for single-stage channels the PDM decisions are principally (b) and (c) above, and in such cases the problem can be seen largely as one of inventory management. We shall be dealing with inventory management in this context in Chapter 17, so here we shall concentrate on the more complex PDM case of multi-stage channels where the approach required is somewhat different because of both (a) above and the more complex situations in (b) and (c).

## Channel decisions

We can identify four important questions to be asked in deciding on 'customer channels':

(a) the question of *level*—the number of levels or stages which should exist in the channel;
(b) the question of *type*—which type or types of intermediary should be employed once the level has been decided;
(c) the question of *intensity*—how many of each type of intermediary are to be used;
(d) the question of *control*—what degree of control should the organization seek to exercise, and where appropriate what degree of control should it accept from others.

### Level (or stages)

Here we are concerned with the length of the customer channel, which to some extent will be influenced by the nature of the operation. For example perishable items, those whose processing requires close liaison with customers, those delivered in bulk, those with high unit value, those which are urgent and those requiring particular services will all best be dealt with through short channels.

Markets which are temporary or which have limited potential will rarely justify the establishment of long channels, and small markets are often best served through short channels. Where communication and/or transportation is difficult or expensive, or where there are numerous 'sources' and 'destinations', an intermediary in the customer channels can reduce the total number of contacts. Where one customer represents a large proportion of total demand there will be pressure to establish relatively direct channels to that customer; conversely, where total demand is spread relatively thinly over many customers, the merit of intermediaries in reducing contact complexity is clear.

### Type

Which types of intermediary are most suited to particular channels? The nature of the 'end' market of customers should influence the choice of 'type' rather than vice versa. Items, transports or services must be available to 'end' customers where they expect to find them. It will therefore be difficult to break with tradition unless service to the end customer is clearly improved, although there are obvious examples of successful innovation, e.g. in new forms of retailing and in direct selling.

### Intensity and control

At one extreme there is the possibility of limited distribution through an exclusive channel, and a move from this situation will involve an organization in dealing with a greater number and range of intermediaries. This, however, may be justified where greater market coverage or 'presence' is required yet where the organization does not aspire to maintain close control over all intermediaries. The increased 'coverage' of the market might justify the use of more intensive distribution through multiple intermediaries at each stage with increased PDM costs. However, the use of a greater number of 'contact' points with the market will influence the stock levels required in order to provide a given level of service (see below).

## Service level decisions

The level of service provided to end customers might be expressed in terms of:

(a) percentage of customer orders satisfied in a given period of time;
(b) average delivery or waiting time before a customer order is satisfied;
(c) percentage of customer orders which are satisfied after a quoted delivery or waiting time;
(d) percentage of total demand satisfied in a given period.

The type of measure employed in setting objectives for, and then in monitoring, customer service will depend on the type of organization, and in particular the type of product or service which is being provided. For example, (a) above will be relevant in a 'manufacture to stock' situation where the customer is normally to be satisfied from stock. Measure (b) above will be relevant where goods or service are provided against a specific order, i.e. where customers will normally expect to wait to be served, or where capacity is insufficient to create output stocks of goods or avoid input queues of customers, even though the nature of customer needs is known in advance.

Whatever the measure of customer service, it will generally be the case that the provision of higher levels of service will incur greater costs to the organization.

Clearly there is a cost penalty in providing high customer service, so the justification for aiming for high service must be demonstrable. The obvious reason is the need to conform to what customers expect, i.e. what competitors provide; indeed this will be essential unless some compensatory satisfaction is provided, e.g. through lower price. Equally, inability to compete in the market through price or specification will necessitate the provision of better service through better delivery, short waiting times, etc. (see Chapter 1).

Where inventories of items exist, clearly service-level decisions can influence inventory decisions in terms of not only the levels of inventory to be provided, but also their location throughout the customer channel. We must now therefore clarify the PDM factors influencing inventory decisions.

## Inventory decisions *(see also Chapter 17)*

Chapter 17 will deal in detail with inventory management decisions. The emphasis there will be on the management of 'single-stage' inventories. Here we must consider inventories *throughout* customer channels. For example in a three-stage distribution channel there may be three levels of inventory of the same type of items, with several different stock-holdings at each level.

Among other purposes, inventories provide service to the next stage in the channel. For example, an input stock of raw materials in a hospital helps to ensure that the medical activities of the hospital are not held up. An output stock in a manufacturing company helps to ensure that those directly served by that organization are able to get what they want when they want it. In other words, for each stock there is an immediate customer and a purpose of the stock is to provide service to that customer. We shall see in Chapter 17 that where demands on stock are uncertain, as is often the case, or when the time required to replenish stocks is uncertain, it is necessary to provide some buffer or safety stock to ensure that most customers get what they want most of the time, i.e. that 'stock out' situations are normally avoided. Two related PDM questions, themselves related to the service-level question, therefore are: what stock levels to provide and where to provide them.

The determination of safety (or buffer) stock levels to provide given levels of service will be dealt with in detail for the 'single-stage' problem in Chapter 17. These single-stage methods can be modified to deal with stocks in multi-stage systems. Here we shall consider only the basic principles to be remembered in making inventory decisions in multi-stage systems.

### The number of stock locations at a given stage

If one stock location is established from which demand throughout a given market is to be satisfied, then a safety stock must be provided in addition to a base stock. The base stock is that amount of inventory necessary to satisfy average demand during a given period of time, while the safety stock is that extra amount provided to protect against uncertainties. The way in which this safety stock can be determined is explained in Chapter 17. If we establish several stock locations *each* for a given sector of the market, e.g. a region, then base stock and safety stock must be provided at each. The sum of the base stocks for each stock location will be the same as the original single base stock, but the sum of the safety stocks at each location to provide the original level of service will exceed the safety stock required for the single location.

The general relationship between the sum of the safety stocks required for $n$ stock-holdings and that required for a single holding can be shown to be as follows:

$$B_n = \frac{B_1 (n)}{\sqrt{n}}$$

where  $B_n$ = total safety or buffer stock for $n$ locations
$B_1$ = safety or buffer stock for 1 location
$n$ = number of locations

The general nature of the relationship is shown in Figure 16.3.

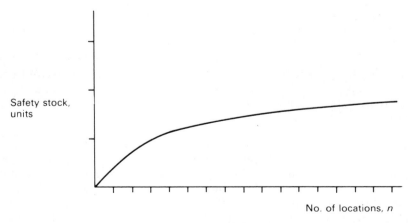

**Figure 16.3**  *Safety stock v. number of stock locations at a given stage or level.*

*Stock-holdings at different levels*

In considering safety stock provision it should be noted that less total safety stock will be needed to provide a given level of end customer service if that stock is provided at a 'higher' level in the customer channel, providing of course that when required it can quickly be deployed to the end customer. For example, in a customer channel which has a wholesale and several retail stocks, safety stock provided at the wholesale level can protect against uncertain demand at all retail outlets, but since high demand at one can be offset by low demand at another, the safety stock-holding at the warehouse level will be less than the total safety stock required by all retailers if each is required to operate entirely separately in its own market sector.

The existence of stocks at 'higher' levels in the customer channel should not simply permit the duplication of stocks held at 'lower' levels, but should complement lower-level stocks. For example, low-usage and/or high-cost items should be stocked at higher levels to reduce cost, while high-usage/low-cost items should be concentrated in lower-level stocks since this permits high customer service at low cost.

## FURTHER READING

Ammer, D. S. (1980) *Materials Management,* 4th edition. Homewood, Illinois: Irwin. A comprehensive treatment of the entire subject.

## QUESTIONS

**16.1** Discuss the merits of centralized purchasing procedure for a series of small retail domestic hardware stores.

**16.2** What factors might influence the make or buy decision for a manufacturing organization, and how might similar considerations operate in a transport or service organization?

**16.3** 'Materials requirements planning is little more than the extension of reverse scheduling from operations to the purchasing function.' Discuss.

**16.4** Give examples of one-stage and two-stage customer channels for:
  (a) a manufacturing organization;
  (b) a supply organization;
  (c) a transport organization;
  (d) a service organization.
  Explain why such channels are employed in these cases.

**16.5** Select *one* of the following organizations and outline and explain the types of decision likely to be required in PDM in that organization (i.e. in the planning, management and control of flows through the customer channels):
  (a) a book publisher dealing with college books;
  (b) a micro-computer manufacturer.

# CHAPTER 17

# Inventory Management

We discussed the management of inventories in the context of physical distribution management in Chapter 16. There we concentrated on multi-stage systems. Here we shall concentrate on the management of single-stage inventories. All of what will be discussed will be relevant in the context of PDM, since not only in some cases will it be appropriate to manage each stock-holding as a separate entity, but also in many cases each stock-holding will be the property or responsibility of a different organization, and thus there will be little opportunity for co-ordinated control of inventories at different levels.

## THE NATURE AND PURPOSES OF SINGLE-STAGE INVENTORIES

For our purposes we can consider stocks to comprise either *consumed* or *non-consumed* items. Consumed items (e.g. materials or products) are utilized by the operating system or taken by the customer and must therefore be replaced. Non-consumed items (e.g. capital equipment and labour) are used repeatedly by the system and need repair and maintenance. In this chapter we deal only with consumed items, and therefore with three types of inventory:

(a) *system output inventory* (in manufacturing and supply systems) e.g. of goods produced or provided by the operating system;
(b) *system input resource inventory* (in manufacturing, supply, transport or service systems), e.g. of materials which will be consumed by the operating system;
(c) *customer input queues* (in transport or service systems) i.e. in effect, the input stocks of customers that will be processed through the system. (They are a resource which is input to the operating system, since the system cannot operate without them.)

Notice that 'work-in-progress' inventory, i.e. partially processed items or customers, is really the output stock of one part of the operating system and the input to the next. It is therefore contained within categories (a) and (b) above.

Inventory management is concerned essentially with the use and control of the inventories associated with operating systems. The need for inventory management is influenced by capacity management decisions, since the existence of inventories will, in part, be determined by the capacity management strategies which are to be employed. If inventories exist, they should serve some useful purpose, and therefore must be carefully managed. These 'purposes' might include:

1. *For output stocks* (in manufacture and possibly supply systems):
    (a) to provide good service to customers;
    (b) to protect the function from uncertainties in demand, e.g. permitting stable level of operating of function despite fluctuating demand;
    (c) to permit manufacture or supply of items in economic batches.
2. *For input resource stocks* (in manufacture, supply, transport and service systems):
    (a) to permit favourable purchase/provision arrangements (e.g. price discounts and economic quantities);
    (b) to protect the function from uncertainties in supply, e.g. permitting stable/undisrupted operation despite fluctuating/interrupted supplies.
3. *For customer input queues* (in transport and service systems): to protect functions from uncertainties in demand, e.g. permitting stable level of operating of functions despite fluctuating demand.

From a capacity viewpoint, output inventories provide a form of damper, insulating the function from fluctuations in demand level. The management of output inventories is concerned with regulation of the flow of items, and the management of input stocks of consumed items is much the same type of flow control problem. Output stocks exist to accommodate short-term differences between demand and system output rates. Similarly, input stocks of consumed items exist to accommodate short-term differences between the supply and consumption rates. The extent to which the level and composition of stocks vary is therefore a measure of their usefulness; lack of variation might suggest that stock is not needed.

## INVENTORIES OF CONSUMED ITEMS

### System output inventory

Certain operating system structures provide for output stocks. Customer demand is satisfied from such stocks, which in turn are replenished from the function. The information flows in the opposite direction to the physical flow; hence, in the case of intermittent stock replenishment, customer orders will be received at output inventory, depletion of which will give rise to the dispatch of replenishment orders to the function.

Stocks may be replenished *intermittently* or *continuously*, although in some cases the distinction is more evident in the type of inventory management decisions that are required than in the physical flow into stock.

For our purposes we can consider the nature of customer demand to be given; however, a knowledge or estimate of the nature of demand, in particular the demand level and fluctuations, will influence inventory management. The stock levels maintained and/or the amount of buffer (or safety) stock provided will reflect expected demand levels and fluctuation.

The complexity of the inventory management problem and the likely effectiveness of inventory management depend on the variability or unpredictability of stock input and output levels and also on the opportunities for, and the extent of, control. Thus in certain systems inventory management is likely to be more effective than in others simply because there is the opportunity for the exercise of closer control.

The classic stock control problem is that of establishing an inventory policy based on some *control over stock inputs* to satisfy unpredictable demand or output. Given a forecast output or usage rate per unit time and the variability of that output rate, the following inventory parameters might be established:

1. For intermittent stock replenishment:
   (a) either re-order level *or* interval; and
   (b) order quantities.
2. For continuous replenishment:
   (a) input rate; and
   (b) average stock level required.

## System input resource inventory

Certain systems require input stocks. The problem of managing the stocks of input resources closely resembles that of system output inventory management. If the function is considered as the customer for input resource stocks then, as with output stocks, demand is satisfied from stock, which in turn is replenished from supply. The activity scheduling function will be responsible for the manner in which input stocks are depleted. Either consumable resources will be scheduled intermittently through the function or a regular throughput rate will have been fixed. In either case we can again consider the nature of demand on stocks to be given; however, a knowledge or estimate of the nature of demand, in particular demand level and fluctuations, will again influence input inventory management. As with output stocks, the amount of buffer (or safety) stock provided will reflect expected demand levels and fluctuation as well as the predictability and degree of control available over *inputs to stock*.

Again the following parameters might be established:

1. For intermittent stock replenishment:
   (a) either re-order level *or* interval; and
   (b) order quantities.
2. For continuous replenishment:
   (a) input rate; and
   (b) average stock level required.

## Customer input queues

Two operating system structures require input queues (or stocks) of customers (see Chapter 1). In such systems, customers, or items provided by them, are consumed resources. We have argued that in transport and service systems the customers themselves, or something provided by them, are an input which differs from other consumed resources only in being beyond the direct control of system management. In other words there is little or no control over the input or arrival of such resources, i.e. their input is unpredictable. Since there is no opportunity for control over inputs, the inventory is in effect managed through *control over the output*.

Given an estimate of the input rate and the variability of that rate, the following inventory parameters might be established.

1. For intermittent depletion:
   (a)  output intervals *or* the stock levels at which output is to occur; and
   (b)  output quantities.

## INVENTORY MANAGEMENT STRATEGIES

The strategies available in inventory management, from above, are summarized in Table 17.1.

**Table 17.1**  *Inventory management strategies (consumed items).*

|  | Location of flow control | |
|---|---|---|
| Nature of flow | On stock inputs | On stock outputs |
| Intermittent | Determine stock replenishment level *or* interval | Determine stock levels *or* intervals at which output is to take place |
|  | Determine input quantity | Determine output quantity |
| Continuous | Determine average (or safety) stock levels required | Determine average stock levels required |
|  | Determine stock replenishment (input) rate | Determine stock output rate |

In the later part of this chapter we will outline procedures and techniques for inventory management. We shall concentrate on the control of inputs to stocks and we shall deal explicitly with the management of system output stocks and input stocks of consumed items other than consumer queues.

## COSTS IN INVENTORY MANAGEMENT

Two sets of parameters are of immediate relevance: inventory costs and customer service costs.

### Inventory costs

Items held in stock incur costs. *Holding costs* comprise the costs of storage facilities, provision of services to such facilities, insurance on stocks, costs of loss, breakage, deterioration, obsolescence, and the opportunity cost or notional loss of interest on the capital tied up. In general, an increase in the quantity of stocks held will be reflected in an increase in holding costs although the relationships may not be linear. For example, costs for increasing stock-holdings may be in the form of a step function, since increased space is required when stocks reach certain levels. The cost of capital, insurance, etc., may also be discontinuous through the effect of price breaks or quantity discounts. Stock-holdings of a certain level may permit replenishment in quantities sufficient to attract quantity discounts. Other things being equal, higher costs of holding will result in lower stock quantities and vice versa. Certain stock-change costs apply particularly in intermittent flow systems, e.g. in input control systems change costs will consist of the cost of *ordering* replenishment, and in some cases the cost of delivery of replenishment items and the cost of receipt, inspection, placing in stock, etc. In output control systems change costs will constitute the cost of ordering or initiating depletion and the cost of dispatch, etc.

## Customer service costs

Customer service considerations influence inventory decisions in customer 'pull' systems, in which output stocks exist. Here customer service might be measured in terms of the number of occasions over a given period on which customer orders cannot immediately be satisfied from stock, i.e. the number of 'stock-out' situations. Equally the *probability* of such stock-outs might also provide a measure of customer service. In such a situation, customers are in effect being starved by the system. In customer push systems, customer service may be measured by the occurrence or duration of queuing. Where queuing is required, customer service may be measured by the average time spent in the queue or the number of items in the queue. Where queuing is not normally required, customer service may be measured by the probability that queuing will occur. In such situations customers are in effect being 'blocked' by the system. This customer service, whether in input or output control systems, has inventory cost implications, e.g. costs of shortage, loss of trade, etc.

## Which items to control

Many companies subject all items, purchased and produced, irrespective of their value, usage or quantity, to the same type of stock-control procedure. Such a policy can be a waste of time and effort.

Although a high usage rate does not necessarily mean high stock levels, fast-moving items (i.e. those for which the usage rate is high) and expensive items are likely to incur greater storage costs than slow-moving, inexpensive items. Consequently it should be our primary aim in stock control to control the 'fast-moving/expensive' items, since, by doing so, greater potential savings are possible than by concentrating on inexpensive items, the usage of which is small.

One of the ubiquitous phenomena of business is expressed by the so-called '80/20 law'. In relation to inventory stock, the law reads as follows: '80 per cent of the firm's total inventory cost is caused by only 20 per cent of all items'. In other words, the 20 per cent high-cost/high-usage items account for 80 per cent of total inventory costs. This 'law' or relationship can be expressed by the ABC or Pareto curve, and often such curves are used by companies to divide stock items into three classes, A, B and C, i.e. those accounting for 80, 13 and 7 per cent approximately of total inventory costs (Figure 17.1). Such a classification, once achieved, enables appropriate stock control 'rules' for each type of product or item to be implemented. Thus, a comprehensive and regular stock control procedure should be designed for items of type A. Less rigorous control is necessary for type B, whereas for C a simple procedure is probably sufficient.

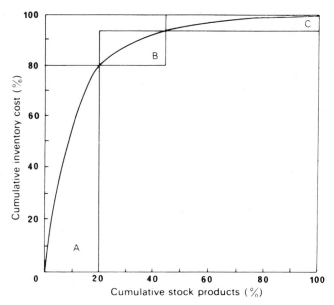

**Figure 17.1** *ABC chart for stock items.*

## INVENTORY MANAGEMENT SYSTEMS

We can now look more closely at the types of problem posed by the adoption of the inventory management strategies outlined in Table 17.1. We shall focus on the more usual case of intermittent flow/input control.

### Intermittent flow input control

Most published treatments of inventory management deal with input control of intermittent flow systems, that is, they deal with the management of inventory through manipulation of supply with the objective of satisfying a given output need or criterion. There are basically two approaches that might be adopted (see Table 17.1):

(a) fixed input level and quantity;
(b) fixed input interval.

The two approaches are compared in Figure 17.2. Fixed input level control relies on the replenishment of stock by a given input quantity, actuated at a given inventory level. In other words, inventory will fall to a re-order level, whereupon replenishment is initiated or takes place. This approach is sometimes known as the 'maximum–minimum' or 'two-bin' system.

The fixed input interval approach relies on the replenishment of inventory at fixed intervals of time. The replenishment quantity in such situations is often determined such as to replenish inventory to a given maximum level. Replenishment of stock in input control/intermittent flow systems might take place instantaneously or over a period of time. The stock level traces on Figure 17.2 rely on instantaneous

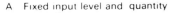

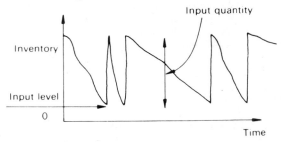

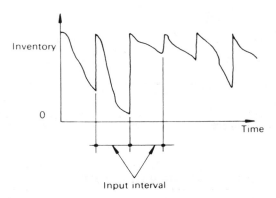

**Figure 17.2** *Input control inventory: types of control.*

replenishment, i.e. replenishment of stock by a whole quantity at an instant in time. Figure 17.3 compares (A) intermittent input/instantaneous with (B) intermittent input/with usage. The latter relies on replenishment of stock intermittently yet over a period of time during which usage or output continues to occur.

The input level approach to inventory control is in effect a form of *perpetual* inventory management. Stock is replenished when it falls to a particular level, so it will be necessary to maintain some 'perpetual' monitoring of the inventory in order to ensure that action is taken when the appropriate stock level is reached. The input interval system is in effect a *periodic* inventory control system. There will be no need to check stock level except at the times when the replenishment order is to be placed. The type of system which is employed will depend largely on the circumstances. In some situations it will be very difficult, or expensive, to maintain a perpetual check on inventory levels in order to be able to operate the order level approach. However, where the number of transactions, i.e. the number of times the stock is depleted, is low compared with the annual usage, or where the unit cost of items is high, it may be more appropriate to use the perpetual inventory control system.

Table 17.2 compares the two systems. In many cases the cost of running a perpetual inventory control system (order level approach) will be greater than that of running a periodic inventory control system (order interval approach). However, the cost of carrying inventory may be less with the perpetual inventory control system than with the periodic system, especially where the periodic control system involves the replenishment of stock by a fixed quantity. As a guide, the order level approach, i.e. the perpetual inventory control system, may be more appropriate where:

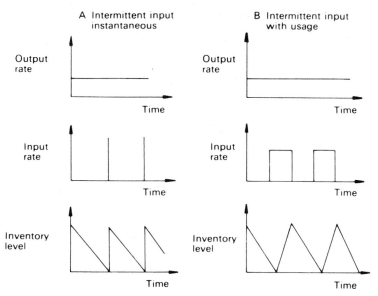

**Figure 17.3** *Input control inventory: types of input flow. (Figures 17.2 and 17.3 from Wild, R. (1977)* Concepts for Operations Management. *New York: Wiley. Reproduced with permission.)*

**Table 17.2** *'Periodic' (order interval) v. 'perpetual' (order quantity) inventory control systems.*

| (Probable) merits of 'periodic' system | (Probable) merits of 'perpetual' system |
|---|---|
| 1. Less cost to operate system (i.e. less checking, recording, etc.)<br>2. Administratively easier in multi-item situations, i.e. easier to place order for each item at same time | 1. Less buffer stock required for protection against stock-outs<br>2. Fewer stock-outs when demand is unusually high<br>3. No need to determine order quantity for each replenishment<br>4. Inventory carrying costs lower than for periodic system |

(a) the number of transactions (i.e. stock depletions) is low compared with the annual usage;
(b) the processing cost of transactions is low compared with the ordering cost;
(c) the unit price of items is high;
(d) the required service level or degree of protection against stock-outs is high;
(e) sales fluctuations are high and difficult to predict;
(f) inventory carrying costs are high;
(g) the use of a computer-based system permits frequent stock level updating (e.g. after every transaction), thus minimizing the disadvantage of the high operating cost of 'perpetual' inventory control.

Where demand is constant and replenishment is instantaneous or where the replenishment lead time is known, the fixed input level approach will resemble the fixed input interval approach. Only where either replenishment lead time or demand is uncertain will the adoption of each approach lead in practice to different inventory behaviour (e.g. Figure 17.2, in which the diagrams show the effect of each policy against the same demand patterns). Virtually all inventory control quantitative models deal with intermittent flow and input control, i.e. batch ordering, and in most cases the objective is cost minimization, i.e. the minimization of the total of holding and inventory change costs. Most such models are deterministic, i.e. they assume a known constant demand and either known input rate or instantaneous input. In such deterministic situations (which rarely, if ever, occur) there will be no need for provision of buffer or safety stocks. Such stocks will be provided only to protect against uncertain demand and/or replenishment lead times (see below). Probabilistic models are available, as are models aimed at profit maximization, etc. Figure 17.4 provides a taxonomy of intermittent flow inventory models. (Models B, C and D are not discussed in the text.)

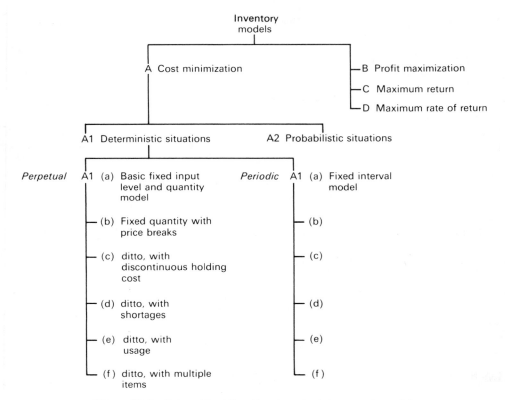

**Figure 17.4** *Intermittent flow/input control inventory models.*

## A1 Deterministic models: perpetual control

*The order quantity approach*

As we have already pointed out, the act of replenishing inventories is costly. Such replenishment costs are normally proportionate only to the number of orders placed and not to the size of the orders.

The ordering cost is equivalent to the set-up cost considered during our discussion of batch quantities in Chapter 14.

The order quantity decision involves the determination of the most economical order quantity—the quantity which minimizes total variable costs. Various economic order quantity (EOQ) models have been developed over the past fifty years so that now not only formulae but also tables, graphs, charts, etc., are available for calculating optimum order sizes in a variety of situations. The following are those commonly adopted and of most value.

*Model A1(a)*

1. Known constant demand
2. Complete deliveries
3. No shortages

The derivation of the economic order quantity formula for this model is unecessary, since it was presented in Chapter 14.
The notation adopted is:

$Q$ = Order quantity
$C_s$ = Ordering cost/order
$C_1$ = Holding cost/item/unit of time
$r$ = Usage rate

$$EOQ = Q^* = \sqrt{\frac{2C_s r}{C_1}}$$

*Model A1 (d)*

As Model A1 (a) *except shortages allowed.*
Notation as before.
Plus $C_2$ = Shortage or stock-out cost per item per unit of time

$$EOQ = Q^* = \sqrt{\frac{2rC_s}{C_1}} \sqrt{\frac{C_1 + C_2}{C_2}}$$

The total variable cost associated with this ordering policy is:

$$C^* = \sqrt{2rC_1C_s} \sqrt{\frac{C_2}{C_1 + C_2}}$$

*Model A1(e) for fixed quantity with usage*

1. Known constant demand
2. Delivery of order at a known and constant rate
3. No shortages
4. Buffer stock

Notation: $Q$ = Order quantity
$C_s$ = Ordering cost
$C_1$ = Holding cost/item/unit of time
$q$ = Delivery or production rate
$r$ = Usage or consumption rate

$$\text{EOQ} = Q^* = \sqrt{\frac{2C_sr}{C_1\left(1 - \dfrac{r}{q}\right)}}$$

The total variable cost associated with this ordering policy is:

$$C^* = \sqrt{2C_srC_1}\;\sqrt{1 - \frac{r}{q}}$$

---

## EXAMPLE

A company which uses a maximum–minimum stock-ordering policy orders 2500 of purchased item A at a time. They wish to determine what annual saving might be made by ordering this item in different quantities. An examination of previous stock records indicates that the annual usage of these items is constant at 7000. They further find that the cost of making an order, which is independent of the order size, is £10. The purchase price of the items is £0.5 and the cost of holding stock is 7 per cent of item price per item per year. The supplier undertakes to deliver the items at a constant rate of 50 per day.

$q = 50 \times 250/\text{year}$ (assuming that there are 250 working days per year)
$r = 7000/\text{year}$
$C_s = £10$
$C_1 = 0.07(0.05) = £0.035/\text{item/year}$

$$\text{EOQ} = Q^* = \sqrt{\frac{2 \times 10 \times 7000}{0.07(0.5) \times \left(1 - \dfrac{7000}{12\,500}\right)}}$$

$$Q^* = 3015 \text{ units}$$

Total annual variable cost associated with this policy $C^*$:

$$= \sqrt{2 \times 7000 \times 10 \times 0.07\,(0.5)}\;\sqrt{1 - \frac{7000}{12\,500}}$$

$$= £46.4 \text{ p.a.}$$

Total annual variable cost associated with present policy:

$$= \frac{C_1Q}{2}\left(1 - \frac{r}{q}\right) + \frac{C_sr}{Q}$$

$$= \frac{0.035 \times 2500}{2}(0.44) + \left(10 \times \frac{7000}{2500}\right)$$

$$= £47.25 \text{ p.a.}$$

Potential annual saving on item A $= £0.25$

---

*The re-order level approach*

We decided earlier that in the fixed quantity (two-bin or order quantity) ordering system, two questions must be answered: what is the fixed order quantity ($Q$) and what is the re-order level? We have decided how, in a few typical situations, the fixed order quantity can be determined and we must now look at the problem of re-order levels.

If the usage or consumption of items is perfectly constant and accurately known and if stock replenishment time is zero, then the stock order level may be zero and orders for stock replenishments can be placed when stock falls to this level. Thus in a deterministic situation the order level decision is easily made.

Unfortunately such an ideal situation rarely, if ever, exists. In practice two complications can arise. First, the usage rate may not be absolutely constant and consequently there is the risk that stock may be prematurely exhausted. Even so, if replenishment of stock is instantaneous, no problems arise because exhausted stock can immediately be replaced. The second complication concerns replenishment. If this is not immediate, it becomes necessary to place orders some time prior to the items being needed and replenishment times may fluctuate. The occurrence of both these complications necessitates the maintenance of buffer or safety stocks.

If both of these complications arise in any magnitude then we cannot reasonably use any of the ordering models discussed in the previous section, since all of those assume a static and deterministic state. However, if these fluctuations are not excessive then these models can be used, since only a slight, and usually tolerable, error is introduced.

To summarize, then, the need to consider order levels other than zero arises because of uncertainty, i.e. the probabilistic nature of demand and/or replenishment lead time. Such uncertainty is alien to the ordering models we have discussed but they can nevertheless be used, with only minor error, provided demand and lead time vary only marginally. The approaches which might be employed are outlined under a discussion of probabilistic models later in this chapter.

## A1 Deterministic models: periodic control

If, to begin with, we again assume that usage or demand is constant and known, then this system of ordering is, in both practice and theory, identical to the maximum–minimum or order quantity system. In the maximum–minimum system, when stocks fall to a predetermined level (which can be zero if order delivery is instantaneous), a further predetermined quantity of items is ordered. In the order interval system, at predetermined intervals, a quantity of goods sufficient to restore stock to a given level is ordered. In the ideal conditions the results of using the order quantity and the order cycle systems would be the same. Consequently, for such cases the answers to our two basic questions—when to order and how much to order—can be found in the previous section, i.e.

$$\text{Order interval} = \frac{\text{Order quantity}}{\text{Usage rate}}$$

$$\text{Optimum order interval} = \frac{\text{EOQ}}{\text{Usage rate}}$$

$$\text{i.e.} \qquad t^* = \frac{Q^*}{r}$$

For the models we examined in the previous section the optimum order intervals are given by the following formulae:

Model A1(a)

$$t^* = \sqrt{\frac{2C_s}{rC_1}}$$

Model A1(d)

$$t^* = \sqrt{\frac{2C_s}{rC_1}} \sqrt{\frac{C_1 + C_2}{C_2}}$$

Model A1(e)

$$t^* = \sqrt{\frac{2C_s}{rC_1\left(1 - \dfrac{r}{q}\right)}}$$

It is only during conditions of uncertainty that these two methods of ordering differ. The fundamental characteristic of the order interval system is that the stock status of each item is examined at regular and fixed intervals, at which time the following questions are asked:

1. Should an order be placed to replenish stock now?
2. If so, how many units must be ordered.

The order interval system is clerically more convenient than the maximum–minimum system. Since stocks are reviewed and orders placed at regular intervals, the stock control department can more easily plan their activities and make better use of their time; however, the penalty for this administrative convenience is that, generally, the use of such a system involves the adoption of higher stock levels. The system is particularly suitable where stocks consist of a larger number of different products, since in such cases the ordering cost is often less than the equivalent cost for variable interval (maximum–minimum) ordering.

## Continuous flow/input control

Conventional inventory control theory also largely ignores the case of continuous, as opposed to intermittent, input flow. In this case input control is again a means for the management of inventory to satisfy expected output needs, and one problem for inventory management is the determination of an input rate (or average rate). Other problems will generally relate to the determination of average, minimum or safety inventory levels, and inventory capacity. Given deterministic output (or full control of output) and full control of input, input rate can be matched to output and inventory problems are obviated. Here, therefore, we must deal with problems deriving from probabilistic output and/or incomplete control of input.

The problem can be considered to be one of matching two probability distributions (i.e. for input and output rates). A mismatch may give rise to:

1. *Output starving*, i.e. depletion of stock due to excess of demand over input (i.e. shortage, etc.).
2. (a) *Input blocking*, i.e. insufficient space or capacity for inputs due to excess of input over output; or
   (b) *Excess stock-holding*, if inventory capacity is not limited.

The required average inventory capacity will be influenced by input and output rate variability (mean input rate must equal mean output rate). The higher the variability, the greater the stock capacity required to accommodate short-term differences in input and output sales. Hence, as a general rule of thumb, the greater the possible short-term difference between rates (i.e. assuming symmetrical distributions, the upper end of one distribution minus the lower end of the other), the greater the stock capacity required. For a given (known or forecast) output rate distribution, inventory levels can be determined for alternative input rate distributions, and vice versa. Simulation techniques will normally be employed.

## FURTHER READING

Compton, H. K. (1968) *Supplies and Materials Management.* London: Business Books. A largely descriptive treatment of inventory management in a supply/purchasing context.
Thomas, A. B. (1980) *Stock Control in Manufacturing Industries.* (2nd ed.) Aldershot: Gower.
Van Hees, R. N. and Monhemius, W. (1972) *An Introduction to Production and Inventory Control.* London: Macmillan.

## QUESTIONS

**17.1** Describe the principles of maximum–minimum and order cycle systems of stock control. In what circumstances is the use of each of these types of system appropriate? In what circumstances would the use of either system give rise to basically the same stock control system (i.e. the same ordering decision)?

**17.2** In a certain situation, demand for goods is both known and stable. The goods are ordered from an 'outside' supplier, they are delivered in complete batches and no quantity discount arrangements apply. No buffer stock is to be maintained. Determine:

(a) the economic order quantity, given:

| | |
|---|---|
| ordering cost per order | = £20 |
| holding cost per item per annum | = £0.05 |
| demand per annum | = 10 000 |
| price per item | = £15 |

(b) the economic order quantity, given:

| | |
|---|---|
| ordering cost per order | = £20 |
| holding cost per item per annum | = 5 per cent of item price |
| demand per annum | = 10 000 |
| price per item | = £15 |

(c) the regular economic ordering interval, given:

| | |
|---|---|
| ordering cost per order | = £50 |
| holding cost per item per annum | = 5 per cent of item price |
| demand per annum | = 15 000 |
| price per item | = £25 |

**17.3** Refer to Figure 17.4. In comparison with model A1(a) what additional factor(s) must be taken into account in determining the economic batch size for model A1(b)? Comment on how the economic batch size might be determined in such a situation.

**17.4** Using the following information determine the approximate economic order quantity. NB. In obtaining your answer either use a graphical approach, i.e. plot the 'change' and the 'holding' cost curves, and thus obtain the total cost curve and therefore the minimum total cost batch, or develop your own numerical approach.

$r = 2500$ units/year
$C_1 = 10$ per cent of unit price/unit/year
$C_2 = £100$

| Order quantity | 100–499 | 500–2499 | 2500–4999 | ⩾5000 |
|---|---|---|---|---|
| Unit price/unit | £5 | £4.75 | £4.6 | £4.5 |

# THE CONTROL OF OPERATING SYSTEMS

# INTRODUCTION TO PART 8

*This section deals with control. The principal topics covered are: the control of the quality of the goods or services provided by the operating systems and the reliability of those goods and services; the maintenance and/or replacement of the system, and its constituent parts; and the control of the system through performance monitoring.*

*The introductory chapter sets the scene for chapters on the three principal topics. These topics are interrelated as well as having relationships with topics dealt with in other sections of the book, in particular The Management of Capacity (Part 5), Operations Scheduling (Part 6) and Inventory Management and the Supply of Resources (Part 7).*

*Finally we consider some aspects of performance measurement.*

# CHAPTER 18

# The Nature of Operations Control

In Chapter 11 we distinguished between operations planning and operations control and chose to deal with the two aspects separately. Part 6 considered planning problems. In this chapter we shall consider operations control in a general manner before considering particular aspects of the control of operating systems within the remaining chapters in this section.

Few operating systems will operate continuously and effectively without the exercise of a certain amount of external control. The Government, as well as planning, must also exercise control in order to maintain a healthy national economy; within the economy, managements must exercise control to maintain or improve the performance of their companies, and within such companies control must be exercised over the various functions and systems.

Rarely within organizations will there be operations control departments. Normally the control function will be invested in departments alongside responsibilities for planning. For example, those responsible for inventory management decisions will be concerned with and responsible for both planning and control. Certainly in manufacturing it is common to find production control departments, although, as previously noted, this title is probably a misnomer, since the emphasis will again be on both planning and control, i.e. on pre-activity decisions and during-activity decisions (see Chapter 11). Financial control will be exercised within most organizations; however, again, those involved will be responsible for financial planning and budgeting, as well as for financial and cost control.

We have noted (in Chapter 11) that the general purpose of control is to ensure, as far as possible, the implementation of plans. Thus those involved in control, and those procedures established for the purposes of control, will, in general, seek to monitor activities with a view to ensuring that these activities correspond to some intended situation or state. Control derives from this process of monitoring activities and the comparison of actual and intended states. The need for the exercise of control derives from the fact that it is rarely possible to ensure in advance that certain things will happen in a particular way, at a particular time, etc. Control is necessary because of the existence of uncertainties. A purely deterministic situation is unlikely to

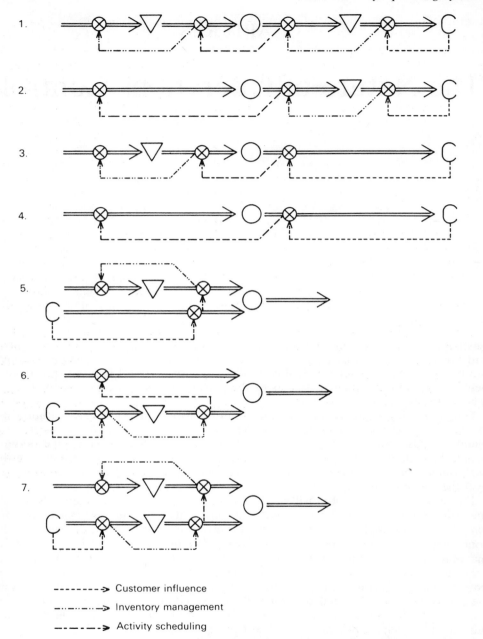

**Figure 18.1**    *Operations control relationships. From Wild, R. (1977)* Concepts for Operations Management. *New York: Wiley. Reproduced with permission.*

necessitate control since, in such circumstances, planning in itself is sufficient. In practice such deterministic situations will rarely exist and thus control is an essential link in the circle or cycle which begins with planning and involves monitoring, action and correction, and possible revision of planning for future events. Most control actions are 'information dependent' in that they derive from the acquisition and use of information on the nature or state of the operating system. As we saw in Chapter 1, operating systems are in effect 'covered' by links such that, together, there is adequate information available for the control of activities and events at all stages in the system. We have seen in fact that flow control in operating systems is exercised through a combination of activity scheduling and inventory control decisions (Chapter 1). This situation can best be illustrated in the manner shown in Figure 18.1. The diagrams in this figure show the principal points in the system at which control of flow is exercised and the decision loops associated with such control. Thus in a 'function from stock to stock system' (1), information in terms of order or delivery requirements goes from the customer to a point equivalent to inventory output. Flow at this stage is monitored, and information, through the inventory management system, passes to the flow control point on inventory input, from where, through the activity scheduling system, information passes to a flow control point on function input, and so on through to resource supply. A similar chain of information loops and a similar series of control points exist for all systems. For example, in a 'function from stock from customer queue' system (7), the customer influences the input to customer queues, which are monitored in order to ensure that appropriate decisions are made in respect of flow from customer queues through to the system. The flow into the system is monitored through the activity scheduling system in order that the flow of resources to the system is appropriate. This flow in turn is monitored through the inventory management system in order to ensure that flow into (i.e. replenishment of) resource stocks is appropriate.

Flow control is an essential responsibility of operations management. Such flow control is associated with the inventory management system(s) and the activity scheduling system. Supplementing this flow control there will be a need to consider the *nature* of the items or customers which are flowing in the system, in order to ensure, for example, that intended quality levels are maintained and that resources are used in the intended fashion. Chapter 17 dealt with control decisions relating to inventory management. In this part we shall consider control associated with activity schedules, quality control and also controls associated with resource utilization, i.e. with resource maintenance, replacement and repair. Finally we shall take a somewhat broader approach and consider performance measurement, i.e. the manner in which the performance of the whole operating system might be monitored for both planning and control purposes.

## CONTROL CONCEPTS

Diagrammatically a control system may be represented in the manner shown in Figure 18.2. It will be seen that there are four components:

(a) a means of sensing output;
(b) a means of comparing actual output with intended output;
(c) a means of recording intended output (memory);
(d) a means of exercising control.

A *closed system*, as shown in Figure 18.2, is directly influenced by its own past behaviour. Its own outputs are monitored or observed in order that some purposeful control might be exercised over its inputs. The operation of the system is dependent on direct feedback of information. The normal domestic central heating system is an example of such control, since the thermostat monitors room temperature and controls the boiler to maintain a given room temperature.

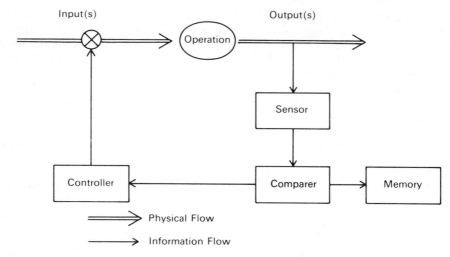

**Figure 18.2**   *Feedback control system (closed).*

In contrast, an *open system* exists where outputs have no direct influence over earlier parts of the system. In other words an open system does not react to its own performance. Its past actions have no influence over current or future actions. There is no feedback of information on its outputs for the control of its inputs. The simple clock is an example of such an open system.

In practice most operations control will be of the closed system type, although the mechanism by which the system is closed will differ, and will vary in its degree of sophistication. For example, in process control, i.e. the control of flow processes such as chemical processes using computers, several types of application exist, their principal differences being the manner in which information is fed back and control is exercised. Figure 18.3, for example, shows a simple data logging system. A computer is used here to scan very rapidly and frequently the information displayed by numerous instruments connected to the process, e.g. flow metres, transducers, thermometers, etc., this information being recorded, printed out and often used to calculate performance indices or guides which subsequently might be used by those concerned with the manual control of the process. Alarm systems are frequently

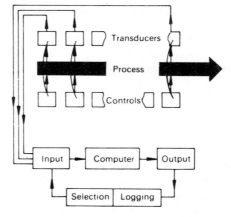

**Figure 18.3**   *A data logging system.*

incorporated, so the computer will signal the occurrence of faults or other unusual conditions in the process and also carry out simple diagnostic procedures using the input data to determine and indicate the cause of such conditions. Data logging systems are often the first stage in the application of computer control to operating systems. They are concerned both with monitoring and, indirectly, with control. The feedback loop, however, comprises both electronic and manual elements. The electronic monitoring of the condition of patients in hospital intensive-care units is an example of such control, since the medical staff responsible for the patient must, of necessity, take any remedial action.

In contrast, supervisory control systems provide for the application of computers through the whole feedback and control system. One of the main reasons for the emergence and development of methods of computer-based process control was the increasing complexity of both equipment and systems such that efficient manual control was increasingly difficult to achieve. Furthermore, in complex and expensive installations, penalties for inferior or poor performance are considerable, consequently expensive control systems are readily justifiable. Sequentially dependent processes such as those found in the chemical industries depend entirely for their efficient operation upon the near optimum control and the stable operation of their parts, since any disturbance in any part will be reflected and perhaps amplified in subsequent parts of the process. Conditions such as these militate against manual control and necessitate some form of automatic monitoring and control system capable of monitoring performance and compensating for changes in operations. Figure 18.4 represents such a supervisory control system. The efficiency of supervisory

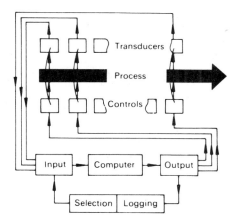

**Figure 18.4**   *A supervisory control system.*

systems depends on their being fed with the correct information, i.e. efficient data logging, and on the speed with which the control system works. Such systems must be carefully designed to accord with the characteristics of the process. The nature of the inputs must correspond to known and foreseeable disturbances of the process and the speed of the computer to the nature of the process, since there is little point in installing a control system whose reaction time is greatly in excess of the erection time of the process being controlled.

It is inappropriate here to enter into a detailed discussion of control theory; however, it is worth noting that in the development of feedback control systems, whether manual, automatic or mixed, it is essential that the feedback mechanism be matched to the characteristics and capability of the process. It is essential also that control be exercised at appropriate stages within the process and that each of the important variables be monitored for control purposes. In practice, therefore, control systems will often be complex, multi-stage and multi-level.

## CONTROL OF ACTIVITIES

The control of activities associated with activity scheduling is one aspect of flow control within a system. Inventory control, the complementary aspect of flow control, has been dealt with in Chapter 17. Here, therefore, we shall deal briefly with the elements of activity control. Essentially three steps are necessary in achieving control of activities: (a) monitoring and recording flows or activities; (b) analysing flows and/or progress by comparison with plans or schedules, and (c) control, that is, modification of plans or a rearrangement of schedules in order to conform as nearly as possible to original targets. To some extent the manner in which these steps are accomplished will depend on the nature and manner of activity scheduling and the nature of the activity schedules. Thus if schedules have been developed in order to achieve a particular flow or particular state at certain points in the system at particular times, then performance will be recorded and monitored by reference to these same points. The manner in which plans and schedules have been expressed and drawn up will influence the way in which step (b) above is achieved, i.e. the analysis of progress by comparison with plans and schedules. The extent and nature of control will of course depend on the variance identified between actual progress or flows and intended progress or flows. The manner in which this control will be achieved will depend to some extent on the nature of the system and the opportunities for the exercise of control. Thus, for example, if a particular procedure has been established for scheduling purposes then control will be linked to the use of the same procedure. If bar charts have been used then progress and monitoring will utilize such charts. If network analysis has been used then similar calculations and procedures will be employed for purposes of control.

## FURTHER READING

Eilon, S. (1971) *Management Control*. London: Macmillan. A study of management systems and control with emphasis on information processing and control theory.

Mize, J. H., White, C. R. and Brooks, S. G. H. (1971) *Operations Planning and Control*. Englewood Cliffs, NJ: Prentice-Hall. A detailed treatment of operations/inventory systems, planning and control. Brief treatments on control system design and control system concepts (Chapters 8 and 9).

## QUESTIONS

**18.1** Show diagrammatically the principal control feedback loops which will be used for the control of flows through the following systems:
(a)  a small jobbing engineering production works;
(b)  a restaurant;
(c)  a specialist retail delicatessen store.

Identify and explain any simplifying assumption that you make.

**18.2** Explain the main features of, and identify the difference between, a closed and an open loop feedback control system.

**18.3** Consider one of the scheduling procedures outlined in the chapters in Part 6 and show how a related control system might work.

# CHAPTER 19

# Quality Management and Reliability

As consumers of *products* we expect our supplier to provide only those goods which we find acceptable. This in turn requires suppliers to try to ensure that they themselves receive from manufacturers only goods or items which are acceptable, and that these items do not deteriorate or get damaged while being held by the suppliers. Manufacturers in turn must ensure that they receive and use only materials and items which are of an acceptable quality, and that their manufacturing processes are used in such a way as to ensure that the goods that they produce are of a quality that is acceptable to their customers.

As consumers of *services and transports* we are again concerned with quality. For example, if we want to be transported by an organization we expect to be taken from an agreed place to an agreed destination, possibly by an agreed route, with an agreed duration. In being treated by a service system we expect the quality of the service to be acceptable. Thus both transport and service organizations must ensure that they use items and products which are of an acceptable quality and that their operations conform to some acceptable standards so that we, the customers, when leaving the system, will express some satisfaction with the treatment that we have received there.

Thus as customers we will have some expectation of the quality of the goods or services with which we are to be provided. There will be an agreed *specification*. Agreement on this specification will have been reached with the organization. They will have accepted the specification which we have laid down, or we will have accepted the specification which the organization has offered, or there will be agreement from discussion and compromise. Given an agreed or acceptable specification we will expect the product or service which is provided to *conform* to that specification.

These two factors—specification which is to do with the 'design quality' of an item, and conformity, which is to do with manufacture or process quality which is achieved—are of particular importance to customers. Ultimately they are the two factors which determine the quality levels provided by an organization to its customers. These two factors, however, are themselves determined by other factors, as shown in Figure 19.1. Consider first the specification. This will have been determined as a result of an organization's product or service policy, which in turn will

324

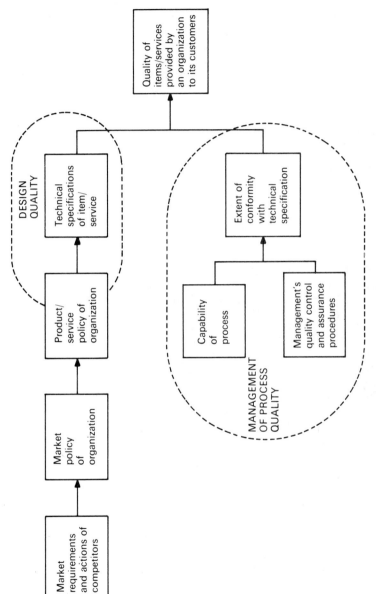

**Figure 19.1** *Factors influencing the quality of items/services, as provided to customers.*

result from decisions on its market policy, which in turn will result from its consideration of the market or customer needs and requirements, and the activities of competitors. This is the process of *designing quality* into the product or service.

The degree to which the product or service conforms to the technical specification will be influenced by the capability of the conversion process. If the conversion process is incapable of producing products or services at the level required by the specification then it must follow that the products or services provided to customers will in some way be inferior. However, the fact that a conversion process is inherently capable of producing or providing products/services according to a specification will not in itself ensure that all products or services are of an acceptable standard, for some management control will be required to ensure that the conversion process is used in the appropriate fashion in order to ensure that the product/service specification is achieved. This is all to do with the *management of process quality*.

In this chapter we shall deal primarily with the *management of process quality*, i.e.

(a) management's quality control and assurance procedures;
(b) capability of the process.

## THE NATURE OF QUALITY

Quality, reliability and cost are all interconnected. With enough expenditure anything can be endowed with high quality (whether through high specification and/or high conformity to specification during manufacture), and with adequate expenditure almost anything can be made to be very reliable. It follows, then, that a company can provide a product or a service at different quality levels, each of which necessitates a different price. There is no single level of quality; nor is there an absolute quality level. Nothing will be perfect, no matter how much it costs. In general, costs rise steeply for increasing quality, but beyond a certain level value to the customers increases more slowly. Thus it is possible to identify, notionally at least, a point at which the difference of value and cost is maximized.

### Definitions

From the above we can develop simple definitions as follows:

*Quality:* The quality of a product or service is the degree to which it satisfies customers' requirements. This is influenced by:

*Design quality:* The degree to which the specification of the product or service satisfies customers' design requirements.
*Manufactured quality*: the degree to which the product or service, when made available to the customer, conforms to specifications.

### Quality costs

The two main aspects of quality-related costs are as follows:

1. *Cost of 'original' quality*, i.e. all costs incurred in providing a product or service with a particular quality level. These might include:
   (a) prevention and appraisal costs associated with the design of the product or service and the specification of the operations processes, including the cost of the quality control system, e.g. the inspection and testing procedures and the training and payment of quality control staff;
   (b) internal failure costs associated with the rejection, scrapping, rectification, etc., of items found to be defective before being offered to the customer.

2. *Usage costs*, i.e. all costs associated with failure of products or services in use, which might include:
   (a) providers' costs associated with repair and replacement under warranty, the cost of operating service and spares systems, etc.;
   (b) user costs, e.g. cost of lost time due to breakdowns, cost of replacements, service and repair.

## QUALITY CONTROL AND ASSURANCE

We shall assume that item specifications have been established and that an appropriate process is available. Hence it is now our task to ensure conformity to the specifications.

To achieve this objective three stages can be defined. We must first ensure that only materials and parts which conform to the given specifications are accepted from suppliers. Second, we must implement control procedures to attempt to ensure that during the conversion of these items only products which conform to the specifications are produced. And finally, we must ensure that only those items which conform to the specifications are offered to the customers. These procedures are outlined diagrammatically in Figure 19.2 and are discussed below.

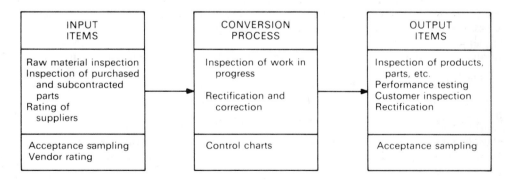

**Figure 19.2**   *The stages, processes and procedures of quality control and assurance.*

### Control of inputs

An organization may adopt one or (usually) both of the following procedures in an attempt to ensure that it uses only items which fully conform to the required specifications and standards.

1. Items used by the organization will be inspected. The items which are supplied to the firm will normally have been subjected by the supplier to some form of quality control. The purchasing firm will institute its own procedure, carried out in the receiving department on its own premises, and/or monitor the quality controls conducted by the supplier. It may ask to be supplied with regular information about the quality of the items as they are prepared, ask for copies of all the final inspection documents to be supplied, or ask a third party (e.g. an insurance company) to ensure that the items conform to the required minimum quality. However, despite such precautionary steps, inspection of purchased items will normally be conducted on receipt, and before use. One or both of the following procedures will normally be adopted:

   (a) exhaustive inspection of every item received;
   (b) an inspection of a sample of the items received—this procedure, which is commonly adopted, is referred to as *acceptance sampling* and is discussed in some detail later in the chapter.

2. The organization will purchase only from those suppliers which are known to be likely to provide acceptable items. To ensure this the purchaser may undertake some form of *vendor rating* (VR) i.e. a comparative rating of suppliers taking into account quality-related factors such as:

   (a) percentage of acceptable items received in the past;
   (b) quality of packaging;
   (c) price;
   (d) percentage of warranty claims which can be traced to defective items provided by the vendor.

   The commonest VR procedures will be discussed below.

### Control of process

Inspection of items between operations is undertaken, not only to ensure that faulty or defective items do not proceed to the subsequent operations, but also in order to predict when the process is likely to produce defective items so that necessary preventive adjustments can be made. Quality control during the process often involves the use of *control charts*, which will be discussed in some detail shortly. The number and location of inspections should reflect both the probability of faults or defectives occurring and the consequences of such occurrences, as well as the cost of conducting inspection. Frequently, technical considerations determine the position and number of inspection operations, but nevertheless, within certain limitations, operations management is usually able to design the inspection procedure.

   Well-defined procedures should be established for the selection and inspection of the items, for the recording and analysis of data, for reprocessing, rectifying or scrapping of defectives, and for the feedback of information. We have tended to assume that a group of people attached to a separate department within the organization is involved in these quality control procedures, but two other alternatives exist. First, automatic 'on-line' inspection or gauging could be used. Such procedures are increasingly used for automatic inspection and checking of variables (dimensions); often the equipment involves a 'feedback' to the machine, which is self-correcting. A second alternative is for workers to be responsible for checking and inspecting their own work. In such cases appropriate time allowances must be provided.

## Control of outputs

Quality inspection of output items is essential because unless defective output is identified by the producer it will be passed on to the consumer. Final inspection is unfortunate, since the purpose of all previous inspection has been to ensure that defective or faulty output is not produced. However, it is not a reflection on the ineffectiveness of earlier inspection, since items can be damaged at any time during the entire process.

Final inspection may involve only a sampling procedure, or exhaustive checks. Suitable procedures must be designed for the collection and retention of inspection data, for the correction, replacement or further examination of faulty items and, if necessary, for the adjustment or modification of either previous inspection or processing operations to ensure that faulty items do not continue to be produced—at least not for the same reasons.

Inspection of output is normally conducted in a similar manner to the inspection of input items, the procedures being referred to as *acceptance sampling*.

## Control of inspection

Quality control and inspection procedures almost invariably involve the use of equipment. If output is to be satisfactory, we must ensure that the means by which it is checked is adequate. A periodic examination and recalibration of all instruments should be undertaken.

## QUALITY CONTROL PROCEDURES

We have identified three basic stages in quality control (Figure 19.2), i.e.

1. Control of quality of input items.
2. Control of quality during operations.
3. Control of quality of output items.

These three stages are complementary. Inadequate control at one stage will necessitate greater effort at subsequent stages. In the remainder of this chapter we shall focus on quality control procedures, and shall discuss three procedures:

1. Vendor rating
2. Acceptance sampling $\Big\}$ involving the *inspection* of items.
3. Control charts

Vendor rating is concerned with the monitoring of the performance and the selection of suppliers. Acceptance sampling is of relevance for the control of input and output quality. Control charts are of relevance for the control of quality during operations.

## Vendor rating

The supplies received by an organization are normally evaluated and used in purchasing decision-making. In vendor rating, this evaluation process is formalized to provide a quantitative measure of 'vendor quality'. Such ratings are meant primarily to provide an overall rating of a vendor for use in reviewing, comparing and selecting vendors. Vendor rating is therefore an integral part of a rigorous purchasing procedure, and an aspect of quality assurance for use alongside, or in some cases instead of, acceptance sampling.

It will often be difficult to create a single numerical quality/rating score because of the different factors which must be taken into account. These may include:

(a) the lot quality (number of lots rejected);
(b) the parts qualities (percentage of items defective);
(c) the 'characteristic' quality of items (e.g. percentage active ingredient, performance, etc.).

Because such factors differ in importance in different companies and for different items, the vendor rating method employed must be tailored for specific applications. However, in general such methods will fall into one of the following four categories:

1. Categorical plan: a non-quantitative system in which those responsible for buying hold a periodic meeting to discuss vendors and rate each one, usually only as 'plus', 'minus' or 'neutral'.
2. Weighted point plan: each vendor is scored on quality, price and service. These factors are weighted and a composite rating is then calculated for each vendor. An example is shown in Table 19.1.

**Table 19.1** *Example of a 'weighted point' vendor rating plan. A hospital purchases sterile supplies from three companies. Data are collected over a one-year period so that the three suppliers can be compared.*

|  | Supplier A | Supplier B | Supplier C |
|---|---|---|---|
| 1. Lots received[a] | 60 | 60 | 20 |
| 2. Lots accepted[a] | 54 | 56 | 16 |
| 3. Percentage accepted[b] | 90.0 | 93.3 | 80.0 |
| 4. Quality rating $((3) \times 0.4)^b$ | 36 | 37.3 | 32 |
| 5. Net price[a] | 0.93 | 1.12 | 1.23 |
| 6. $\dfrac{\text{Lowest price}}{\text{Net price}} \times 100^b$ | 100 | 83 | 75.6 |
| 7. Price rating $((6) \times 0.35)^b$ | 35 | 29 | 26.5 |
| 8. Delivery promises kept[a] | 90% | 95% | 100% |
| 9. Service rating $((8) \times 0.25)^b$ | 22.5 | 23.8 | 25 |
| 10. Total rating $(4) + (7) + (9)^b$ | 93.5 | 90.1 | 83.5 |

[a] Data
[b] Calculations
*Note.* Here the relative importances of quality, price and service have been judged to be 0.4, 0.35 and 0.25.

3. Cost ratio plan: compares vendors on the *total* cost involved for a specific purchase. This will include:
   (a) price quotation;
   (b) quality costs (e.g. repair, return or replacement of defectives);
   (c) delivery costs.
4. Quality only rating plans: the first three types of plans above recognize item quality in the rating of vendors but in no case is the rating restricted to quality alone. In the fourth type of plan *only* quality is taken into account.

Many such vendor rating systems exist. In selecting a system for a particular situation, a basic decision must be whether the rating will be based solely on quality performance or on additional considerations such as cost and delivery.

True vendor ratings (for the purpose of making decisions on retaining or dropping vendors) are published infrequently. These ratings are not to be confused with monthly publications of 'vendor performance', which serve mainly as product rating rather than vendor rating.

It is important that vendor ratings be used as an *aid*, and not as the sole criterion in vendor decision-making. It should be remembered that:

1. A single index will often hide important detail.
2. The specific purpose of the rating should be kept in mind.

Most vendor rating plans involve some degree of subjectivity and guesswork. The mathematical treatment of data in the plans often tends to obscure the fact that the results are no more accurate than the assumptions on which the quantitative data are based. In the final analysis, therefore, supplier evaluation must represent a combined appraisal of facts, quantitative computations and value judgements. In most cases vendor rating will be used along with an acceptance sampling plan.

Vendor rating is an important defect prevention device if it is used in an atmosphere of interdependence between vendor and customer. This means that the customer must:

(a) make the investment of time, effort and special skills to help the poor vendors to improve;
(b) be willing to change the specifications when warranted (in some companies 20 to 40 per cent of rejected purchases can be used without any quality compromise).

Finally, in cases of consistently poor vendors who cannot respond to help, the rating highlights them as candidates to be dropped as vendors.

## Inspection

In this section we shall consider both acceptance sampling and control chart procedures. Both procedures will involve the *inspection* of items so that a decision can be made on whether an item, or the batch from which a sample of items is drawn, is acceptable or not. The planning of inspection may involve deciding *where* to inspect. These problems will be considered before we look at acceptance sampling and control chart techniques.

### *The location of inspection*

There will normally be some choice of the location of quality inspection points in operating systems. For example, we may choose to locate inspection before or after the inventories which exist in operating systems, or between an operation and its supplier, and its customer. This will provide a wide choice of locations but, additionally, since most businesses are multi-stage, it will usually be necessary to decide where to inspect within a sequence of operations. Rarely will items be inspected formally after every stage in the system, since to do so would be expensive. The problem, therefore, is to locate inspection operations, taking into account the cost of inspection and the benefits of inspecting (or the risks of not inspecting).

In practice such decisions are often based on empirical and quantitative rules. For example, good 'rules of thumb' are:

1. Inspect before costly operations in order to avoid high processing costs for defective items.
2. Inspect before any series of operations during which inspection will be difficult and/or costly.
3. Inspect after operations which generally result in a high rate of defectives.
4. Inspect before operations which would conceal defects previously caused.
5. Inspect before a 'point of no return', i.e. after which any rectification is impossible.
6. Inspect before points at which potential damage may be caused, i.e. before the use of equipment which would be damaged through the processing of faulty items.
7. Inspect before a change in quality responsibility, e.g. between departments.

## Acceptance sampling

Inspection of each critical feature of every item received may be a very desirable procedure in that, by so doing, no defective items would pass unnoticed, except by a mistake or error in the inspection procedure. There are, however, several reasons why such a procedure may be uneconomical or even impossible:

1. Inspection may cause damage or even complete destruction of the items (e.g. the testing of electrical fuses).
2. The accuracy of inspection may be diminished after frequent repetition. For example, an inspection task may take only a few seconds to complete but if this is undertaken continually over a long period, it may be excessively fatiguing and boring for the inspector, whose accuracy and judgement might then be affected.
3. Handling of the item may result in deterioration, or, alternatively, items may naturally deteriorate rapidly prior to use, and lengthy inspection procedures may be undesirable.
4. Inspection may be a particularly expensive procedure involving the unpacking or dismantling of items, the use of special machines, etc.
5. Inspection may be a hazardous, even dangerous procedure (e.g. the testing of pressure vessels).

For these reasons, some form of *sampling inspection* is often required. In acceptance sampling, decisions about the quality of batches of items are made after inspection of only a portion of those items. If the sample of items conforms to the requisite quality levels then the whole batch from which it came is accepted. If the sample does not conform to the requisite quality level, then the whole batch is rejected or subjected to further inspection. Adopting this procedure, decisions about the quality levels of items can be made fairly quickly, easily and cheaply. However, a certain amount of risk is involved, since there is the possibility that the sample taken will not be of the same quality as the batch from which it came. A greater proportion of defectives in the sample will lead us erroneously to attribute a lower quality level to the batch and vice versa.

Several types of acceptance sampling plan may be used. For example, some necessitate taking a *single* sample lot from a batch, upon which a quality decision is made, while others may necessitate the use of *multiple* samples from the same batch. Plans will also vary in the types of measurement that are involved. The most common, and simplest, type of inspection decision involves classifying items as good or bad, as acceptable or unacceptable. This is referred to as acceptance sampling by *attributes*.

Less often, acceptance sampling by *variables* is used, in which the purpose of inspection is to obtain exact measurements for dimensions. We shall concentrate on the more usual procedure, which is *single acceptance sampling* by *attributes*.

Acceptance sampling by attributes is suitable not only for items whose critical features cannot easily be measured, such as the quality of finish of furniture, the power of light bulbs, etc., but may also be used where inspection is concerned with dimensions, since such dimensions ultimately are either acceptable or not. For example, the size of a hole in a component will either fall within the upper and lower tolerance specified, and hence be acceptable, or if it does not then it will be rejected. In such cases Go/No go gauges are often used to check the acceptability of variables.

Customers would ideally like 100 per cent of the products which they purchase to be acceptable but this, as we have pointed out previously, is impractical. Therefore some lower quality level must, of necessity, be agreed. Even so only by 100 per cent inspection (and even then, only if there are no errors during inspection) can we be absolutely certain that a batch conforms to this agreed standard. In Figure 19.3 100 per cent inspection has been used, so we can be 100 per cent certain that batches do, or do not, conform to the agreed quality level, which is a maximum of 20 per cent defectives per batch (again assuming no mistakes during inspection).

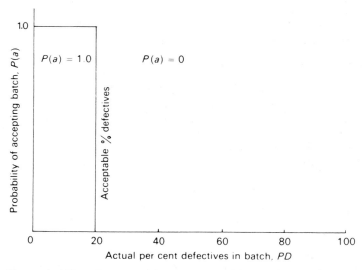

**Figure 19.3** *The probability of accepting batches, with 100 per cent inspection. (Acceptable per cent defectives = 20 per cent or less.)*

A curve such as this is known as an *operating characteristic* curve and shows the probability of accepting batches with various percentage defectives. Operating characteristic (OC) curves can be calculated and drawn for any sampling plan if we specify:

(a) the sample size ($n$);
(b) the acceptance number, i.e. the maximum allowance number of defects in the sample ($c$).

An example for a sampling plan with $c \leqslant 1$ and $n = 10$ is shown in Figure 19.4.

For simplicity, the calculations may be performed with the assistance of the *Thorndike chart*. This chart, as shown in Figure 19.5, gives the probability of $c$ or less defectives ($P(a)$ on the vertical axis) for given values of $PD \times n/100$ (on the horizontal axis)

where $PD$ = actual per cent defectives in a batch or lot
$\quad\quad n$ = sample size

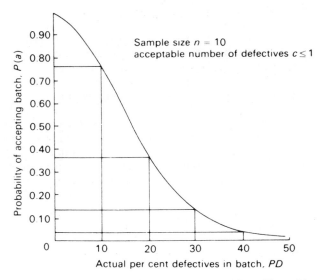

**Figure 19.4**   *Operating characteristic curve (n = 10; c≤1).*

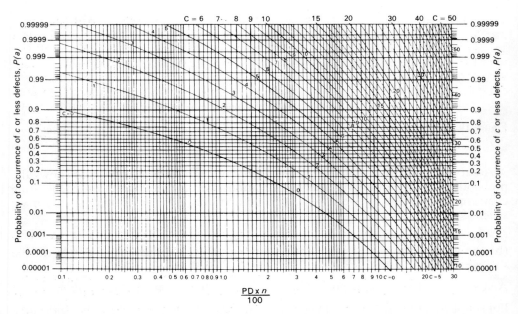

**Figure 19.5**   *Thorndike chart. (From Dodge, H. F. and Romig, H. G. (1959)* Sampling Inspection Tables. *London: Wiley. Adapted with permission.)*

## EXAMPLE 19.1

Use the Thorndike chart to construct an operating characteristic curve for

$n = 100$ sample size
$c \leqslant 3$ allowable number of defects

Answer:

| Actual per cent defectives in batch (PD) | $\dfrac{PD \times n}{100}$ | P(a) |
|:---:|:---:|:---:|
| 1 | 1 | 0.98 |
| 2 | 2 | 0.86 |
| 3 | 3 | 0.65 |
| 4 | 4 | 0.44 |
| 5 | 5 | 0.26 |
| 6 | 6 | 0.15 |
| 7 | 7 | 0.08 |
| 8 | 8 | 0.04 |
| 9 | 9 | 0.02 |
| 10 | 10 | 0.01 |

These figures can now be used to plot an OC curve of the type shown previously.

---

The ability of a sampling procedure to distinguish between good and bad batches is primarily a function of the sample size. If three sampling processes are designed to test the quality level of batches of components for which the acceptable quality level is 1 per cent or less defectives, then the procedure using the largest sample will be more accurate than those using smaller samples, particularly where the actual percentage of defectives in the batch is high. Figure 19.6 shows three such OC curves, each of which is fairly accurate up to a percentage defective level just below the acceptable level but, above that point, curve 3 is superior. As the sample size is increased, the curves become steeper and begin to approach the perfectly discriminating OC curve given in Figure 19.3.

### The design of single acceptance sampling plans

The merit of any sampling plan depends on the relationship of sampling cost to risk. As the cost of inspection decreases and the cost of accepting defective items increases, then the merit of inspection increases and the more willing we are to use larger samples. The OC curve shows, for any plan, both the probability of accepting batches with more than the acceptable number of defects, as well as the probability of rejecting batches with less than the acceptable number of defects.

It is the consumer's desire to reduce the probability of accepting batches including too many defects and the producer's desire to minimize the probability of rejecting

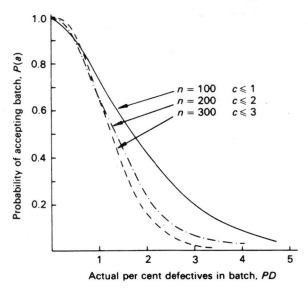

**Figure 19.6**   *Operating characteristic curves.*

batches including an acceptable number of defectives. These are called respectively the *consumer's risk (β)* and the *producer's risk (α)*. These two values are used in order to design acceptance sampling plans and, in addition, two further points are used:

1. *Acceptable quality level (AQL)*—the desired quality level, at which probability of acceptance should be high.
2. *Lot tolerance per cent defective (LTPD)*—a quality level below which batches are considered unacceptable, and a level at which probability of acceptance should be low.

These four values are shown on the OC curve in Figure 19.7. The consumer's risk *(β)* is usually specified at about 10 per cent and the producer's risk *(α)* at approximately 5 per cent. Acceptable quality level is often around 2 per cent and lot tolerance per cent defective around 10 per cent. These four figures are specified in designing the sampling plan. All that then remains is to construct an OC curve which passes through the two points *(AQL; α)* and *(LTPD; β)*. This can be done by trial and error, selecting various values for the sample size *(n)* and acceptable number of defectives *(c)* and substituting into the binomial probability formula until an acceptable curve is obtained, or by use of the Thorndike chart. The OC curve constructed in this way determines the sample size *n* and the value of *c* to be used in the acceptance sampling procedure.

   Defective items found in the *samples* will always be either rectified or replaced. If, during inspection, samples are drawn from the batch which include more than the acceptable number of defectives, then two alternatives are available:

1. Reject and scrap the complete *batch*.
2. Subject the complete *batch* to 100 per cent inspection and replace or rectify all faulty items found in it.

The choice of alternative (1) or (2) will depend on the value of the items concerned and the cost to replace or rectify them, but often, in order to obtain a high-quality level for batches with a minimum of inspection, the second alternative is adopted.

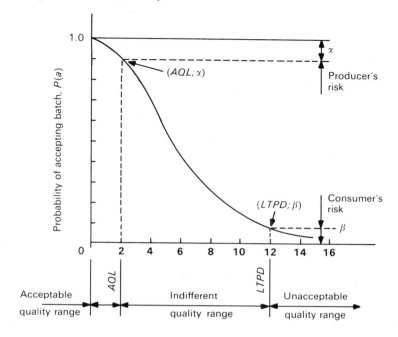

**Figure 19.7** *Operating characteristic curve and points specifying a sampling plan.*

## Double and multiple sampling

The total amount of inspection required to obtain a certain output quality level can be reduced if *double* or *multiple sampling* is used.

In single acceptance sampling as described above, the decision to accept or to reject the batch of items is dependent on the inspection of a single random sample from that batch. In *double* sampling there exists the possibility of delaying that decision until a second sampling has been taken. A random sample of $n$ items is drawn from the batch, each item is inspected and the number of defectives ($c$) is counted. If this number is less than or equal to a given acceptance number ($c1$) then the batch is accepted. Alternatively, if it is greater than a larger given acceptance number ($c2$) the batch is rejected. If, however, the number of defectives in the sample falls between these two levels, then the result is inconclusive and a second sample is drawn from the same batch. Again, the number of defectives is counted and this number is added to the number of defectives found in the first sample. If the total number is less than $c2$, the batch is accepted, but if the total number is greater than $c2$, the batch is rejected.

*Multiple* sampling is a similar procedure, but here there is the possibility of taking more than two samples from the same batch. An initial sample is drawn from the batch and, depending on the number of defectives found, the batch is accepted ($c \leqslant c1$), rejected ($c > c2$) or a decision is deferred ($c1 < c < c2$). The number of defectives in the second sample is added to the number found in the first and the total is compared with two further acceptance numbers, the batch being accepted or rejected or the decision deferred as before. This procedure is repeated until a decision can be made. A multiple sampling plan is depicted diagrammatically in Figure 19.8.

*Sequential* sampling is a similar procedure but involves taking one at a time from the batch and basing acceptance or rejection decisions on the number of defectives accumulated.

Double or multiple sampling permits smaller-sized samples to be taken. Consequently, on the occasions when the items or material inspected are well within, or well beyond, acceptable quality levels, fewer items need to be inspected. In such cases double or multiple sampling is more economical than single acceptance sampling.

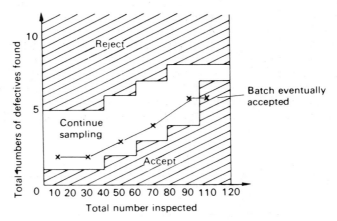

**Figure 19.8** *Multiple (sequential) sampling plan (for batch sizes of 500 to 799 for 3 per cent AQL).*

## Control charts

Irrespective of how well designed or maintained manufacturing equipment is, or how skilfully it is used, the items produced by such equipment will inevitably be subject to some variation, e.g. the length of steel bars cut on a cropping press will vary slightly, as will the diameter of holes drilled on a drilling machine and the diameter of shafts turned on a lathe. It is not only variables such as these (length, diameter, etc.) but also other attributes which will be subject to some variations. These variations might be caused by numerous factors, but we can classify the variations into two categories:

(a) *usual or chance* variations, which are likely to occur in a random manner and about which comparatively little can be done;
(b) *unusual or assignable* variations, which occur less frequently and which can normally be traced to some 'external' cause, such as wear on tools or faulty materials.

'Usual' variations are normally of a lesser magnitude than 'unusual' variations and, since they result from some inherent process variability, they occur randomly and can be described by the normal probability distribution. Quality controllers define *limits* within which variations are acceptable and beyond which they are either unacceptable, or necessitate some examination. Such limits are called *control limits*. For example, for a normal probability distribution, 99.73 per cent of all chance or usual variations would be expected to occur within limits placed three standard deviations larger and smaller then the mean value of the variable. Therefore any variation occurring beyond such limits would probably have resulted from some other unusual or assignable cause and would merit some investigation.

For example, after a pilot investigation of the length of rods produced by a cropping press, we discover that the mean length ($\bar{x}$) is 100 cm, and that after excluding the faulty rods that were produced when the setting on the press was accidentally altered, the standard deviation ($\sigma$),[1] which is a measure of the variability of the rods produced, was 2.1 cm. We could then set up a control chart with a mean of 100 and control limits of plus and minus three standard deviations. Such a chart (Figure 19.9) might then be used to test the quality of rods produced by this press. Rather than examine every rod, we take a sample rod every hour and examine it, then plot our result on the control chart, and by so doing we are able to discover that the process, while initially 'in control', is now running 'out of control' and often producing rods which are too long.

A process is considered to be statistically 'under' or 'in control' if it regularly produces items whose attributes or variables fall within the acceptable or tolerable range, whereas a process is said to be 'out of control' if items are produced whose attributes or variables are beyond the acceptable or tolerable range. In this case (Figure 19.9) the process appears to have gone out of control because of the change in the mean value ($\bar{x}$).

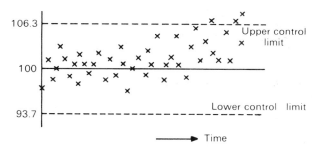

**Figure 19.9** *A simple control chart for the lengths of rods.*

This is only one of the three possible types of change which might occur in a process, i.e. in Figure 19.10, (1) has resulted from a change in the value of the mean, (2) has resulted from a change in the standard deviation, and (3) has resulted from a change in both of these characteristics. Each of these changes or disturbances in the process might lead to the production of defective items, but in each case the use of a control chart to monitor output will enable such items to be observed and action to be taken to prevent the production of defective items.

Control charts would therefore be used as follows:

Step 1  Decide which characteristics of the items are to be controlled.
Step 2  Conduct a pilot study of the process to determine the mean and the standard deviation of the characteristics.
Step 3  Design the control chart(s) using these data.

---

[1] The standard deviation ($\sigma$) is calculated using the formula:

$$\sigma = \sqrt{\frac{\Sigma(\bar{x}-x)^2}{N}}$$

where $x$ = length of individual bar
$\bar{x}$ = mean length of all bars measured
$N$ = number of bars measured

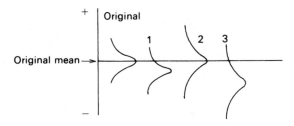

**Figure 19.10** *Frequency distributions showing types of change which might occur in a process.*

Step 4 Check these control limits to ensure that they are economically feasible and realistic.
Step 5 Take samples of the process output and plot the characteristics on the control charts.
Step 6 Whenever points fall beyond the control limits:
    (a) investigate causes;
    (b) take corrective action;
    (c) inspect remainder of batch if necessary.

### Control charts for variables

Control charts for variables are usually based on the normal probability distribution and are most frequently designed to test the *means* of samples rather than individual measurements. In practice, therefore, the dimensions of individual components are not plotted separately on control charts; only the *mean*, or average value of the dimensions in the sample, is plotted.

Two upper and two lower control limits are normally used, these being referred to as the *upper and lower warning limit* and the *upper and lower action limit*. If points fall beyond the warning limits, this is taken to indicate that the process may be going out of control and that careful observation or additional sampling is required. Points falling beyond the action limits indicate the need to take immediate steps to establish and eliminate the causes. Action limits are normally set so as to exclude only 0.2 per cent of the points through usual or random variations. Warning limits are set so as to exclude 5 per cent of the points through usual or random variation.

The following formulae are used

where $\sigma$ = standard deviation of individual items produced by process
    $\bar{w}_x$ = mean range of several samples
    $d_n$ = a constant depending on the sample size

$$\sigma = \frac{\bar{w}_x}{d_n}$$

Upper action limit $\qquad = \bar{X} + \dfrac{3.09(\bar{w}_x/d_n)}{\sqrt{n}}$

Upper warning limit $\qquad = \bar{X} + \dfrac{1.96(\bar{w}_x/d_n)}{\sqrt{n}}$

Centre $\qquad\qquad\qquad = \bar{X}$

$$\text{Lower warning limit} \quad = \bar{X} - \frac{1.96(\bar{w}_x/d_n)}{\sqrt{n}}$$

$$\text{Lower action limit} \quad = \bar{X} - \frac{3.09(\bar{w}_x/d_n)}{\sqrt{n}}$$

(where $\bar{X}$ = overall process mean value).

To simplify such calculations even further, tables for $3.09/\sqrt{n}d_n$ and $1.96/\sqrt{n}d_n$ can be used (see Table 19.2).

**Table 19.2**  *Factors for calculating control limits for control charts for means.*

| Sample size $n$ | Constant $d_n$ | Factors ($m$) for warning limits $= \dfrac{1.96}{\sqrt{n}d_n}$ | Factors ($m$) for action limits $= \dfrac{3.09}{\sqrt{n}d_n}$ |
|---|---|---|---|
| 2 | 1.128 | 1.23 | 1.94 |
| 3 | 1.693 | 0.67 | 1.05 |
| 4 | 2.059 | 0.48 | 0.75 |
| 5 | 2.236 | 0.38 | 0.59 |
| 6 | 2.334 | 0.32 | 0.50 |
| 7 | 2.704 | 0.27 | 0.43 |
| 8 | 2.847 | 0.24 | 0.38 |
| 9 | 2.970 | 0.22 | 0.35 |
| 10 | 3.078 | 0.20 | 0.32 |

*Note:* To calculate control limits, multiply $w_x$ by factor ($m$) and add or subtract from $\bar{X}$.

Even though the mean value is constant, we have seen how the process might produce defective items by an increase in variability (Figure 19.10). Consequently, a process cannot be said to be fully under control unless *both* mean and standard deviation are under control. We should, therefore, also construct a control chart on which to plot standard deviations, but, for the same reasons as before, it is found to be easier to use the range as a measure of variability. In much the same way as for control limits for means, factors can be calculated from which control limits for ranges can be established. These are shown in Table 19.3.

**Table 19.3**  *Factors for calculating control limits for control charts for ranges.*

| Sample size $n$ | Factor ($R$) for warning limits | | Factor ($R$) for action limits | |
|---|---|---|---|---|
| | Upper | Lower | Upper | Lower |
| 2 | 2.81 | 0.04 | 4.12 | 0.00 |
| 3 | 2.17 | 0.18 | 2.98 | 0.04 |
| 4 | 1.93 | 0.29 | 2.57 | 0.10 |
| 5 | 1.81 | 0.37 | 2.34 | 0.16 |
| 6 | 1.72 | 0.42 | 2.21 | 0.21 |
| 7 | 1.66 | 0.46 | 2.11 | 0.26 |
| 8 | 1.62 | 0.50 | 2.04 | 0.29 |
| 9 | 1.58 | 0.52 | 1.99 | 0.32 |
| 10 | 1.56 | 0.54 | 1.94 | 0.35 |

Note: To calculate control limit, multiply $w_x$ by the appropriate factor ($R$).

EXAMPLE 19.2

Again referring to a cropping press on which bars are to be cut continually to a length of 12 cm, a random sample of five bars is taken from each hour's production, and for each sample the mean and range are calculated, i.e.

| Sample (size $n = 5$) | Sample mean ($\bar{x}$) | Sample range ($w_x$) |
|---|---|---|
| 9.00 a.m. | 12.005 | 0.007 |
| 10.00 a.m. | 12.001 | 0.008 |
| 11.00 a.m. | 11.993 | 0.010 |
| 12.00 | 11.991 | 0.003 |
| 1.00 p.m. | 12.001 | 0.006 |
| 2.00 p.m. | 12.003 | 0.015 |
| 3.00 p.m. | 11.995 | 0.011 |
| 4.00 p.m. | 12.004 | 0.008 |
| 5.00 p.m. | 12.003 | 0.009 |
| 6.00 p.m. | 12.000 | 0.010 |
| 7.00 p.m. | 11.999 | 0.006 |
| 8.00 p.m. | 11.997 | 0.013 |
| 9.00 p.m. | 11.999 | 0.011 |
| 10.00 p.m. | 12.000 | 0.010 |
| *Total* | 167.991 | 0.127 |

From an earlier pilot study the overall mean ($\bar{X}$) and average range ($\bar{W}$) have been found to be:

$$\bar{X} = 11.9994 \qquad \bar{W} = 0.0091$$

Now using the factors from Table 19.2 and Table 19.3, control limits for means and ranges can be calculated.

Mean
- UAL = $11.9994 + 0.59(0.0091) = 12.0048$
- UWL = $11.9994 + 0.38(0.0091) = 12.0029$
- Centre = $11.9994$
- LWL = $11.9994 - 0.38(0.0091) = 11.9959$
- LAL = $11.9994 - 0.59(0.0091) = 11.9940$

Range
- UAL = $0.0091 \times 2.34$ = $0.0213$
- UWL = $0.0091 \times 1.81$ = $0.0165$
- Centre = $0.0091$
- LWL = $0.0091 \times 0.37$ = $0.0034$
- LAL = $0.0091 \times 0.16$ = $0.0015$

The control charts can now be constructed using these figures and the individual sample means and ranges plotted (Figure 19.11). The charts indicate that the process is beginning to settle down. The mean lengths from early

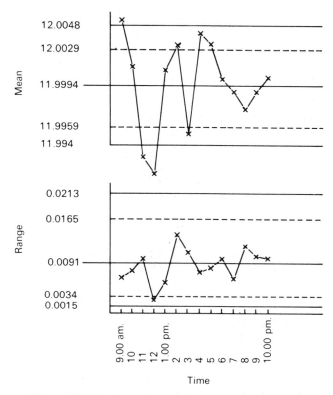

**Figure 19.11** *Control chart for means and for range.*

samples were probably unacceptable, but towards the end of the day the process was under better control.

## Design limits and control limits

The control limits we have discussed do not necessarily bear any relationship to the design limits, since in constructing the control charts no account was taken of the dimensional tolerance specified on component drawings, etc. It is possible then, using the control charts, to accept items which are *not* manufactured to design specifications. To avoid such a situation the design limits, i.e. the tolerances on a dimension, must fall outside the action limits of the control chart, i.e. the dimensional tolerance should be a minimum of $6.18\sigma$. During design it is important, therefore, to ensure that manufacturing equipment is capable of producing parts to the required tolerance so that (say) 99.8 per cent of the items should be within such tolerances. During the design of the control charts it is essential to ensure that the limits constructed after a pilot study are within the design limits.

## Control charts for attributes

Often, as was the case in acceptance sampling, it is possible after inspecting items to classify them only as 'good' or 'bad', as 'acceptable' or 'not acceptable', and it is for reasons such as these that control charts for attributes have been devised. Such charts are developed in much the same way as were control charts for variables.

Two types of chart are most popular:

1. Control chart for *proportion* or *per cent* defective.
2. Control chart for *number* of defects.

The method of using the charts is similar to that outlined previously, except that, in this case, rather than calculating the mean and range of all the items in each random sample, only the number, or the percentage, of defective items in the sample is calculated.

Control charts for *proportion* or *per cent defective* are known as *p-charts*. Control limits are constructed after a pilot investigation and if, during production, the proportion of defectives in a sample falls within these limits the process is considered to be 'under control', whereas, if the proportion of defectives in a sample falls beyond these limits, this is taken to be a good indication that the process is, for some reason, out of control and that some investigation and corrective action are required.

An estimate of the proportion defective produced by the process ($\bar{p}$) is obtained after a pilot study consisting of several samples, i.e.

$$\bar{p} = \frac{\text{Total number of defectives in 10 to 20 samples}}{\text{Total number inspected}}$$

0.2 per cent (and less frequently 5 per cent) control limits are set in the usual way, using the following formulae:

$$\text{Upper action limit: } \bar{p} + 3.09 \sqrt{\frac{\bar{p}(1 - \bar{p})}{n}}$$

$$\text{Lower action limit: } \bar{p} - 3.09 \sqrt{\frac{\bar{p}(1 - \bar{p})}{n}}$$

$$\text{where } n = \text{sample size}$$

---

EXAMPLE 19.3

| Time of sample | Sample size (n) | Numbers of defectives in sample | p |
|---|---|---|---|
| 9.00 a.m. | 205 | 12 | 0.0585 |
| 10.00 a.m. | 206 | 14 | 0.07 |
| 11.00 a.m. | 195 | 12 | 0.0615 |
| 12.00 | 200 | 15 | 0.075 |
| 1.00 p.m. | 210 | 14 | 0.0665 |
| 2.00 p.m. | 195 | 12 | 0.0615 |
| 3.00 p.m. | 200 | 15 | 0.075 |
| 4.00 p.m. | 200 | 16 | 0.080 |
| 5.00 p.m. | 205 | 13 | 0.0635 |
| 6.00 p.m. | 195 | 14 | 0.0715 |
| 7.00 p.m. | 200 | 15 | 0.075 |
| 8.00 p.m. | 195 | 14 | 0.0715 |

Output for previous week                                    = 10 000
Number of defectives included in this output = 370

The proportion defective produced by the process can in this case be estimated from the figures given for the previous week's production, i.e.

$$\bar{p} = \frac{370}{10\ 000} = 0.037$$

Therefore upper action limit is:

$$\bar{p} + 3.09 \sqrt{\frac{\bar{p}(1 - \bar{p})}{n}}$$
$$= 0.037 + 3.09 \sqrt{\frac{0.037(0.963)}{200}}$$
$$= 0.079$$

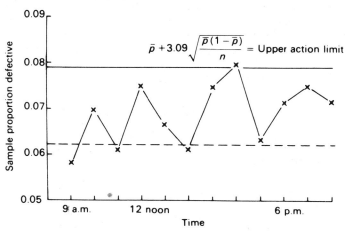

**Figure 19.12**  p-*chart.*

This action limit is shown on the *p*-chart in Figure 19.12. The proportion defective in each of the 12 samples is plotted on the chart, from which it can be seen that, compared with the previous week's production, the proportion of defectives in the batches has increased, and the process is almost 'out of control'.

Since the control limits for a *p*-chart are a function of *n* (the sample size), when the sample size changes the control limits must also change (e.g. Figure 19.13). In the above example, the sample size was nearly constant, hence a mean $n = 200$ was taken.

Control charts for *number* of defects are known as *c-charts* and are of particular value for controlling the number of defects in, or on, a particular unit, i.e. a single item, a group of items, or a part of an item. For example, the *c*-chart might be used to control the quality of cloth by counting the number of defects in a roll, to control the quality of a riveted structure by counting the number of faulty rivets, etc. Conditions such as these enable the Poisson distribution to be used. The symbol $\bar{c}$ is the average number of defects per unit obtained after a pilot investigation. The standard deviation of the Poisson distribution is given by $\sqrt{\bar{c}}$; consequently, the control limits are set at:

$$\text{Upper action} = \bar{c} + 3.09 \sqrt{\bar{c}}$$
$$\text{Lower action} = \bar{c} - 3.09 \sqrt{\bar{c}}$$

The manner in which *c*-charts are constructed and used is very similar to the construction and use of *p*-charts.

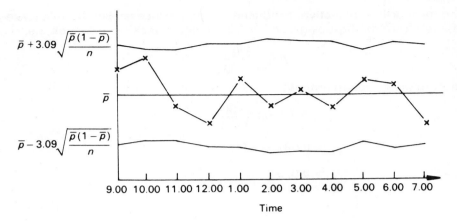

**Figure 19.13**  *A proportion defective control chart (p-chart) in which the sample size, n, has changed.*

## PROCESS CAPABILITY

### Control limits and design limits

The use of control charts permits us to determine whether a process is 'statistically' in control or not. By establishing action limits and plotting observations on a chart we can determine when to take appropriate remedial action or, using warning limits, appropriate preventive action. The positioning of these limits, however, is based on observations of the actual items received, or items output from a process. If we consider the latter, i.e. items produced by a process, then the establishment of the control chart involves us in considering the normal performance of the processes in order to establish limits beyond which output can be considered to be abnormal for those same circumstances. Thus if a process is highly reliable and extremely accurate, the control chart limits will be set relatively close to the mean. If, perhaps many years later, the same process becomes unreliable, the equipment worn, etc., then the normal variability in, for example, the dimensions of an item produced by the process will be greater, and thus the action and warning limits will be set further away from the overall mean.

We have noted earlier that the limits set on control charts may bear no direct relationship to the limits set in the specification for items. If a process is capable of producing items with considerable accuracy and extremely reliably, but the design specification for those items is very 'loose', then it is possible that, by using control charts designed in the manner described above, we will reject items which are acceptable under the original design specification. Conversely, if a process is not consistently capable of producing items to fine tolerances, yet the design tolerances for the item are very narrow, then it is possible, in using a control chart, to accept items which are not acceptable against the original design specification.

For these reasons we must consider the relationship between control chart limits and design or specification limits, and in doing so we must consider the question of *process capability*.

The use of the mean and range charts shows us whether a process is in statistical control or not, but does not necessarily give any adequate indication of whether individual items are acceptable within specification limits. Organizations are concerned primarily with ensuring that items are within the intended specification tolerance rather than being under 'statistical' control overall.

It will be recalled that in discussing the design of control charts for items we chose to use charts for mean values for reasons of convenience. Ideally we would have liked to set up control charts for individual observations in the manner shown below:

$$UAL_{individuals} = Overall\ mean + 3.09\sigma$$

$$LAL_{individuals} = Overall\ mean - 3.09\sigma$$

We chose instead to set up a control chart for mean values as follows:

$$UAL_{means} = Overall\ mean + 3.09\ \frac{\sigma}{\sqrt{n}}$$

$$LAL_{means} = Overall\ mean - 3.09\ \frac{\sigma}{\sqrt{n}}$$

In fact the action limits for a control chart based on mean values are somewhat narrower than those that would be established for the same population of individuals. It follows, therefore, that if in using control charts based on mean values we are to be sure that individual items conform to design specifications, the design limits must be placed well beyond the action limits of a mean control chart. This relationship is shown in Figure 19.14. If the design limits are within the action limits for the mean chart, or even just beyond those limits, then it is possible that, using the means chart, individual items will be accepted which do not conform to the specification limits.

## Process capability measurement

In studying process capability we shall be concerned with the extent to which a process is capable of processing items which correspond to the design specification limits.

A measure of process capability can be obtained as follows:

$$PC = \frac{USL - LSL}{\sigma}$$

where   PC = Process capability
         USL = Upper specification limit
         LSL = Lower specification limit
         $\sigma$ = Standard deviation of individual items

Strictly, this measure of process capability applies only where the specification tolerances are distributed symmetrically about the intended dimension, and where the overall mean dimension produced by a process is the same as the intended dimension. In these circumstances, where the value of PC is less than 6, more than 2 per cent of defective items will be produced, hence either the process variability must be improved or the specification tolerances must be increased. For a value between 6 and 11 the process may be controlled in the manner described above using a mean control chart. Where the value is greater than 11 then the use of a mean control chart may imply the use of a quality control procedure which is far tighter than is actually required. In these circumstances it may be appropriate to use modified action limits in the manner described later. Alternatively it may be appropriate, or indeed necessary, to retain action limits which are very much narrower than the specification limits in order to allow some 'drift' in the mean value.

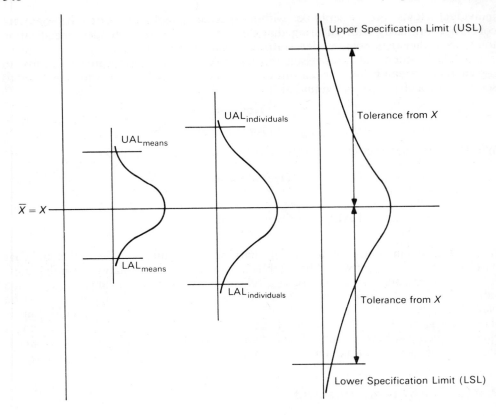

where $X$ = specified dimension
$\overline{X}$ = overall process mean dimension

**Figure 19.14**   *Comparison of action limits and possible specification limits.*

## BEHAVIOURAL AND ORGANIZATIONAL FACTORS IN QUALITY MANAGEMENT

### People as inspectors

Despite the fact that increasing use is being made of automatic devices, the principal method of inspection, and hence of quality control and assurance, is still the human inspector. We have taken care throughout this chapter to indicate that 100 per cent inspection does not necessarily ensure the complete absence of defects from the output, because inspectors, being human, are liable to make mistakes. It will now be appropriate to look briefly at the problem of error during inspection. What sort of decisions are inspectors asked to make? Essentially, there are two types: first, those connected with the inspection of variables (i.e. measurement); and second, those connected with the inspection of attributes (i.e. assessment).

In measurement, an inspector compares a characteristic of the item with a defined standard. Often this involves the use of a gauge or instrument against or within which the item is placed. Greater opportunity for error or mistake exists as the ease of comparison of characteristic and standard decreases.

A similar situation exists with respect to assessment. It is not too difficult to make decisions about the acceptability of certain noise levels, and of attributes such as brightness, because the inspector, conceptually at least, is able to compare such attributes with a known standard. In fact these could be considered as only slightly more difficult problems of *measurement* since it is possible to use decibel meters to measure noise levels and light meters to measure light levels. More difficult is the assessment of colour quality, since it is more difficult to define colour standards. The assessment of smell and taste is even more difficult because for such characteristics standards are virtually impossible to define.

The more remote and ill-defined the standard the more difficult the comparison of characteristic and standard and, consequently, the more difficult and the more equivocal the decision. It should be clear, therefore, that in order to ensure adequate and consistent inspection procedures, instruments should be used which ensure easy and accurate comparison of characteristic and standard. Furthermore, standards for which instruments cannot be used should be clearly defined, e.g. colour shade cards might be used and inspectors could be trained and retrained to recognize standard noise levels, brightness levels, etc., in much the same way that time study practitioners are trained ro recognize a notional concept of standard performance. Workplaces should be designed to permit and, preferably, emphasize the comparison of characteristic and standard.

The following notes will illustrate how the equipment and the situation might be designed to facilitate accurate and consistent inspection.

1. Ideally the standard itself should be used during the inspection process as, for example, in the physical comparison of dimensions while using Go/No go gauges.
2. The standard, if not used during inspection, should be prominently displayed so that comparison of characteristic and standard is easy or, alternatively, so that inspectors might regularly refer to the standard in order to 'recalibrate their perception'.
3. Where possible, inspection procedures might be 'reconstructed' as pattern recognition procedures. For example, in the design of instrument displays, dials are often arranged so that when each instrument is reading correctly all pointers appear horizontal or vertical. Consequently, when one instrument shows an unusual or wrong reading, the pattern is disrupted and recognition of the fact is made easier. In such a case the acceptable standard has been redefined, acceptability now being associated with consistency of appearance.
4. Wherever possible the workplace conditions should be arranged to emphasize the characteristic being measured or assessed. For example, lighting might be arranged to emphasize irregularities or roughness of surfaces.

## 'Zero defects' programmes

The original 'zero defects' programme was established by the Martin-Marietta Corporation in the USA around 1962. It was introduced to augment the established statistical quality control programme in order to try to improve product quality beyond that level which might economically be achieved by the statistical procedures. The programme was in large part a 'motivational' device which sought to organize and motivate direct and indirect workers to achieve higher levels of quality in their work. The slogan 'zero defect' was an important part of this motivational exercise.

This original zero defects programme was considered to be highly successful, and the company was able to demonstrate significant improvements in product quality as a result of its introduction. This in turn led other companies in similar industries, e.g. defence and aerospace, to adopt this motivational/organizational approach to quality assurance and, in time, 'zero defects' programmes became well established. It has been suggested that the principal features of such programmes were as follows:

'1. A motivational package aimed at reducing individual operator controlled defects. The contents of this package were such things as the 'Big Meeting Rally', 'Pledge Cards', 'Posters', 'Attention getters', 'Scoreboards' etc.
2. A prevention package aimed at reducing management controlled defects. This package centred around 'error cause removal' (ECR) suggestions to be made by employers for subsequent analysis and action by supervisors. These suggestions were submitted to the supervisor on ECR forms which defined the probable error cause and proposed action.
3. Procedures to provide for prompt feedback to the worker.'

Basic behavioural science principles and practices are the basis of 'zero defects' programmes. Such programmes are based on efforts to motivate workers, and the approaches employed, e.g. providing clear objectives, participation in decision-making and positive feedback on performance, are established principles which have widespread use in other applications. Thus the development of 'zero defects' programmes demonstrates a sensible application of established theories in a relatively new field.

Effective ZD programmes would probably involve the following:

(a) some methods of establishing agreement on the quality problems or quality goals to be achieved, or the reasons behind these problems and/or goals;
(b) the use of a well-structured approach to establishing a motivational programme aimed at solving these problems and/or achieving these goals;
(c) the participation of all those involved, i.e. all those who might in some way contribute to the solving of quality problems/achievement of quality objectives, in both the establishment and running of the programme;
(d) the setting of clear targets against which to measure improvements;
(e) the establishment of formalized, regular, simple procedures for reporting achievement on goals;
(f) the establishment of procedures for reinforcing effort in connection with the above;
(g) the organization of jobs, e.g. of workers, quality controllers, supervisors, management, etc., in such a way as to facilitate the above.

## 'Quality circles'

The quality circle approach to quality assurance was widely established in Japan before being adopted in Europe and North America. Wherever employed the QC approach rests upon the motivation of individuals and the organization of efforts to improve quality through error reduction, etc., and as such the procedure is designed to supplement conventional quality control procedures as previously discussed in this chapter.

A quality circle comprises a group of workers and supervisors in a single area or department within an organization, which meets regularly to study ways of improving quality and to monitor progress towards such goals. Thus it is a participative device, perhaps fundamentally more in tune with Japanese culture than with Western culture. A company will seek to establish quality circles largely on a voluntary basis. Those volunteering will often be up to half of the direct and indirect workers involved in the activities of a particular department. They are offered training in the analysis and identification of quality problems and problem-solving procedures. Once this training is completed the circle is formed and is invited to tackle particular quality problems nominated by management or identified by the circle itself. Each quality circle will normally tackle a series of projects, one at a time, identifying quality problems and means of eliminating such problems and establishing targets (often financial targets) to be achieved through quality improvement.

There will be numerous quality circles within an organization and their work will be monitored and co-ordinated by company management, who will be responsible for establishing overall objectives and monitoring the progress towards the achievement of these objectives. Thus the quality control effort within the organization is diffused through all levels rather than being seen as the responsibility of managers and indirect, often specialist, staff.

The *original* concept of QC may be of relevance only in a Japanese type of culture. For example, originally most of the training for those involved in QC and the meetings of the circles themselves took place out of working hours and on a voluntary and often unpaid basis. Normally there was no financial incentive in the improvement of quality except that obtained indirectly through improvements in the performance and financial status of the organization as a whole. The only major incentive was that of obtaining further training and of recognition within the organization. This analysis, however, conceals the fundamental nature of the programme, i.e. that of motivating individuals through participation in decision-making and reinforcing by positive feedback of results. Fundamentally such an approach is 'culture free' and can possibly be employed with benefit in other situations where quality performance is largely a function of individual effort and attention. Certainly the use of QC in Europe and North America does not follow exactly the pattern established in Japan, and interest in this type of approach to quality 'assurance' is increasing.

Quality circles have some similarity to ZD programmes; however, the former is essentially a group approach and the latter individual. The QC methodology (which is almost a ritualistic approach in Japan) probably requires considerable effort to establish and sustain, and it is perhaps for this reason that those companies which have adopted the approach, especially in Japan, have tended to concentrate on this one concept, rather than trying to sustain several different types of programme or campaign.

## RELIABILITY

The reliability of items has been considered above in connection with the specification and achievement of quality. We have seen that quality, reliability and cost are linked, higher quality being associated with higher reliability and normally higher cost. In Chapter 20 we shall consider the maintenance and replacement facilities. Here, again, consideration of reliability is relevant, since the higher the reliability the less is the need for replacement and maintenance. We shall also have cause to mention reliability in a slightly different context in discussing performance measurement in Chapter 21.

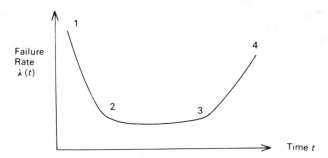

**Figure 19.15**   *Reliability distributions.*

Clearly, therefore, the reliability of items, products and facilities is an important consideration during design. It is of relevance to the user, and is a factor to consider in quality management and in maintenance and replacement.

The curve in Figure 19.15 shows the classic 'bath tub' pattern. It shows the failure rate, i.e. the number of failures per unit time, expressed as a fraction of the number of survivors. Three phases are evident:

1–2 'burn-in' or 'infant mortality' or 'early life' failures;
2–3 'random' or 'normal operating' or 'middle life' failures;
3–4 'wear-out' or 'old age' failures.

In analysing item reliability we must consider each of the three phases of reliability. Following a period of low but improving reliability during the 'infant mortality' period, reliability would be expected to be relatively high during 'middle age' and to reduce again during the 'old age' period. Analysis of reliability during these periods necessitates the use of appropriate formulae to describe these three essentially different curves.

## System reliability

The characteristics discussed above apply both to single items or components and to products comprising several components. The latter may fail if any one of their component parts fails unless the failed part is redundant, i.e is not required for effective system operation. This of course raises the possibility of deliberately introducing redundant components as a design feature. Thus it may be possible to design a product such that, initially, certain components are redundant and are brought into operation only when other components fail.

The reliability of complex products, or systems of components, is clearly a function of the number and the reliability of their components. Thus in a system without redundancy, which fails when any of its components, A, B, C and D, fail:

$$R_{\text{SYSTEM}} = R_Z \times R_B \times R_C \times R_D$$

For example, in a system comprising ten components, each essential for satisfactory system operation (i.e. without redundancy), if component reliability is 0.99:

$$R_{\text{SYSTEM}} = 0.99^{10}$$
$$= 0.904 \text{ approximately}$$

Now if in this example, because of built-in redundancy, five of the components would instantly be replaced by parallel components if they fail, the system might be shown as in Figure 19.16.

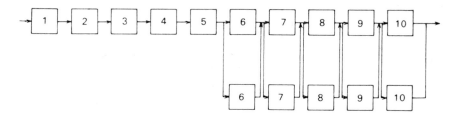

**Figure 19.16** *Diagrammatic representation of a ten-component system with redundancy.*

The reliability of components 1–5 = 0.99; the reliability of components 6–10 = 0.99; but since these are each arranged in parallel, the reliability of each pair is:

$$1 - (1 - R_{6,7 \text{ etc.}})^2$$

$$\text{Thus } R_{\text{SYSTEM}} = 0.99^5 \times (1 - (1 - 0.99)^2)^5$$
$$- 0.950$$

Such system reliability considerations are relevant in design and in planning maintenance and replacement.

## FURTHER READING

Caplan, R. H. (1972) *A Practical Approach to Reliability*. London: Business Books. A comprehensive and comparatively easy-to-read treatment of reliability theory and management.
Crosby, P. B. (1979) *Quality is Free: The Art of Making Quality Certain*. New York: McGraw Hill.
HMSO (1981) *Quality Assurance*, British Standards Institution Handbook, No. 22. London: HMSO.
Price, F. (1984) *Right First Time*. Aldershot: Gower.

## QUESTIONS

**19.1** (a) What is the purpose of acceptance sampling?
(b) What is an operating characteristic curve?
(c) Use the binomial probability expression to calculate the probability of finding two or fewer defectives in a sample of size 12, if the actual percentage defectives in the batch from which the sample was drawn is 20 per cent.

**19.2** Construct an operating characteristic curve to show the probability of accepting batches of varying percentage actual defective levels, if sample sizes of 80 items are drawn from the batches and if batches are accepted when two or fewer defectives are found in the samples.

**19.3** Distinguish between and describe double acceptance sampling and multiple acceptance sampling.

**19.4** (a) Distinguish between quality assurance and quality control.
(b) Distinguish between quality control as regards the 'attributes' of items and the 'variables' of items.
(c) Distinguish between design limits and control limits.
(d) Distinguish between usual or chance variation and unusual or assignable variation, in respect of quality control.
(e) Distinguish between warning limits and action limits in respect of control charts.

**19.5** (a) A machine produces components at a rate of 100 per hour. Every hour a random sample of five components is taken and their lengths are measured. After ten hours the data given below have been collected. Use these data to design control charts for the sample mean and range of the dimension concerned.

| Sample number | Measurements (cm) | | | | |
|---|---|---|---|---|---|
| 1 | 9.00 | 9.10 | 9.00 | 9.05 | 8.95 |
| 2 | 9.10 | 9.10 | 9.00 | 9.05 | 9.05 |
| 3 | 9.00 | 9.05 | 9.00 | 9.05 | 9.00 |
| 4 | 9.00 | 9.00 | 8.95 | 9.00 | 9.05 |
| 5 | 9.00 | 9.05 | 9.05 | 9.05 | 9.00 |
| 6 | 9.00 | 9.10 | 9.10 | 9.05 | 9.00 |
| 7 | 9.00 | 9.10 | 9.05 | 9.15 | 9.05 |
| 8 | 9.00 | 9.10 | 9.10 | 9.00 | 9.05 |
| 9 | 9.00 | 9.00 | 8.95 | 9.00 | 9.00 |
| 10 | 9.00 | 9.05 | 9.00 | 9.10 | 8.95 |

(b) Following the construction of the charts, the same sampling procedure is followed and the data shown below are obtained. Plot these data on the control charts and comment on the quality 'performance' of the process.

| Sample number | Mean length (cm) | Range | Sample number | Mean length (cm) | Range |
|---|---|---|---|---|---|
| 1 | 9.020 | 0.100 | 11 | 9.040 | 0.150 |
| 2 | 9.030 | 0.100 | 12 | 9.040 | 0.125 |
| 3 | 9.025 | 0.050 | 13 | 9.035 | 0.100 |
| 4 | 9.030 | 0.100 | 14 | 9.040 | 0.055 |
| 5 | 9.035 | 0.025 | 15 | 9.030 | 0.100 |
| 6 | 9.040 | 0.105 | 16 | 9.025 | 0.050 |
| 7 | 9.020 | 0.050 | 17 | 9.030 | 0.125 |
| 8 | 9.030 | 0.100 | 18 | 9.025 | 0.100 |
| 9 | 9.040 | 0.050 | 19 | 9.025 | 0.150 |
| 10 | 9.035 | 0.065 | 20 | 9.030 | 0.150 |

**19.6** Phragyle Products Ltd supply imitation glass decanters to the hotel trade. Because of the delicate nature of the manufacturing process, each decanter is expected to have some minor blemishes, most of which are completely invisible to the naked eye. These very minor blemishes may occur almost anywhere on the product and are not usually sufficient to lead to the rejection of the item. Nevertheless, the sales manager of Phragyle Products is anxious to investigate the effects of recent efforts that the manufacturers claim to have made to improve the manufacturing process and the quality of the products supplied to Phragyle.

Prior to the modifications to the process, each decanter had an average of five almost imperceptible blemishes. The table below shows the number of blemishes on every fifth decanter for a short period after the claimed improvement in manufacture. Comment on the success of the supposed adjustments to the manufacturing process.

---

Number of blemishes per product: 6, 7, 6, 5, 6, 7, 7, 6, 8, 7, 7, 7, 6, 8, 9, 8, 7, 8, 9, 8, 8, 7

**19.7** (a) Even if 100 per cent acceptance sampling is adopted, it is likely that a certain number of defective items will be accepted. Discuss.

(b) What measures can be taken, and in what circumstances, to decrease the error of human inspectors?

**19.8** Three phases are often evident in the reliability of items. Describe them and explain the reasons for their existence. Use examples.

# CHAPTER 20

# Maintenance and Replacement

Our discussion of quality in the previous chapter led us to consider the question of reliability. We noted that quality and reliability were related: in general, higher-quality items were likely to be more reliable. We noticed also that quality level and cost were related, higher quality often being associated with higher costs. Since few purchases are made irrespective of cost, most products or items in use will have less than perfect reliability. At some time most items will cease to function satisfactorily. On such occasions they will have to be repaired or replaced. To some extent, however, the need for repair or replacement may be reduced through effective servicing and maintenance. Thus:

1. Most items will be *inspected* regularly, in order to detect any signs of reduced effectiveness or impending failure. And additionally
2. Items will normally be *serviced* regularly, e.g. readjusted, lubricated, etc., also to try to ensure continued effective operation.
3. *Preventive maintenance* will often be provided on a regular basis and/or as seen to be required in order to try to sustain satisfactory operation of items or equipment. During preventive maintenance, components which are liable to failure may be changed prior to the end of their working life. But nevertheless
4. *Breakdown maintenance (i.e. repair)* will normally be required so that items and equipment might be returned to satisfactory operation. And eventually
5. *Replacement* of items and equipment will occur when they are no longer capable of satisfactory operation and are beyond economic repair.

The relationship of these five activities is outlined in Figure 20.1: activities 1 to 4 above can be seen to be part of the maintenance function, while 5 is concerned with replacement. Initially in this chapter we shall consider maintenance, and then the problem of replacement.

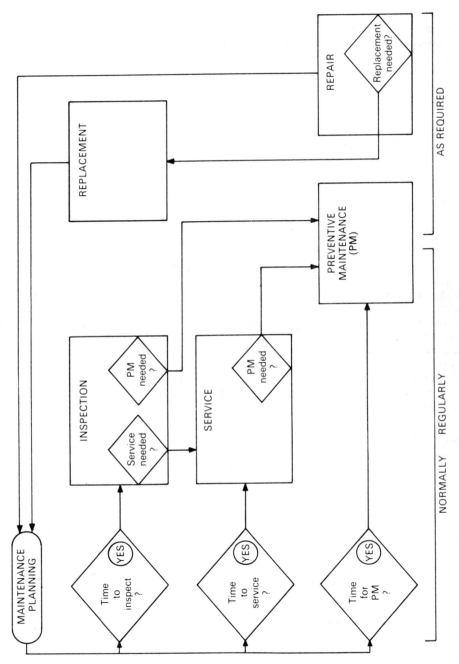

**Figure 20.1** *Maintenance and replacement activities.*

## THE MAINTENANCE FUNCTION

Equipment of whatever type, however complex or simple, however cheap or expensive, is liable to breakdown. Thus in manufacture, supply, transport and service not only must procedures exist for equipment maintenance, but also the inevitability of breakdowns and disruption of operation must be considered during capacity planning and activity scheduling. The effective operation of any system is dependent on the maintenance of all parts of the system, e.g. machines, buildings, services. In this chapter we shall be concerned only with the maintenance of mechanical rather than human facilities, although, in concept at least, the maintenance requirement also applies to workers. Indeed, company welfare or personnel practice may be designed partly as a maintenance activity, e.g. training and retraining to maintain the availability of appropriate skills, medical facilities to maintain human capacity, counselling to maintain interest and motivation.

A UK Government Report[1] has shown that manufacturing industry wastes large sums of money each year because of ineffective and badly organized maintenance. The report indicated that although the loss to manufacturing industry directly attributable to poor performance was estimated at £550 million, the total loss to British industry deriving from similar causes was probably several times this figure. The report recognized that improvements in performance could be achieved only by the co-ordinated application of several disciplines which had not previously been brought together in such a way, and because no existing word adequately described this multi-disciplinary approach to the specification, design, installation, commissioning, use and disposal of facilities, equipment and buildings, the name 'terotechnology' was chosen. Terotechnology is a combination of management, financial, engineering and other practices applied to physical assets in pursuit of economic life-cycle costs. In practice it is concerned with the selection and provision of permanent physical resources used for the provision of goods and services, for the care of the resources, and for their co-ordination and improvement. Thus terotechnology comprises the practice of design, maintenance, replacement and repair. It is therefore a somewhat broader concept than discussed in this chapter; however, some consideration of this function will provide an adequate background for our discussion.

Figure 20.2 shows a typical life-cycle for a facility. The diagram indicates those activities required in conceiving, creating, providing, operating, maintaining and disposing of a physical facility. Taking maintenance from this set, it will be seen that many decisions and activities will affect the nature and amount of maintenance required. The design of the facility, both with regard to its design 'for function' and its design 'for maintainability and reliability', will influence operation, as will its installation and commissioning. The effectiveness of maintenance will influence the time available for and the time spent in operation. Thus the need for maintenance and the nature of the maintenance required are determined by a variety of factors. The maintenance function within an organization is therefore influenced by many other activities within the organization.

### The objectives of maintenance

The purpose of maintenance is to attempt to maximize the performance of production equipment by ensuring that such equipment performs regularly and efficiently, by

---

[1] Department of Industry's Report on Maintenance Engineering, HMSO, London, 1970.

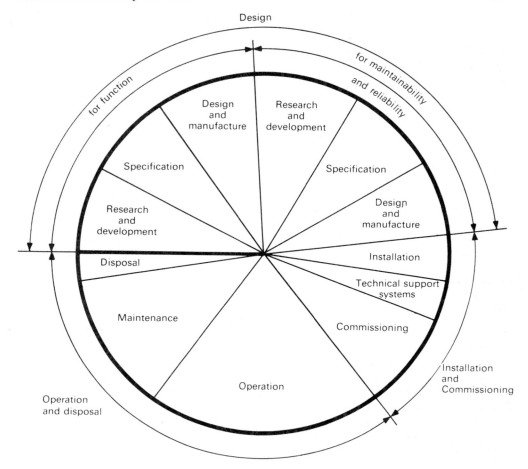

**Figure 20.2**   *The operating life-cycle of a facility.*

attempting to prevent breakdowns or failures, and by minimizing the loss resulting from breakdowns or failures. In fact it is the objective of the maintenance function to maintain or increase the reliability of the operating system as a whole.

Many steps can be taken to ensure that such an objective is achieved, but only a few of these are normally considered to be the responsibility of the maintenance department. For example, each of the following will contribute to the reliability of the operating system:

(a) improvement of the quality of equipment and components through improved design and or 'tighter' manufacturing standards;
(b) improvements in the design of equipment to facilitate the replacement of broken items and inspection and routine maintenance work;
(c) improvements in the layout of equipment to facilitate maintenance work, i.e. providing space around or underneath equipment;
(d) providing 'slack' in the operating system, i.e. providing excess capacity so that the failure of equipment does not affect the performance of other equipment;
(e) using 'work-in-progress' to ensure that the failure of equipment is not immediately reflected in a shortage of materials or parts for a subsequent piece of equipment;

(f) establishing a repair facility so that, through speedy replacement of broken parts, equipment downtime is reduced;
(g) undertaking preventive maintenance, which, through regular inspection and/or replacement of critical parts, reduces the occurrence of breakdowns.

These points may be summarized in two overall objectives, which are:

(a) to attempt to ensure that breakdowns or failures do not occur (see (a) and (g) above);
(b) to attempt to minimize the disruption or loss caused by the breakdowns which do occur (see (b), (c), (d), (e) and (f) above).

Excluding the influence of improvements in equipment design and layout, discussion of which is not appropriate to this chapter, it is clear that two distinct facets of maintenance may contribute to the increased reliability of the operating system: preventive maintenance and repair.

We can, of course, draw the total cost curve as shown in Figure 20.3. Clearly, increased effort in preventive maintenance should reduce the cost of repair maintenance. Were we able to define both these curves mathematically or graphically, then it would be a simple matter to determine the minimum cost maintenance policy. However, as might be expected, the problem is not as simple as this, and consequently maintenance policy is substantially more difficult to determine.

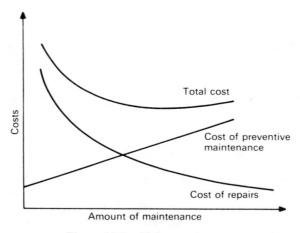

**Figure 20.3**   *Maintenance costs.*

## MAINTENANCE DECISIONS

It will be seen from the above that several decisions are required in the establishment of a comprehensive maintenance policy for any set of facilities. We can consider the establishment of a maintenance policy as comprising three necessary and interdependent decisions:

1. Which items, facilities, etc., are to be maintained?
2. What kind of maintenance will be applied in each case?
3. How is this maintenance work to be organized?

## What is to be maintained?

Any maintenance activity incurs some cost. Inspection is costly in that it involves someone devoting some time to looking at an item or a facility, and that may mean that the operation of that facility has to be interrupted. Service work will be expensive and will not normally be possible while the facility is operating. Preventive maintenance will normally be undertaken while the facility is out of operation. To some extent all this work can be planned to take place at a time when the disruption caused by the inoperation of the facility is minimized, but of course breakdown maintenance can occur at any time and can be very disruptive, and can therefore be expensive in terms of both the direct effort involved and the time lost while the facility is repaired. If the cost of any of this maintenance exceeds the cost benefits obtained, then it may be cheaper simply to dispose of items when they eventually break down. Indeed in some situations the way in which the items work and the conditions in which they are employed necessitate such an approach. There will, therefore, be situations in which it will be decided that some items will not be maintained, except perhaps through regular inspection and service to avoid safety and health hazards. Furthermore, the manner in which items break down or are subject to failure may make it difficult to develop an effective preventive maintenance strategy. For example if the cost per unit of time of undertaking preventive maintenance is greater than the cost per unit of time of breakdown maintenance, then there will be a tendency to rely on the latter.

Although in some cases preventive maintenance may be inappropriate, and even breakdown maintenance, i.e. repair, may not be employed, in most cases facilities will require one or both of these approaches in addition to inspection and service. In these situations we must decide on the size of 'unit' to be maintained. Here there are three possible approaches:

1. A large system comprising several interdependent facilities can be considered as one 'unit' for maintenance purposes.
2. Single facilities can be considered to be the 'unit'.
3. Parts or subsections of a particular facility can be considered to be the 'unit' for which maintenance must be planned.

For example, in a manufacturing situation an entire system may comprise all the interdependent and interlinked machines on an assembly line, whereas the single-facility approach may involve the development of a maintenance plan for each of the separate machine tools and/or facilities in that system. The third approach would involve the planning of maintenance for appropriate parts of these separate facilities, e.g. electric motors. As a non-manufacturing example, a complete computer installation can be considered as a 'unit' for maintenance, or alternatively each device in that system, e.g. the central processor, terminals, printers, can be seen as a 'unit' for the development of separate maintenance plans, or a maintenance policy can be developed for the components, e.g. the printer circuit boards, within certain facilities. An entire hospital operating theatre can be considered as a 'unit' for manufacture, but if more appropriate a maintenance plan can be developed for the separate facilities within that system or for components within those facilities.

The extent to which the facilities within a larger system are interdependent, i.e. the extent to which the breakdown of one can cause disruption of the others, will influence the approach which will be employed. A system comprising similar facilities all installed at around the same time would perhaps be treated as an entire unit for maintenance purposes, whereas a system in which items, although linked together in some interdependent way, were installed at different times and have quite different reliability characteristics might encourage us to adopt the second approach. If an entire configuration of facilities operates continuously, then the entire system must be stopped when any part requires maintenance, and again there will be a tendency to see the entire system as the 'unit' for maintenance. On the other hand, where facilities operate intermittently, different facilities being idle at different times, then there will be a tendency to see each facility as a 'unit' for maintenance, since this provides the greatest opportunity for scheduling maintenance work. Where a system comprises several facilities, and where each facility has similar component parts, e.g. electric motors, and where the reliability and/or breakdown characteristics of these parts are known, the third approach above may be appropriate.

## Types of maintenance

### Inspection

Facilities will normally be inspected at intervals in order to determine whether service and/or preventive maintenance is required or is likely to be required in the near future. Such work may involve visual inspection or the measurement of certain of the physical characteristics of a facility. Inspection may involve the whole facility or simply those parts which are known to be liable to failure. One of the problems in planning inspection is to decide on the *inspection interval*. This problem will be tackled in the next section.

### Service

This will involve the routine readjustment of equipment, lubrication, cleaning, etc. Such work will often be undertaken, if seen to be required, alongside inspection.

### Preventive maintenance

Preventive maintenance is precautionary and is undertaken to try to prevent or delay breakdowns, and therefore the need for repair. Such preventive action may be undertaken according to a predetermined and regular schedule or when required. A regular schedule can be established for items which have known and fairly predictable reliability or breakdown characteristics. Preventive maintenance can be undertaken as and when required in circumstances where there is some evidence of deteriorating efficiency or impending breakdown. One of the problems, therefore, in planning preventive maintenance is to identify the type of approach which will be suitable in particular circumstances.

### Repair

Breakdown maintenance or repair is remedial, taking place after an item has ceased to operate. The need for repair is not necessarily the result of inefficient or insufficient inspection, service and preventive maintenance, since in some cases the cost of repairs will be less than the accumulated cost of preventive work. One of the major problems in planning repair work is to decide on the amount of resources to be made available, since the larger the repair 'team' the shorter the repair time, but also the larger the amount of repair team idle time.

## The organization of maintenance

Maintenance work can be performed by:

(a) the personnel who normally use the equipment;
(b) staff employed in a maintenance department by and within the organization;
(c) external maintenance personnel, e.g. under service contracts from equipment suppliers.

The first approach will often be employed for inspection and sometimes for service work. It may also be an appropriate approach where preventive maintenance activities are relatively straightforward and are undertaken as and when required, i.e. where some urgent preventive action is required without prior warning. It may be employed for repair work where the facility operator has specialist skills and knowledge, perhaps acquired through the use of the facility, which are not available to other personnel.

More often an organization will have a specialist 'maintenance department'. The staff and resources of this department will be employed in inspection, service, preventive maintenance and repair work, some of which can be undertaken on a scheduled basis. The main problems in organizing maintenance in this way are to decide on the size of the maintenance 'crew', the range of skills required, the amount of stocks to be held, the amount of standby equipment to be held in stock, etc.

Maintenance will be the responsibility of an external organization either where specialist equipment is involved or where a service or maintenance contract has been provided as a compulsory or normal part of the purchase contract for that equipment. Such situations are normal for computer installations, etc. The approach may also be appropriate where maintenance work is highly specialized or hazardous, but infrequent, e.g. the maintenance of complex installations or underwater installations.

The planning of effective maintenance, however undertaken, will require collection and maintenance of certain data. For example, a complete list of all facilities in use, their date of purchase and their maintenance history to date will normally be maintained. Statistics on operating life between failures, the time required to perform repair operations, etc., will be maintained so that decisions can be made about the scheduling of preventive work and the merits of preventive compared with repair maintenance.

The 'data base' of information on each facility will be updated regularly so that appropriate statistics, etc., can be extracted. Often such data will be held on a computer-based system, such a system being used to schedule maintenance, allocate maintenance resources, etc. (These will be discussed towards the end of this chapter.)

## INSPECTION

Often inspection is disruptive, e.g. the operation of facilities may have to be halted while inspection is undertaken. On the other hand inspection might reasonably be expected to reduce the amount of time lost (downtime) through breakdowns. One problem, therefore, is to decide how much time to devote to inspection so that total downtime is minimized.

> *If* $T_T$ = total downtime per unit time
> $t_I$ = downtime per inspection
> $t_s$ = downtime per breakdown
> $N$ = number of inspections per facility per unit time
> $k$ = a constant for a particular facility

If the total time lost through inspection is a function of $t_I$ and $N$, and if we assume that the total time lost through breakdowns is a function of $t_s$ and inversely related to $N$, then:

$$T_T = t_I N + t_s \frac{k}{N}$$

Differentiating this equation with respect to $N$ and equating to zero will give the optimum value of $N$. If $t_I$ and $t_s$ are constants:

$$N \text{ to minimize } T_T = \sqrt{t_s \times \frac{k}{t_I}}$$

---

**EXAMPLE**

$$t_s = 0.9 \text{ weeks}$$
$$t_1 = 0.2 \text{ weeks}$$

From experience it has been found that $k = 2$. Hence:

$$N_{\text{opt}} = \sqrt{0.9 \times \frac{2}{0.2}} = 3 \text{ per week}$$

---

## PREVENTIVE AND BREAKDOWN MAINTENANCE

Preventive maintenance is used to delay or prevent the breakdown of equipment, and also to reduce the severity of any breakdowns that occur. Two aspects of preventive maintenance can be identified:

1. *Inspection.* Inspection of critical parts will often indicate the need for replacement or repair well in advance of probable breakdown. (Inspection forms an important part of motor vehicle maintenance, regular inspection of tyres, radiator, battery, brakes, etc., being called for by all maintenance schedules.) Regular inspection, conducted either by the equipment operator or by the maintenance department, is the most important direct means of increasing equipment reliability.
2. *Servicing.* Routine cleaning, lubrication and adjustment may reduce wear significantly and hence prevent breakdowns. Frequently such duties belong to the equipment operator rather than being the direct responsibility of the maintenance department; however, irrespective of responsibility, servicing or routine

preventive maintenance must be conducted regularly according to schedules constructed from both operating experience and manufacturers' recommendations.

No matter how much preventive maintenance is undertaken, failures will still occur, if only because of the use of defective or sub-standard parts, or the misuse of equipment. It will always be necessary, therefore, to provide breakdown maintenance. Repair policy may involve the use of subcontractors, the repair of equipment immediately upon breakdown or later, the replacement of parts or sub-assemblies, or even the replacement of whole pieces of equipment. Repairs may be conducted on equipment in situ or equipment may be removed to a more appropriate situation. Standby equipment may be available for permanent or temporary replacement in cases of breakdown.

## REPAIRS

Consider now the situation in which several machines of the same type are to be maintained. Furthermore, let us consider a policy which provides only for repair maintenance and not preventive maintenance (a policy which might have been adopted because of large variability in breakdown time distributions).

Providing appropriate assumptions are made about the nature of breakdowns and repair time, the design of a maintenance system for such a situation can be accomplished by using conventional queuing theory.

## REPLACEMENT POLICIES

### Replacement policies for items subject to sudden failure

When a machine stops because of the failure of one component, then the maintenance team may simply go along to the machine and effect a repair by replacing the broken component. An alternative strategy is to replace not only the broken component but also all other similar components, on the assumption that since they have all been in service for some length of time, because one has already failed, the others are also likely to fail in the near future. A third strategy might be adopted, namely the replacement of the broken component and *certain* of the other similar components.

As an example, consider the problem faced by someone whose job it is to replace, when necessary, the bulbs in the lights of every room of a multi-storey building. The replacement strategies may be as follows:

1. Replace only those bulbs that fail. Such a strategy may involve an excessive amount of work, since replacing a bulb takes an average of 30 minutes erecting a ladder, obtaining new bulbs from stores, etc. Because of the difference between the comparatively low cost of a new bulb and the comparatively high cost of replacement, an alternative strategy may be preferred.
2. When one bulb fails, replace *all* bulbs in that room, or on that floor.
3. Alternatively, as a compromise, replace the bulb that has failed *and* a proportion of other bulbs, say those that have been in service for longer than six months, in other words those that are expected to fail fairly shortly.

The problem then is to decide which of these strategies to adopt, a decision which must, of course, be made on a basis of cost considerations. The cost involved in replacement is dependent on the probability of component failure. In the case of strategy 1 the total cost of maintenance over, say, a year is given by the following:

$$\text{Cost of making a single replacement} \times \text{Probable number of failures during year}$$

In the case of strategy 2 the total cost is determined by the number of components replaced each time and the number of 'first failures' during the period. In the final strategy (3) the cost would depend on the number of 'first failures' and the number of components at every replacement period which have been in service longer than a given time.

Although it is possible to develop formulae for the replacement problem in which items are subject to sudden failure, such formulae are often inadequate for the practical situation; consequently the choice of replacement strategy is often made with the aid of a simulation exercise.

## Replacement policies for items which deteriorate

The cost of operating equipment and machinery normally increases with the increasing age of the equipment. Such increasing cost may be caused by: (a) the increasing cost of the maintenance necessary to obtain continuing reliability of the equipment, and (b) the obsolescence of the equipment, making its continued operation comparatively more costly when compared with the equipment which might be used to replace it. There comes a time, therefore, when it is not economically justifiable to replace the present ageing equipment, but economically beneficial in order to obtain equipment which has greater output, reliability, etc.

Our present problem, then, is to decide at what time such equipment should be replaced. Such a decision must obviously be made on economic grounds, by a comparison of the net economic benefit of retaining present equipment and the net economic benefit of replacing present equipment.

As regards *present* equipment we must consider the following:

(a)  its life;
(b)  its current and future salvage or sale value;
(c)  the revenue produced throughout the rest of its life;
(d)  the expenditure incurred throughout the rest of its life.

As regards the *proposed* replacement equipment we must consider:

(a)  the purchase price of the equipment;
(b)  its life;
(c)  the salvage or sale value at various times in its life;
(d)  the revenue produced by the equipment;
(e)  the expenditure incurred throughout its life.

In considering the replacement of equipment it is important to remember that money has a time value. For example £100 is of more value to us now that it would be next year. The evaluation of the economic worth of equipment therefore depends on both its earning potential and time considerations. We must therefore make our replacement decisions by considering the *present value* of the net revenue associated with its use.

If $i$ = annual rate of interest, then £100 now is worth

$$\frac{100}{(1 + i)^n} \text{ in } n \text{ years' time}$$

e.g. £100 is worth $100/1.1^2 = $ £82.6 in two years' time.

Suppose that the investment of £10 000 in a new piece of equipment results in a net income of £5000 for each of the following three years. If we assume that the 'cost of capital', or the rate of interest which might have been achieved had the £10 000 been invested, is 10 per cent, then the *present value* of this income is £12 434, i.e.

$$\frac{5000}{(1.1)} + \frac{5000}{(1.1)^2} + \frac{5000}{(1.1)^3}$$

$$= £12\ 434$$

The calculation of present values in this way, by *discounting* future sums of money at a given rate, is the basis of the *discounted cash flow* technique for investment appraisal.

When concerned with equipment replacement, this discounting procedure can be expressed by the following equation:

$$NPV = \left( \sum_{n\ =\ 1}^{N} \frac{I_n - E_n}{(1 + i)^n} \right) + \frac{S_N}{(1 + i)^N}$$

**Table 20.1** *Compound interest table* $(1/(1 + i)^n)$.

| n | i = 1% | 2 | 3 | 4 | 5 | 6 | 7 | 8 | 9 | 10 |
|---|---|---|---|---|---|---|---|---|---|---|
| 1 | 0.9901 | 0.9804 | 0.9709 | 0.9615 | 0.9524 | 0.9434 | 0.9346 | 0.9259 | 0.9174 | 0.9091 |
| 2 | 0.9803 | 0.9612 | 0.9426 | 0.9246 | 0.9070 | 0.8900 | 0.8734 | 0.8573 | 0.8417 | 0.8264 |
| 3 | 0.9706 | 0.9423 | 0.9151 | 0.8890 | 0.8638 | 0.8396 | 0.8163 | 0.7938 | 0.7722 | 0.7513 |
| 4 | 0.9610 | 0.9238 | 0.8885 | 0.8548 | 0.8227 | 0.7921 | 0.7629 | 0.7350 | 0.7084 | 0.6830 |
| 5 | 0.9515 | 0.9057 | 0.8626 | 0.8219 | 0.7835 | 0.7473 | 0.7130 | 0.6806 | 0.6499 | 0.6209 |
| 6 | 0.9420 | 0.8880 | 0.8375 | 0.7903 | 0.7462 | 0.7050 | 0.6663 | 0.6302 | 0.5963 | 0.5645 |
| 7 | 0.9327 | 0.8706 | 0.8131 | 0.7599 | 0.7107 | 0.6651 | 0.6227 | 0.5835 | 0.5470 | 0.5132 |
| 8 | 0.9235 | 0.8535 | 0.7894 | 0.7307 | 0.6768 | 0.6274 | 0.5820 | 0.5403 | 0.5019 | 0.4665 |
| 9 | 0.9143 | 0.8368 | 0.7664 | 0.7026 | 0.6446 | 0.5919 | 0.5439 | 0.5002 | 0.4604 | 0.4241 |
| 10 | 0.9053 | 0.8302 | 0.7441 | 0.6756 | 0.6139 | 0.5584 | 0.5083 | 0.4632 | 0.4224 | 0.3588 |
| 11 | 0.8963 | 0.8043 | 0.7224 | 0.6496 | 0.5847 | 0.5268 | 0.4751 | 0.4289 | 0.3875 | 0.3505 |
| 12 | 0.8874 | 0.7885 | 0.7014 | 0.6246 | 0.5568 | 0.4970 | 0.4440 | 0.3971 | 0.3555 | 0.3186 |
| 13 | 0.8787 | 0.7730 | 0.6810 | 0.6006 | 0.5303 | 0.4688 | 0.4150 | 0.3677 | 0.3262 | 0.2897 |
| 14 | 0.8700 | 0.7579 | 0.6611 | 0.5775 | 0.5051 | 0.4423 | 0.3878 | 0.3405 | 0.2992 | 0.2633 |
| 15 | 0.8613 | 0.7430 | 0.6419 | 0.5553 | 0.4810 | 0.4173 | 0.3624 | 0.3152 | 0.2745 | 0.2394 |
| 16 | 0.8528 | 0.7284 | 0.6232 | 0.5339 | 0.4581 | 0.3936 | 0.3387 | 0.2919 | 0.2519 | 0.2176 |
| 17 | 0.8444 | 0.7142 | 0.6050 | 0.5134 | 0.4363 | 0.3714 | 0.3166 | 0.2703 | 0.2311 | 0.1978 |
| 18 | 0.8360 | 0.7002 | 0.5874 | 0.4936 | 0.4155 | 0.3503 | 0.2959 | 0.2502 | 0.2120 | 0.1799 |
| 19 | 0.8277 | 0.6864 | 0.5703 | 0.4746 | 0.3957 | 0.3305 | 0.2765 | 0.2317 | 0.1945 | 0.1635 |
| 20 | 0.8195 | 0.6730 | 0.5537 | 0.4564 | 0.3769 | 0.3118 | 0.2584 | 0.2145 | 0.1784 | 0.1486 |
| 21 | 0.8114 | 0.6598 | 0.5375 | 0.4388 | 0.3589 | 0.2942 | 0.2415 | 0.1987 | 0.1637 | 0.1351 |
| 22 | 0.8034 | 0.6468 | 0.5219 | 0.4220 | 0.3418 | 0.2775 | 0.2257 | 0.1839 | 0.1502 | 0.1228 |
| 23 | 0.7954 | 0.6432 | 0.5067 | 0.4057 | 0.3256 | 0.2618 | 0.2109 | 0.1703 | 0.1378 | 0.1117 |
| 24 | 0.7876 | 0.6217 | 0.4919 | 0.3901 | 0.3101 | 0.2470 | 0.1971 | 0.1577 | 0.1264 | 0.1015 |
| 25 | 0.7798 | 0.6095 | 0.4776 | 0.3751 | 0.2953 | 0.2330 | 0.1842 | 0.1460 | 0.1160 | 0.0923 |
| 26 | 0.7720 | 0.5976 | 0.4637 | 0.3607 | 0.2812 | 0.2198 | 0.1722 | 0.1352 | 0.1064 | 0.0839 |
| 27 | 0.7644 | 0.5859 | 0.4502 | 0.3468 | 0.2678 | 0.2074 | 0.1696 | 0.1252 | 0.0976 | 0.0763 |
| 28 | 0.7568 | 0.5744 | 0.4371 | 0.3335 | 0.2551 | 0.1956 | 0.1504 | 0.1159 | 0.0895 | 0.0693 |
| 29 | 0.7493 | 0.5631 | 0.4243 | 0.3207 | 0.2429 | 0.1846 | 0.1406 | 0.1073 | 0.0822 | 0.0630 |
| 30 | 0.7419 | 0.5521 | 0.4120 | 0.3083 | 0.2314 | 0.1741 | 0.1314 | 0.0994 | 0.0754 | 0.0573 |

where     $NPV$ = net present value
          $I_n$ = income for year $n$
          $E_n$ = expenditure for year $n$
          $i$ = discount rate
          $N$ = life of equipment or number of years being considered
          $S_N$ = sale or scrap value at end of life, i.e. year $N$

Clearly, to be economically beneficial the net present value ($NPV$) must be equal to or greater than zero.

To assist discounted cash flow calculations, tables for $1/(1+i)^n$ have been prepared (see Table 20.1).

The replacement decision normally takes the following form: whether to replace existing equipment now, or at a later date, up to and including the last year in the life of the existing equipment. The problem, then, is one of comparing, at *present value*, the cash flows associated with the use of the present and the proposed equipment over the common period, from the present time to the end of the life of the present equipment. Naturally cash flows that have already occurred do not enter into the decision, for example past operating costs of present equipment. We are concerned only with the cash flows that will result from the decision to retain the equipment and the decision to replace it, i.e. the operating costs, the revenues and the changes in disposal values.

## FURTHER READING

Husband, T. M. (1976) *Maintenance Management and Terotechnology*. London: Saxon House.
UK Department of Industry (1975) *Terotechnology—Case Histories*. London: HMSO. Simple descriptions and examples of terotechnology, principles and practices.

## QUESTIONS

**20.1** Define and differentiate between preventive maintenance and repair. What are the objectives of maintenance? In what circumstances is preventive maintenance particularly appropriate?

**20.2** Describe briefly how you would collect and analyse data in order to assist in the determination of a maintenance policy for a small jobbing machine shop.

Having determined the policy, what data would you collect regularly in order to ensure that the maintenance procedures were adjusted to conform to changes in the characteristics of the equipment in the shop?

**20.3** What are the principal factors which contribute to the effective operation of a facility throughout its entire life-cycle? In what way might decisions on or the management of certain of these factors reduce the need for maintenance of the facility during its operating life and/or delay the need for its replacement?

**20.4** Show, by a simple numerical example, how the present value of future costs and revenues can be taken into account in comparing alternative replacement and maintenance policies for a facility.

# CHAPTER 21

# Performance Measurements

Two basic objectives for operating systems and operations management were identified in Chapter 1, i.e. the provision of customer service and resource productivity. If operating systems are intended to achieve certain objectives in respect of both customer service and resource productivity it is appropriate that system performance should be measured against both objectives. Performance measurement in respect of resource productivity is common in operations management. The measurement of performance in respect of customer service is less common.

Here we shall again consider the nature of both customer service and resource productivity and the manner in which objectives in each area are established and performance against them is measured.

## CUSTOMER SERVICE

The items, movement or treatment provided by the operating system must match customers' needs if these customers are to be satisfied. The provision of customer service and the creation of customer satisfaction is a multi-dimensional problem, three principal factors having been identified in Chapter 1.

### The dimensions of customer service

These three customer service factors are general factors only; they each comprise several dimensions and in most cases it will be more practical and appropriate to assess or measure performance on these narrower dimensions.

1. The *specification* of goods may be considered in terms of their design features and

performance characteristics. Together these dimensions define what the item is and how it is intended to perform its purpose. Similarly, the specification of a transport may be expressed in terms of its 'design' and performance. In this context design, i.e. the nature of the transport, movement may be expressed in terms of the origin, destination and route of movement. The performance can be considered synonymous with 'means', i.e. the means or method by which the movement is achieved. A service treatment may be defined in similar terms. The nature of the treatment can be considered to be the design characteristic or dimension, and the means by which the treatment is provided can be considered to be the performance characteristic. Two main dimensions can therefore be identified for the specification of items, movement or treatment. They are the 'what' and 'how' dimensions. In designing an item, a movement or a treatment an organization will define these two characteristics. In assessing the performance of an organization the customer will again consider these two dimensions. They are summarized in Table 21.1.

**Table 21.1**   *The specifications of items, movement and treatment.*

| Dimensions for 'specification' | Items | Movement | Treatment |
|---|---|---|---|
| *Design*, i.e. what is the item/movement/ treatment? | e.g. comprising *Appearance* and *dimensions* *Material* specifications Design and manufacture *quality* | e.g. comprising *Source, destination* and *route* | e.g. comprising *Nature* of treatment |
| *Performance*, i.e. *how* is the purpose achieved? — the means or method employed | e.g. comprising *Operating* characteristics or *performance* characteristics, or *operating principles* or means | e.g. comprising *Means* of transport | e.g. comprising Means of treatment or *procedures* employed, or *form* of *treatment* |

2. The general dimension of *cost* identified above may similarly be broken down into important components. The customer—theoretically at least—will evaluate an item of a given specification in terms of its total expected costs, i.e. acquisition price plus any necessary additional expenses associated with an item, e.g. installation, running and maintenance costs, all discounted to the present time in order to take account of cash flows over a period of time. Similarly the cost of a transport movement or service may be expressed in terms of the original price of acquisition plus any additional and necessary costs or expenses. We can therefore distinguish, for our purposes, two aspects of costs, i.e. price and expenses. In seeking to provide customer service an organization will consider these two dimensions. In evaluating an organization, customers will consider or respond to these two dimensions. These cost dimensions of customer service are summarized in Table 21.2.

3. The third factor identified above—*timing*—may also be subdivided. Consider first the cost of goods. A customer will take into account the delay or wait involved between the expression of a want and the subsequent satisfaction of that want. This delay or wait will normally be evident as the period of time between placing an order and receiving the goods. This is clearly an important dimension of customer service, since delay greatly in excess of that which is acceptable will give rise to reduced overall customer satisfaction and loss of customers. Again this is a dimension which is, to some extent, within the control of the organization. It can,

**Table 21.2** *The cost of items, movement and treatment.*

| Dimensions for *cost* | Items | Movement | Treatment |
|---|---|---|---|
| *Price*, i.e. intended or quoted cost | e.g. comprising *Purchase price*, or initial cost of good | e.g. comprising *Cost of journey or fare* | e.g. comprising *Cost of treatment or charge* |
| *Expenses*, i.e. expected additional costs | e.g. comprising Cost of installation Cost of maintenance and replacement Running costs | e.g. comprising Additional costs such as insurance, etc. | e.g. comprising Additional costs such as insurance, etc. |

for example, set out deliberately to provide goods virtually on demand, or alternatively might choose to provide goods for which customers are expected to wait, perhaps for some considerable time. This delay dimension is also relevant in the provision of both transport and service. However, a further dimension is also important in these two functions. Both transport (i.e. movement) and service (i.e. treatment) are time consuming. In both cases, therefore, the customers will consider their likely duration or the time required for their performance, i.e. to move from source to destination, or to be treated or accommodated. In assessing an organization the customer will therefore have regard to this dimension, and equally, in seeking to achieve customer service, an organization will seek to provide an appropriate or acceptable duration for its transport or service. The timing factor can therefore be subdivided into the dimensions of delay and duration, summarized in Table 21.3.

**Table 21.3** *The timing of the provision of items, movement and treatment.*

| Dimensions for *timing* | Items | Movement | Treatment |
|---|---|---|---|
| *Delay*, i.e. intended or quoted delay or waiting time | e.g. comprising *Delivery time* or waiting time for delivery of goods | e.g. comprising Time spent waiting for transport | e.g. comprising Time spent waiting for treatment |
| *Duration*, i.e. intended or quoted duration | | e.g. comprising Travel time or duration of journey | e.g. comprising Treatment time or duration of treatment |

Customers, in appraising the specification of an item, will be aware that it may perform differently in practice than had been intended at design. Design and performance characteristics may therefore be seen as intended features. There will be some probability that items will perform unsatisfactorily. An item may fail to function as intended, i.e. to achieve its intended purpose. It may function for some time and then fail, i.e. break down. It may break down regularly. It may function, but not at a desired level of performance. The customer must therefore consider the probability of an item satisfactorily achieving its intended purpose or continuing to achieve that purpose, i.e. its reliability. An organization must recognize this as a dimension of customer service and a characteristic of the product. The manner in which this reliability might be measured will depend on the nature of the item. It could, for example, be measured in terms of mean time between failures, or average operating life, or simply the probability that it will work at all. Similarly, in the specification of a transport or service, it is necessary to consider reliability, namely the probability of the required destination being reached and the probability of the movement being achieved as intended. The cost factor will also be seen in terms of its reliability. Price and expenses, as outlined above, can be considered to be quoted or intended costs. In practice, actual costs may differ, hence the probability of such changes will be an important customer service dimension and characteristic.

In considering the timing of goods, transport and service it is necessary to consider reliability issues. Both delay and duration, as discussed above, can be considered as intended times. The customer must consider the likelihood of the quoted or intended delay occurring and the likelihood of the quoted or intended duration occurring. In many cases in the provision of goods a delivery time is quoted, but both parties realize that there is a probability that in practice a longer delay will occur. Similarly, in the provision of transport, both parties will realize that, while the normal intended or quoted duration for a journey may be $x$ hours, due to a variety of factors the actual duration may be greatly in excess of $x$ hours. In this case, therefore, it is necessary again to consider reliability, i.e. the probability that the intended or quoted duration will in fact be achieved and the probability that the intended delay will in fact occur.

These three reliability dimensions (reliability of specification, cost and timing) are of major concern to operations management. The reliability of intended specification, cost and timing will depend to a considerable extent upon the effectiveness of operations management. Inadequate management of capacity, inventories, and poor scheduling may give rise to cost, timing and specification changes. Poor resource utilization will add to costs, bring delays, and increase durations. Inadequate execution of design intentions may give rise to poor performance. Since the responsibility for achieving customer service in these three areas is primarily the responsibility of operations management, operations management must have a major influence on the formulation of objectives on these three reliability dimensions.

Nine basic customer service dimensions can therefore be identified (Table 21.4). The intended specification, cost and timing of goods, transports and services will be largely determined by policy decisions within the organization. In some cases organizations will seek to maximize customer service on each of the six main dimensions, but in most cases different importance will be attached to each of these six dimensions. For this reason there can be no valid absolute measure of the performance of operations on design, performance, price, expenses, delay and duration. It is relevant only to measure the extent to which intended objectives are achieved, i.e. specification, cost and timing reliability.

**Table 21.4**  *The principal dimensions of customer service.*

| Factors | Dimensions | |
| --- | --- | --- |
| *Specifications*<br>of goods, movement<br>or treatment | i.e.<br>1. *Design*<br>2. *Performance* | 7. *Specification reliability* |
| *Cost*<br>of goods, movement<br>or treatment | i.e.<br>3. *Price*<br>4. *Expenses* | 8. *Cost reliability* |
| *Timing*<br>of goods, movement<br>or treatment | i.e.<br>5. *Delay*<br>6. *Duration* | 9. *Timing reliability* |

Tables 21.1 to 21.4 from Wild, R. (1979) *Operations Management—A Policy Framework.* Oxford: Pergamon.

## RESOURCE PRODUCTIVITY

Here we are on more familiar ground, for in most situations the intensity of the utilization of resources will be accepted as a legitimate measure of the performance of the operating system.

A useful approach to the discussion of resource productivity as a concept is the identification of the manner in which various interested parties might apply measurement. From the engineer's standpoint, productivity and efficiency are synonymous and efficiency is the measure of the amount of energy supplies converted into useful work. Productivity would be seen as the quotient obtained by dividing output by a factor of production, whether capital or raw material. Input generates output, and in a physical sense at least the quotient cannot exceed unity, although in a financial sense it must do so if the business is to secure a profit to survive.

An economist might take a different approach and might emphasize labour rather than capital productivity. Emphasis on the former encourages one to express inputs in terms of labour or labour equivalent, with attendant risks of estimation, averaging, etc. In an attempt to overcome this, the United Kingdom Department of Trade and Industry developed the idea of net output per employee as a productivity measure, i.e.

$$\text{Net output per employee} = \frac{\text{Added value per annum}}{\text{Total number of employees}}$$

'Added value' represents the value added to materials by the process of production and from which wages, salaries, rent, rates, tax reserves and dividends, selling distribution, and advertising costs have to be met.

An accountant might take yet another view. Many contemporary productivity measures are financially oriented because many firms evaluate the worth and effectiveness of their enterprise by using 'financial ratio analysis'. A variety of ratios might be developed, but it is essential that those adopted be seen to be useful and relevant. The following are among those commonly employed:

(a) profit/capital employed;
(b) profit/sales;
(c) sales/capital employed;
(d) sales/fixed assets;
(e) sales/stocks;
(f) sales/employee;
(g) profits/employee.

In such an approach an emphasis is placed on sales revenue and profit; however, it is possible that both are affected by market supply and demand factors as well as being influenced by the efficiency of operations.

## Integrated productivity measurement

Each of these approaches to the measurement of productivity may be seen as parts of a composite or integrated productivity model. Such a model has been developed and presented by Norman and Bahiri (see 'Further Reading'). Figure 21.1 presents an integrated productivity model through which can be identified various means for the measurement of the productivity of operating systems. The notation is given in Table 21.5. All inputs and outputs are measured in financial units, and while the model is particularly relevant in the measurement of resource productivity in conversion or creation systems, it can be modified for use in service, and even non-profit, systems. Referring back to the above, the engineer's measure of efficiency might be seen to be equivalent to a measure of total earnings productivity, i.e. $\frac{T}{C}$ in Figure 21.1. The economist's measure may be seen to be equivalent to added value productivity, i.e.

**Table 21.5** *Notation for integrated productivity measurement model* (From Norman, R. G. and Bahiri, S. (1972) *Productivity Measurement and Incentives.* London: Butterworth. Adapted with permission.)

| | |
|---|---|
| $S$ | = Sales revenue or gross output |
| $T$ | = Total earnings |
| $AV$ | = Added value or net output |
| $H$ | = Net earnings |
| | |
| $M$ | = Materials throughput |
| $Cx$ | = Indirect external expenses |
| $X$ | = Total external purchase |
| $K$ | = Capital charges |
| $N$ | = Non-labour factorial cost |
| $L$ | = Employment or labour charges |
| $P$ | = Profits |
| | |
| $C$ | = Operations costs |
| $F$ | = Total factorial inputs |
| $R$ | = Internal expenses |

$\dfrac{AV}{R}$, while the accountant's measure of productivity may be seen to be equivalent to the measure of gross efficiency shown in Figure 21.1, i.e. $\dfrac{S}{F}$.

## The 'physical' dimensions of resource productivity

The above integrated approach takes a largely financial approach to resource productivity measurement. Returning, however, to the operations management objectives developed in Chapter 1, we might alternatively logically consider three

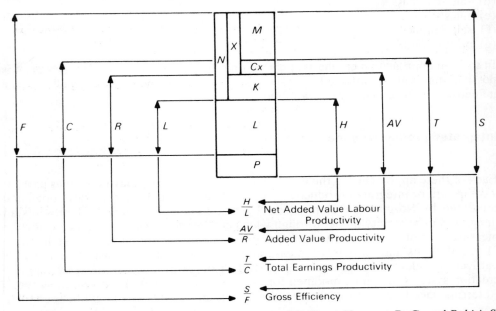

**Figure 21.1** *Integrated productivity measurement model. (From Norman, R. G. and Bahiri, S. (1972)* Productivity Measurement and Incentives. *London: Butterworth. Adapted with permission.)*

dimensions of resource productivity, and in so doing take a largely 'physical' approach to the measurement of productivity. In Chapter 1 we identified three principal types of operating system resource: machines, labour and materials. We shall now consider these dimensions of productivity measurement. They offer another means for productivity measurement. Capital or money will often be considered, as above, although since all resources can be measured and expressed in financial terms it may, on occasions, be logical to consider money as a common denominator resource, and as a unit for the measurement of productivity for each resource and overall productivity.

**Table 21.6** *Resource productivity and measurement.*

| Resource | Productivity objectives | Productivity measures |
|---|---|---|
| | e.g. | |
| *Machines* | *Maximize* | |
| i.e. all physical items, e.g. equipment, tools, buildings, space, etc., directly and indirectly used by the system. | Output/distance/throughput per machine hour | Output/distance/throughput /machine hour |
| | Proportion of total available time utilized | Time(s) used or percentage |
| | Effectiveness of utilization (e.g. capacity utilized) | Capacity used or percentage |
| | Occupancy/space utilization | Occupancy/space utilization or percentage |
| | *Minimize* | |
| | Idle time and downtime | Idle time and/or downtime or percentage |
| | Under-utilized/unoccupied space | Percentage utilized/occupied space |
| | Machine cost content | Machine cost content or percentage |
| | e.g. | |
| *Labour* | *Maximize* | |
| i.e. those people who directly or indirectly necessarily provide or contribute to the operation of the system, e.g. manual labour, supervision, etc. | Output/distance/throughput per work hour | Output/distance/throughput work hours |
| | Proportion of total available time utilized | Time(s) used or percentage |
| | Effectiveness of utilization (e.g. capacity utilized) | Capacity used or percentage |
| | *Minimize* | |
| | Idle and ineffective time | Idle and/or ineffective time or percentage |
| | Labour cost content | Labour cost content or percentage |
| | e.g. | |
| *Materials* | *Maximize* | |
| i.e. those physical items directly or indirectly consumed or converted by the system. | Yield (i.e. output/distance/throughput) per unit weight volume, etc. | Yield quantity, weight, etc. |
| | *Minimize* | |
| | Wastage, losses or scrap | Wastage, losses or scrap quantity or percentage Rework/rectification quantity or percentage |
| | Material cost content | Material cost content or percentage |

Each of our three main physical resources must be used effectively, hence we must consider productivity on each of these three 'dimensions'. Table 21.6 outlines some objectives for each resource and some means of measuring productivity against these objectives. In each case the achievement of high productivity can be considered in terms of maximizing resource utilization or, of course, minimizing loss or waste. The precise objectives and hence also the performance standards employed will depend on the nature of the resource in each area, as will also the amount of detail necessary in both stating and measuring the achievement of objectives in these areas.

## FURTHER MEASURES OF PERFORMANCE

Finally in this chapter it is worth reminding ourselves that we have in previous chapters dealt both directly and indirectly with the measurement of system performance-related factors and dimensions. In fact in most decision areas of operations management there will be means for either indirect or direct assessment of outcomes, and thus for the measurement not only of system performance in particular respects, but also for the measurement of the effectiveness of operations management decisions.

## FURTHER READING

Norman, R. G. and Bahiri, S. (1972) *Productivity Measurement and Incentives*. London: Butterworth. A detailed treatment of productivity measurement techniques and procedures. A comparative productivity study and a discussion of productivity bargaining and incentives.

## QUESTIONS

**21.1** Describe and compare the customer service objectives which might be expected to influence the operation of the following systems:
(a) a small bespoke (i.e. 'made to measure') gents' manufacturing tailor;
(b) a dentist's practice;
(c) a city bus service.

How might system performance in respect of these objectives be measured in each case?

**21.2** Show how (a) added value productivity; (b) gross efficiency and (c) total earnings productivity would be measured in a small batch production to stock manufacturing organization.

**21.3** Compare the notion of reliability introduced in this chapter with that discussed in Chapter 20. How might measures of item performance reliability and techniques for maintenance management be of value in performance measurement?

# APPENDIX

# APPENDIX

# Answers to Analytical Questions

**Chapter 4**

**4.2** Break-even sales = 16,500 p.a.

**Chapter 5**

**5.2** Select A.

**Chapter 6**

**6.1**

Receiving
Stores
Turning
Milling
Grinding
Assembly
Testing
General office
Drawing office
Personnel department

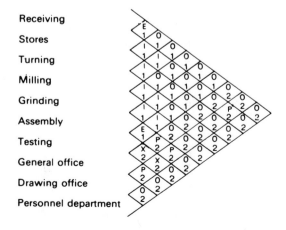

| Closeness | |
|---|---|
| E | Essential |
| I | Important |
| P | Preferable |
| O | Ordinarily close |
| X | Undesirable |

| Reason | |
|---|---|
| 1 | MH |
| 2 | Others |

**6.3**

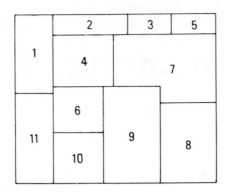

[This question is based on the example used by E. S. Buffa in 'Sequence analysis for functional layouts', *Journal of Industrial Engineering*, March/April, pp. 12–24 (1955).]

## Chapter 7

**7.3**

(a)

Workplace

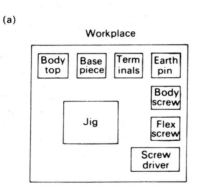

| (b) Left hand | | Right hand | |
|---|---|---|---|
| Reach for base piece | ⇨ | Reach for earth pin | ⇨ |
| Grasp base | ○ | Grasp/orient in fingers | ○ |
| Carry to jig | ⇨ | Carry to jig/orient in fingers | ⇨ |
| Place in jig | ○ | Position in base | ○ |
| Reach to terminal | ⇨ | Reach to terminal | ⇨ |
| Grasp/orient | ○ | Grasp/orient | ○ |
| Carry to base | ⇨ | Carry to jig/orient | ⇨ |
| Place in base | ○ | Place in base | ○ |
| Reach to body top | ⇨ | Delay | D |
| Grasp | ○ | Delay | D |
| Carry to jig | ⇨ | Delay | D |
| Place in jig | ○ | Reach to body screw | ⇨ |
| Grasp assembly | ○ | Grasp/orient | ○ |

| Left hand | | Right hand |
|---|---|---|
| Remove from jig | ○ | Carry to assembly/orient ⇨ |
| Place inverted on bench | ○ | Place screw in hole ○ |
| Hold | ○ | Reach to two screws ⇨ |
| &#124; | | Grasp ○ |
| &#124; | | Carry/orient ⇨ |
| &#124; | | Place one screw in hole ○ |
| &#124; | | Place second screw in hole ○ |
| &#124; | | Reach for screw driver ⇨ |
| &#124; | | Grasp ○ |
| &#124; | | Carry to assembly ○ |
| &#124; | | Tighten body screw ○ |
| &#124; | | Tighten one flex screw ○ |
| Grasp plug ○ | | Tighten second flex screw ○ |
| Carry to bin ⇨ | | Return screw driver ⇨ |
| Release ○ | | Release screw driver ○ |

**7.4**

| Left hand | Therblig | Therblig | Right hand |
|---|---|---|---|
| Reach for bolt | TE | TE | Reach for nut |
| Select and grasp a bolt head | S,G | S,G | Select and grasp nut |
| Carry bolt to central position | TL | TL | Carry to central position |
| Position bolt | P | P | Position nut |
| Hold head | H | A | Assemble nut onto bolt |
| Release assembly | RL | G | Grasp assembly |
| Idle | | TL | Carry assembly to box |
| Idle | | RL | Release assembly into box |

## Chapter 8

**8.1** $N^1 = 4.9$, therefore sufficient observations have been made.

**8.2** 49.2 (1/100 minutes)

**8.3** 2262 pieces

**8.4** Output per shift at standard performance = 200.
Production cost per piece = 9 p.

**8.6** 10.2 SM

**8.7** Worker A E1 1   BM = 0.09 } 0.23/item
           E1 2   BM = 0.14

     Worker B E1 3   BM = 0.15 } 0.20/item
           E1 4   BM = 0.05

     Worker C E1 5   BM = 0.20 } 0.20/item

(This question is based on an example given in Chapter 6 of Graham, C. F. (1965) *Work Measurement and Cost Control*. Oxford: Pergamon. This excellent little book gives a good description of the uses of rated systematic sampling.)

## Chapter 9

**9.8** (a) 45.9 hours
    (b) 51.2 hours
    (c) 16

## Chapter 10

**10.1** 2530 p
**10.3** (a) 13 500 p
    (b) 18 000 p
    (c) 12 150 p
    (d) 14 000 p

## Chapter 12

**12.2** (a)

| Job | Priority rule | | | | | | | | |
|-----|---|---|---|---|---|---|---|---|---|
|     | 1 | 2 | 3 | 4 | 5 | 6 | 7 | 8 | 9 |
| 1   | 4 | 4 | 4 | 3 | 7 | 4 | 3 | 7 | 1 |
| 2   | 1 | 1 | 1 | 5 | 3 | 1 | 1 | 4 | 10 |
| 3   | 5 | 4 | 8 | 3 | 7 | 5 | 3 | 9 | 2 |
| 4   | 2 | 1 | 2 | 9 | 2 | 2 | 2 | 6 | 4 |
| 5   | 3 | 3 | 3 | 1 | 9 | 3 | 6 | 3 | 9 |
| 6   | 10 | 8 | 9 | 5 | 3 | 10 | 8 | 7 | 3 |
| 7   | 8 | 7 | 10 | 1 | 9 | 8 | 3 | 10 | 5 |
| 8   | 5 | 6 | 4 | 10 | 1 | 5 | 9 | 2 | 8 |
| 9   | 5 | 8 | 7 | 5 | 3 | 5 | 7 | 4 | 6 |
| 10  | 8 | 10 | 6 | 5 | 3 | 8 | 10 | 1 | 7 |

(b)

| Job | Priority rule (+ FCFS) | | | | | | | | |
|-----|---|---|---|---|---|---|---|---|---|
|     | 1 | 2 | 3 | 4 | 5 | 6 | 7 | 8 | 9 |
| 1   | 4 | 4 | 4 | 3 | 7 | 4 | 3 | 7 | 1 |
| 2   | 1 | 2 | 1 | 8 | 6 | 1 | 1 | 4 | 10 |
| 3   | 5 | 5 | 8 | 4 | 8 | 5 | 4 | 9 | 2 |
| 4   | 2 | 1 | 2 | 9 | 2 | 2 | 2 | 6 | 4 |
| 5   | 3 | 3 | 3 | 2 | 10 | 3 | 6 | 3 | 9 |
| 6   | 10 | 8 | 9 | 5 | 3 | 10 | 8 | 8 | 3 |
| 7   | 8 | 7 | 10 | 1 | 9 | 8 | 5 | 10 | 5 |
| 8   | 7 | 6 | 5 | 10 | 1 | 7 | 9 | 2 | 8 |
| 9   | 6 | 9 | 7 | 6 | 4 | 6 | 7 | 5 | 6 |
| 10  | 9 | 10 | 6 | 7 | 5 | 9 | 10 | 1 | 7 |

**12.4**

| Order number | Number of products | Machine | | | | | |
|---|---|---|---|---|---|---|---|
| | | A | | B | | C | |
| | | I | Hours | I | Hours | I | Hours |
| 1 | 50 | 0.33 | | 0.67 | | 0 | 150 |
| 2 | 75 | 0.5 | | 0 | 150 | 1.0 | |
| 3 | 25 | 0.67 | | 0.33 | 100 | 0 | |
| 4 | 80 | 0 | 160 | 1.5 | | 1.0 | |
| | | | 175 (91%) | | 275 (91%) | | 175 (86%) |

**Chapter 13**

**13.1**

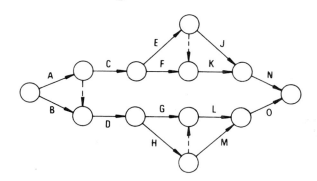

**13.2**

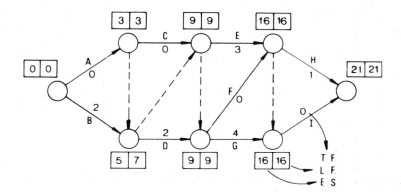

**13.3** Critical path = A, C, F, I
Critical path = A, B, F, H, for which $t = 28$ and $\sigma^2 = 7.23$. From tables $p = 2$ per cent, i.e. considering critical path only, probability of finishing on or before 22.5 days = 2 per cent. *But* minimum duration for path A, C, D, G $= 2 + 9 + 5 + 7 = 23$. Therefore actual probability = 0.

**13.4** (a)

| Activity | TF |
|----------|-----|
| 0–1      | 0  |
| 1–2      | 0  |
| 1–3      | 1  |
| 2–4      | 0  |
| 3–5      | 1  |
| 4–5      | 0  |
| 4–6      | 3  |
| 5–7      | 9  |
| 5–8      | 7  |
| 5–9      | 0  |
| 6–10     | 3  |
| 7–10     | 9  |
| 8–10     | 3  |
| 9–10     | 0  |
| 10–11    | 0  |

Critical path = 0, 1, 2, 4, 5, 9, 10, 11

(b)  (i) Delay project by five days.
  (ii) The new critical path is 6, 10, 11 since these are the only activities whose delay will delay the project.

**13.7** (a) 31 days
  (b)

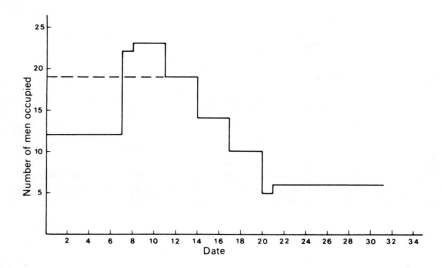

(c)

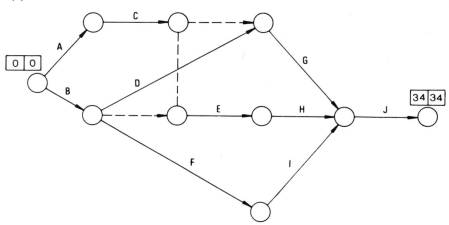

(d) Three days

**Chapter 14**

**14.2** (a) (i) 1435
(ii) 1.4 months
(b) Since demand rate now exceeds processing rate, processing rate must be continuous and even then all demand cannot be satisfied.

**14.3** 21 000 litres (equivalent)

**Chapter 15**

**15.1** $n_{min.} = 28$
$C = 0.4$ minutes
**15.3** Cycle time $= 20$ minutes

| Station | Work elements | Station time |
|---------|---------------|--------------|
| 1 | 0, 1, 2, 4 | 20 min |
| 2 | 3, 5, 7, 8 | 20 min |
| 3 | 6, 9, 10, 11 | 20 min |

Balancing loss = zero

**15.4**

|  | Station |  |  |  |  |  |
|--|---|---|---|---|---|---|
|  | 1 | 2 | 3 | 4 | 5 | 6 |
| 4.61 per hour $C = 13$ minutes | 0, 1, 2 | 3, 4 | 5, 6 | 7 | 8, 10 | 9 |
| Balancing loss $= 25.7$ per cent | | | | | | |
| 5 per hour $C = 12$ minutes | | | | | | |
| Balancing loss $= 19.6$ per cent | 0, 1, 2 | 3, 4 | 5, 6 | 7 | 8, 10 | 9 |

**Chapter 17**

**17.2** (a) 2830
   (b) 633
   (c) 0.64 months

**17.4** $Q^* = 2500$ units

**Chapter 19**

**19.1** (c) 0.56

**19.5**

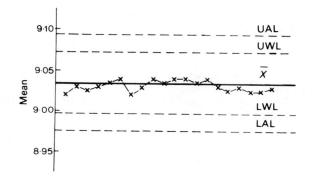

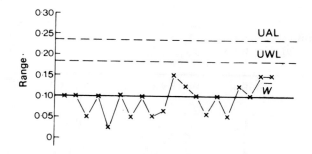

**19.6**

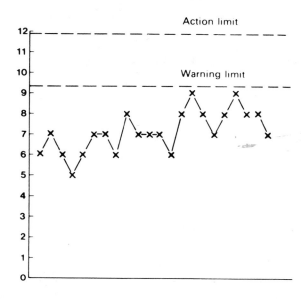

# Author Index

# Subject Index